A SOURCE BOOK OF
IRISH GOVERNMENT

POBLACHT NA H EIREANN.

THE PROVISIONAL GOVERNMENT
OF THE
IRISH REPUBLIC
TO THE PEOPLE OF IRELAND.

IRISHMEN AND IRISHWOMEN : In the name of God and of the dead generations from which she receives her old tradition of nationhood, Ireland, through us, summons her children to her flag and strikes for her freedom.

Having organised and trained her manhood through her secret revolutionary organisation, the Irish Republican Brotherhood, and through her open military organisations, the Irish Volunteers and the Irish Citizen Army, having patiently perfected her discipline, having resolutely waited for the right moment to reveal itself, she now seizes that moment, and, supported by her exiled children in America and by gallant allies in Europe, but relying in the first on her own strength, she strikes in full confidence of victory.

We declare the right of the people of Ireland to the ownership of Ireland, and to the unfettered control of Irish destinies, to be sovereign and indefeasible. The long usurpation of that right by a foreign people and government has not extinguished the right, nor can it ever be extinguished except by the destruction of the Irish people. In every generation the Irish people have asserted their right to national freedom and sovereignty ; six times during the past three hundred years they have asserted it in arms. Standing on that fundamental right and again asserting it in arms in the face of the world, we hereby proclaim the Irish Republic as a Sovereign Independent State, and we pledge our lives and the lives of our comrades-in-arms to the cause of its freedom, of its welfare, and of its exaltation among the nations.

The Irish Republic is entitled to, and hereby claims, the allegiance of every Irishman and Irishwoman. The Republic guarantees religious and civil liberty, equal rights and equal opportunities to all its citizens, and declares its resolve to pursue the happiness and prosperity of the whole nation and of all its parts, cherishing all the children of the nation equally, and oblivious of the differences carefully fostered by an alien government, which have divided a minority from the majority in the past.

Until our arms have brought the opportune moment for the establishment of a permanent National Government, representative of the whole people of Ireland and elected by the suffrages of all her men and women, the Provisional Government, hereby constituted, will administer the civil and military affairs of the Republic in trust for the people.

We place the cause of the Irish Republic under the protection of the Most High God, Whose blessing we invoke upon our arms, and we pray that no one who serves that cause will dishonour it by cowardice, inhumanity, or rapine. In this supreme hour the Irish nation must, by its valour and discipline and by the readiness of its children to sacrifice themselves for the common good, prove itself worthy of the august destiny to which it is called.

Signed on Behalf of the Provisional Government,

THOMAS J. CLARKE,

SEAN Mac DIARMADA, THOMAS MacDONAGH,
P. H. PEARSE, EAMONN CEANNT,
JAMES CONNOLLY. JOSEPH PLUNKETT.

The Proclamation of the Irish Republic, Easter 1916

A SOURCE BOOK OF
IRISH GOVERNMENT

edited by
BASIL CHUBB

DUBLIN
INSTITUTE OF PUBLIC ADMINISTRATION
1964

PUBLISHED BY THE
INSTITUTE OF PUBLIC ADMINISTRATION
59 LANSDOWNE ROAD
DUBLIN 4

First published 1964

© Institute of Public Administration
1964

Printed in the Republic of Ireland by Mount Salus Press Ltd., Sandymount, Dublin 4

TABLE OF CONTENTS

PREFACE

Anyone who teaches government or public administration in Ireland is only too well aware of the paucity of books available to students and particularly of the difficulties facing those who might wish to consult official material. For the many students, often young professional people, working alone or in small groups for professional or other examinations throughout the country, these difficulties must sometimes seem almost insurmountable. A growing awareness of their problems has led me to prepare this collection of extracts drawn largely from official and semi-official documents for publication by the Institute of Public Administration. In doing it, I have had the encouragement and help of the Director of the Institute and of the members of the Institute's Publications and Research Committee who share my concern at the plight of students, particularly among their own Institute members.

The main purpose of this collection is to provide students of government with an adequate yet manageable collection of documentary material to aid a study of the machinery and working of Irish government. It is composed largely of extracts from legal instruments, Oireachtas debates, official reports and other official documents, supplemented with passages from authoritative semi-official articles or from articles by public servants about matters with which they are or were concerned. In only one or two places have I had recourse to secondary descriptive material. Being a source book, it is inevitably confined to a large extent to formal structure. In any case, material of any sort on ' the structure of politics ' or political sociology is still sadly lacking and it will be some time yet before a collection of ' readings ' of that nature will be possible.

In quoting statutes, I have so far as possible set down the law as it is, putting in amendments and omitting repealed portions. Occasionally, it has been convenient to include statutory provisions which no longer apply, but where this has been done, the fact has been pointed out. However, although I hope that the extracts are accurate and up-to-date, it cannot be too much stressed that the book is intended to help a study of government and is not a handy reference book of the law, the extracts being both 'snippety' and put together by a layman. In the case of long extracts, I have in some cases inserted explanatory subheadings which are not in the original in order to assist the reader. The introductions at the beginning of each chapter are intended only to provide brief notes on the subject matter of the chapters and to put each document into context. The bibliographies are confined to comparatively accessible books and journals.

I have had much help and advice from many public servants and officials of the major political parties which I gratefully acknowledge. In particular, my thanks are due to Mr Tom Barrington, Mr Vincent Grogan, Mr Brendan Kiernan, Mrs C. Mac Aonghusa, Mr C. H. Murray, Mr D. Nally, Senator Tomas O Maoláin, Mr J. C. Smyth and the Secretariat of the Fine Gael Party. My thanks are due also to Mrs Máire de Paor for her help in preparing the manuscript, to Miss Geraldine Counahan for her help in the later stages, to Mr James O'Donnell of the Institute of Public Administration for his help in seeing the work through the press, and to my wife for her help throughout. Finally, I have to thank the staff of the Library of Trinity College for their many services.

Works of this sort cannot be published without the cooperation of authors and publishers. I thank the following authors and publishers — the Controller of the Stationery Office for permission to reprint extracts from the Irish Statutes, Oireachtas Debates, official reports and other official material and from H. A. Street, *The Law Relating to Local Government;* Mr T. de Valera for permission to reprint extracts from D. Macardle, *The Irish Republic;* Mr J. A. Costello, S.C., T.D., for permission to print an extract from his speech to the Canadian Bar Association printed in *Ireland in International Affairs;* Mr Michael McDunphy and Browne and Nolan Ltd. for permission to reprint an extract from *The President of Ireland;* the Incorporated Council of Law Reporting for Ireland for permission to reprint extracts from the *Irish Reports;* Mr Paul Jackson and the Editor of *Public Law* for permission to reprint from Mr Jackson's 'Delegated legislation in Ireland' ; the Editor of *Political Studies* and the Clarendon Press, Oxford, for permission to reprint extracts from an article of my own which has appeared in that journal; to Mr J. C. Smyth for permission to reprint extracts from his *Houses of the Oireachtas;* to the late Professor V. T. H. Delany for permission to reprint extracts from

The Administration of Justice in Ireland; to Mr Vincent Grogan for permission to reprint an extract from his *Administrative Tribunals in the Public Service;* to Mr M. O'Muimhneacháin, Mr Michael Lawless and Mr T. Troy for permission to reprint extracts from articles by them which have appeared in *Administration.*

BASIL CHUBB

Trinity College, Dublin.

Chapter 1

THE REPUBLIC AND COMMONWEALTH STATUS

INTRODUCTION

The independence movement, which was to culminate in the emergence of the Irish Free State, was a republican movement. It was republican in the sense that the Irish nation, in whose name the struggle was waged, was envisaged not only as an entity on whose behalf actions were taken and a Government claimed allegiance (Documents 1.1 and 1.2), but also as the people of Ireland who had democratic rights to choose their leaders and to participate in government. In this sense, it was bitterly opposed by the majority in the North-east who adhered to the United Kingdom, the symbol of which was the Crown. Neither Nationalist aspirations nor Northern loyalty were to be satisfied by the expedients envisaged in the Government of Ireland Act, 1920, which, while providing for the eventual appearance of common political organs, proposed to set up two parliaments, two administrations and two judicial systems, one for most of Ulster, the other for the rest of Ireland. (Document 1.3). Nevertheless, it is on those portions of the Act which apply to the six Ulster counties that the Northern Ireland Parliament and Government rest today. In looking forward to partition, this Act both rendered Northern Ireland secure and opened the way to independence for the South. In doing so, it made it inevitable that the struggle for independence once won, nationalist feeling in Ireland would be transformed into an irredentist movement.

The movement was republican also in the sense that a sovereign and democratic Irish state might be expected, in the manner of newly emerging states to assume the form, and set up the institutions, of a republic rather than of a constitutional monarchy. However, although the events of 1916 to 1922 were enough to force the British Government to concede independence, that Government did insist not only on partition but on independence in the form regarded by Great Britain as natural and proper for nation states emerging from her empire, namely Commonwealth status. Accordingly, the Constitution of the Irish Free State and the Treaty with

1

Great Britain (Document 1.4) embody Commonwealth status, which at that time involved the recognition of the British Crown. The Irish Free State Constitution thus reflects two different political theories, including as it does assertions of popular sovereignty together with the forms and symbols of the very different British and Commonwealth tradition. For many Irishmen the substance of independence was sufficient for the moment; for some, it was not; for a few, such an attitude was a betrayal of 'The Republic', even of solemn vows. Disagreement as to whether to accept the Treaty or not, and over the constitutional arrangements embodied in the Constitution, precipitated a division in the independence movement which has been a major influence in the subsequent political and social history of the country.

With the coming to power of Mr de Valera and Fianna Fáil, who were the great majority of the 'anti-treaty' party, a radical revision of the constitutional forms naturally took place. At first by constitutional amendment and ordinary legislation and then by the substitution of Bunreacht na hÉireann (Constitution of Ireland) for the Irish Free State Constitution, Mr de Valera replaced Commonwealth status by a looser form of association. In 1933, the oath of allegiance was removed; in 1936 the office of Governor General was abolished; while the occasion of the abdication of King Edward VIII in 1936 was taken to remove the Crown from the constitutional machinery of the state, reinstating it on a simple statutory basis as an instrument which might be used by the Irish Government for purposes connected with the conduct of external affairs. (Documents 1.5 and 1.6). In 1937, Mr de Valera proposed his own constitution to replace the Irish Free State Constitution, now much amended.

Bunreacht na hÉireann, which was expounded and defended at length by Mr de Valera in the Dáil, states the republican position unqualified by British Commonwealth theory and forms, the Crown, disguised as an 'organ, instrument or method of procedure', being retained as envisaged in the External Relations Act for as long as the Government should find convenient. However, though republican in spirit, in form and in language, the new Constitution did not explicitly declare the state to be a republic. This was deliberate — a consequence of Mr de Valera's policy of 'external association' with Britain and the Commonwealth and of the existence of the problem of partition (Documents 1.7 to 1.9).

While, on the one hand, it might be thought curious that a matter so basic as the nature and status of the state should be left vague in the fundamental law of that state (Document 1.10), on the other hand, this arrangement did, it was claimed, have the advantage of flexibility, allowing for changes to be made easily to conform with altered circumstances. When in 1948, Mr Costello's ' Inter-party ' Government decided that the time had come to declare the state a republic (Document 1.11), an ordinary statute sufficed (Document 1.12). Even so, although Commonwealth status had probably never been well suited to Irish conditions, the formal declaration of a Republic did not alter the ineluctable fact of Irish-British ties so close, and social, economic and political interests so tightly interwoven, that Ireland and Great Britain must of necessity have special relations one with another. (Document 1.13).

DOCUMENTS

1. THE DECLARATION OF EASTER 1916

Document 1.1 — The Declaration of the Republic as printed in D. Macardle, *The Irish Republic,* 4th edition, 1951, pp. 167-8.

Poblacht na h-Éireann

The Provisional Government

of the

IRISH REPUBLIC

To the people of Ireland

IRISHMEN AND IRISHWOMEN: In the name of God and of the dead generations from which she receives her old tradition of nationhood, Ireland, through us, summons her children to her flag and strikes for her freedom.

Having organised and trained her manhood through her secret revolutionary organisation, the Irish Republican Brotherhood, and through her open military organisations, the Irish Volunteers and the Irish Citizen Army, having patiently perfected her discipline, having resolutely waited for the right moment to reveal itself, she now seizes that moment and, supported by her exiled children in America and by gallant allies in Europe, but relying in the first on her own strength, she strikes in full confidence of victory.

We declare the right of the people of Ireland to the ownership of Ireland and to the unfettered control of Irish destinies, to be sovereign and indefeasible.

The long usurpation of that right by a foreign people and government has not extinguished the right, nor can it ever be extinguished except by the destruction of the Irish people. In every generation the Irish people have asserted their right to national freedom and sovereignty: six times during the past three hundred years they have asserted it in arms. Standing on that fundamental right and again asserting it in arms in the face of the world, we hereby proclaim the Irish Republic as a Sovereign Independent State, and we pledge our lives and the lives of our comrades-in-arms to the cause of its freedom, of its welfare and of its exaltation among the nations.

The Irish Republic is entitled to, and hereby claims, the allegiance of every Irishman and Irishwoman. The Republic guarantees religious and civil liberty, equal rights and equal opportunities to all its citizens, and declares its resolve to pursue the happiness and prosperity of the whole nation and of all its parts, cherishing all the children of the nation equally, and oblivious of the differences, carefully fostered by an alien government, which have divided a minority from the majority in the past.

Until our arms have brought the opportune moment for the establishment of a permanent National Government, representative of the whole people of Ireland, and elected by the suffrages of all her men and women, the Provisional Government, hereby constituted, will administer the civil and military affairs of the Republic in trust for the people. We place the cause of the Irish Republic under the protection of the Most High God, Whose blessing we invoke upon our arms, and we pray that no one who serves that cause will dishonour it by cowardice, inhumanity or rapine. In this supreme hour the Irish nation must, by its valour and discipline, and by the readiness of its children to sacrifice themselves for the common good, prove itself worthy of the august destiny to which it is called.

Signed on Behalf of the Provisional Government,

THOMAS J. CLARKE

SEAN MAC DIARMADA	THOMAS MACDONAGH
P. H. PEARSE	ÉAMONN CEANNT
JAMES CONNOLLY	JOSEPH PLUNKETT.

2. OATH TAKEN BY MEMBERS OF THE FIRST DAIL

Document 1.2 — Extract from *Minutes of Proceedings of the First Parliament of the Republic of Ireland*, 1919-1921, col. 151 (20 August, 1919).

I, A.B., do solemnly swear (or affirm) that I do not and shall not yield a voluntary support to any pretended Government, authority or power within Ireland hostile and inimical thereto, and I do further swear (or affirm) that to the best of my knowledge and ability I will support and defend the Irish

Republic and the Government of the Irish Republic, which is Dáil Éireann, against all enemies, foreign and domestic, and I will bear true faith and allegiance to the same, and that I take this obligation freely without any mental reservation or purpose of evasion, so help me, God.

3. THE GOVERNMENT OF IRELAND ACT

Document 1.3 — Extracts from The Government of Ireland Act, 1920 (10 and 11 Geo. 5, ch. 67) in *The Public General Acts Passed in the Tenth and Eleventh Years of The Reign of H.M. King George the Fifth* (1920).

PARLIAMENTS OF SOUTHERN AND NORTHERN IRELAND

1.—(1) On and after the appointed day there shall be established for Southern Ireland a Parliament to be called the Parliament of Southern Ireland consisting of His Majesty, the Senate of Southern Ireland, and the House of Commons of Southern Ireland, and there shall be established for Northern Ireland a Parliament to be called the Parliament of Northern Ireland consisting of His Majesty, the Senate of Northern Ireland, and the House of Commons of Northern Ireland.

(2) For the purposes of this Act, Northern Ireland shall consist of the parliamentary counties of Antrim, Armagh, Down, Fermanagh, Londonderry and Tyrone, and the parliamentary boroughs of Belfast and Londonderry, and Southern Ireland shall consist of so much of Ireland as is not comprised within the said parliamentary counties and boroughs.

COUNCIL OF IRELAND

2.—(1) With a view to the eventual establishment of a Parliament for the whole of Ireland, and to bringing about harmonious action between the parliaments and governments of Southern Ireland and Northern Ireland, and to the promotion of mutual intercourse and uniformity in relation to matters affecting the whole of Ireland, and to providing for the administration of services which the two parliaments mutually agree should be administered uniformly throughout the whole of Ireland, or which by virtue of this Act are to be so administered, there shall be constituted, as soon as may be after the appointed day, a Council to be called the Council of Ireland.

(2) Subject as hereinafter provided, the Council of Ireland shall consist of a person nominated by the Lord Lieutenant acting in accordance with instructions from His Majesty who shall be President and forty other persons, of whom seven shall be members of the Senate of Southern Ireland, thirteen shall be members of the House of Commons of Southern Ireland, seven shall be members of the Senate of Northern Ireland, and thirteen shall be members of the House of Commons of Northern Ireland.

The members of the Council of Ireland shall be elected in each case by the members of that House of the Parliament of Southern Ireland or Northern Ireland of which they are members. [*Remainder of SS. 2 omitted.*]

(3) The constitution of the Council of Ireland may from time to time be varied by identical Acts passed by the Parliament of Southern Ireland and the Parliament of Northern Ireland, and the Acts may provide for all or any of the members of the Council of Ireland being elected by parliamentary electors, and determine the constituencies by which the several elective members are to be returned and the number of the members to be returned by the several constituencies and the method of election.

POWER TO ESTABLISH A PARLIAMENT FOR THE WHOLE OF IRELAND

3.—(1) The Parliaments of Southern Ireland and Northern Ireland may, by identical Acts agreed to by an absolute majority of members of the House of Commons of each Parliament at the third reading (hereinafter referred to as constituent Acts), establish, in lieu of the Council of Ireland, a Parliament for the whole of Ireland consisting of His Majesty and two Houses (which shall be called and known as The Parliament of Ireland), and may determine the number of members thereof and the manner in which the members are to be appointed or elected, and the constituencies for which the several elective members are to be returned, and the number of members to be returned by the several constituencies, and the method of appointment or election, and the relations of the two Houses to one another; and the date at which the Parliament of Ireland is established is hereinafter referred to as the date of Irish union:

Provided that the Bill for a constituent Act shall not be introduced except upon a resolution passed at a previous meeting of the House in which the Bill is to be introduced.

(2) On the date of Irish union the Council of Ireland shall cease to exist and there shall be transferred to the Parliament and Government of Ireland all powers then exerciseable by the Council of Ireland, and (except so far as the constituent Acts otherwise provide) the matters which under this Act cease to be reserved matters at the date of Irish union, and any other powers for the joint exercise of which by the Parliaments or Governments of Southern and Northern Ireland provision has been made under this Act.

(3) There shall also be transferred to the Parliament and Government of Ireland, except so far as the constituent Acts otherwise provide, all the powers and duties of the Parliaments and Governments of Southern Ireland and Northern Ireland, including all powers as to taxation, and, unless any powers and duties are retained by the Parliament and Governments of Southern Ireland and Northern Ireland under the constituent Acts, those Parliaments and Governments shall cease to exist. [*Remainder of SS. 3 omitted.*]

(4) If by the constituent Acts any powers and duties are so retained as aforesaid, the Parliaments of Southern Ireland and Northern Ireland may subsequently by identical Acts transfer any of those powers and duties to the

Government and Parliament of Ireland, and, in the event of all such powers and duties being so transferred, the Parliaments and Governments of Southern Ireland and Northern Ireland shall cease to exist.

LEGISLATIVE POWERS OF IRISH PARLIAMENTS

4.—(1) Subject to the provisions of this Act, the Parliament of Southern Ireland and the Parliament of Northern Ireland shall respectively have power to make laws for the peace, order, and good government of Southern Ireland and Northern Ireland with the following limitations, namely, that they shall not have power to make laws except in respect of matters exclusively relating to the portion of Ireland within their jurisdiction, or some part thereof, and (without prejudice to that general limitation) that they shall not have power to make laws in respect of the following matters in particular, namely:—

(1) The Crown or the succession to the Crown, or a regency, or the property of the Crown (including foreshore vested in the Crown), or the Lord Lieutenant, except as respects the exercise of his executive power in relation to Irish services as defined for the purposes of this Act; or

(2) The making of peace or war, or matters arising from a state of war; or the regulation of the conduct of any portion of His Majesty's subjects during the existence of hostilities between foreign states with which His Majesty is at peace, in relation to those hostilities; or

(3) The navy, the army, the air force, the territorial force, or any other naval, military, or air force, or the defence of the realm, or any other naval, military, or air force matter (including any pensions and allowances payable to persons who have been members of or in respect of service in any such force or their widows or dependants, and provision for the training, education, employment and assistance for the reinstatement in civil life of persons who have ceased to be members of any such force); or

(4) Treaties, or any relations with foreign states, or relations with other parts of His Majesty's dominions, or matters involving the contravention of treaties or agreements with foreign states or any part of His Majesty's dominions, or offences connected with any such treaties or relations, or procedure connected with the extradition of criminals under any treaty, or the return of fugitive offenders from or to any part of His Majesty's dominions; or

(5) Dignities or titles of honour; or

(6) Treason, treason felony, alienage, naturalization, or aliens as such, or domicile; or

(7) Trade with any place out of the part of Ireland within their jurisdiction, except so far as trade may be affected by the exercise of the powers of taxation given to the said parliaments, or by regulations made for the sole purpose of preventing contagious disease, or by steps taken by means of inquiries or agencies out of

the part of Ireland within their jurisdiction for the improvement of the trade of that part or for the protection of traders of that part from fraud; the granting of bounties on the export of goods; quarantine; navigation, including merchant shipping (except as respects inland waters, the regulation of harbours, and local health regulations); or

(8) Submarine cables; or

(9) Wireless telegraphy; or

(10) Aerial navigation; or

(11) Lighthouses, buoys, or beacons (except so far as they can consistently with any general Act of the Parliament of the United Kingdom be constructed or maintained by a local harbour authority); or

(12) Coinage; legal tender; negotiable instruments (including bank notes) except so far as negotiable instruments may be affected by the exercise of the powers of taxation given to the said Parliaments; or any change in the standard of weights and measures; or

(13) Trade marks, designs, merchandise marks, copyright, or patent rights; or

(14) Any matter which by this Act is declared to be a reserved matter, so long as it remains reserved.

Any law made in contravention of the limitations imposed by this section shall, as far as it contravenes those limitations, be void. [*SS. 2 omitted.*]

5.—(1) In the exercise of their power to make laws under this Act neither the Parliament of Southern Ireland nor the Parliament of Northern Ireland shall make a law so as either directly or indirectly to establish or endow any religion, or prohibit or restrict the free exercise thereof, or give a preference, privilege, or advantage, or impose any disability or disadvantage, on account of religious belief or religious ceremony a condition of the validity of any marriage, or affect prejudicially the right of any child to attend a school receiving public money without attending the religious instruction at that school, or alter the constitution of any religious body except where the alteration is approved on behalf of the religious body by the governing body thereof, or divert from any religious denomination the fabric of cathedral churches, or, except for the purpose of roads, railways, lighting, water, or drainage works, or other works of public utility upon payment of compensation, any other property, or take any property without compensation.

Any law made in contravention of the restrictions imposed by this subsection shall, so far as it contravenes those restrictions, be void. [*SS. 2 and S. 6 omitted.*]

POWERS OF THE COUNCIL OF IRELAND

7.—(1) The Council of Ireland shall have power to make orders with respect to matters affecting interests both in Southern Ireland and Northern Ireland, in any case where the matter—

(*a*) is of such a nature that if it had affected interests in one of those areas only it would have been within the powers of the Parliament for that area; and

(*b*) is a matter to affect which, it would, apart from this provision, have been necessary to apply to the Parliament of the United Kingdom by petition for leave to bring in a private Bill.

[*SSs. 2 and 3 omitted.*]

EXECUTIVE POWERS

8.—(1) The executive power in Southern Ireland and in Northern Ireland shall continue vested in His Majesty the King, and nothing in this Act shall affect the exercise of that power, except as respects Irish services as defined for the purposes of this Act.

(2) As respects Irish services, the Lord Lieutenant or other chief executive officer or officers for the time being appointed in his place, on behalf of His Majesty, shall exercise any prerogative or other executive power of His Majesty the exercise of which may be delegated to him by His Majesty:

Provided that, if any such power is delegated to the Lord Lieutenant in respect of Southern Ireland or Northern Ireland, the power shall also be delegated to him in respect of Northern Ireland or Southern Ireland.

(3) Subject to the provisions of this Act relating to the Council of Ireland, powers so delegated shall be exercised—

(*a*) In Southern Ireland, through such departments as may be established by Act of the Parliament of Southern Ireland, or, subject to any alteration by Act of that Parliament, by the Lord Lieutenant; and

(*b*) in Northern Ireland, through such departments as may be established by Act of the Parliament of Northern Ireland, or, subject to any alteration by Act of that Parliament, by the Lord Lieutenant;

and the Lord Lieutenant may appoint officers to administer those departments, and those officers shall hold office during the pleasure of the Lord Lieutenant.

(4) The persons who are for the time being heads of such departments of the Government of Southern Ireland as may be determined by Act of the Parliament of Southern Ireland or, in the absence of any such determination, by the Lord Lieutenant, and such other persons (if any) as the Lord Lieutenant may appoint, shall be the ministers of Southern Ireland:

Provided that—

(*u*) no such person shall be a minister of Southern Ireland or a minister of Northern Ireland unless he is a member of the Privy Council of Ireland; and

(*b*) no such person shall hold office as a minister of Southern Ireland or as a minister of Northern Ireland for a longer period than six months, unless he is or becomes a member of the Parliament of Southern Ireland or of Northern Ireland, as the case may be, but in reckoning those six months any time prior to the date of the first meeting of the Parliament of Southern Ireland or of Northern Ireland, as the case may be, or during which that Parliament stands prorogued shall be excluded; and

(c) any such person not being the head of a department of the Government of Southern Ireland or a department of the Government of Northern Ireland shall hold office as a minister of Southern Ireland or a minister of Northern Ireland during the pleasure of the Lord Lieutenant in the same manner as the head of a department of the Government of Southern Ireland or a department of the Government of Northern Ireland holds his office. [*SSs. 5 and 6 omitted.*]

(7) The seats of the Governments of Southern Ireland and Northern Ireland shall be at Dublin and Belfast, respectively, or such places as the Parliaments of Southern Ireland and Northern Ireland may respectively determine.

(8) For the purposes of this Act, "Irish services" in relation to Southern Ireland and Northern Ireland respectively are all public services in connection with the administration of civil government in Southern Ireland and Northern Ireland, except the administration of matters with respect to which the Parliament of Southern Ireland and the Parliament of Northern Ireland have under the provisions hereinbefore contained no power to make laws, including in this exception all public services in connection with the administration of matters by this Act declared to be reserved matters so long as they continue to be reserved; and the public services in connection with the matters so reserved are in this Act referred to as reserved services.

9.—(1) The Royal Irish Constabulary and the Dublin Metropolitan Police and the management and control of those forces and the administration of the Acts relating thereto, including appointments remuneration and removal of magistrates thereunder, shall be reserved matters until such date, not being later than the expiration of three years after the appointed day, as His Majesty in Council may determine, and on the date so determined the public services in connection with the administration of those Acts and the management and control of those forces shall, by virtue of this Act, be transferred from the Government of the United Kingdom to the Government of Southern Ireland as respects Southern Ireland and to the Government of Northern Ireland as respects Northern Ireland, and shall then cease to be reserved services and become Irish services. [*Remainder of SS. 1 omitted.*]

(2) The following matters, namely,—

(a) the postal service;

(b) the Post Office Savings Bank and Trustee Savings Banks;

(c) designs for stamps, whether for postal or revenue purposes;

(d) the registration of deeds; and

(e) the Public Record Office of Ireland;

shall be reserved matters until the date of Irish union. . . [*Remainder of SS. 2 omitted.*]

(3) The general subject-matter of the Acts relating to land purchase in Ireland shall be a reserved matter unless and until otherwise provided by any Act of the Parliament of the United Kingdom relating to land purchase in Ireland, passed in the present or any future session of that Parliament. . . [*Remainder of S. 9 omitted.*]

FURTHER POWERS OF THE COUNCIL OF IRELAND

10.—(1) The Parliaments of Southern Ireland and Northern Ireland may, by identical Acts, delegate to the Council of Ireland any of the powers of the Parliaments and Governments of Southern Ireland and Northern Ireland, and such Acts may determine the manner in which the powers so delegated are to be exerciseable by the Council.

(2) With a view to the uniform administration throughout Ireland of public services in connection with railways and fisheries, and the administration of the Diseases of Animals Acts any powers (not being powers relating to reserved matters) exerciseable by any department of the Government of the United Kingdom at the appointed day with respect to railways and fisheries and the contagious diseases of animals in Ireland and the power of making laws with respect to railways and fisheries and the contagious diseases of animals shall, as from the appointed day, become powers of the Council of Ireland, and not of the Governments and Parliaments of Southern Ireland and Northern Ireland. [*Remainder of SS. 2 omitted.*]

(3) The Council may consider any questions which may appear in any way to bear on the welfare of both Southern Ireland and Northern Ireland, and may, by resolution, make suggestions in relation thereto as they may think proper, but suggestions so made shall have no legislative effect, and in particular it shall be the duty of the Council of Ireland as soon as may be after the constitution thereof to consider what Irish services ought in the common interest to be administered by a body having jurisdiction over the whole of Ireland, and what reserved services which are transferable on the passing of identical Acts ought to be so transferred, and to make recommendations to the Parliaments of Southern Ireland and Northern Ireland as to the advisability of passing identical Acts delegating to the Council of Ireland the administration of any such Irish services, with a view to avoiding the necessity of administering them separately in Southern Ireland or Northern Ireland, and providing for the transfer of any such reserved services at the earliest possible date. [*Remainder of S. 10 and Ss. 11-74 omitted.*]

SUPREME AUTHORITY TO REMAIN WITH UK PARLIAMENT

75. Notwithstanding the establishment of the Parliaments of Southern and and Northern Ireland, or the Parliament of Ireland, or anything contained in this Act, the supreme authority of the Parliament of the United Kingdom shall remain unaffected and undiminished over all persons, matters, and things in Ireland and every part thereof. [*Remainder of Act omitted.*]

4. THE TREATY AND THE IRISH FREE STATE CONSTITUTION

Document 1.4 — The Constitution of The Irish Free State (Saorstát Éireann) Act, 1922.

AN ACT TO ENACT A CONSTITUTION FOR THE IRISH FREE STATE (SAORSTAT EIREANN) AND FOR IMPLEMENTING THE TREATY BETWEEN GREAT BRITAIN AND IRELAND SIGNED AT LONDON ON THE 6th DAY OF DECEMBER, 1921.

Dáil Éireann sitting as a Constituent Assembly in this Provisional Parliament, acknowledging that all lawful authority comes from God to the people and in the confidence that the National life and unity of Ireland shall thus be restored, hereby proclaims the establishment of The Irish Free State (otherwise called Saorstát Éireann) and in the exercise of undoubted right, decrees and enacts as follows : —

1. The Constitution set forth in the First Schedule hereto annexed shall be the Constitution of The Irish Free State (Saorstát Éireann).

2. The said Constitution shall be construed with reference to the Articles of Agreement for a Treaty between Great Britain and Ireland set forth in the Second Schedule hereto annexed (hereinafter referred to as " the Scheduled Treaty ") which are hereby given the force of law, and if any provision of the said Constitution or of any amendment thereof or of any law made thereunder is in any respect repugnant to any of the provisions of the Scheduled Treaty, it shall, to the extent only of such repugnancy, be absolutely void and inoperative and the Parliament and the Executive Council of the Irish Free State (Saorstát Éireann) shall respectively pass such further legislation and do all such other things as may be necessary to implement the Scheduled Treaty.

3. This Act may be cited for all purposes as the Constitution of The Irish Free State (Saorstát Éireann) Act, 1922.

FIRST SCHEDULE ABOVE REFERRED TO.

CONSTITUTION OF
THE IRISH FREE STATE
(SAORSTAT EIREANN)

Article 1.

The Irish Free State (otherwise hereinafter called or sometimes called Saorstát Eireann) is a co-equal member of the Community of Nations forming the British Commonwealth of Nations.

Article 2.

All powers of government and all authority, legislative, executive, and judicial, in Ireland are derived from the people of Ireland, and the same shall be exercised in the Irish Free State (Saorstát Eireann) through the organisations established by or under, and in accord with, this Constitution. [*Article 3 omitted.*]

Article 4.

The National language of the Irish Free State (Saorstát Eireann) is the Irish language, but the English language shall be equally recognised as an official language. Nothing in this Article shall prevent special provisions being made by the Parliament of the Irish Free State (otherwise called and herein generally referred to as the " Oireachtas ") for districts or areas in which only one language is in general use. [*Rest of Schedule I omitted.*]

SECOND SCHEDULE ABOVE REFERRED TO.

(Articles of Agreement for a Treaty between Great Britain and Ireland).

---

1. Ireland shall have the same constitutional status in the Community of Nations known as the British Empire as the Dominion of Canada, the Commonwealth of Australia, the Dominion of New Zealand, and the Union of South Africa, with a Parliament having powers to make laws for the peace, order and good government of Ireland, and an Executive responsible to that Parliament, and shall be styled and known as the Irish Free State.

2. Subject to the provisions hereinafter set out the position of the Irish Free State in relation to the Imperial Parliament and Government and otherwise shall be that of the Dominion of Canada, and the law, practice and constitutional usage governing the relationship of the Crown or the representative of the Crown and of the Imperial Parliament to the Dominion of Canada shall govern their relationship to the Irish Free State.

3. The representative of the Crown in Ireland shall be appointed in like manner as the Governor-General of Canada and in accordance with the practice observed in the making of such appointments.

4. The oath to be taken by Members of the Parliament of the Irish Free State shall be in the following form : —

I . . . . . do solemnly swear true faith and allegiance to the Constitution of the Irish Free State as by law established and that I will be faithful to H.M. King George V., his heirs and successors by law, in virtue of the common citizenship of Ireland with Great Britain and her adherence to and membership of the group of nations forming the British Commonwealth of Nations. [*Articles 5 and 6 omitted*].

7. The Government of the Irish Free State shall afford to His Majesty's Imperial Forces : —

(*a*) In time of peace such harbour and other facilities as are indicated in the Annex hereto, or such other facilities as may from time to time be agreed between the British Government and the Government of the Irish Free State; and

(*b*) In time of war or of strained relations with a Foreign Power such harbour and other facilities as the British Government may require for the purpose of such defence as aforesaid. [*Articles* 8-10 *omitted*].

11. Until the expiration of one month from the passing of the Act of Parliament for the ratification of this instrument, the powers of the Parliament and the government of the Irish Free State shall not be exercisable as respects Northern Ireland and the provisions of the Government of Ireland Act, 1920, shall, so far as they relate to Northern Ireland, remain of full force and effect, and no election shall be held for the return of members to, serve in the Parliament of the Irish Free State for constituencies in Northern Ireland, unless a resolution is passed by both Houses of the Parliament of Northern Ireland in favour of the holding of such elections before the end of the said month.

12. If before the expiration of the said month an address is presented to His Majesty by both Houses of the Parliament of Northern Ireland to that effect, the powers of the Parliament and Government of the Irish Free State shall no longer extend to Northern Ireland, and the provisions of the Government of Ireland Act, 1920, (including those relating to the Council of Ireland) shall, so far as they relate to Northern Ireland, continue to be of full force and effect, and this instrument shall have effect subject to the necessary modifications.

Provided that if such an address is so presented a Commission consisting of three persons, one to be appointed by the Government of the Irish Free State, one to be appointed by the Government of Northern Ireland and one, who shall be Chairman, to be appointed by the British Government shall determine in accordance with the wishes of the inhabitants, so far as may be compatible with economic and geographic conditions, the boundaries between Northern Ireland and the rest of Ireland, and for the purposes of the Government of Ireland Act, 1920, and of this instrument, the boundary of Northern Ireland shall be such as may be determined by such Commission.

13. For the purpose of the last foregoing article, the powers of the Parliament of Southern Ireland under the Government of Ireland Act, 1920, to elect members of the Council of Ireland shall after the Parliament of the Irish Free State is constituted be exercised by that Parliament.

14. After the expiration of the said month, if no such address as is mentioned in Article 12 hereof is presented, the Parliament and Government of Northern Ireland shall continue to exercise as respects Northern Ireland the powers conferred on them by the Government of Ireland Act, 1920, but the Parliament and Government of the Irish Free State shall in Northern Ireland have in relation to matters in respect of which the Parliament of

Northern Ireland has not power to make laws under that Act (including matters which under the said Act are within the jurisdiction of the Council of Ireland) the same powers as in the rest of Ireland subject to such other provisions as may be agreed in manner hereinafter appearing. [*Article 15 omitted*].

16. Neither the Parliament of the Irish Free State nor the Parliament of Northern Ireland shall make any law so as either directly or indirectly to endow any religion or prohibit or restrict the free exercise thereof or give any preference or impose any disability on account of religious belief or religious status or affect prejudicially the right of any child to attend a school receiving public money without attending the religious instruction at the school or make any discrimination as respects state aid between schools under the management of different religious denominations or divert from any religious denomination or any educational institution any of its property except for public utility purpose and on payment of compensation.

17. By way of provisional arrangement for the administration of Southern Ireland during the interval which must elapse between the date hereof and the constitution of a Parliament and Government of the Irish Free State in accordance therewith, steps shall be taken forthwith for summoning a meeting of members of Parliament elected for constituencies in Southern Ireland since the passing of the Government of Ireland Act, 1920, and for constituting a provisional Government, and the British Government shall take the steps necessary to transfer to such provisional Government the powers and machinery requisite for the discharge of its duties, provided that every member of such provisional Government shall have signified in writing his or her acceptance of this instrument. But this arrangement shall not continue in force beyond the expiration of twelve months from the date hereof.

18. This instrument shall be submitted forthwith by His Majesty's Government for the approval of Parliament and by the Irish signatories to a meeting summoned for the purpose of the members elected to sit in the House of Commons of Southern Ireland, and if approved shall be ratified by the necessary legislation.

On behalf of the British
Delegation
(*Signed*)

D. LLOYD GEORGE
AUSTEN CHAMBERLAIN
BIRKENHEAD
WINSTON S. CHURCHILL
L. WORTHINGTON-EVANS
HAMAR GREENWOOD
GORDON HEWART

December 6, 1921

On behalf of the Irish
Delegation
(*Signed*)

ART O GRIOBHTHA
(Arthur Griffith)
MICHEAL O COILEAIN
RIOBARD BARTUN
EUDHMONN S. O DUGAIN
SEORSA GHABHAIN UI
              DHUBHTHAIGH

ANNEX

1. The following are the specific facilities required.

DOCKYARD PORT AT BEREHAVEN

(a) Admiralty property and rights to be retained as at the date hereof. Harbour defences to remain in charge of British care and maintenance parties.

QUEENSTOWN

(b) Harbour defences to remain in charge of British care and maintenance parties. Certain mooring buoys to be retained for use of His Majesty's ships.

BELFAST LOUGH

(c) Harbour defences to remain in charge of British care and maintenance parties.

LOUGH SWILLY

(d) Harbour defences to remain in charge of British care and maintenance parties.

AVIATION

(e) Facilities in the neighbourhood of the above Ports for coastal defence by air.

OIL FUEL STORAGE

(f) Haulbowline ...
    Rathmullen ... { To be offered for sale to commercial companies under guarantee that purchasers shall maintain a certain minimum stock for Admiralty purposes. [*Remainder of Annex omitted.*]

5. THE EXTERNAL RELATIONS ACT

(a) *Mr de Valera explains the Bill*

Document 1.5 — Extract from *Dáil Debates,* vol. 64, cols. 1279-80 (11 December, 1936).

. . . We propose to continue the King for the functions which he in fact directly exercises and for these only. The functions provided for here are the only functions which in fact the King exercises. We are providing for the continuance of these functions on the advice and authority—as in the past and in the future—of the Executive Council. We are clearing up the political constitutional situation. We are making clear to everyone what the situation is, and we are removing fiction. Whatever justification there might be in British history or British constitutional theory for such fiction, there is no justification in our case. It is very much better that our people should see clearly, with no fog and no mist of constitutional theory about it, what the situation is. That is what is being proposed in this Bill.

What is happening, then is that from the King are being taken away any functions internal, either direct or indirect, in the Administration of the Government and in the internal Executive of the country, and we are retaining the King for those purposes for which he was used hitherto. He is being retained for these purposes because he is recognised as the symbol of this particular co-operation in the States of the Commonwealth. If the Irish people do not wish to continue him for these purposes they can end that by legislation. They can end the whole situation by law or limit the exercise of these powers by law.

(b) *The Act*

Document 1.6 — The Executive Authority (External Relations) Act, 1936 (no. 58).

AN ACT TO MAKE PROVISION, IN ACCORDANCE WITH THE CONSTITUTION, FOR THE EXERCISE OF THE EXECUTIVE AUTHORITY OF SAORSTAT EIREANN IN RELATION TO CERTAIN MATTERS IN THE D O M A I N OF EXTERNAL RELATIONS AND FOR OTHER MATTERS CONNECTED WITH THE MATTERS AFORESAID. [*12th December*, 1936.]

BE IT ENACTED BY THE OIREACHTAS OF SAORSTAT EIREANN AS FOLLOWS:—

1.—(1) The diplomatic representatives of Saorstát Eireann in other countries shall be appointed on the authority of the Executive Council.

(2) The consular representatives of Saorstát Eireann in other countries shall be appointed by or on the authority of the Executive Council.

2.—Every international agreement concluded on behalf of Saorstát Eireann shall be concluded by or on the authority of the Executive Council.

3.—(1) It is hereby declared and enacted that, so long as Saorstát Eireann is associated with the following nations, that is to say, Australia, Canada, Great Britain, New Zealand, and South Africa, and so long as the king recognised by those nations as the symbol of their co-operation continues to act on behalf of each of those nations (on the advice of the several Governments thereof) for the purposes of the appointment of diplomatic and consular representatives and the conclusion of international agreements, the king so recognised may, and is hereby authorised to, act on behalf of Saorstát Eireann for the like purposes as and when advised by the Executive Council so to do.

(2) Immediately upon the passing of this Act, the instrument of abdication executed by His Majesty King Edward the Eighth on the 10th day of December, 1936, (a copy whereof is set out in the Schedule to this Act) shall have effect according to the tenor thereof and His said Majesty shall, for the purposes of the foregoing subsection of this section and all other (if any) purposes, cease to be king, and the king for those purposes shall henceforth be the person who, if His said Majesty had died on the 10th day of December, 1936, unmarried, would for the time being be his successor under the law of Saorstát Eireann.

4.—This Act may be cited as the Executive Authority (External Relations) Act, 1936.

SCHEDULE

I, Edward the Eighth, of Great Britain, Ireland, and the British Dominions beyond the Seas, King, Emperor of India, do hereby declare My irrevocable determination to renounce the Throne for Myself and for My descendants, and My desire that effect should be given to this Instrument of Abdication immediately

In token whereof I have hereunto set My hand this tenth day of December, Nineteen hundred and thirty-six, in the presence of the witnesses whose signatures are subscribed.

EDWARD R.I.

SIGNED AT FORT BELVEDERE
IN THE PRESENCE OF
  ALBERT
  HENRY
  GEORGE

6. BUNREACHT NA hEIREANN

(a) *The Debate on the Constitution*

  Document 1.7 — Extract from speech by the President of the Executive Council (Mr de Valera) in *Dáil Debates,* vol. 67, cols. 60-75 (11 May, 1937).

. . . The next portion of importance in the Constitution is that which deals with the question of international relations. With regard to international relations generally, it does not make a change. It is not intended to make a change, except this change, that it puts the question of our international relations in their proper place—and that is outside the Constitution. It is clearly to the interests of our people that there should be in regard to the fundamental law the greatest possible amount of unanimity, the greatest possible amount of agreement. These are the rules under which all our political institutions are to work. We shall have advanced a great distance indeed if we can get the rules under which we are to work, the things that prescribe all our institutions and the manner of their operation. If we can get substantial agreement on these, a great deal will have been done. The idea of this Constitution is to put this matter of our external relations in its proper position relatively to the Constitution, and that is outside it, as a matter of foreign policy, to be determined from time to time, according as the people's interests suggest to them that they should put this Government or that Government into office with powers to implement their will. That is what is done here. It is done by giving to the executive authority, namely the Government, which is the fundamental executive authority, power to use any organ, instrument or method of procedure which may be used for similar purposes by other nations with whom we may be associated, no matter what it is. Although it is giving a power which has been clearly and obviously suggested by the exact circumstances in which we find ourselves at the moment, nevertheless if we were a completely isolated State in the world, looking around us, and if we thought there was going to be instituted a league which was going to hold itself together by an agreement amongst its members to operate in a certain way, we should have power, if we wanted to, to join such a league. I am not saying that that idea—although I think it is a perfect one in the Constitution, and ought to be there—would have been suggested to me or anybody else except in the context of the existing situation, but there is nothing in it that is derogatory to the powers of the people, of the people's Parliament, of the Government, to do that. Consequently, dealing with our external relations, it enables the Executive Government of the day to make use of it, provided that there is a law passed by the national Parliament which would make that possible. Now, the law can exactly prescribe the conditions. In our case the law has already been passed, and this Constitution takes over that law. Therefore, when this Constitution is passed, as far as our external relations are concerned, no change is made, but the external relations are kept in a position in which they can be dealt with and handled as a matter of public policy, without bringing them across the fundamental rights which govern the working of our institutions. . . .

I do not at this Stage want to follow Deputy Costello into another mistaken argument of his that this is an amendment of the old Constitution. It is not. I do not think we could amend the old Constitution in this way. The only way in which you can get a Constitution is to get the people themselves to enact it or get them to elect a Constituent Assembly to enact it. That is my view. I do not think there would be any Deputy more quickly on his feet than Deputy Costello if I suggested I was moving in that direction. Deputy Costello would be telling us that he would have a grand time going to the Supreme Court asking them to say that the Constitution was *ultra vires*. But neither Deputy Costello nor anybody else can tell us that this Draft Constitution is *ultra vires* for it is the people themselves who will enact it. They are the authority. The people have power to determine from time to time who their rulers will be and also what their Government will be. The Government can go back to the people and the people can effect that revolution and change their form of government as long as it is referred to themselves. In this case they will be doing that and I would like to see the lawyers who would stand in their way. This Draft Constitution, if passed at all, is going to be passed by the sovereign people who are above the lawyers and above the Government and all others. Their will is the final decision and once they have voted on it and their elected representatives come together this Draft becomes, in accordance with its own terms, law within a certain date.

If the new Dáil passes a resolution that this Constitution is to come into operation, then before six months it comes into operation. If the new Dáil neglect their duty, even whether they like it or not, it becomes law within six months from the date of the plebiscite. Therefore, it is that in this case we are not bothering very much about what the lawyers think or say about this Constitution. I know, however, that the lawyers would have a lot to say about it if it were brought in as an amendment of the old Constitution. This is a new Constitution put before the people and the people will enact it with such amendments as we may make here. When it is enacted it is the foundation law of the sovereign people of this country and, I, therefore, put it before the Dáil.

Document 1.8 — Extract from the Debate in *Dáil Debates,* vol. 68, col. 430 (14 June, 1937).

Mr. MacDermot: What is there in this Constitution in the way of concession that would not be there if the Northern problem did not exist at all?

The President: The Deputy had better not ask me to go into the origin of a number of other things that would possibly be in this Constitution if the Northern problem were not there. If it was not there, in all probability there would be a flat, downright proclamation of the republic in this. That is one.

(b) *The Constitution*

Document 1.9 — Extracts from Bunreacht na hÉireann (Constitution of Ireland).

In the Name of the Most Holy Trinity, from Whom is all authority and to Whom, as our final end, all actions both of men and States must be referred,
We, the people of Éire,
Humbly acknowledging all our obligations to our Divine Lord, Jesus Christ, Who sustained our fathers through centuries of trial,
Gratefully remembering their heroic and unremitting struggle to regain the rightful independence of our Nation,
And seeking to promote the common good, with due observance of Prudence, Justice and Charity, so that the dignity and freedom of the individual may be assured, true social order attained, the unity of our country restored, and concord established with other nations,
Do hereby adopt, enact, and give to ourselves this Constitution.

Article 1.
    The Irish nation hereby affirms its inalienable, indefeasible, and sovereign right to choose its own form of Government, to determine its relations with other nations, and to develop its life, political, economic and cultural, in accordance with its own genius and traditions.

Article 2.
    The national territory consists of the whole island of Ireland, its islands and the territorial seas.

Article 3.

Pending the re-integration of the national territory, and without prejudice to the right of the Parliament and Government established by this Constitution to exercise jurisdiction over the whole of that territory, the laws enacted by that Parliament shall have the like area and extent of application as the laws of Saorstát Éireann and the like extra-territorial effect.

Article 4.

The name of the State is Éire, or in the English language, *Ireland.*

Article 5.

Ireland is a sovereign, independent, democratic state.

[*Articles 6 and 7 omitted*]

Article 8.

1. The Irish language as the national language is the first official language.
2. The English language is recognised as a second official language.
3. Provision may, however, be made by law for the exclusive use of either of the said languages for any one or more official purposes, either throughout the State or in any part thereof.

[*Articles 9-28 and Article 29.1-3 omitted*]

Article 29.

4. 1° The executive power of the State in or in connection with its external relations shall in accordance with Article 28 of this Constitution be exercised by or on the authority of the Government.

2° For the purpose of the exercise of any executive function of the State in or in connection with its external relations, the Government may to such extent and subject to such conditions, if any, as may be determined by law, avail of or adopt any organ, instrument, or method of procedure used or adopted for the like purpose by the members of any group or league of nations with which the State is or becomes associated for the purpose of international co-operation in matters of common concern.

[*Remainder of Article 29 and Articles 30-40.1 omitted.*]

Article 40.

2. 1° Titles of nobility shall not be conferred by the State.

2° No title of nobility or of honour may be accepted by any citizen except with the prior approval of the Government.

[*Remainder omitted*]

7. REPUBLIC OR COMMONWEALTH ?

Document 1.10 — Extracts from a speech by the Taoiseach, Mr de Valera, in *Dáil Debates*, vol. 97, cols. 2568-75 (14 July, 1945).

. . . Last week Deputy Dillon wanted to know if we were a republic, and pretended that I was the only person who knew the answer. He asked in fact two questions, one of which was easy to answer, the other not so easy. He asked was this State a republic, and were we a member State of the British Commonwealth. When I told him that we were a republic his surprise was, as a friend remarked, like that of Molière's *Bourgeois Gentilhomme* when he learned that he had been speaking prose all his life. Of course the pretence that I alone could answer is plainly ráiméis. The State is what it is, not what I say or think it is. How a particular State is to be classified politically is a matter not to be settled by the *ipse dixit* of any person but by observation of the State's institutions and an examination of its fundamental laws.

Our one fundamental law is the Constitution. A written Constitution, it was submitted to and enacted by the people in a plebiscite taken on adult suffrage on July 1st, 1937. It came into operation on the 29th December, 1937. The first President, Dr. Hyde, entered upon office on the 25th June, 1938, and the organs of State provided for by the Constitution were all fully functioning from that date. A period of three years was allowed during which with the President's consent amendments to the Constitution might be made by the Legislature simply. That period has long since expired, and no change in the Constitution can now be made except by a vote of the people in a Referendum.

Let us glance for a moment at some of the provisions of that fundamental law so that we may realise its character, and the character of our State. Article 5 declares the State to be "sovereign", "independent" and "democratic". Article 6 (1) declares that "all powers of Government, legislative, executive and judicial, derive under God, from the people, whose right it is to designate the rulers of the State and, in final appeal, to decide all questions of national policy, according to the requirements of the common good". Article 6 (2) declares that "these powers of Government are exercisable only by or on the authority of the organs of State established by this Constitution". Article 12 provides for a President to be elected by direct vote of the people for a period of seven years "who shall take precedence over all other persons in the State and who shall exercise and perform the powers and functions conferred on the President by this Constitution and by law". Article 15 states that the National Parliament shall consist of the President and two Houses —the House of Representatives, Dáil Eireann, and a second, Seanad Eireann —constituting, all three together, the Oireachtas, in which is vested "the sole and exclusive power of making laws for the State". Article 28 provides that "the executive power of the State shall, subject to the provisions of this Constitution, be exercised by, or on the authority of, the Government".

The State, whose institutions correspond to these Articles is, it seems to me, demonstrably a republic. Let us look up any standard text on political theory, look up any standard book of reference and get from any of them any definition of a republic or any description of what a republic is and judge whether our State does not possess every characteristic mark by which a republic can be distinguished or recognised. We are a democracy with the ultimate sovereign power resting with the people—a representative democracy with the various organs of State functioning under a written Constitution, with the executive authority controlled by Parliament, with an independent judiciary functioning under the Constitution and the law, and with a Head of State directly elected by the people for a definite term of office.

To save members of the Dáil the trouble of looking up references, I have collected a few. I give first a relevant passage from the *Encyclopedia Britannica* (14th Edition): —

"REPUBLIC.—A State in which the supreme power rests in the people, or in officers elected by them, to whom the people have delegated power sufficient to enable them to perform the duties required of them. In the small republics of antiquity the people usually expressed their preference directly, but in the larger republics of modern times representatives are elected to sit in law-making bodies. The Head of the State is usually elected directly, and in modern usage this fact distinguishes a republic from a monarchy in which the Head is hereditary . . ."

The *Encyclopedia Americana* (1937 Edition) says: —
"REPUBLIC.—A word signifying a State in which the people are the source of power."

I give next a similar passage from the *Shorter Oxford English Dictionary* (Second Edition): —

"REPUBLIC.—A State in which the supreme power rests in the people and their elected representatives or officers, as opposed to one governed by a king or the like; a commonwealth."

Here is what *Webster's International Dictionary* says: —
"REPUBLIC.—A State in which the sovereign power resides in the whole body of the people, and is exercised by representatives elected by them; a commonwealth . . ."

The following is from the *New Standard Dictionary of the English Language*: —

"REPUBLIC.—A State in which the sovereignty resides in the people and the administration is lodged in officers elected by and representing the people; a representative democracy". . . .

Is it argued that, because we have the External Relations Act of 1936, our State is a monarchy? I do not think any constitutional lawyer of repute would attempt to maintain such a thesis. By this Act, so long as we are "associated with the following nations, that is to say, Australia, Canada, Great Britain, New Zealand and South Africa, and so long as the King, recognised by those nations as the symbol of their co-operation, continues to act on behalf of each of those nations (on the advice of the several Governments thereof) for the purposes of the appointment of diplomatic and consular representatives and the conclusion of international agreements, the King so recognised" is permitted and authorised to act on our behalf for like purposes as and when advised by the Government.

This External Relations Act is a simple statute repealable by the legislature and not a fundamental law. As a law it is, in fact, null and void to any extent whatever in which it conflicts with our only fundamental law, the Constitution. It is a simple enabling Act to permit of the carrying out of the external policy of the State in the field of international relations as indicated and provided for in Article 29 (4) of the Constitution and nothing more. This may be regarded as a unique arrangement. I am not disposed to question a statement of this sort. The situation which it was designated to fit, and for a number of years has effectively fitted, was likewise unique. The position, as I conceive it to be, is this: We are an independent republic, associated as a matter of our external policy with the States of the British Commonwealth. To mark this association, we avail ourselves of the procedure of the External Relations Act just quoted, by which the King recognised by the States of the British Commonwealth therein named acts for us, under advice, in certain specified matters in the field of our external relations.

And now, to Deputy Dillon's second question—are we or are we not a member of the British Commonwealth? That is a question for which the material necessary for a conclusive answer is not fully available. It depends on what the essential element is in the constitution of the British Commonwealth.

The British Commonwealth claims to be an elastic, growing, developing organism and the statesmen of the Commonwealth have, I think, adopted the view of Joseph de Maistre that "In all political systems there are relationships which it is wiser to leave undefined." I can only say that, without any request or reference or suggestion from us, on the day on which our Constitution came into force, viz., 29th December, 1937, the following communication was issued from 10 Downing Street, and published in the Press on the following day: —

"His Majesty's Government in the United Kingdom have considered the position created by the new Constitution which was approved by the Parliament of the Irish Free State in June, 1937, and came into force on December 29.

They are prepared to treat the new Constitution as not effecting a fundamental alteration in the position of the Irish Free State—in future to be described under the new Constitution as 'Éire' or 'Ireland' — as a member of the British Commonwealth of Nations.

His Majesty's Government in the United Kingdom have ascertained that His Majesty's Government in Canada, the Commonwealth of Australia, New Zealand, and the Union of South Africa are also prepared so to treat the new Constitution."

8. THE REPUBLIC OF IRELAND

(a) *Speech by Mr J. A. Costello*

Document 1.11 — Extracts from a speech by Mr J. A. Costello to the Canadian Bar Association on 1 September, 1948, printed in John A. Costello, *Ireland in International Affairs,* Monument Press, Dublin and Bray, n.d.

. . . In British constitutional theory the Crown was the link which bound the self-governing parts of the British Commonwealth to the mother country. That Crown was regarded as one and undivided, and recognition of that link a prerequisite to continued membership or of association with the British Commonwealth of Nations. The Crown was a symbol, a rallying point for peoples who sprang from and recognized the common origin and the common motherland. The British Empire, certainly before it developed into the British Commonwealth of Nations, was really a close family circle. It consisted on the one hand of the mother country, Great Britain, and the daughters, grown or growing up, Canada, Australia and New Zealand on the other. The daughters were rapidly developing in independence and self-expression as nations, but their rapid development did not necessarily carry with it any weakening in their sense of family, or any lessening of their pride in the family connexion. . . .

By reason of Ireland's seven centuries of struggle with England and because of the fact that the political institutions, which grew up naturally in Great Britain and her Dominions as the expression of their national individuality, were imposed upon Ireland, those institutions could never be really acceptable to Irishmen or be expected to earn the respect of Irishmen, much less their loyalty. Irish national instincts, deep-rooted in history, recoiled from the forms which were to them, not the embodiment of their national pride in the social structure, but the symbol of centuries of civil and religious persecution and confiscation.

To understand the Irish attitude a knowledge and appreciation of the historical relations between Great Britain and Ireland is essential. . . .

It has never been denied as it could not be challenged that Ireland is a mother country. No nation has contributed so generously of its life blood to the enrichment of other countries and no nation has produced so many exiles who, while never forgetting their debt to the motherland, have discharged with unstinted loyalty and devotion their obligations to the lands of their adoption. Throughout dark and oppressive decades the Irish have left their homes to go into exile. After the Great Famine of a hundred years ago a tide of emigration began, which threatened to destroy our nation for ever. What Ireland lost other countries gained: Canada, the United States of America, Australia, South Africa, New Zealand and South America. But even before the Famine our exiles had spread themselves and made themselves felt across the Continent of Europe. They left their homes because of the oppression and persecution of an alien Government, which had hoped that the day would dawn when a 'native Irishman on the banks of the Shannon would be as rare as a Red Indian on the banks of the Potomac'.

During all that period the Crown was a symbol of a political and religious ascendancy and became anathema to the vast majority of the Irish people. The harp without the Crown symbolized the ideal of Irish independence and nationhood. The harp beneath the Crown was the symbol of conquest. The bitter facts of history have inevitably prevented our people from having that outlook which the people of the great self-governing members of the British Commonwealth of Nations may have for the Crown as their traditional link. Whatever other conclusions may be drawn from the long and varied history of our national struggle, it established certain historical facts which are of great importance as marking a sharp distinction between us and the other members of the group of nations with which we became associated by the Treaty of 1921 . . . The characteristic marks of the community into which Ireland entered by that Treaty were constitutional forms which had their roots far back in British constitutional history. The member states of that community had attained their membership and reached nationhood by a process of gradual constitutional evolution within the framework of British constitutional traditions and ideas. . . .

Michael Collins, one of the signatories of the Treaty, described the Treaty as giving us the freedom necessary to enable us to achieve freedom. That phrase aptly describes the purpose and direction of our national policy in the years that followed. . . .

With the passage of the Statute of Westminster, the sovereignty of Ireland and the other members of the Commonwealth was beyond all question complete and absolute. There was no bond or fetter, practical or theoretical, on their powers to order their destinies in accordance with the wishes of their own people. So far as our constitutional structure and our relationship with the Commonwealth was concerned, it was no longer a question of whether or not changes required to be made to establish the fact of our sovereignty beyond all legal doubt; any possibility of doubt as to our sovereignty had been removed; the question had become *not* whether our association with the Commonwealth and the constitutional provisions in which it was expressed represented a limitation of our freedom or sovereignty, but whether our Constitutional arrangements relating to these matters were in a *form* which the people as a whole could accept as being compatible with our national sentiment and historical tradition. . . .

The Irish Constitution of 1937 is radically different from that of Canada, Australia, New Zealand or South Africa. Instead of a Governor General, we have a President of Ireland elected by universal popular suffrage. The executive power of the State is to be exercised by or on the authority of the Government and the Crown is nowhere mentioned in the Constitution. Article 5 of the Constitution declares that Ireland is a sovereign, independent, democratic state, and Article 29 which recognizes that the State is, or may become, associated with a group or league of nations for the purposes of international co-operation in matters of common concern would seem to be a constitutional authority for our association as a sovereign, independent, democratic state with the community of nations known as the Commonwealth of Nations.

By the External Authority (External Relations) Act, 1936, it is declared that so long as the State is associated with Australia, Canada, Great Britain, New Zealand and South Africa, and so long as the King recognized by those nations as the *symbol of their co-operation* continues to act on behalf of each of those nations (on the advice of the several governments thereof) for the purposes of the *appointment* of diplomatic and consular representatives and the conclusion of international agreements, the King, so recognized, may act on behalf of the State for the like purpose and act when advised by the Government to do so. The inaccuracies and infirmities of these provisions are apparent. The Crown was the symbol of free association and not the symbol of co-operation; the formalities of the issue of Full Powers to negotiate or sign treaties are ignored; and the statutory provisions deal only with the appointment and not with the reception of diplomatic representatives.

In the time at my disposal it has been possible only to sketch the merest outline of the Constitutional structure as it was fashioned and altered during the quarter of a century which has elapsed since the foundation of the Irish State. We have to deal with the existing position. The reasons for or the wisdom of the changes are not now in issue.

In any event is it fruitful, with the mentality of the person who 'would peep and botanize upon his mother's grave', to enquire too legalistically into the nature of Ireland's association with the Commonwealth; to insist that it does not conform to an existing pattern; or that the association has no common factor with traditional constitutional concepts?

The answers to these questions affect or may affect not merely Ireland but other States who are or may become hereafter associated with the League of Free Nations, the Commonwealth of Nations.

(b) *The Republic of Ireland Act*

Document 1.12 — The Republic of Ireland Act, 1948 (no. 22).

BE IT ENACTED BY THE OIREACHTAS AS FOLLOWS:—

1.—The Executive Authority (External Relations) Act, 1936 (No. 58 of 1936), is hereby repealed.

2.—It is hereby declared that the description of the State shall be the Republic of Ireland.

3.—The President, on the authority and on the advice of the Government, may exercise the executive power or any executive function of the State in or in connection with its external relations.

4.—This Act shall come into operation on such day as the Government may by order appoint.

5.This Act may be cited as The Republic of Ireland Act, 1948.

(c) *The Ireland Act*

Document 1.13 — The Ireland Act, 1949 (12 and 13, Geo. 6, ch. 41) in *The Public General Acts and the Church Assembly Measures of 1949,* vol. 1.

An Act to recognise and declare the constitutional position as to the part of Ireland heretofore known as Eire, and to make provision as to the name by which it may be known and the manner in which the law is to apply in relation to it; to declare and affirm the constitutional position and the territorial integrity of Northern Ireland and to amend, as respects the Parliament of the United Kingdom, the law relating to the qualifications of electors in constituencies in Northern Ireland; and for purposes connected with the matters aforesaid.   [2nd June 1949]

Be it enacted by the King's most Excellent Majesty, by and with the advice and consent of the Lords Spiritual and Temporal, and Commons, in this present Parliament assembled, and by the authority of the same, as follows: —

1.—(1) It is hereby recognized and declared that the part of Ireland heretofore known as Eire ceased, as from the eighteenth day of April, nineteen hundred and forty-nine, to be part of His Majesty's dominions.

(2) It is hereby declared that Northern Ireland remains part of His Majesty's dominions and of the United Kingdom and it is hereby affirmed that in no event will Northern Ireland or any part thereof cease to be part of His Majesty's dominions and of the United Kingdom without the consent of the Parliament of Northern Ireland.

(3) The part of Ireland referred to in subsection (1) of this section is hereafter in this Act referred to, and may in any Act, enactment or instrument passed or made after the passing of this Act be referred to, by the name attributed thereto by the law thereof, that is to say, as the Republic of Ireland.

2.—(1) It is hereby declared that, notwithstanding that the Republic of Ireland is not part of His Majesty's dominions, the Republic of Ireland is not a foreign country for the purposes of any law in force in any part of the United Kingdom or in any colony, protectorate or United Kingdom trust territory, whether by virtue of a rule of law or of an Act of Parliament or any other enactment or instrument whatsoever, whether passed or made before or after the passing of this Act, and references in any Act of Parliament, other enactment or instrument whatsoever, whether passed or made before or after the passing of this Act, to foreigners, aliens, foreign countries, and foreign or foreign-built ships or aircraft shall be construed accordingly.

(2) The person who, in the United Kingdom, is the chief representative of the Republic of Ireland or of the Government thereof shall, whatever the style of his office, have the same privileges and exemptions as to taxation and otherwise as fall to be accorded under the law for the time being in force to

High Commissioners and Agents General within the meaning of section nineteen of the Finance Act, 1923, and his staff shall have the same privileges and exemptions as to taxation and otherwise as fall to be accorded under the law for the time being in force to their staffs.

[Remainder omitted]

READING

V. Grogan: 'Irish Constitutional Development' in *Studies*, vol. 40, pp. 385-98.

A. G. Donaldson: *Some Comparative Aspects of Irish Law*, Durham N.C. and London, 1957.

W. K. Hancock: *Survey of British Commonwealth Affairs*, vol. 1. *Problems of Nationality, 1918-36*, London, 1937.

D. Macardle: *The Irish Republic*, Dublin, 1951.

N. Mansergh: *Survey of British Commonwealth Affairs*: *Problems of External Policy, 1931-39*, London, 1952.

N. Mansergh: *Survey of British Commonwealth Affairs*: *Problems of Wartime Cooperation and Post-war Change, 1939-52*, London, 1958.

In Addition:

A number of works deal in a general way with Irish constitutional development and government and cover the subject matter of a number of chapters in this work. Among them are:—

B. Chubb: *The Constitution of Ireland*, Dublin, 1963.

L. Kohn: *The Constitution of the Irish Free State*, London, 1932.

N. Mansergh: *The Irish Free State, its Government and Politics*, London, 1934.

Chapter 2

THE SOVEREIGN PEOPLE AND THE PRESIDENT

INTRODUCTION

Irish nationalism was by and large liberal democratic, seeking the source of political authority in the people. The Irish Free State Constitution contained, however, as we have observed, an internal contradiction. On the one hand, it declared that all power and authority derive from the people and, on the other, it included the Crown and, hence, imported a piece of British political mythology concerning the source of authority. Bunreacht na hÉireann contains no such equivocation: indeed, it was part of the case for a new constitution that there was need to make perfectly clear that the source of authority in Ireland and of the fundamental law of the country is the people of Ireland (Document 2.1.; and see also the last words of the preamble to the Constitution in Document 1.9 above).

This assertion is not simply a matter of high-sounding generalizations or of statements of abstract rights of a mystical entity called ' the Nation '. The Constitution asserts the right of the people to choose their Government and ' in final appeal ' to decide political issues, and it provides for machinery for this by way of free election and referendum (Document 2.2).

The declaration of popular sovereignty is not wholly unqualified however. Bunreacht na hÉireann is clearly a 'Christian constitution', giving explicit recognition of God as the ultimate source of authority. While the people have a right to decide finally questions of policy, they must do so 'according to the requirements of the common good ' (Article 6).

The ability of the body of citizens to play an active role in government is, of course, limited to such activities as casting their votes at elections and referenda. Their interests are, or should be, actively pursued by their Governments and Representatives, and their rights jealously guarded by the courts. But the Governments and Representatives whom they choose and who are in theory responsible to them, might misread public opinion or even seek inadvertently to change the fundamental law of the Constitution enacted by the people themselves. Also political crises might occur, necessitating speedy decision and action, perhaps involving restraining even the Government. Can the mastery of the people be exerted on these occasions ? Mr de Valera attempted to accomplish this by casting the President of Ireland in the role of the agent of the people at such times. (Document 2.3). The Constitution envisages a role for the President that is not merely that of a ceremonial head of state who performs a number of formal acts of government at the behest of the competent political authorities. He is also invested with real powers to act on behalf of the people in certain circumstances, powers which involve him in using his own judgement. (Document 2.4). His powers to refer bills to the Supreme Court to be tested for repugnancy, to decline, if petitioned by a majority of the Senate and not less than one third of the Dáil, to sign a bill until it shall have been approved by the people at a referendum, and to summon the Oireachtas, all enable him in effect to call in the people or their Representatives. His most important discretionary power, however, (Article 13.2.2°), permits him, on the contrary, to *exclude* the people, for he may, in his absolute discretion, refuse a dissolution to a Taoiseach who has ceased to retain the support of a majority of the Dáil. (Document 2.5).

As it happens, the machinery of referendum provided by the Constitution and subsequent legislation (Document 2.6) was not used for more than twenty years. The first two amendments of the Constitution, in 1939 and 1941, were effected by the Oireachtas alone under transitory provisions contained in the Constitution itself. This does not, however, mean that the referendum is of little practical importance. The occasion of the first use of the device indeed proves how vital it is. A proposal to replace the single transferable vote system of proportional representation and multi-member constituencies by a simple majority system in single member constituencies (see Document 7.5 below), having passed the Oireachtas (though only by the Dáil overriding the rejection of the Senate), was rejected by the people. (Document 2.9).

The preparation for this referendum involved another important matter, the enacting of legislation to provide a suitable form of ballot paper to be used at a referendum. The debate on this measure (Document 2.7) brings out the great importance for democracy of such matters as the amount of information to be given about proposals which are to be placed before the people and the manner in which questions are posed on the ballot paper. (Document 2.8).

1. THE CONSTITUTION STRESSES THE SOVEREIGNTY OF THE PEOPLE
   (a) *Mr de Valera's Speech to the Dáil*
   Document 2.1—Extracts from *Dáil Debates,* vol. 67, cols. 38-40 (11 May 1937).

In the second section, dealing with the State, the most important matters dealt with are the name of the State; the fact that under God the power of government comes from the people, the people designating the rulers. It is, therefore, from the people that the rulers get, not their authority for ruling, because that authority comes from a higher source, but their immediate designation as rulers. . . . .

Now, once you determine upon a democratic form of government, representative government, government responsible to the elected representatives of the people, the main lines of your Constitution are set. We here have always made clear that we believed in the fundamental right of our people to choose their own Government, the form of their State even, and, believing in that right, we naturally enshrined it in the Constitution.

(b) *The Constitution*
Document 2.2—Extracts from Bunreacht na hÉireann (Constitution of Ireland).

Article 6.
1.   All powers of government, legislative, executive and judicial, derive, under God, from the people, whose right it is to designate the rulers of the State and, in final appeal, to decide all questions of national policy, according to the requirements of the common good.

[*Articles 7-26 omitted*]

REFERENCE OF BILLS TO THE PEOPLE

Article 27.
     This Article applies to any Bill, other than a Bill expressed to be a Bill containing a proposal for the amendment of this Constitution, which shall have been deemed, by virtue of Article 23 hereof, to have been passed by both Houses of the Oireachtas.

1.   A majority of the members of Seanad Éireann and not less than one-third of the members of Dáil Éireann may by a joint petition addressed to the President by them under this Article request the President to decline to sign and promulgate as a law any Bill to which this Article applies on the ground that the Bill contains a proposal of such national importance that the will of the people thereon ought to be ascertained.

2.   Every such petition shall be in writing and shall be signed by the petitioners whose signatures shall be verified in the manner prescribed by law.

3.   Every such petition shall contain a statement of the particular ground or grounds on which the request is based, and shall be presented to the President not later than four days after the date on which the Bill shall have been deemed to have been passed by both Houses of the Oireachtas.

4.   1° Upon receipt of a petition addressed to him under this Article, the President shall forthwith consider such petition and shall, after consultation with the Council of State, pronounce his decision thereon not later than ten days after the date on which the Bill to which such petition relates shall have been deemed to have been passed by both Houses of the Oireachtas.

[SS. 2° omitted.]

5.   1° In every case in which the President decides that a Bill the subject of a petition under this Article contains a proposal of such national importance that the will of the people thereon ought to be ascertained, he shall inform the Taoiseach and the Chairman of each House of the Oireachtas accordingly in writing under his hand and Seal, and shall decline to sign and promulgate such Bill as a law unless and until the proposal shall have been approved either

   i. by the people at a Referendum in accordance with the provisions of section 2 of Article 47 of this Constitution within a period of eighteen months from the date of the President's decision, or

   ii. by a resolution of Dáil Éireann passed within the said period after a dissolution and re-assembly of Dáil Éireann.

[SS. 2, S. 6 and Articles 28-45 omitted.]

AMENDMENT OF THE CONSTITUTION

Article 46.

1.   Any provision of this Constitution may be amended, whether by way of variation, addition, or repeal, in the manner provided by this Article.

2.   Every proposal for an amendment of this Constitution shall be initiated in Dáil Éireann as a Bill, and shall upon having been passed or deemed to have been passed by both Houses of the Oireachtas, be submitted by Referendum to the decision of the people in accordance with the law for the time being in force relating to the Referendum.

3.   Every such Bill shall be expressed to be "An Act to amend the Constitution".

4.   A Bill containing a proposal or proposals for the amendment of this Constitution shall not contain any other proposal.

[S. 5 omitted.]

THE REFERENDUM

Article 47.

1.   Every proposal for an amendment of this Constitution which is submitted by Referendum to the decision of the people shall, for the purpose of Article 46 of this Constitution, be held to have been approved by the people, if, upon having been so submitted, a majority of the votes cast

at such Referendum shall have been cast in favour of its enactment into law.

2.   1°   Every proposal, other than a proposal to amend the Constitution, which is submitted by Referendum to the decision of the people shall be held to have been vetoed by the people if a majority of the votes cast at such Referendum shall have been cast against its enactment into law and if the votes so cast against its enactment into law shall have amounted to not less than thirty-three and one-third per cent. of the voters on the register.

2°   Every proposal, other than a proposal to amend the Constitution, which is submitted by Referendum to the decision of the people shall for the purposes of Article 27 hereof be held to have been approved by the people unless vetoed by them in accordance with the provisions of the foregoing sub-section of this section.

3.   Every citizen who has the right to vote at an election for members of Dáil Éireann shall have the right to vote at a Referendum.

4.   Subject as aforesaid, the Referendum shall be regulated by law.

[Remainder omitted]

2. THE PRESIDENT AS THE GUARDIAN OF THE PEOPLE'S RIGHTS
(a) *Mr de Valera's Speech to the Dáil*
Document 2.3—Extract from *Dáil Debates*, vol. 67, cols. 40 and 51, (11 May 1937).

If there is one thing more than another that is clear and shining through this whole Constitution, it is the fact that the people are the masters. They are the masters at the time of an election, and their mastery is maintained during the period from election to election through the President, who has been chosen definitely to safeguard their interests, to see that nothing that they have not in a general way given approval of is passed by the small majority which used to be threatened here as a danger to the country as a whole. . . . In exercising these powers he is acting on behalf of the people who have put him there for that special purpose. He is there to guard the people's rights and mainly to guard the Constitution.

(b) *The Constitution*
Document 2.4—Extracts from Bunreacht na hÉireann (Constitution of Ireland).

THE PRESIDENT

Article 12.

1.   There shall be a President of Ireland (*Uachtarán na hÉireann*), herein-after called the President, who shall take precedence over all other

persons in the State and who shall exercise and perform the powers and functions conferred on the President by this Constitution and by law.

2. 1° The President shall be elected by direct vote of the people.

2° Every citizen who has the right to vote at an election for members of Dáil Éireann shall have the right to vote at an election for President.

3° The voting shall be by secret ballot and on the system of proportional representation by means of the single transferable vote.

3. 1° The President shall hold office for seven years from the date upon which he enters upon his office, unless before the expiration of that period he dies, or resigns, or is removed from office, or becomes permanently incapacitated, such incapacity being established to the satisfaction of the Supreme Court consisting of not less than five judges.

2° A person who holds, or who has held, office as President, shall be eligible for re-election to that office once, but only once.

[Remainder of S. 3 omitted.]

4. 1° Every citizen who has reached his thirty-fifth year of age is eligible for election to the office of President.

2° Every candidate for election, not a former or retiring President, must be nominated either by
  i. not less than twenty persons, each of whom is at the time a member of one of the Houses of the Oireachtas, or
  ii. by the Councils of not less than four administrative Counties (including County Boroughs) as defined by law.

3° No person and no such Council shall be entitled to subscribe to the nomination of more than one candidate in respect of the same election.

4° Former or retiring Presidents may become candidates on their own nomination.

5° Where only one candidate is nominated for the office of President it shall not be necessary to proceed to a ballot for his election.

5. Subject to the provisions of this Article, elections for the office of President shall be regulated by law.

6. 1° The President shall not be a member of either House of the Oireachtas.

2° If a member of either House of the Oireachtas be elected President, he shall be deemed to have vacated his seat in that House.

3° The President shall not hold any other office or position of emolument.

[Ss. 7 and 8 omitted.]

9. The President shall not leave the State during his term of office save with the consent of the Government.

10.   1°   The President may be impeached for stated misbehaviour.

      2°   The charge shall be preferred by either of the Houses of the Oireachtas, subject to and in accordance with the provisions of this section.

[Remainder of Article 12 omitted]

Article 13.

1.   1°   The President shall, on the nomination of Dáil Éireann, appoint the Taoiseach, that is, the head of the Government or Prime Minister.

      2°   The President shall, on the nomination of the Taoiseach with the previous approval of Dáil Éireann, appoint the other members of the Government.

      3°   The President shall, on the advice of the Taoiseach, accept the resignation or terminate the appointment of any member of the Government.

2.   1°   Dáil Éireann shall be summoned and dissolved by the President on the advice of the Taoiseach.

      2°   The President may in his absolute discretion refuse to dissolve Dáil Éireann on the advice of a Taoiseach who has ceased to retain the support of a majority in Dáil Éireann.

      3°   The President may at any time, after consultation with the Council of State, convene a meeting of either or both of the Houses of the Oireachtas.

3.   1°   Every Bill passed or deemed to have been passed by both Houses of the Oireachtas shall require the signature of the President for its enactment into law.

      2°   The President shall promulgate every law made by the Oireachtas.

4.   The supreme command of the Defence Forces is hereby vested in the President.

5.   1°   The exercise of the supreme command of the Defence Forces shall be regulated by law.

      2°   All commissioned officers of the Defence Forces shall hold their commissions from the President.

6.   The right of pardon and the power to commute or remit punishment imposed by any court exercising criminal jurisdiction are hereby vested in the President, but such power of commutation or remission may, except in capital cases, also be conferred by law on other authorities.

7.   1°   The President may, after consultation with the Council of State, communicate with the Houses of the Oireachtas by message or address on any matter of national or public importance.

      2°   The President may, after consultation with the Council of State, address a message to the Nation at any time on any such matter.

3° Every such message or address must, however, have received the approval of the Government.

8. 1° The President shall not be answerable to either House of the Oireachtas or to any court for the exercise and performance of the powers and functions of his office or for any act done or purporting to be done by him in the exercise and performance of these powers and functions.

2° The behaviour of the President may, however, be brought under review in either of the Houses of the Oireachtas for the purposes of section 10 of Article 12 of this Constitution, or by any court, tribunal or body appointed or designated by either of the Houses of the Oireachtas for the investigation of a charge under Section 10 of the said Article.

9. The powers and functions conferred on the President by this Constitution shall be exercisable and performable by him only on the advice of the Government, save where it is provided by this Constitution that he shall act in his absolute discretion or after consultation with or in relation to the Council of State, or on the advice or nomination of, or on receipt of any other communication from, any other person or body.

[*S. 10 omitted.*]

11. No power or function conferred on the President by law shall be exercisable or performable by him save only on the advice of the Government.

Article 14.

1. In the event of the absence of the President or his temporary incapacity, or his permanent incapacity established as provided by section 3 of Article 12 hereof, or in the event of his death, resignation, removal from office, or failure to exercise and perform the powers and functions of his office or any of them, or at any time at which the office of President may be vacant, the powers and functions conferred on the President by or under this Constitution shall be exercised and performed by a Commission constituted as provided in section 2 of this Article.

2. 1° The Commission shall consist of the following persons, namely, the Chief Justice, the Chairman of Dáil Éireann (*An Ceann Comhairle*), and the Chairman of Seanad Éireann.

2° The President of the High Court shall act as a member of the Commission in the place of the Chief Justice on any occasion on which the office of Chief Justice is vacant or on which the Chief Justice is unable to act.

3° The Deputy Chairman of Dáil Éireann shall act as a member of the Commission in the place of the Chairman of Dáil Éireann on any occasion on which the office of Chairman of Dáil Éireann is vacant or on which the said Chairman is unable to act.

4°   The Deputy Chairman of Seanad Éireann shall act as a member of the Commission in the place of the Chairman of Seanad Éireann on any occasion on which the office of Chairman of Seanad Éireann is vacant or on which the said Chairman is unable to act.

3.   The Commission may act by any two of their number and may act notwithstanding a vacancy in their membership.

4.   The Council of State may by a majority of its members make such provision as to them may seem meet for the exercise and performance of the powers and functions conferred on the President by or under this Constitution in any contingency which is not provided for by the foregoing provisions of this Article.

5.   1°   The provisions of this Constitution which relate to the exercise and performance by the President of the powers and functions conferred on him by or under this Constitution shall subject to the subsequent provisions of this section apply to the exercise and performance of the said powers and functions under this Article.

2°   In the event of the failure of the President to exercise or perform any power or function which the President is by or under this Constitution required to exercise or perform within a specified time, the said power or function shall be exercised or performed under this Article, as soon as may be after the expiration of the time so specified.

[Articles 15-25 omitted]

REFERENCE OF BILLS TO THE SUPREME COURT

Article 26.

This Article applies to any Bill passed or deemed to have been passed by both Houses of the Oireachtas other than a Money Bill, or a Bill expressed to be a Bill containing a proposal to amend the Constitution, or a Bill the time for the consideration of which by Seanad Éireann shall have been abridged under Article 24 of this Constitution.

1.   1°   The President may, after consultation with the Council of State, refer any Bill to which this Article applies to the Supreme Court for a decision on the questions as to whether such Bill or any specified provision or provisions of such Bill is or are repugnant to this Constitution or to any provision thereof.

2°   Every such reference shall be made not later than the seventh day after the date on which such Bill shall have been presented by the Taoiseach to the President for his signature.

3°   The President shall not sign any Bill the subject of a reference to the Supreme Court under this Article pending the pronouncement of the decision of the Court.

2.   1°   The Supreme Court consisting of not less than five judges shall consider every question referred to it by the President under this Article for a decision, and having heard arguments by or on behalf of the

Attorney General and by counsel assigned by the Court, shall pronounce its decision on such question in open court as soon as may be, and in any case not later than sixty days after the date of such reference.

2° The decision of the majority of the judges of the Supreme Court shall, for the purposes of this Article, be the decision of the Court and shall be pronounced by such one of those judges as the Court shall direct, and no other opinion, whether assenting or dissenting, shall be pronounced nor shall the existence of any such other opinion be disclosed.

3.   1° In every case in which the Supreme Court decides that any provision of a Bill the subject of a reference to the Supreme Court under this Article is repugnant to this Constitution or to any provision thereof, the President shall decline to sign such Bill.

2° If, in the case of a Bill to which Article 27 of this Constitution applies, a petition has been addressed to the President under that Article, that Article shall be complied with.

3° In every other case the President shall sign the Bill as soon as may be after the date on which the decision of the Supreme Court shall have been pronounced.

[*Articles 27-30 omitted*]

THE COUNCIL OF STATE
Article 31.

1.   There shall be a Council of State to aid and counsel the President on all matters on which the President may consult the said Council in relation to the exercise and performance by him of such of his powers and functions as are by this Constitution expressed to be exercisable and performable after consultation with the Council of State, and to exercise such other functions as are conferred on the said Council by this Constitution.

2.   The Council of State shall consist of the following members:

    i. As *ex-officio* members: the Taoiseach, the Tánaiste, the Chief Justice, the President of the High Court, the Chairman of Dáil Éireann, the Chairman of Seanad Éireann, and the Attorney General.

    ii. Every person able and willing to act as a member of the Council of State who shall have held the office of President or the office of Taoiseach, or the office of Chief Justice, or the office of President of the Executive Council of Saorstát Éireann.

    iii. Such other persons, if any, as may be appointed by the President under this Article to be members of the Council of State.

3.   The President may at any time and from time to time by warrant under his hand and Seal appoint such other persons as, in his absolute discretion, he may think fit, to be members of the Council of State, but not more than seven persons so appointed shall be members of the Council of State at the same time.

[*S. 4 omitted.*]

5. Every member of the Council of State appointed by the President, unless he previously dies, resigns, becomes permanently incapacitated, or is removed from office, shall hold office until the successor of the President by whom he was appointed shall have entered upon his office.
6. Any member of the Council of State appointed by the President may resign from office by placing his resignation in the hands of the President.
7. The President may, for reasons which to him seem sufficient, by an order under his hand and Seal, terminate the appointment of any member of the Council of State appointed by him.
8. Meetings of the Council of State may be convened by the President at such times and places as he shall determine.

Article 32.

The President shall not exercise or perform any of the powers or functions which are by this Constitution expressed to be exercisable or performable by him after consultation with the Council of State unless, and on every occasion before so doing, he shall have convened a meeting of the Council of State and the members present at such meeting shall have been heard by him.

(c) *The President's Power to Refuse a Dissolution*
Document 2.5—Extract from M. McDunphy, *The President of Ireland*,
Browne and Nolan Ltd., Dublin, 1945, pp. 51-2.

The President, however, may, in his absolute discretion, refuse to dissolve Dáil Éireann on the advice of a Taoiseach who has ceased to retain the support of a majority in Dáil Éireann. This provision reserves to the President the right to decide whether, in such circumstances, it would be better in the public interest that he should proclaim a general election, or, by refusing to do so, oblige the Taoiseach to resign, thus giving the Dáil an opportunity, if it so desired, of choosing a new head of the Government.

The Constitution gives no indication as to the evidence which would entitle the President to decide that a Taoiseach had in fact ceased to retain the support of a majority in Dáil Éireann. Nor is there yet available any empirical material which might enlighten the student of Constitutional law on this point, as no case has so far occurred of a refusal by the President to grant a dissolution.

Granted that such a situation has arisen, the President has to consider which of the two decisions open to him, to grant or to refuse a dissolution, is likely to be the better for the country. For such a case no rules can be laid down. The responsibility rests entirely with the President. He is not required to consult with any other person or authority, not even with the Council of State, which figures so largely in other important matters. The decision is his own, made entirely on his own judgment, and he is not bound to state his reasons. At the same time it must be assumed that the President would be slow to refuse a dissolution except for very adequate reasons.

This power is unique in the Irish Constitution. It is the only case in which the President has an absolute and unquestionable right to act in direct opposition to a constitutional request from the Head of the Government, to reject an advice which in other matters is equivalent to a direction, which must be complied with as a matter of course.

3. THE REFERENDUM

(a) *The Act*

Document 2.6—Extracts from Referendum Act, 1942 (No. 8).

8.—(1) Whenever a Bill containing a proposal for the amendment of the Constitution shall have been passed or be deemed to have been passed by both Houses of the Oireachtas it shall be lawful for the Minister to appoint by order the day (in this Act also referred to as the polling day) upon which the polling at the referendum on such proposal shall take place.

[SSs. (2) and (3) omitted]

9.—(1) Whenever a Bill containing a proposal for the amendment of the Constitution shall have been passed, or deemed to have been passed, by both Houses of the Oireachtas, and Dáil Éireann is dissolved before the Minister has made under the next preceding section an order appointing the polling day at the referendum on such proposal, the Minister, if he so thinks fit, may (notwithstanding anything contained in the said next preceding section) appoint by his order under that section the polling day at the general election consequent on such dissolution of Dáil Éireann to be the polling day at such referendum.

(2) Whenever a Bill containing a proposal for the amendment of the Constitution shall have been passed, or deemed to have been passed, by both Houses of the Oireachtas, and Dáil Éireann is dissolved after the Minister has made his order (in this sub-section referred to as the original order) under the next preceding section in relation to the referendum on such proposal and before the polling day appointed by that order, the Minister, if he so thinks fit, may by order amend the original order by substituting the day which is the polling day at the general election consequent on such dissolution of Dáil Éireann for the day named in the original order as the polling day at such referendum.

10.—(1) Whenever—

    (*a*) the President informs the Taoiseach in accordance with Article 27 of the Constitution that he has decided that a Bill to which that Article applies contains a proposal of such national importance that the will of the people thereon ought to be ascertained, and

(b) the Government determines that a referendum for the purpose of ascertaining the will of the people on such proposal shall be taken,

the Minister shall, within one week after such determination by the Government, appoint by order the day (in this Act also referred to as the polling day) upon which the polling at such referendum shall take place.

(2) The polling day appointed by an order made by the Minister under this section shall not be less than thirty days and not more than ninety days after the date of such order.

(3) Whenever the Government determines that an ordinary referendum shall be taken, the Government shall cause notice of such determination to be published in the *Iris Oifigiúil,* and thereupon such publication shall be conclusive evidence of such determination....

(4) Every order made by the Minister under this section shall be published in the *Iris Oifigiúil* as soon as may be after it is made.

[The remainder is omitted]

(b) *Debate on the Referendum (Amendment) Bill,* 1959.
Document 2.7 — Extract from *Dáil Debates,* vol. 172, cols. 17-21
(7 January 1959).

The Minister for Local Government: . . . . Under the Referendum Act, 1942, the form of ballot paper to be used at a referendum contains a space in which the proposal which is the subject of the referendum is to be set out. The voter is asked to state whether he approves or disapproves of the proposal becoming law. The Act provides that in the case of a constitutional referendum the proposal must "be stated on the ballot paper in the same terms as nearly as may be as such proposal is stated in the Bill containing such proposal passed or deemed to have been passed by both Houses of the Oireachtas". I am advised that in order to comply with this provision it would be necessary to set out in the appropriate space in the ballot paper virtually the whole text of the Bill to amend the Constitution, in both official languages.

This would be quite impracticable in the case of a Constitutional Amendment Bill running to several pages, such as the Third Amendment of the Constitution Bill, 1958. It would, obviously, be unreasonable to expect a voter to read a long document of that kind in the polling booth. Copies of the Bill to amend the Constitution will be provided for inspection and purchase in post offices in accordance with the provisions of the Referendum Act, 1942, so that voters can study the terms of the proposed constitutional amendment before polling day.

The First Schedule of the Bill sets out the new form of ballot paper at a constitutional referendum. The proposal which is the subject of the referendum will be stated by citing by its Short Title the Bill to amend the Constitution and the voter will be asked to vote "Yes" or "No" to the question, "Do you approve of the proposal to amend the Constitution contained in the under-mentioned Bill?" . . . .

Mr. J. A. Costello: I move the following amendment : —

To delete all words after the word "That" and substitute therefor the words :

Dáil Éireann declines to give a Second Reading to the Bill as it proposes to deprive the voter of that knowledge of the issue on which he is asked to express an opinion, as would otherwise be set out on the ballot paper as required by Section 15 (4) of the Referendum Act, 1942.

Having regard to the manner in which the proposals for the amendment of the Constitution were brought before the House and are being hurried to the country, this amending Bill, which appears, according to the Minister's statement, to be very simple—perhaps in his view, it is entirely unobjection-able—is regarded by us with extreme suspicion.

The Act of 1942 was passed at a time when calm and objective consideration could be given, and doubtless was given, to the necessary details in connection with the holding of a referendum, be it constitutional or otherwise. We want to know why it is that this Bill now is so framed as to deprive the electorate going in to vote on the referendum and reading the ballot paper of at least a certain amount of information as to what they are voting on and to give them no information.

We must approach the consideration of this Bill on the basis that, under the existing law as contained in the Referendum Act of 1942, a considerable amount of information was set forth on the ballot paper. Under the proposal put forward by the Minister in this Bill, the electorate is to get no information —good, bad or indifferent. The proposal is to change the form of the ballot paper from what is required under the Referendum Act of 1942 to merely putting in the Short Title of the Bill. If Deputies will look at the Short Title of the Constitution Amendment Bill, the first thing that will strike them is that the Short Title is very much longer than the Long Title of the Bill, which is a rather absurd situation. All that the elector will be told on the ballot paper is that the proposal is "The Third Amendment of the Constitution Act, 1959". . . . .

In the 1942 Act, there is a reasonable provision that the voter, when voting, should be told what he is voting on. Section 15, sub-section (4) of that Act provided that every ballot paper in a constitutional referendum should contain a statement of the subject of the referendum. Sub-section (5) proposed that that statement should consist in stating on the ballot paper the proposal in the same terms, as nearly as may be, as those in which such proposal is stated in the Bill containing such proposal passed by the Oireachtas. That Act required that the ballot paper on which the voter was casting his vote should contain a statement of the proposals of the Bill. I see no reason why there should not be an obligation on the Government to state on the ballot paper, as nearly as may be possible, a statement of the proposals contained in this Bill. It could be reduced to a pretty simple form that could be understood by the voters being asked to vote on this proposal, radical as indeed it is.

Instead of having this statement, apparently in the interests of simplicity, the voter is to be told nothing. Under the existing law, the voter had in front of him a statement giving him some information—in fact, considerable information—as to what he was voting on. Here he is to be told nothing. Deputies voting on this Bill must realise and understand the significance of that. Voters are to be told what is the Short Title of the Bill, and the Short Title of the Bill gives no information, good, bad or indifferent, except that it is the Third Amendment of the Constitution Act, 1959. . . .

(c) *Forms of Ballot Papers*
   Document 2.8—Extracts from Electoral Act, 1963 (No. 19).

70.—(1) Subject to the subsequent provisions of this section, every person whose name is on the register of Dáil electors for the time being in force for a constituency, and no other person, shall be entitled to vote in that constituency at the poll at a referendum.

[Remainder of Article 70 omitted]

71.—(1) At a constitutional referendum—

   (*a*) every ballot paper shall be in the form set out in Part I of the Fourth Schedule to this Act, and

   (*b*) the proposal which is the subject of the referendum shall be stated on the ballot paper by citing by its short title the Bill containing such proposal passed or deemed to have been passed by both Houses of the Oireachtas.

(2) At an ordinary referendum every ballot paper shall be in the appropriate form set out in Part II of the Fourth Schedule to this Act, and—

   (*a*) in the case of a ballot paper in respect of one referendum it shall contain a reference to the Bill or the portion of the Bill containing the proposal which is the subject of the referendum, and

   (*b*) in the case of a ballot paper in respect of two or more referenda having the same polling day, it shall contain, in respect of each referendum, a reference to the Bill or the portion of the Bill containing the proposal which is the subject of the referendum.

[Other sections omitted]

FOURTH SCHEDULE
FORMS OF BALLOT PAPERS AT REFERENDA
PART I.
FORM OF BALLOT PAPER AT CONSTITUTIONAL REFERENDUM
(Front of Paper)

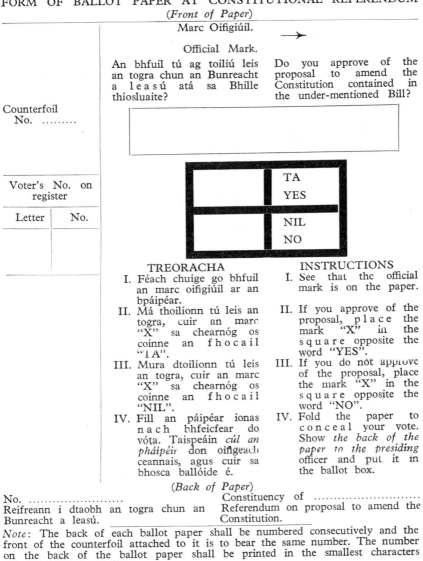

Marc Oifigiúil.

Official Mark. →

An bhfuil tú ag toiliú leis an togra chun an Bunreacht a leasú atá sa Bhille thíosluaite?

Do you approve of the proposal to amend the Constitution contained in the under-mentioned Bill?

Counterfoil No. ....

Voter's No. on register

Letter | No.

TA
YES

NIL
NO

TREORACHA	INSTRUCTIONS
I. Féach chuige go bhfuil an marc oifigiúil ar an bpáipéar.	I. See that the official mark is on the paper.
II. Má thoilíonn tú leis an togra, cuir an marc "X" sa chearnóg os coinne an fhocail "TA".	II. If you approve of the proposal, place the mark "X" in the square opposite the word "YES".
III. Mura dtoilíonn tú leis an togra, cuir an marc "X" sa chearnóg os coinne an fhocail "NIL".	III. If you do not approve of the proposal, place the mark "X" in the square opposite the word "NO".
IV. Fill an páipéar ionas nach bhfeicfear do vóta. Taispeáin *cúl an pháipéir* don oifigeach ceannais, agus cuir sa bhosca ballóide é.	IV. Fold the paper to conceal your vote. Show *the back of the paper to the presiding* officer and put it in the ballot box.

(Back of Paper)

No. ....
Reifreann i dtaobh an togra chun an Bunreacht a leasú.

Constituency of ....
Referendum on proposal to amend the Constitution.

Note: The back of each ballot paper shall be numbered consecutively and the front of the counterfoil attached to it is to bear the same number. The number on the back of the ballot paper shall be printed in the smallest characters compatible with legibility.

PART II.

FORMS OF BALLOT PAPERS AT ORDINARY REFERENDA

1.

FORM OF BALLOT PAPER WHERE ONE REFERENDUM ONLY IS BEING TAKEN

(*Front of Paper*)

Marc Oifigiúil.

Official Mark.

$\longrightarrow$

An bhfuil tú ag toiliú le dlí a dhéanamh den togra thíosluaite?

Do you approve of the undermentioned proposal becoming law?

Counterfoil No. ....

Voter's No. on register

Letter   No.

	TA
	YES
	NIL
	NO

TREORACHA	INSTRUCTIONS
I. Féach chuige go bhfuil an marc oifigiúil ar an bpáipéar.	I. See that the official mark is on the paper.
II. Má thoilíonn tú leis an togra, cuir an marc "X" sa chearnóg os coinne an fhocail "TA".	II. If you approve of the proposal, place the mark "X" in the square opposite the word "YES".
III. Mura dtoilíonn tú leis an togra, cuir an marc "X" sa chearnóg os coinne an fhocail "NIL".	III. If you do not approve of the proposal, place the mark "X" in the square opposite the word "NO".
IV. Fill an páipéar ionas nach bhfeicfear do vóta. Taispeáin *cúl an pháipéir* don oifigeach ceannais, agus cuir sa bhosca ballóide é.	IV. Fold the paper to conceal your vote. Show *the back of the paper to the presiding* officer and put it in the ballot box.

(*Back of Paper*)

No. ....   Constituency of ....

Reifreann i dtaobh an togra go ....   Referendum on proposal that ....

....

....

Note: The back of each ballot paper shall be numbered consecutively and the front of the counterfoil attached to it shall bear the same number. The number on the back of the ballot paper shall be printed in the smallest characters compatible with legibility.

(d) *Notice of Result of a Referendum*

Document 2.9—Notice published in *Iris Oifigiúil*, 23 June 1959.

REFERENDUM ACT, 1942

CONSTITUTIONAL REFERENDUM

PROVISIONAL REFERENDUM CERTIFICATE stating the result of the voting in the Referendum taken on the 17th day of June, 1959, under the Referendum Act, 1942, prepared by the Referendum Returning Officer from the reports furnished to him by the several local returning officers in all the constituencies.

I. The number of votes recorded at the Referendum in each constituency in favour of the proposal, and against the proposal, contained in the Bill entitled

---

AN BILLE UM AN TRIU LEASU AR AN MBUNREACHT, 1958

THIRD AMENDMENT OF THE CONSTITUTION BILL, 1958

---

are shown respectively, for each such constituency, in columns 2 and 3 of the table set out hereunder, that is to say : —

[*Table showing results constituency by constituency omitted.*]

II. (*a*) The total number of votes recorded at the Referendum in favour of the proposal is 453,322.

(*b*) The total number of votes recorded at the Referendum against the proposal is 486,989.

III. A majority of the votes recorded at the Referendum is not recorded in favour of the proposal.

MICHAEL LAWLESS,

Date 22 June, 1959.   *Referendum Returning Officer.*

The foregoing provisional referendum certificate will become final and incapable of being questioned when I am informed by the Master of the High Court either that no referendum petition has been duly presented in respect thereof, or that every such petition so presented has become null and void.

MICHAEL LAWLESS,

Date 22 June, 1959.   *Referendum Returning Officer.*

READING

D. Barrington: 'The Irish Constitution' in *Irish Monthly*, vols. 80 and 81.

B. Chubb: *The Constitution of Ireland*, Dublin, 1963.

M. McDunphy: *The President of Ireland*, Dublin, 1945.

Chapter 3

RIGHTS AND DUTIES OF THE CITIZENS

INTRODUCTION

The enunciation of the rights and duties of the citizens, which is usually an integral part of the Constitution of a country, was one among a number of declarations made by the First Dáil in January 1919 as part of its programme for taking over the state. By enacting a Constitution (see Documents 4.1 and 4.2 below), adopting a social programme and setting up the framework of a state, it hoped to give positive meaning to the declaration of independence to which it was committed and, thus, to attract the loyalty and obedience of the people to its administration. In this way it would drain away the power of established authority.

The Democratic Programme (Document 3.1) should be seen in this light rather than as a carefully considered enunciation of rights which were intended to be strictly enforced forthwith. It is clear that the Programme did not represent the views of all. The independence movement included people of diverse social attitudes, among them some who felt great concern for education, social welfare and social equality. This was particularly marked amongst the labour wing of the movement where there were avowed socialists, including Marxist socialists. Some of the views of this more left-wing element that found expression in the document were not congenial to others in the movement, including many of the leaders.

The rights mentioned in the Constitution of the Irish Free State (Document 3.2) reflect a more conservative attitude. Compared not only with the Democratic Programme but also with some of the new constitutions of the time, the list is conventional in the liberal democratic tradition rather than social democratic. It combined a declaration of personal and civil rights, couched in terms reflecting British legal concepts, with special concern to provide safeguards against religious discrimination which looked like secular indifference but, in fact, reflected the need to guarantee the

48

religious minority. The important principle that the courts should have the function of declaring on the constitutionality of legislation was specifically stated. From the Democratic Programme only two of the positive duties of the state survived — the obligation to provide free elementary education and the declaration that all the natural resources of the country belong to the state. The latter, though widely drawn, did not in fact presage large-scale nationalization and, in practice, governments pursued conservative policies.

The rights articles in Bunreacht na hÉireann (Document 3.3) confirm this conservatism, and the liberal democratic attitude is largely retained in the enunciation of personal and civil rights. An expression of Catholic principles, particularly in articles dealing with such matters as education, property and the family, is an important addition and a most marked feature, distinguishing this declaration from that of the Irish Free State Constitution. In much longer and more elaborate articles than in the previous document, there is in Bunreacht na hÉireann a combination of traditional liberal principles and the teaching of the Encyclicals.

Some commentators, particularly lawyers, have remarked that these articles of the Constitution are a good example of giving with one hand and taking back with the other. Qualifying phrases such as ' save in accordance with law ' or ' subject to public order and morality ' are indeed unsatisfactory from a lawyer's point of view. This does not, however, mean that articles containing such phrases are not valuable as statements intended as guides for the community and particularly its legislators. Articles 40 to 44 might be seen in this light : certainly Article 45 (Document 3.4) must be so regarded, since it is specifically stated that it is a declaration of principles of social policy for the guidance of the Oireachtas and ' shall not be cognisable in any court '.

If some of the citizens' rights seem uncertain, it is quite the reverse in respect of the authority accorded to the Oireachtas to deal with emergencies, both war and civilian (Documents 3.5 and 3.7). The wide powers given by statute to the Government (Documents 3.8 and 3.9) and the continuation in force of the resolution of the Oireachtas declaring an emergency in 1939, which gives the Oireachtas almost unlimited powers to legislate what it will (Document 3.6), mean that a formidable collection of weapons are to hand for any Government which needs, or is minded, to use them. That is not to say that the courts are not some safeguard. They are, and, in fact, they are specifically assigned the role of protecting the Constitution. Much depends on what attitude they take in the cases which are brought before them. It is not possible in a work of this sort to abstract their rulings. In one case, however, *In re Article* 26 *and the Offences against the State (Amendment) Bill, 1940,* important general principles seem to have been enunciated by the Supreme Court, and an extract from the judgement in this case is included (Document 3.10).

Important additions to the rights, and guarantees of the rights, of the citizen given in the domestic law of the state, are to be found in international law, though these are often overlooked. As a member of the Council of Europe, Ireland has, with fourteen other members, accepted the Convention for the Protection of Human Rights and Fundamental Freedoms agreed in Rome in November, 1950, and to some subsequent additions (Documents 3.11 and 3.12). Moreover, she has bound herself by declaration to accept the competence and jurisdiction of the judicial bodies (The European Commission of Human Rights and the European Court of Human Rights) set up under that Convention. Many of the rights enunciated in the Convention are of course guaranteed by domestic law, but in so far as they are not, there is presumably a duty on the Irish Government and Oireachtas to bring the law of the land into accord with the Convention. Certainly, in preparing legislative proposals, it is incumbent on Irish Governments to have regard to the Convention.

It is important to notice, in this respect, that the Convention itself as a whole is no part of the domestic law of the land. While eight states have made the Convention part of their national law, under Article 29.6 of Bunreacht na hÉireann, 'no international agreement shall be part of the domestic law of the State save as may be determined by the Oireachtas'. The Oireachtas has not yet so determined, though it might well appear to be the Government's duty to ask it to do so. As a consequence of this, the rights conferred in the Convention and subsequent Protocol cannot be pleaded in an Irish court. However, Ireland having made the declarations mentioned above, Irish individuals and non-governmental organizations can proceed against the state itself before the Commission, and, through the Commission, before the Court. One citizen of Ireland, Mr Gerard Lawless, has in fact done this: (see Articles by A. H. Robertson, in *British Year Book of International Law,* vol. 36, pp. 343 ff. and vol. 37, pp. 536 ff.) This is an important diminution of sovereignty which five states, including Britain and Italy, were not prepared to accept.

These rights in international law are, then, of very real importance to the individual in extending his chances of obtaining recognition of his claim to satisfactory conditions of life. In the end, however, the liberties a person can enjoy depend upon the attitudes of his fellow men and on the willingness and ability of public representatives both to interpret public opinion and gently to lead it.

DOCUMENTS

1. THE DEMOCRATIC PROGRAMME
   Document 3.1—Extract from *Dáil Éireann: Minutes of Proceedings of the First Parliament of The Republic of Ireland, 1919-1921*, pp. 22-23.

We declare in the words of the Irish Republican Proclamation the right of the people of Ireland to the ownership of Ireland, and to the unfettered control of Irish destinies to be indefeasible, and in the language of our first President, Pádraig Mac Phiarais, we declare that the Nation's sovereignty extends not only to all men and women of the Nation, but to all its material possessions, the Nation's soil and all its resources, all the wealth and all the wealth-producing processes within the Nation, and with him we affirm that all right to private property must be subordinated to the public right and welfare.

We declare that we desire our country to be ruled in accordance with the principles of Liberty, Equality, and Justice for all, which alone can secure permanence of Government in the willing adhesion of the people.

We affirm the duty of every man and woman to give allegiance and service to the Commonwealth, and declare it is the duty of the Nation to assure that every citizen shall have opportunity to spend his or her strength and faculties in the service of the people. In return for willing service, we, in the name of the Republic, declare the right of every citizen to an adequate share of the produce of the Nation's labour.

It shall be the first duty of the Republic to make provision for the physical mental and spiritual well-being of the children, to secure that no child shall suffer hunger or cold from lack or food, clothing, or shelter, but that all shall be provided with the means and facilities requisite for their proper education and training as Citizens of a Free and Gaelic Ireland.

The Irish Republic fully realises the necessity of abolishing the present odious, degrading and foreign Poor Law System, substituting therefor a sympathetic native scheme for the care of the Nation's aged and infirm, who shall not be regarded as a burden, but rather entitled to the Nation's gratitude and consideration. Likewise it shall be the duty of the Republic to take such measures as will safeguard the health of the people and ensure the physical as well as the moral well-being of the Nation.

It shall be our duty to promote the development of the Nation's resources, to increase the productivity of its soil, to exploit its mineral deposits, peat bogs, and fisheries, its waterways and harbours, in the interests and for the benefit of the Irish people.

It shall be the duty of the Republic to adopt all measures necessary for the recreation and invigoration of our Industries, and to ensure their being developed on the most beneficial and progressive co-operative and industrial lines. With the adoption of an extensive Irish Consular Service, trade with foreign Nations shall be revived on terms of mutual advantage and goodwill, and while undertaking the organisation of the Nation's trade, import and export, it shall be the duty of the Republic to prevent the shipment from Ireland of food and other necessaries until the wants of the Irish people are fully satisfied and the future provided for.

It shall also devolve upon the National Government to seek co-operation of the Governments of other countries in determining a standard of Social and Industrial Legislation with a view to a general and lasting improvement in the conditions under which the working classes live and labour.

2. RIGHTS IN THE IRISH FREE STATE CONSTITUTION
Document 3.2 — Extracts from the Constitution of the Irish Free State (Saorstát Éireann) Act, 1922.

Article 5.

No title of honour in respect of any services rendered in or in relation to the Irish Free State (Saorstát Éireann) may be conferred on any citizen of the Irish Free State (Saorstát Éireann) except with the approval or upon the advice of the Executive Council of the State.

Article 6.

The liberty of the person is inviolable, and no person shall be deprived of his liberty except in accordance with law. Upon complaint made by or on behalf of any person that he is being unlawfully detained, the High Court and any and every judge thereof shall forthwith enquire into the same and may make an order requiring the person in whose custody such person shall be detained to produce the body of the person so detained before such Court or judge without delay, and to certify in writing as to the cause of the detention and such Court or judge shall thereupon order the release of such person unless satisfied that he is being detained in accordance with the law:

Provided, however, that nothing in this Article contained shall be invoked to prohibit, control or interfere with any act of the military forces of the Irish Free State (Saorstát Éireann) during the existence of a state of war or armed rebellion.

Article 7.

The dwelling of each citizen is inviolable and shall not be forcibly entered except in accordance with law.

Article 8.

Freedom of conscience and the free profession and practice of religion are, subject to public order and morality, guaranteed to every citizen, and no law may be made either directly or indirectly to endow any religion, or prohibit or restrict the free exercise thereof or give any preference, or impose any disability on account of religious belief or religious status, or affect prejudicially the right of any child to attend a school receiving public money without attending the religious instruction at the school, or make any discrimination as respects State aid between schools under the management of different religious denominations, or divert from any religious denomination or any educational institution any of its property except for the purpose of roads, railways, lighting, water or drainage works or other works of public utility, and on payment of compensation.

Article 9.

The right of free expression of opinion as well as the right to assemble peaceably and without arms, and to form associations or unions is guaranteed for purposes not opposed to public morality. Laws regulating the manner in which the right of forming associations and the right of free assembly may be exercised shall contain no political, religious or class distinction.

Article 10.

All citizens of the Irish Free State (Saorstát Éireann) have the right to free elementary education.

Article 11.

All the lands and waters, mines and minerals, within the territory of the Irish Free State (Saorstát Éireann) hitherto vested in the State, or any department thereof, or held for the public use or benefit, and also all the natural resources of the same territory (including the air and all forms of potential energy), and also all royalties and franchises within that territory shall, from and after the date of the coming into operation of this Constitution, belong to the Irish Free State (Saorstát Éireann), subject to any trusts, grants, leases or concessions then existing in respect thereof, or any valid private interest therein, and shall be controlled and administered by the Oireachtas, in accordance with such regulations and provisions as shall be from time to time approved by legislation, but the same shall not, nor shall any part hereof, be alienated, but may in the public interest be from time to time granted by way of lease or licence to be worked or enjoyed under the authority and subject to the control of the Oireachtas: Provided that no such lease or licence may be made for a term exceeding ninety-nine years, beginning from the date thereof, and no such lease or licence may be renewable by the terms thereof. [*Articles* 12-42 *omitted.*]

Article 43.

The Oireachtas shall have no power to declare acts to be infringements of the law which were not so at the date of their commission. [*Articles* 44-64 *omitted.*]

Article 65.

The judicial power of the High Court shall extend to the question of the validity of any law having regard to the provisions of the Constitution. In all cases in which such matters shall come into question, the High Court alone shall exercise original jurisdiction. [*Remainder omitted.*]

3. BUNREACHT NA hEIREANN

(a) *Fundamental Rights*

> Document 3.3—Extracts from Bunreacht na hÉireann (Constitution of Ireland).

Article 15.

> [*Ss.* 1-4 *omitted.*]

5. The Oireachtas shall not declare acts to be infringements of the law which were not so at the date of their commission. [*Articles* 16 *to* 34.2 *omitted.*]

Article 34.

3. 1° The Courts of First Instance shall include a High Court invested with full original jurisdiction in and power to determine all matters and questions whether of law or fact, civil or criminal.

2° Save as otherwise provided by this Article, the jurisdiction of the High Court shall extend to the question of the validity of any law having regard to the provisions of this Constitution, and no such question shall be raised (whether by pleading, argument or otherwise) in any Court established under this or any other Article of this Constitution other than the High Court or the Supreme Court.

3° No Court whatever shall have jurisdiction to question the validity of a law, or any provision of a law, the Bill for which shall have been referred to the Supreme Court by the President under Article 26 of this Constitution, or to question the validity of a provision of a law where the corresponding provision in the Bill for such law shall have been referred to the Supreme Court by the President under the said Article 26.

4° The Courts of First Instance shall also include Courts of local and limited jurisdiction with a right of appeal as determined by law. [*Articles* 35-38 *omitted.*]

Article 39.

Treason shall consist only in levying war against the State, or assisting any State or person or inciting or conspiring with any person to levy war against the State, or attempting by force of arms or other violent means to overthrow the organs of government established by this Constitution, or taking part or being concerned in or inciting or conspiring with any person to make or to take part or be concerned in any such attempt.

PERSONAL RIGHTS

Article 40.

1.   All citizens shall, as human persons, be held equal before the law.

This shall not be held to mean that the State shall not in its enactments have due regard to differences of capacity, physical and moral, and of social function.

2.   1° Titles of nobility shall not be conferred by the State.

2° No title of nobility or of honour may be accepted by any citizen except with the prior approval of the Government.

3.   1° The State guarantees in its laws to respect, and, as far as practicable, by its laws to defend and vindicate the personal rights of the citizen.

2° The State shall, in particular, by its laws protect as best it may from unjust attack and, in the case of injustice done, vindicate the life, person, good name, and property rights of every citizen.

4.   1° No citizen shall be deprived of his personal liberty save in accordance with law.

2° Upon complaint being made by or on behalf of any person to the High Court or any judge thereof alleging that such person is being unlawfully detained, the High Court and any and every judge thereof to whom such complaint is made shall forthwith enquire into the said complaint and may order the person in whose custody such person is detained to produce the body of such person before the High Court on a named day and to certify in writing the grounds of his detention, and the High Court shall, upon the body of such person being produced before that Court and after giving the person in whose custody he is detained an opportunity of justifying the detention, order the release of such person from such detention unless satisfied that he is being detained in accordance with the law.

3° Where the body of a person alleged to be unlawfully detained is produced before the High Court in pursuance of an order in that behalf made under this section and that Court is satisfied that such person is being detained in accordance with a law but that such law is invalid having regard to the provisions of this Constitution, the High Court shall refer the question of the validity of such law to the Supreme Court by way of case stated and may, at the time of such reference or at any time thereafter, allow the said person to be at liberty on such bail and subject to such conditions as the High Court shall fix until the Supreme Court has determined the question so referred to it.

4° The High Court before which the body of a person alleged to be unlawfully detained is to be produced in pursuance of an order in that behalf made under this section shall, if the President of the High Court or, if he is not available, the senior judge of that Court who is available so directs in respect of any particular case, consist of three judges and shall, in every other case, consist of one judge only.

5° Where an order is made under this section by the High Court or a judge thereof for the production of the body of a person who is under sentence of death, the High Court or such judge thereof shall further order that the execution of the said sentence of death shall be deferred until after the body of such person has been produced before the High Court and the lawfulness of his detention has been determined and if, after such deferment, the detention of such person is determined to be lawful, the High Court shall appoint a day for the execution of the said sentence of death and that sentence shall have effect with the substitution of the day so appointed for the day originally fixed for the execution thereof.

6° Nothing in this section, however, shall be invoked to prohibit, control, or interfere with any act of the Defence Forces during the existence of a state of war or armed rebellion.

5.   The dwelling of every citizen is inviolable and shall not be forcibly entered save in accordance with law.

6.   1° The State guarantees liberty for the exercise of the following rights, subject to public order and morality: —

   i. The right of the citizens to express freely their convictions and opinions.

       The education of public opinion being, however, a matter of such grave import to the common good, the State shall endeavour to ensure that organs of public opinion, such as the radio, the press, the cinema, while preserving their rightful liberty of expression, including criticism of Government policy, shall not be used to undermine public order or morality or the authority of the State.

       The publication or utterance of blasphemous, seditious, or indecent matter is an offence which shall be punishable in accordance with law.

  ii. The right of the cizitens to assemble peaceably and without arms.

       Provision may be made by law to prevent or control meetings which are determined in accordance with law to be calculated to cause a breach of the peace or to be a danger or nuisance to the general public and to prevent or control meetings in the vicinity of either House of the Oireachtas.

 iii. The right of the citizens to form associations and unions.

       Laws, however, may be enacted for the regulation and control in the public interest of the exercise of the foregoing right.

2° Laws regulating the manner in which the right of forming associations and unions and the right of free assembly may be exercised shall contain no political, religious or class discrimination.

THE FAMILY

Article 41.

1. 1° The State recognises the Family as the natural primary and fundamental unit group of Society, and as a moral institution possessing inalienable and imprescriptible rights, antecedent and superior to all positive law.

2° The State, therefore, guarantees to protect the Family in its constitution and authority, as the necessary basis of social order and as indispensable to the welfare of the Nation and the State.

2. 1° In particular, the State recognises that by her life within the home, woman gives to the State a support without which the common good cannot be achieved.

2° The State shall, therefore, endeavour to ensure that mothers shall not be obliged by economic necessity to engage in labour to the neglect of their duties in the home.

3. 1° The State pledges itself to guard with special care the institution of Marriage, on which the Family is founded, and to protect it against attack.

2° No law shall be enacted providing for the grant of a dissolution of marriage.

3° No person whose marriage has been dissolved under the civil law of any other State but is a subsisting valid marriage under the law for the time being in force within the jurisdiction of the Government and Parliament established by this Constitution shall be capable of contracting a valid marriage within that jurisdiction during the lifetime of the other party to the marriage so dissolved.

EDUCATION

Article 42.

1. The State acknowledges that the primary and natural educator of the child is the Family and guarantees to respect the inalienable right and duty of parents to provide, according to their means, for the religious and moral, intellectual, physical and social education of their children.

2. Parents shall be free to provide this education in their homes or in private schools or in schools recognised or established by the State.

3. 1° The State shall not oblige parents in violation of their conscience and lawful preference to send their children to schools established by the State, or to any particular type of school designated by the State.

2° The State shall, however, as guardian of the common good, require in view of actual conditions that the children receive a certain minimum education, moral, intellectual and social.

4.   The State shall provide for free primary education and shall endeavour to supplement and give reasonable aid to private and corporate educational initiative, and, when the public good requires it, provide other educational facilities or institutions with due regard, however, for the rights of parents, especially in the matter of religious and moral formation.

5.   In exceptional cases where the parents for physical or moral reasons fail in their duty towards their children, the State as guardian of the common good, by appropriate means, shall endeavour to supply the place of the parents, but always with due regard for the natural and imprescriptible rights of the child.

PRIVATE PROPERTY

Article 43.

1.   1° The State acknowledges that man, in virtue of his rational being, has the natural right, antecedent to positive law, to the private ownership of external goods.

2° The State accordingly guarantees to pass no law attempting to abolish the right of private ownership or the general right to transfer, bequeath, and inherit property.

2.   1° The State recognises, however, that the exercise of the rights mentioned in the foregoing provisions of this Article ought, in civil society, to be regulated by the principles of social justice.

2° The State, accordingly, may as occasion requires delimit by law the exercise of the said rights with a view to reconciling their exercise with the exigencies of the common good.

RELIGION

Article 44.

1.   1° The State acknowledges that the homage of public worship is due to Almighty God. It shall hold His Name in reverence, and shall respect and honour religion.

2° The State recognises the special position of the Holy Catholic Apostolic and Roman Church as the guardian of the Faith professed by the great majority of the citizens.

3° The State also recognises the Church of Ireland, the Presbyterian Church in Ireland, the Methodist Church in Ireland, the Religious Society of Friends in Ireland, as well as the Jewish Congregations and the other religious denominations existing in Ireland at the date of the coming into operation of this Constitution.

2.   1° Freedom of conscience and the free profession and practice of religion are, subject to public order and morality, guaranteed to every citizen.

2° The State guarantees not to endow any religion.

3° The State shall not impose any disabilities or make any discrimination on the ground of religious profession, belief or status.

4° Legislation providing State aid for schools shall not discriminate between schools under the management of different religious denominations, nor be such as to affect prejudicially the right of any child to attend a school receiving public money without attending religious instruction at that school.

5° Every religious denomination shall have the right to manage its own affairs, own, acquire and administer property, movable and immovable, and maintain institutions for religious or charitable purposes.

6° The property of any religious denomination or any educational institution shall not be diverted save for necessary works of public utility and on payment of compensation.

(b) Directive Principles of Social Policy.
Document 3.4 — Article 45 of Bunreacht na hÉireann (Constitution of Ireland).

Article 45.

The principles of social policy set forth in this Article are intended for the general guidance of the Oireachtas. The application of those principles in the making of laws shall be the care of the Oireachtas exclusively, and shall not be cognisable by any Court under any of the provisions of this Constitution.

1. The State shall strive to promote the welfare of the whole people by securing and protecting as effectively as it may a social order in which justice and charity shall inform all the institutions of the national life.

2. The State shall, in particular, direct its policy towards securing
    i. That the citizens (all of whom, men and women equally, have the right to an adequate means of livelihood) may through their occupations find the means of making reasonable provision for their domestic needs.
    ii. That the ownership and control of the material resources of the community may be so distributed amongst private individuals and the various classes as best to subserve the common good.
    iii. That, especially, the operation of free competition shall not be allowed so to develop as to result in the concentration of the ownership or control of essential commodities in a few individuals to the common detriment.
    iv. That in what pertains to the control of credit the constant and predominant aim shall be the welfare of the people as a whole.
    v. That there may be established on the land in economic security as many families as in the circumstances shall be practicable.

3.   1° The State shall favour and, where necessary, supplement private initiative in industry and commerce.

2° The State shall endeavour to secure that private enterprise shall be so conducted as to ensure reasonable efficiency in the production and distribution of goods and as to protect the public against unjust exploitation.

4.   1° The State pledges itself to safeguard with especial care the economic interests of the weaker sections of the community, and, where necessary, to contribute to the support of the infirm, the widow, the orphan, and the aged.

2° The State shall endeavour to ensure that the strength and health of workers, men and women, and the tender age of children shall not be abused and that citizens shall not be forced by economic necessity to enter avocations unsuited to their sex, age or strength.

(4) EMERGENCY POWERS
(a) *The Constitution*

Document 3.5 — Extracts from Bunreacht na hÉireann (Constitution of Ireland).

Article 28. [*Ss. 1 to 3.2° omitted.*]

3.   3° Nothing in this Constitution shall be invoked to invalidate any law enacted by the Oireachtas which is expressed to be for the purpose of securing the public safety and the preservation of the State in time of war or armed rebellion, or to nullify any act done or purporting to be done in time of war or armed rebellion in pursuance of any such law. In this sub-section " time of war " includes a time when there is taking place an armed conflict in which the State is not a participant but in respect of which each of the Houses of the Oireachtas shall have resolved that, arising out of such armed conflict, a national emergency exists affecting the vital interests of the State and " time of war or armed rebellion " includes such time after the termination of any war, or of any such armed conflict as aforesaid, or of an armed rebellion, as may elapse until each of the Houses of the Oireachtas shall have resolved that the national emergency occasioned by such war, armed conflict, or armed rebellion has ceased to exist. [*Remainder of Article 28 and Articles 29-38.3 omitted.*]

Article 38.

4.   1° Military tribunals may be established for the trial of offences against military law alleged to have been committed by persons while subject to military law and also to deal with a state of war or armed rebellion. [*Remainder omitted.*]

(b) *Resolution of the Dáil declaring a State of Emergency*

Document 3.6 — Extract from *Dáil Debates*, vol. 77, col. 19 (2 September 1939)[1].

That Dáil Eireann hereby resolves, pursuant to sub-section 3° of section 3 of Article 28 of the Constitution, that, arising out of the armed conflict now taking place in Europe, a national emergency exists affecting the vital interests of the State.

(c) *Special Courts*

Document 3.7—Extracts from Article 38 of Bunreacht na hÉireann (Constitution of Ireland).

TRIAL OF OFFENCES

Article 38.

1. No person shall be tried on any criminal charge save in due course of law.

2. Minor offences may be tried by courts of summary jurisdiction.

3. 1° Special courts may be established by law for the trial of offences in cases where it may be determined in accordance with such law that the ordinary courts are inadequate to secure the effective administration of justice, and the preservation of public peace and order.

   2° The constitution, powers, jurisdiction and procedure of such special courts shall be prescribed by law. [*Ss. 4 and 5 omitted.*]

6. The provisions of Articles 34 and 35[2] of this Constitution shall not apply to any court or tribunal set up under section 3 or section 4 of this Article.

(d) *Offences Against the State Act,* 1939

Document 3.8—Extracts from Offences Against the State Act, 1939 (No. 13).

AN ACT TO MAKE PROVISION IN RELATION TO ACTIONS AND CONDUCT CALCULATED TO UNDERMINE PUBLIC ORDER AND THE AUTHORITY OF THE STATE, AND FOR THAT PURPOSE TO PROVIDE FOR THE PUNISHMENT OF PERSONS GUILTY OF OFFENCES AGAINST THE STATE, TO REGULATE AND CONTROL

---

[1]On the same day, Seanad Eireann passed a resolution in the same terms (Seanad Debates, vol. 23, cols. 1044-47). These resolutions have not yet been rescinded.—Editor.

[2]For the text of Articles 34 and 35, see Document 11.4 below.—Editor.

IN THE PUBLIC INTEREST THE FORMATION OF ASSOCIATIONS, TO ESTABLISH SPECIAL CRIMINAL COURTS IN ACCORDANCE WITH ARTICLE 38 OF THE CONSTITUTION AND PROVIDE FOR THE CONSTITUTION, POWERS, JURISDICTION, AND PROCEDURE OF SUCH COURTS, TO REPEAL CERTAIN ENACTMENTS AND TO MAKE PROVISION GENERALLY IN RELATION TO MATTERS CONNECTED WITH THE MATTERS AFORESAID. [*14th June, 1939.*]

BE IT ENACTED BY THE OIREACHTAS AS FOLLOWS:—

USURPATION OR OBSTRUCTION OF THE GOVERNMENT

6.—(1) Every person who usurps or unlawfully exercises any function of government, whether by setting up, maintaining, or taking part in any way in a body of persons purporting to be a government or a legislature but not authorised in that behalf by or under the Constitution, or by setting up, maintaining, or taking part in any way in a purported court or other tribunal not lawfully established, or by forming, maintaining, or being a member of an armed force or a purported police force not so authorised, or by any other action or conduct whatsoever, shall be guilty of felony and shall be liable on conviction thereof to suffer penal servitude for a term not exceeding ten years or to imprisonment for a term not exceeding two years. [*SS. 2 omitted.*]

7.—(1) Every person who prevents or obstructs, or attempts or is concerned in an attempt to prevent or obstruct, by force of arms or other violent means or by any form of intimidation the carrying on of the government of the State or any branch (whether legislative, judicial, or executive) of the government of the State or the exercise or performance by any member of the legislature, the judiciary, or the executive or by any officer or employee (whether civil (including police) or military) of the State of any of his functions, powers or duties shall be guilty of felony and shall be liable on conviction thereof to suffer penal servitude for a term not exceeding seven years or to imprisonment for a term not exceeding two years. [*SS. 2 omitted.*]

8.—(1) Every person who prevents or obstructs, or attempts or is concerned in an attempt to prevent or obstruct, by force of arms or other violent means or by any form of intimidation the exercise or performance by the President of any of his functions, powers, or duties shall be guilty of felony and shall be liable on conviction thereof to suffer penal servitude for a term not exceeding seven years or to imprisonment for a term not exceeding two years. [*SS. 2 omitted.*]

9.—(1) Every person who shall with intent to undermine public order or the authority of the State commit any act of violence against or of interference with a member of a lawfully established military or police force (whether such member is or is not on duty) or shall take away, injure, or otherwise interfere with the arms or equipment, or any part of the arms or equipment, of any such member shall be guilty of a misdemeanour and shall be liable on conviction thereof to imprisonment for a term not exceeding two years.

(2) Every person who shall incite or encourage any person employed in any capacity by the State to refuse, neglect, or omit (in a manner or to an extent calculated to dislocate the public service or a branch thereof) to perform his duty or shall incite or encourage any person so employed to be negligent or insubordinate (in such manner or to such extent as aforesaid) in the performance of his duty shall be guilty of a misdemeanour and shall be liable on conviction thereof to imprisonment for a term not exceeding two years. [*SS. 3 omitted.*]

PROHIBITIONS ON PRINTING AND FOREIGN NEWSPAPERS ETC.

10.—(1) It shall not be lawful to set up in type, print, publish, send through the post, distribute, sell, or offer for sale any document—

(*a*) which is or contains or includes an incriminating document, or

(*b*) which is or contains or includes a treasonable document, or

(c) which is or contains or includes a seditious document.
[*SSs. 2-5 omitted.*]

11.—(1) Whenever the Minister for Justice is of opinion, in respect of a newspaper or other periodical publication ordinarily printed outside the State, that a particular issue of such publication either is seditious or contains any matter the publication of which is a contravention of this Act, the said Minister may by order, if he considers that it is in the public interest so to do, do either or both of the following things, that is to say : —

(*a*) authorise members of the Gárda Síochána to seize and destroy all copies of the said issue of such publication wherever they may be found;

(*b*) prohibit the importation of any copy of any issue of such publication published within a specified period (not exceeding three months) after the publication of the said issue of such publication.
[*SSs. 2 and 3 omitted.*]

POSSESSION OF TREASONABLE ETC. DOCUMENTS

12.—(1) It shall not be lawful for any person to have any treasonable document, seditious document, or incriminating document in his possession or on any lands or premises owned or occupied by him or under his control. [*Other SSs. and Ss. 13 and 14 omitted.*]

UNAUTHORISED MILITARY EXERCISES

15.—(1) Save as authorised by a Minister of State under this section, and subject to the exceptions hereinafter mentioned, it shall not be lawful for any assembly of persons to practise or to train or drill themselves in or be trained or drilled in the use of arms or the performance of military exercises, evolutions, or manoeuvres nor for any persons to meet together or assemble for the purpose of so practising or training or drilling or being trained or drilled. [*SSs. 2-5 omitted.*]

SECRET SOCIETIES AND UNLAWFUL ORGANIZATIONS

16.—(1) Every person who shall—

(a) form, organise, promote, or maintain any secret society amongst or consisting of or including members of any military or police force lawfully maintained by the Government, or

(b) attempt to form, organise, promote, or maintain any such secret society, or

(c) take part, assist, or be concerned in any way in the formation, organisation, promotion, management, or maintenance of any such society, or

(d) induce, solicit, or assist any member of a military or police force lawfully maintained by the Government to join any secret society whatsoever,

shall be guilty of a misdemeanour and shall be liable on conviction thereof to suffer penal servitude for any term not exceeding five years or imprisonment for any term not exceeding two years. [*SS. 2 and S. 17 omitted.*]

18.—In order to regulate and control in the public interest the exercise of the constitutional right of citizens to form associations, it is hereby declared that any organisation which—

(a) engages in, promotes, encourages, or advocates the commission of treason or any activity of a treasonable nature, or

(b) advocates, encourages, or attempts the procuring by force, violence, or other unconstitutional means of an alteration of the Constitution, or

(c) raises or maintains or attempts to raise or maintain a military or armed force in contravention of the Constitution or without constitutional authority, or

(d) engages in, promotes, encourages, or advocates the commission of any criminal offence or the obstruction of or interference with the administration of justice or the enforcement of the law, or

(e) engages in, promotes, encourages, or advocates the attainment of any particular object, lawful or unlawful, by violent, criminal, or other unlawful means, or

(f) promotes, encourages, or advocates the non-payment of moneys payable to the Central Fund or any other public fund or the non-payment of local taxation,

shall be an unlawful organisation within the meaning and for the purposes of this Act, and this Act shall apply and have effect in relation to such organisation accordingly. [*Ss. 19-26 omitted.*]

PROHIBITIONS OF PUBLIC MEETINGS

27.—(1) It shall not be lawful to hold a public meeting which is held or purports to be held by or on behalf of or by arrangement or in concert with an unlawful organisation or which is held or purports to be held for the purpose of supporting, aiding, abetting, or encouraging an unlawful organisation or of advocating the support of an unlawful organisation. [*SSs. 2-5 omitted.*]

28.—(1) It shall not be lawful for any public meeting to be held in, or any procession to pass along or through, any public street or unenclosed place which or any part of which is situate within one-half of a mile from any building in which both Houses or either House of the Oireachtas are or is sitting or about to sit if either—

(*a*) an officer of the Gárda Síochána not below the rank of chief super-intendent has, by notice given to a person concerned in the holding or organisation of such meeting or procession or published in a manner reasonably calculated to come to the knowledge of the persons so concerned, prohibited the holding of such meeting in or the passing of such procession along or through any such public street or unenclosed place as aforesaid, or

(*b*) a member of the Gárda Síochána calls on the persons taking part in such meeting or procession to disperse.

[*Other SSs. and Ss. 29-34 omitted.*]

35.—(2) If and whenever and so often as the Government is satisfied that the ordinary courts are inadequate to secure the effective administration of justice and the preservation of public peace and order and that it is therefore necessary that this Part of the Act should come into force, the Government may make and publish a proclamation declaring that the Government is satisfied as aforesaid and ordering that this Part of this Act shall come into force. [*SSs.* 1 *and* 3-6 *omitted.*]

SCHEDULED OFFENCES

36.—(1) Whenever while this Part of this Act is in force the Government is satisfied that the ordinary courts are inadequate to secure the effective administration of justice and the preservation of public peace and order in relation to offences of any particular class or kind or under any particular enactment, the Government may by order declare that offences of that particular class or kind or under that particular enactment shall be scheduled offences for the purpose of this Part of this Act. [*Other Sub-sections and S.* 37 *omitted.*]

SPECIAL COURTS

38.—(1) As soon as may be after the coming into force of this Part of this Act, there shall be established for the purposes of this Part of this Act, a court which shall be styled and known and is in this Act referred to as a Special Criminal Court. [*SS.* 2 *and* 3 *omitted.*]

39.—(1) Every Special Criminal Court established under this Part of this Act shall consist of such uneven number, (not being less than three) of members as the Government shall from time to time determine, and different numbers of members may be so fixed in respect of different Special Criminal Courts.

(2) Each member of a Special Criminal Court shall be appointed, and be removable at will, by the Government.

(3) No person shall be appointed to be a member of a Special Criminal Court unless he is a judge of the High Court or the Circuit Court, or a justice of the District Court, or a barrister of not less than seven years standing, or a solicitor of not less than seven years standing, or an officer of the Defence Forces not below the rank of commandant. [*Remainder omitted.*]

(e) *Special Powers of Arrest and Detention*
Document 3.9—Extracts from Offences Against the State (Amendment) Act, 1940 (No.2).

3.—(2) If and whenever and so often as the Government makes and publishes a proclamation declaring that the powers conferred by this Part of this Act are necessary to secure the preservation of public peace and order and that it is expedient that this Part of this Act should come into force immediately, this Part of this Act shall come into force forthwith. [*SSs. 3-5 omitted.*]

4.—(1) Whenever a Minister of State is of opinion that any particular person is engaged in activities which, in his opinion, are prejudicial to the preservation of public peace and order or to the security of the State, such Minister may by warrant under his hand and sealed with his official seal order the arrest and detention of such person under this section.

(2) Any member of the Gárda Síochána may arrest without warrant any person in respect of whom a warrant has been issued by a Minister of State under the foregoing sub-section of this section.

(3) Every person arrested under the next preceding sub-section of this section shall be detained in a prison or other place prescribed in that behalf by regulations made under this Part of this Act until this Part of this Act ceases to be in force or until he is released under the subsequent provisions of this Part of this Act whichever first happens. [*SSs. 4 and 5 and S. 5 omitted.*]

6.—A Minister of State may by writing under his hand, if and whenever he so thinks proper, order the release of any particular person who is for the time being detained under this Part of this Act, and thereupon such person shall forthwith be released from such detention.

7.—(1) A Minister of State may by order make regulations for all or any of the following purposes, that is to say: —
    (*a*) prescribing the prisons, internment camps, and other places in which persons may be detained under this Part of this Act;
    (*b*) providing for the efficient management, sanitation, control and guarding of such prisons, internment camps, and other places;
    (*c*) providing for the enforcement and preservation of discipline amongst the persons detained in any such prison, internment camp, or other place as aforesaid;

(*d*) providing for the punishment of persons who contravene the regulations;

(*e*) prescribing or providing for any other matter or thing incidental or ancillary to the efficient detention of persons detained under this Part of this Act.

(2) Every regulation made under this section shall be laid before each House of the Oireachtas as soon as may be after it is made, and if a resolution annulling such regulation is passed by either House of the Oireachtas within the next subsequent twenty-one days on which such House has sat after such regulation is laid before it, such regulation shall be annulled accordingly, but without prejudice to the validity of anything previously done under such regulation. [*Remainder omitted.*]

(f) *Advice of the Supreme Court in respect of the Offences Against the State (Amendment) Bill, 1940.*

Document 3.10—Extracts from *In re Article 26 and The Offences Against the State (Amendment) Bill, 1940, Irish Reports, 1940, pp. 470-82* (usually cited as [1940] I.R. 470).

The President having referred to the Supreme Court, under Art. 26 of the Constitution, a Bill entitled "An Act to repeal Part VI of the Offences Against the State Act, 1939, and to make other provisions in relation to the detention of certain persons," for a decision on the question whether the said Bill was repugnant to the Constitution or to any provision thereof,

The Court (by a majority) was of opinion:—

1. That s. 4 of the Bill, which provides, *inter alia*, that "whenever a Minister of State is of opinion that any particular person is engaged in activities which, in his opinion, are prejudicial to the preservation of public peace and order or to the security of the State, such Minister may by warrant under his hand and sealed with his official seal order the arrest and detention of such person under this section," does not confer upon the Minister power to administer justice, and is not repugnant to Art. 34 of the Constitution, which provides that justice shall be administered in public Courts.

2. That the detention of persons provided for in the Bill is not in the nature of punishment but of preventive justice, being a precautionary measure taken for the purpose of preserving the public peace and order and the security of the State, and did not contravene the provision of Art. 38 of the Constitution providing that no person be tried on any criminal charge save in due course of law.

R. (Zadig) v. *Halliday*, [1917] A. C. 260; and *The King (O'Connell)* v. *The Military Governor of Hare Park Camp*, [1924] 2 I. R. 104, on appeal [1935] I. R. 247, applied.

3. That the provisions of the Bill are not repugnant to the provisions of Art. 40, clause 3, of the Constitution by which the State guarantees by its laws to respect and, as far as practicable, by its laws to defend and vindicate the personal rights of the citizen.

4. That the Bill does not take away the right to *habeas corpus*.

5. That the provisions of s. 5 of the Bill, as to the interrogation and searching of persons, and of s. 7, authorising the making of regulations as to the place and

mode of detention of persons arrested under the Bill, and other matters incidental thereto, and as to the punishment of persons so detained who contravene the regulations, were made necessary by reason of the provisions of s. 4 and that there is nothing in these sections to suggest that any regulation made thereunder would contravene any Article of the Constitution.

The Court accordingly advised the President that the said Bill was not repugnant to the Constitution or to any provision thereof.

EXTRACT FROM THE COURT'S OPINION

In the opinion of this Court neither s. 4 nor s. 5 of the Bill creates or purports to create a criminal offence. The only essential preliminary to the exercise by a Minister of the powers contained in s. 4 is that he should have formed opinions on the matters specifically mentioned in the section. The validity of such opinions is not a matter that could be questioned in any Court. Having formed such opinions, the Minister is entitled to make an order for detention; but this Court is of opinion that the detention is not in the nature of punishment, but is a precautionary measure taken for the purpose of preserving the public peace and order and the security of the State. This distinction has been recognised in several cases. . . .

Article 40 deals with personal rights. Clause 3 thereof provides that the State guarantees by its laws to respect, and, as far as practicable, by its laws to defend and vindicate the personal rights of the citizen, and to protect from unjust attack and, in case of injustice done, to vindicate, the life, person, good name, and property rights of every citizen.

It is alleged that the provisions of the Bill are repugnant to the guarantee contained in this clause. It seems to us impossible to accede to this argument. The guarantee in the clause is not in respect of any particular citizen, or class of citizens, but extends to all the citizens of the State, and the duty of determining the extent to which the rights of any particular citizen, or class of citizen, can properly be harmonised with the rights of the citizens as a whole seems to us to be a matter which is peculiarly within the province of the Oireachtas, and any attempt by this Court to control the Oireachtas in the exercise of this function, would, in our opinion, be a usurpation of its authority. . . .

Clause 4 of the said Article provides that no citizen shall be deprived of his liberty save in accordance with law, and makes provision for the release of any person who is being detained otherwise than in accordance with law.

The phrase "in accordance with law" is used in several Articles of the Constitution, and we are of opinion that it means in accordance with the law as it exists at the time when the particular Article is invoked and sought to be applied. In this Article, it means the law as it exists at the time when the legality of the detention arises for determination. A person in custody is detained in accordance with law if he is detained in accordance with the provisions of a statute duly passed by the Oireachtas; subject always to the qualification that such provisions are not repugnant to the Constitution or to any provision thereof.

5. HUMAN RIGHTS IN INTERNATIONAL LAW

(a) *European Convention on Human Rights*

> Document 3.11—Extracts from *Convention for The Protection of Rights and Fundamental Freedoms,* Rome, 4th November, 1950, Stationery Office, Dublin, Treaty Series, 1953, No. 12[1].

The Governments signatory hereto, being Members of the Council of Europe,

Considering the Universal Declaration of Human Rights proclaimed by the General Assembly of the United Nations on 10th December 1948;

Considering that this Declaration aims at securing the universal and effective recognition and observance of the Rights therein declared;

Considering that the aim of the Council of Europe is the achievement of greater unity between its Members and that one of the methods by which that aim is to be pursued is the maintenance and further realisation of Human Rights and Fundamental Freedoms;

Reaffirming their profound belief in those Fundamental Freedoms which are the foundation of justice and peace in the world and are best maintained on the one hand by an effective political democracy and on the other by a common understanding and observance of the Human Rights upon which they depend;

Being resolved, as the Governments of European countries which are like-minded and have a common heritage of political traditions, ideals, freedom and the rule of law, to take the first steps for the collective enforcement of certain of the Rights stated in the Universal Declaration;

Have agreed as follows:

Article 1.

The High Contracting Parties shall secure to everyone within their jurisdiction the rights and freedoms defined in Section I of this Convention.

SECTION I

Article 2.

(1) Everyone's right to life shall be protected by law. No one shall be deprived of his life intentionally save in the execution of a sentence of a court following his conviction of a crime for which this penalty is provided by law.

(2) Deprivation of life shall not be regarded as inflicted in contravention of this Article when it results from the use of force which is no more than absolutely necessary;

---

[1]This Convention came into force on 3 September 1953 when ten states had signed it. Ireland was amongst these. Ireland also made the declarations referred to in Articles 25 and 46 and is accordingly bound.—Editor.

    (a) in defence of any person from unlawful violence;

    (b) in order to affect a lawful arrest or to prevent the escape of a person lawfully detained;

    (c) in action lawfully taken for the purpose of quelling a riot or insurrection.

Article 3.

No one shall be subjected to torture or to inhuman or degrading treatment or punishment.

Article 4.

(1) No one shall be held in slavery or servitude.

(2) No one shall be required to perform forced or compulsory labour.

(3) For the purpose of this Article the term "forced or compulsory labour" shall not include:

    (a) any work required to be done in the ordinary course of detention imposed according to the provisions of Article 5 of this Convention or during conditional release from such detention;

    (b) any service of a military character or, in case of conscientious objectors in countries where they are recognised, service exacted instead of compulsory military service;

    (c) any service exacted in case of an emergency or calamity threatening the life or well-being of the community;

    (d) any work or service which forms part of normal civic obligations.

Article 5.

(1) Everyone has the right to liberty and security of person.

No one shall be deprived of his liberty save in the following cases and in accordance with a procedure prescribed by law:

    (a) the lawful detention of a person after conviction by a competent court;

    (b) the lawful arrest or detention of a person for non-compliance with the lawful order of a court or in order to secure the fulfilment of any obligation prescribed by law;

    (c) the lawful arrest or detention of a person effected for the purpose of bringing him before the competent legal authority on reasonable suspicion of having committed an offence or when it is reasonably considered necessary to prevent his committing an offence or fleeing after having done so;

    (d) the detention of a minor by lawful order for the purpose of educational supervision or his lawful detention for the purpose of bringing him before the competent legal authority;

    (e) the lawful detention of persons for the prevention of the spreading of infectious diseases, of persons of unsound mind, alcoholics or drug addicts or vagrants;

(*f*) the lawful arrest or detention of a person to prevent his effecting an unauthorised entry into the country or of a person against whom action is being taken with a view to deportation or extradition;

(2) Everyone who is arrested shall be informed promptly, in a language which he understands, of the reasons for his arrest and of any charge against him.

(3) Everyone arrested or detained in accordance with the provisions of paragraph 1 (*c*) of this Article shall be brought promptly before a judge or other officer authorised by law to exercise judicial power and shall be entitled to trial within a reasonable time or to release pending trial. Release may be conditioned by guarantees to appear for trial.

(4) Everyone who is deprived of his liberty by arrest or detention shall be entitled to take proceedings by which the lawfulness of his detention shall be decided speedily by a court and his release ordered if the detention is not lawful.

(5) Everyone who has been the victim of arrest or detention in contravention of the provisions of this Article shall have an enforceable right to compensation.

Article 6.

(1) In the determination of his civil rights and obligations or of any criminal charge against him, everyone is entitled to a fair and public hearing within a reasonable time by an independent and impartial tribunal established by law. Judgment shall be pronounced publicly but the press and public may be excluded from all or part of the trial in the interests of morals, public order or national security in a democratic society, where the interests of juveniles or the protection of the private life of the parties so require, or to the extent strictly necessary in the opinion of the court in special circumstances where publicity would prejudice the interests of justice.

(2) Everyone charged with a criminal offence shall be presumed innocent until proved guilty according to law.

(3) Everyone charged with a criminal offence has the following minimum rights:

(*a*) to be informed promptly, in a language which he understands and in detail, of the nature and cause of the accusation against him;

(*b*) to have adequate time and facilities for the preparation of his defence;

[1] (*c*) to defend himself in person or through legal assistance of his own choosing or, if he has not sufficient means to pay for legal assistance to be given it free when the interests of justice so require;

---

[1] The Irish Instrument of Ratification of the Convention contained a clause to the effect that the Government of Ireland do not interpret Article 6 (3) (*c*) of the Convention as requiring the provision of free legal assistance to any wider extent than is now provided in Ireland.

(*d*) to examine or have examined witnesses against him and to obtain the attendance and examination of witnesses on his behalf under the same conditions as witnesses against him;

(*e*) to have the free assistance of an interpreter if he cannot understand or speak the language used in court.

Article 7.

(1) No one shall be held guilty of any criminal offence on account of any act or omission which did not constitute a criminal offence under national or international law at the time when it was committed. Nor shall a heavier penalty be imposed than the one that was applicable at the time the criminal offence was committed.

(2) This Article shall not prejudice the trial and punishment of any person for any act or omission which, at the time when it was committed, was criminal according to the general principles of law recognised by civilised nations.

Article 8.

(1) Everyone has the right to respect for his private and family life, his home and his correspondence.

(2) There shall be no interference by a public authority with the exercise of this right except such as is in accordance with the law and is necessary in a democratic society in the interests of national security, public safety or the economic well-being of the country, for the prevention of disorder or crime, for the protection of health or morals, or for the protection of the rights and freedom of others.

Article 9.

(1) Everyone has the right to freedom of thought, conscience and religion; this right includes freedom to change his religion or belief and freedom, either alone or in community with others and in public or private, to manifest his religion or belief, in worship, teaching, practice and observance.

(2) Freedom to manifest one's religion or beliefs shall be subject only to such limitations as are prescribed by law and are necessary in a democratic society in the interests of public safety, for the protection of public order, health or morals, or for the protection of the rights and freedoms of others.

Article 10.

(1) Everyone has the right to freedom of expression. This right shall include freedom to hold opinions and to receive and impart information and ideas without interference by public authority and regardless of frontiers. This Article shall not prevent States from requiring the licensing of broadcasting, television or cinema enterprises.

(2) The exercise of these freedoms, since it carries with it duties and responsibilities, may be subject to such formalities, conditions, restrictions or penalties as are prescribed by law and are necessary in a democratic society, in the interests of national security, territorial integrity or public safety, for the prevention of disorder or crime, for the protection of health or morals, for the protection of the reputation or rights of others, for preventing the disclosure of information received in confidence, or for maintaining the authority and impartiality of the judiciary.

Article 11.

(1) Everyone has the right to freedom of peaceful assembly and to freedom of association with others, including the right to form and to join trade unions for the protection of his interests.

(2) No restrictions shall be placed on the exercise of these rights other than such as are prescribed by law and are necessary in a democratic society in the interests of national security or public safety, for the prevention of disorder or crime, for the protection of health or morals or for the protection of the rights and freedoms of others. This Article shall not prevent the imposition of lawful restrictions on the exercise of these rights by members of the armed forces, of the police or of the administration of the State.

Article 12.

Men and women of marriageable age have the right to marry and to found a family, according to the national laws governing the exercise of this right.

Article 13.

Everyone whose rights and freedoms as set forth in this Convention are violated shall have an effective remedy before a national authority notwithstanding that the violation has been committed by persons acting in an official capacity.

Article 14.

The enjoyment of the rights and freedoms set forth in this Convention shall be secured without discrimination on any ground such as sex, race, colour, language, religion, political or other opinion, national or social origin, association with a national minority, property, birth or other status.

Article 15.

(1) In time of war or other public emergency threatening the life of the nation any High Contracting Party may take measures derogating from its obligations under this Convention to the extent strictly required by the exigencies of the situation, provided that such measures are not inconsistent with its other obligations under international law.

(2) No derogation from Article 2, except in respect of deaths resulting from lawful acts of war, or from Articles 3, 4 (paragraph 1) and 7 shall be made under this provision.

(3) Any High Contracting Party availing itself of this right of derogation shall keep the Secretary-General of the Council of Europe fully informed of the measures which it has taken and the reasons therefor. It shall also inform the Secretary-General of the Council of Europe when such measures have ceased to operate and the provisions of the Convention are again being fully executed.

Article 16.

Nothing in Articles 10, 11 and 14 shall be regarded as preventing the High Contracting Parties from imposing restrictions on the political activity of aliens.

Article 17.

Nothing in this Convention may be interpreted as implying for any State, group or person any right to engage in any activity or perform any act aimed at the destruction of any of the rights and freedoms set forth herein or at their limitation to a greater extent than is provided for in the Convention.

Article 18.

The restrictions permitted under this Convention to the said rights and freedoms shall not be applied for any purpose other than those for which they have been prescribed.

SECTION II

Article 19.

To ensure the observance of the engagements undertaken by the High Contracting Parties in the present Convention, there shall be set up:

(1) A European Commission of Human Rights, hereinafter referred to as "the Commission";

(2) A European Court of Human Rights, hereinafter referred to as "the Court".

SECTION III

Article 20.

The Commission shall consist of a number of members equal to that of the High Contracting Parties. No two members of the Commission may be nationals of the same State. [*Articles* 21-23 *omitted.*]

Article 24.

Any High Contracting Party may refer to the Commission, through the Secretary-General of the Council of Europe, any alleged breach of the provisions of the Convention by another High Contracting Party.

Article 25.

(1) The Commission may receive petitions addressed to the Secretary-General of the Council of Europe from any person, non-governmental organisation or group of individuals claiming to be the victim of a violation by one of the High Contracting Parties of the rights set forth in this Conven-

tion, provided that the High Contracting Party against which the complaint has been lodged has declared that it recognises the competence of the Commission to receive such petitions. Those of the High Contracting Parties who have made such a declaration undertake not to hinder in any way the effective exercise of this right. [*Clauses 2-4 and Articles 26 and 27 omitted.*]

Articles 28.
In the event of the Commission accepting a petition referred to it:

    (*a*) it shall, with a view to ascertaining the facts, undertake together with the representatives of the parties an examination of the petition and, if need be, an investigation, for the effective conduct of which the States concerned shall furnish all necessary facilities, after an exchange of views with the Commission;

    (*b*) it shall place itself at the disposal of the parties concerned with a view to securing a friendly settlement of the matter on the basis of respect for Human Rights as defined in this Convention. [*Articles 29-37 omitted.*]

SECTION IV

Article 38.
The European Court of Human Rights shall consist of a number of judges equal to that of the Members of the Council of Europe. No two judges may be nationals of the same State. [*Articles 39-43 omitted.*]

Article 44.
Only the High Contracting Parties and the Commission shall have the right to bring a case before the Court.

Article 45
The jurisdiction of the Court shall extend to all cases concerning the interpretation and application of the present Convention which the High Contracting Parties or the Commission shall refer to it in accordance with Article 48.

Article 46.
(1) Any of the High Contracting Parties may at any time declare that it recognises as compulsory *ipso facto* and without special agreement the jurisdiction of the Court in all matters concerning the interpretation and application of the present Convention.

(2) The declarations referred to above may be made unconditionally or on condition of reciprocity on the part of several or certain other High Contracting Parties or for a specified period.

(3) These declarations shall be deposited with the Secretary-General of the Council of Europe, who shall transmit copies thereof to the High Contracting Parties.

Article 47.

The Court may only deal with a case after the Commission has acknowledged the failure of efforts for a friendly settlement and within the period of three months provided for in Article 32. [*Articles 48-52 omitted.*]

Article 53.

The High Contracting Parties undertake to abide by the decision of the Court in any case to which they are parties. [*Articles 54-56 omitted.*]

SECTION V

Article 57.

On receipt of a request from the Secretary-General of the Council of Europe any High Contracting Party shall furnish an explanation of the manner in which its internal law ensures the effective implementation of any of the provisions of this Convention. [*Remainder omitted.*]

(b) *Additions to the European Convention on Human Rights*

Document 3.12—Extract from *Protocol to the Convention for the Protection of Human Rights and Fundamental Freedoms,* Paris, 20 March 1952, Stationery Office, Dublin, Treaty Series, 1954, No. 3.

The Governments signatory hereto, being Members of the Council of Europe,

Being resolved to take steps to ensure the collective enforcement of certain rights and freedoms other than those already included in Section 1 of the Convention for the Protection of Human Rights and Fundamental Freedoms signed at Rome on 4th November, 1950 (hereinafter referred to as "the Convention),

Have agreed as follows:

Article 1.

Every natural or legal person is entitled to the peaceful enjoyment of his possessions. No one shall be deprived of his possessions except in the public interest and subject to the conditions provided for by law and by the general principles of international law.

The preceding provisions shall not, however, in any way impair the right of a State to enforce such laws as it deems necessary to control the use of property in accordance with the general interest or to secure the payment of taxes or other contributions or penalties.

Article 2.

No person shall be denied the right to education. In the exercise of any functions which it assumes in relation to education and to teaching, the State shall respect the right of parents to ensure such education and teaching in conformity with their own religious and philosophical convictions.

Article 3.

The High Contracting Parties undertake to hold free elections at reasonable intervals by secret ballot, under conditions which will ensure the free expression of the opinion of the people in the choice of the legislature.

[*Remainder omitted.*]

READING

D. Barrington: 'The Irish Constitution' in *Irish Monthly,* vols. 80 and 81.
D. Costello: 'The Natural Law and the Constitution' in *Studies,* vol. 45.
V. Grogan: 'The Constitution and the Natural Law', in *Christus Rex,* vol. 8.
J. M. Kelly: *Fundamental Rights in the Irish Law and Constitution,* Dublin, 1961.
E. McDonagh: 'Church and State in the Constitution of Ireland' in *Irish Theological Quarterly,* vol. 28.
E. McWhinney: *Judicial Review in the English-speaking World,* 2nd edition, Toronto, 1960.
J. Newman: *Studies in Political Morality,* Dublin and London, 1962.

Chapter 4

THE GOVERNMENT AND THE CENTRAL ADMINISTRATION

INTRODUCTION

From the beginning, the architects of the Irish state adopted the political institutions and procedures of Great Britain. In this respect they were like the leaders of many of the states that have emerged from the British Empire, and the Irish system can best be classified as belonging to the British Commonwealth pattern.

The Constitution of Dáil Éireann (1919) provided in a few short articles, couched in non-technical language, for a Parliament, a Prime Minister and a Government and for the relationships between them. (Documents 4.1 and 4.2). The Dáil Constitution was never intended as the basic law of a fully-fledged sovereign state. In contrast, the Constitution of the Irish Free State was so intended, being occasioned by the emergence of the state to full sovereign status. But, although a committee was appointed to draw up a new constitution and assiduously gathered information on the constitutions of many contemporary states throughout the world, and although there was some opinion in favour of avoiding certain features of the British political system, the machinery of government prescribed in the Constitution (Document 4.3) included the most important features of the British system. However, an attempt was made to qualify that system and to mitigate the supposed evils of strong government by a majority-party Government, by providing for a number of checks. These took the form of provisions for referendum and popular initiative, a proportional representation system of election, the appointment of ministers by the Dáil, and the institution of ' extern ministers ', i.e. ministers without seats in the cabinet and in charge of those departments believed to be concerned with activities of a comparatively technical and non-political character. In its original form a novel scheme, it was much modified in the Constituent Assembly, emerged in practice as an arrangement for non-cabinet ministers of a conventional variety and was soon dropped (Document 4.4).

This development is typical of Irish experience in the first decade of the state's existence, which seemed to indicate that the British system working in much the same manner as in Britain was well adapted to Ireland's needs. No doubt the fact that single parties found themselves commanding parliamentary majorities contributed much to this. No doubt also Mr de Valera found the system well suited to his requirements as a strong Prime Minister leading a loyal majority party that looked to him for positive leadership and political initiative. Naturally, then, the Constitution of which he was the chief architect, though it embodied fundamental changes in the status of the state, did not alter the machinery of government in any radical way. (Document 4.5).

It is not possible to convey accurately the functions and responsibilities of the Taoiseach or the Government by way of official documentary material. Much less is it possible to convey the flavour of political office. The extract from an article by Mr Ó Muimhneacháin, a former Secretary to the Government, which we include, is a semi-official description of their roles. (Document 4.6).

Just as the cabinet system of Ireland resembles the British in its main principles and also in practice, given of course the differences occasioned by differences of scale and range of government functions, so too does the structure of the central administration, minister-civil servant relationships and, as we shall see in Chapter 5, the structure and organization of the Civil Service. The administration taken over in 1922 was a complex jumble of offices, some answering via civil service heads to the Chief Secretary, the British cabinet minister responsible for Irish affairs, others controlled more or less directly by parent departments in Whitehall, and yet others conducted by Boards and Commissioners operating with varying degrees of autonomy (Document 4.7). Ireland, it was said, had as many boards as would make her coffin. The new Government consolidated all of these units in, or under the wing of, eleven ministerial departments. The Ministers and Secretaries Act, 1924 is the legal expression of this consolidation and the statutory basis of the central administration to this day. (Document 4.8). Providing as it does not only for the functions, duties and status of the ministers and departments, but also for parliamentary secretaries (i.e. deputy ministers) and the Attorney General (Documents 4.10-4.12), there has apparently been need to do little more than add new departments on the same pattern, as the range of governmental functions has widened. Few new needs seem to have been experienced until recently, though the

Second World War occasioned a Minister without Portfolio (Document 4.9), and the difference between appointing to membership of the Government and assigning to the headship of departments has had to be clarified (Documents 4.13 and 4.14). Development has, however, occurred mainly in the areas of social welfare and, more recently, of economic affairs, and, in recent years, there has been a growing recognition of the necessity for Government planning in order to assure a rate of economic development acceptable to the community and to prepare Ireland for the effects of close integration with Europe. Following the publication in 1958 of *Economic Development,* a remarkable document produced by the Civil Service which both pointed to the needs of the situation and also gave a lead in the direction in which the country should go, (Document 4.15), the Government hurriedly adopted a *Programme for Economic Expansion* and began to concern itself in a serious fashion with planning. As a consequence, there has been a need to adapt existing machinery and to invent new machinery. This has resulted not only in internal changes in government departments, particularly the Department of Finance, but in the creation of new types of public body somewhat akin to advisory bodies (Documents 4.16 and 4.17: see also Organization Charts on pp. 110-111). These bodies have parallels in other countries facing somewhat similar problems, and they represent the first attempts to devise appropriate machinery for full-scale planning in a free and democratic community. Meanwhile, in 1963, the Government produced its *Second Programme for Economic Expansion.* (Document 4.18).

Just as it is not possible to give an adequate picture in documents of the functions of the Government, it is not possible, either, to illustrate the enormous variety of practice that is possible within the terms of the articles of the Constitution dealing with the making and demise of Governments, their conduct, and the appointment and resignation of ministers. In such matters as these, in any case, documents are usually not available. Looking back on Irish Governments, it is obvious that the appointment of ministers and the conduct of government differed markedly with the personality of leaders and with the nature and size of their following. The conditions under which coalition government operates clearly cannot be the same as those obtaining in the case of a Government composed of members of a single party. Hence the replacement, in 1948 and again in 1954, of Mr de Valera and his Fianna Fáil Government by a coalition of diverse groups and individuals led by Mr Costello could not but lead to differences of practice. As it happens, it is possible from published material to get glimpses of the process of the formation of the 'Inter-Party' Governments, including the procedure by which the Labour Party chose its candidates for office (Documents 4.19 to 4.21); of the interpretation by members in that Government of the important concept of collective responsibility (Documents 4.22 and 4.23); and of the attitudes of a leader of one of the component parties of the Inter-party Government and the Taoiseach in the matter of a resignation (Documents 4.24 to 4.26).

DOCUMENTS

1. THE DAIL CONSTITUTION

   (a) *Constitution of Dáil Éireann, January, 1919.*

   Document 4.1—*Constitution of Dáil Éireann as approved provisionally January, 21st, 1919*, translation as it appears in D. Macardle, *The Irish Republic*, 4th edition, Irish Press Ltd., Dublin, 1951, pp. 923-4.

CONSTITUTION OF DAIL EIREANN

As approved provisionally January 21st, 1919.

FIRST SECTION:
   Dáil Éireann shall possess full powers to legislate and shall be composed of Delegates (Teachtaí) chosen by the people of Ireland from the present constituencies of the country.

SECOND SECTION:
   (1) Full executive powers shall be held at any time by the Ministry (Aireacht) in office at the time.
   (2) The Ministry shall be composed of the following: A Prime Minister (Príomh-Aireach) chosen by Dáil Éireann, and four other Ministers, viz.:
      Minister of Finance (Aireach Airgid),
      Minister of Home Affairs (A. Gnóthaí Duthchais),
      Minister of Foreign Affairs (A. Gnóthaí Coigcríoch), and
      Minister of Defence (A. Cosanta).
   The Prime Minister shall nominate the four others, and shall have power to dismiss them from office.
   (3) Every Minister must be a member of the Dáil and shall at all times be answerable to the Dáil.

Prime Minister

(5) The Prime Minister shall hold office as soon as elected and the other Ministers as soon as their appointment is ratified by the Dáil.

(6) The Dáil shall have power by vote to dismiss the Ministry or any of the Ministers from office if a written order in the form of a unanimous resolution be presented for that object seven days previously.

SECTION THREE:

Every meeting of the Dáil shall be presided over by a Chairman (Ceann Cómhairle) or Vice-Chairman (Ceann Ionaid) chosen by the Dáil for the year. Should the Chairman and Vice-Chairman be absent, the Dáil shall select substitutes or elect a Provisional Chairman (Ceann Cómhairle Sealadach).

SECTION FOUR:

The Ministry shall receive whatever money it needs, by vote of the Dáil. The Ministry shall be answerable to the Dáil for such moneys, and the accounts shall be audited with regard to the spending of money for the Dáil twice yearly, viz. at Samhain and Bealtaine (November and May). The auditing shall be carried out by an auditor or auditors chosen by the Dáil. No member of the Dáil shall be chosen as auditor.

SECTION FIVE:

The present is a provisional constitution, and may be altered on a written unanimous order being given to that effect seven days previously.

(b) *Amendment to Article 2 of The Dáil Constitution*
    Document 4.2—Extract from *Dáil Éireann: Minutes of Proceedings of the First Parliament of the Republic of Ireland,* 1919-21, p. 34.

AMENDMENT TO ARTICLE 2 (b)[1]

Eamonn de Valera (East Clare) moved, and M. O Coileain (Cork, South) seconded, that Article 2 (b) of the Constitution should be amended to read as follows:—

"The Ministry shall consist of a President of the Ministry elected by Dáil Éireann, and not more than nine Executive Officers, including:—

A Secretary of Finance,
A Secretary of Home Affairs,
A Secretary of Foreign Affairs,
A Secretary of National Defence,

each of whom the President shall nominate and have power to dismiss."

---

[1] In Miss Macardle's translation above this is referred to as 'Second Section (2)'.

An objection that this motion was not within the terms of the notice was overruled.

The House divided on the proposed amendment, and the motion was declared carried.

2. THE CONSTITUTION OF THE IRISH FREE STATE

Document 4.3—Extract from the Constitution of the Irish Free State (Saorstát Éireann) Act, 1922.

Article 51.

The Executive Authority of the Irish Free State (Saorstát Éireann) is hereby declared to be vested in the King, and shall be exercisable, in accordance with the law, practice and constitutional usage governing the exercise of the Executive Authority in the case of the Dominion of Canada, by the Representative of the Crown. There shall be a Council to aid and advise in the government of the Irish Free State (Saorstát Éireann) to be styled the Executive Council. The Executive Council shall be responsible to Dáil Éireann, and shall consist of not more than seven nor less than five Ministers appointed by the Representatives of the Crown on the nomination of the President of the Executive Council.

Article 52.

Those Ministers who form the Executive Council shall all be members of Dáil Éireann and shall include the President of the Council, the Vice-President of the Council and the Minister in charge of the Department of Finance.

Article 53.

The President of the Council shall be appointed on the nomination of Dáil Éireann. He shall nominate a Vice-President of the Council, who shall act for all purposes in the place of the President, if the President shall die, resign, or be permanently incapacitated, until a new President of the Council shall have been elected. The Vice-President shall also act in the place of the President during his temporary absence. The other Ministers who are to hold office as members of the Executive Council shall be appointed on the nomination of the President, with the assent of Dáil Éireann, and he and the Ministers nominated by him shall retire from office should he cease to retain the support of a majority in Dáil Éireann, but the President and such Ministers shall continue to carry on their duties until their successors shall have been appointed : Provided, however, that the Oireachtas shall not be dissolved on the advice of an Executive Council which has ceased to retain the support of a majority in Dáil Éireann.

Article 54.

The Executive Council shall be collectively responsible for all matters concerning the Departments of State administered by Members of the Executive Council. The Executive Council shall prepare Estimates of the receipts and expenditure of the Irish Free State (Saorstát Éireann) for each financial year, and shall present them to Dáil Éireann before the close of the previous financial year. The Executive Council shall meet and act as a collective authority.

Article 55.

Ministers who shall not be members of the Executive Council may be appointed by the Representative of the Crown, and shall comply with the provisions of Article 17 of this Constitution. Every such Minister shall be nominated by Dáil Éireann on the recommendation of a Committee of Dáil Éireann chosen by a method to be determined by Dáil Éireann, so as to be impartially representative of Dáil Éireann. Should a recommendation not be acceptable to Dáil Éireann, the Committee may continue to recommend names until one is found acceptable. The total number of Ministers, including the Ministers of the Executive Council, shall not exceed twelve.

Article 56.

Every Minister who is not a member of the Executive Council shall be the responsible head of the Department or Departments under his charge, and shall be individually responsible to Dáil Éireann alone for the administration of the Department or Departments of which he is the head: Provided that should arrangements for Functional or Vocational Councils be made by the Oireachtas these Ministers or any of them may, should the Oireachtas so decide, be members of, and be recommended to Dáil Éireann by, such Councils. The term of office of any Minister, not a member of the Executive Council, shall be the term of Dáil Éireann existing at the time of his appointment, but he shall continue in office until his successor shall have been appointed, and no such Minister shall be removed from office during his term otherwise than by Dáil Éireann itself, and then for stated reasons, and after the proposal to remove him has been submitted to a Committee, chosen by a method to be determined by Dáil Éireann, so as to be impartially representative of Dáil Éireann, and the Committee has reported thereon.

Article 57.

Every Minister shall have the right to attend and be heard in Seanad Éireann.

Article 58.

The appointment of a member of Dáil Éireann to be a Minister shall not entail upon him any obligation to resign his seat or to submit himself for re-election.

Article 59.

Ministers shall receive such remuneration as may from time to time be prescribed by law, but the remuneration of any Minister shall not be diminished during his term of office. [*Remainder omitted.*]

3. THE EXTERN MINISTER EXPERIMENT

Document 4.4—Extracts from B. Chubb, *The Government: an Introduction to the Cabinet System in Ireland,* Institute of Public Administration, Dublin, 1961.

In the draft [Constitution] submitted to the Constituent Assembly, the Government attempted . . . to restrict the area of cabinet responsibility to a narrow range of governmental functions. It did so by providing for a new type of extra-parliamentary minister elected by the Dáil itself for the term of its own life. Such 'extern ministers', as they came to be called, were to be members of the Executive Council but were not subject to collective cabinet responsibility, being explicitly responsible directly and individually to the Dáil. They were expected to be administrative experts rather than party politicians, and, to emphasize their separation from party life, it was provided that they 'should so far as possible be generally representative of the Irish Free State as a whole rather than of groups or parties'. The Executive Council was to consist of up to twelve members; four parliamentary or normal cabinet ministers (in charge of defence, home affairs, foreign affairs, and finance) bound together by collective responsibility, and not more than eight 'extern ministers'. By way of exception, up to three of the latter group could be members of either house. The Dáil was thus intended to effect a measure of direct control over some of the departments of state—those which were held to be not vitally concerned with national security and which were somewhat ingenuously thought to administer 'non-political' or 'technical' functions.

This proposal, which reflected the attitude of at least some of those concerned, clearly owed its inspiration to Swiss institutions and its advocates apparently hoped to graft together two dissimilar governmental devices. The scheme ran into difficulties in the Dáil, however; and since it did not in any case please all the members of the Government, it was so amended as to emerge in the Constitution as 'an optional modification of the British system'. The Constitution, as finally approved, provided for a normal cabinet of not less than five or more than seven, all members of the Dáil and collectively responsible. 'Extern ministers', who were not now to be members of the Executive Council, might be appointed up to such a number that the total Ministry would not exceed twelve. They were to be chosen by the Dáil, but they were not, as in the original proposals, required to resign parliamentary seats if they had them. Thus the final scheme was a far less radical modification of the cabinet system than had originally been intended. Even so, it represented a substantial effort to graft something new on to cabinet government as it operated in Britain . . . But in its final form, and with the existence of a strong parliamentary executive, it was from the first no more than 'a torso, bound to be swept away by the technical exigencies of parliamentary government'. In Mr. Cosgrave's first Government, three extern ministers were appointed; in his second, four. In all cases they were active politicians of the Government party and members of the Dáil. Moreover, they were picked by the party leaders, proposed as Government nominees, and approved by a vote along party lines in the Dáil. Thus the most original feature of the scheme—the idea of appointing non-party, extra-parliamentary administrators—was never tried. Moreover, though the Constitution made it clear that these ministers were not responsible with their cabinet colleagues for general government policy, Mr. Cosgrave told the Dáil in 1923 that they did accept such responsibility as though they were cabinet ministers, though he did draw some distinction between their position and that of the members of the Executive Council. When one of them later 'freely availed himself of his undoubted constitutional right to criticize the Executive Council on major matters of policy', the general reaction showed clearly that the normal conventions of cabinet government were felt by most to be altogether more suitable and proper. In any case, however, the arrangement could not have worked. Not only did it depend upon an independent deliberative assembly voting freely, which never existed, but it made an unreal distinction between functions of government which were held to be of vital political significance and others which were not, and which some had even imagined were not 'political' at all but 'technical'. The division of the ministry into 'executive ministers' and 'extern ministers' proved to be unreal: 'extern ministers' were merely a junior non-cabinet grade in a normal ministry. In 1927 a constitutional amendment provided that the total permitted number of twelve ministers might all be members of the Executive Council, and the Government was thus allowed a discretion to dispense with 'extern ministers'. None were appointed after that date.

4. BUNREACHT NA hEIREANN
   Document 4.5—Article 28 of Bunreacht na hÉireann (Constitution of Ireland).

Article 28.
1.   The Government shall consist of not less than seven and not more than fifteen members who shall be appointed by the President in accordance with the provisions of this Constitution.
2.   The executive power of the State shall, subject to the provisions of this Constitution, be exercised by or on the authority of the Government.

3.   1° War shall not be declared and the State shall not participate in any war save with the assent of Dáil Éireann. [*SSs. 2° and 3° omitted.*]

4.   1° The Government shall be responsible to Dáil Éireann.

2° The Government shall meet and act as a collective authority, and shall be collectively responsible for the Departments of State administered by the members of the Government.

3° The Government shall prepare Estimates of the Receipts and Estimates of the Expenditure of the State for each financial year, and shall present them to Dáil Éireann for consideration.

5.   1° The head of the Government, or Prime Minister, shall be called, and is in this Constitution referred to as, the Taoiseach.

2° The Taoiseach shall keep the President generally informed on matters of domestic and international policy.

6.   1° The Taoiseach shall nominate a member of the Government to be the Tánaiste.

2° The Tánaiste shall act for all purposes in the place of the Taoiseach if the Taoiseach should die, or become permanently incapacitated, until a new Taoiseach shall have been appointed.

3° The Tánaiste shall also act for or in the place of the Taoiseach during the temporary absence of the Taoiseach.

7.   1° The Taoiseach, the Tánaiste and the member of the Government who is in charge of the Department of Finance must be members of Dáil Éireann.

2° The other members of the Government must be members of Dáil Éireann or Seanad Éireann, but not more than two may be members of Seanad Éireann.

8.   Every member of the Government shall have the right to attend and be heard in each House of the Oireachtas.

9.   1° The Taoiseach may resign from office at any time by placing his resignation in the hands of the President.

2° Any other member of the Government may resign from office by placing his resignation in the hands of the Taoiseach for submission to the President.

3° The President shall accept the resignation of a member of the Government, other than the Taoiseach, if so advised by the Taoiseach.

4° The Taoiseach may at any time, for reasons which to him seem sufficient, request a member of the Government to resign; should the member concerned fail to comply with the request, his appointment shall be terminated by the President if the Taoiseach so advises.

10.   The Taoiseach shall resign from office upon his ceasing to retain the support of a majority in Dáil Éireann unless on his advice the President dissolves Dáil Éireann and on the reassembly of Dáil Éireann after the dissolution the Taoiseach secures the support of a majority in Dáil Éireann.

11.   1° If the Taoiseach at any time resigns from office the other members of the Government shall be deemed also to have resigned from office, but the Taoiseach and the other members of the Government shall continue to carry on their duties until their successors shall have been appointed.

2° The members of the Government in office at the date of a dissolution of Dáil Éireann shall continue to hold office until their successors shall have been appointed.

12.   The following matters shall be regulated in accordance with law, namely, the organization of, and distribution of business amongst, Departments of State, the designation of members of the Government to be the Ministers in charge of the said Departments, the discharge of the functions of the office of a member of the Government during his temporary absence or incapacity, and the remuneration of the members of the Government.

5. THE ROLE OF THE GOVERNMENT AND THE TAOISEACH

Document 4.6—Extract from M. Ó Muimhneacháin, 'The Functions of the Department of the Taoiseach' in *Administration*, vol. 7. (Also published as a pamphlet under the same title by the Institute of Public Administration, Dublin, 1960).

As the chief executive organ of the State, the Government has a great deal of work to do besides exercising the powers and functions specifically and expressly conferred on it by the Constitution or by statute. It is its function to govern, to see that the peace is kept and the law enforced, to keep the varying needs of the community as a whole and of its different sections constantly in mind, to concert measures, so far as it can, for averting any dangers that may threaten the community and for creating conditions that will help the people to advance in welfare and prosperity. The Agenda for a meeting of the Government does not, therefore, consist merely of a list of formal items, such as Orders to be made, but also includes other items relating to proposals for legislative or administrative measures recommended by Ministers as being, in their opinion, necessary or desirable in the public interest. Indeed, by a long-established practice, the Department of the Taoiseach, as the Government's secretariat, divides the items into two categories, which we call Government items and Cabinet items. Government items are those relating to the performance by the Government of specific functions devolving upon it by express provisions of the Constitution or the law—such as advising the President to make a judicial appointment or making an Imposition of Duties Order. Cabinet items are the others—the miscellaneous matters which come before the Government for decision as the policy-making organ of State.

Government meetings are usually held twice a week. Memoranda on the matters on the Agenda are, normally, submitted, in advance, by the Ministers concerned. Each memorandum sets out the relevant facts and considerations and the decision sought. A procedure has been laid down by the Government which is designed to ensure that every Minister whose Department is particularly affected by a proposal of another Minister will have had an adequate opportunity of considering the matter and of submitting his comments. Acting as the Government's secretariat, the Department of the Taoiseach is responsible, under the Taoiseach's directions, for securing compliance with the prescribed procedure. The Government's decisions are conveyed, in writing, to the Minister primarily concerned and to any other Ministers affected. The decisions are also recorded in formal Minutes, which are read and signed at the next meeting . . .

At this stage, it is well to recall once more the special position of the Taoiseach as the Head of the Government— the captain of the team. In this capacity, he is the central co-ordinating figure, who takes an interest in the work of all Departments, the figure to whom Ministers naturally turn for advice and guidance when faced with problems involving large questions of policy or otherwise of special difficulty and whose leadership is essential to the successful working of the Government as a collective authority, collectively responsible to Dáil Éireann, but acting through members each of whom is charged with specific Departmental tasks. He may often have to inform himself in considerable detail of particular matters with which other members of the Government are primarily concerned. He may have to make public statements on such matters, as well as on general matters of broad policy, internal and external. He answers Dáil Questions where the attitude of the Government towards important matters of policy is involved. He may occasionally sponsor Bills which represent important new developments of policy, even when the legislation, when enacted, will be the particular concern of the Minister in charge of some other Department of State. His Department is the sole channel of communication between Departments generally and the President's secretariat, except in minor and routine matters. Through his Parliamentary Secretary, whose Office is also included in the Department of the Taoiseach, he secures the co-ordination, in a comprehensive Parliamentary programme, of the proposals of the various Ministers for legislative and other measures in the Houses of the Oireachtas . . .

6. MINISTERS AND SECRETARIES ACTS
   (a) *The Inheritance*
   Document 4.7—Extracts from a speech on the Ministers and Secretaries Bill by the President of the Executive Council, Mr W. T. Cosgrave, in *Dáil Debates*, vol. 5, cols. 917-18 (16 November 1923).

As the House well knows, there were, during the British administration, quite a multiplicity of Boards and Statutory bodies, and during the last two years it has not been possible to survey the whole field and to see how better we may construct the Government machine . . . We have had to take over what was left of one Government and what had already been constructed of another. We have had to re-organise what was left of one and to adapt what was there of the other to suit the needs of the country.

(b) *The Principal Act*

Document 4.8—Extracts from Ministers and Secretaries Act, 1924 (No. 16).

ESTABLISHMENT OF DEPARTMENTS OF STATE

1.—There shall be established in Saorstát Éireann the several Departments of State specified and named in the eleven following sub-paragraphs, amongst which the administration and business of the public services in Saorstát Éireann shall be distributed as in the said sub-paragraphs is particularly mentioned, and each of which said Departments and the powers, duties and functions thereof shall be assigned to and administered by the Minister hereinafter named as head thereof, that is to say : —

(*i*) The Department of the President of the Executive Council which shall comprise the business, powers, authorities, duties and functions by the Constitution or by any existing or future Act of the Oireachtas or otherwise conferred on or to be discharged or performed by the Minister, who shall hold the office of and be styled Uachtarán na hArd-Chomhairle or (in English) the President of the Executive Council, and also the custody of and responsibility for all public archives and records and of papers and documents of State and of grants, deeds and other instruments of title relating to the property corporeal and incorporeal, real and personal for the time being vested in Saorstát Éireann and of records of the Executive Council and also the custody of the Seal of the Executive Council and also the responsibility for and control of the official publications of the Executive Council and also the administrative control of and responsibility for such public services and the business, powers, duties and functions thereof as may not for the time being be comprised in any of the Departments of State constituted by this Act.

(*ii*) The Department of Finance which shall comprise the administration and business generally of the public finance of Saorstát Éireann and all powers, duties and functions connected with the same, including in particular the collection and expenditure of the revenues of Saorstát Éireann from whatever source arising (save as may be otherwise provided by law), and the supervision and control of all purchases made for or on behalf of, and all supplies of commodities and goods held by any Department of State and the   disposal thereof, and also the business, powers, duties and functions of the branches and officers of the public service specified in the first part of the Schedule to this Act, and of which Department the head shall be, and shall be styled an t-Aire Airgid or (in English) the Minister for Finance.

(*iii*) The Department of Justice which shall comprise the administration and business generally of public services in connection with law, justice, public order and police, and all powers, duties and functions connected with the same (except such powers, duties and functions as are by law reserved to the Executive Council and such powers, duties and functions as are by the Constitution or by law excepted from the authority of the Executive Council or of an Executive Minister), and shall include in particular the business, powers, duties and functions of the branches and officers of the public service specified in the Second Part of the Schedule to this Act, and of which Department the head shall be, and shall be styled, an t-Aire Dlí agus Cirt or (in English) the Minister for Justice.

(*iv*) The Department of Local Government and Public Health which shall comprise the administration and business generally of public services in connection with local government, public health, relief of the poor, care of the insane (including insane criminals), health insurance, elections to each House of the Oireachtas, elections to local bodies and authorities, registration of voters, maintenance of public roads, and highways, registration of births, deaths and marriages, and vital statistics and all powers, duties and functions connected with the same, and shall include in particular the business, powers, duties and functions of the branches and officers of the public service specified in the Third Part of the Schedule to this Act, and of which Department the head shall be, and shall be styled, an t-Aire Rialtais Aitiúla agus Sláinte Puiblí or (in English) the Minister for Local Government and Public Health.

(*v*) The Department of Education which shall comprise the administration and business generally of public services in connection with Education, including primary, secondary and university education, vocational and technical training, endowed schools, reformatories, and industrial schools, and all powers, duties and functions connected with the same, and shall include in particular the business, powers, duties and functions of the branches and officers of the public services specified in the Fourth Part of the Schedule to this Act, and of which Department the head shall be, and shall be styled, an t-Aire Oideachais or (in English) the Minister for Education.

(*vi*) The Department of Lands and Agriculture which shall comprise the administration and business generally of public services in connection with agriculture and lands, including the fixing of rents and tenure of lands, acquisition by occupying tenants of full ownership by means of public funds, enlargement and other economic improvement of holdings of land, purchase of land for distribution by way of re-sale, relief of rural congestion and like uneconomic conditions, promotion of agriculture by means of educational grants, and of lectures on special subjects, agricultural statistics, forestry, veterinary services, survey and mapping of land, and all powers, duties and functions connected with the same, and shall include in particular the business, powers, duties and functions of the branches and officers of the public services specified in the Fifth Part of the Schedule to this Act, and of which Department the head shall be, and shall be styled, an t-Aire Tailte agus Talmhaíochta or (in English) the Minister for Lands and Agriculture.

(*vii*) The Department of Industry and Commerce which shall comprise the administration and business generally of public services in connection with trade, commerce, industry, and labour, industrial and commercial organisations and combinations, industrial and commercial statistics, transport, shipping, natural resources, and all powers, duties and functions connected with the same, including the promotion of trade and commerce by means of educational grants, and shall include in particular the business, powers, duties and functions of the branches and officers of the public services specified in the Sixth Part of the Schedule to this Act, and of which Department the head shall be, and shall be styled, an t-Aire Tionnscail agus Tráchtála or (in English) the Minister for Industry and Commerce.

(*viii*) The Department of Fisheries which shall comprise the administration and business generally of public services in connection with fisheries, including deep-sea fisheries, tidal waters fisheries, coastal fisheries, inland water fisheries, and industries connected with or auxiliary to the same, and all powers, duties and functions connected with the same, and shall include in particular the business, powers, duties and functions of the branches and officers of the public services specified in the Seventh Part of the Schedule to this Act, and of which Department the head shall be, and shall be styled, an t-Aire Iascaigh or (in English) the Minister for Fisheries.

(*ix*) The Department of Posts and Telegraphs which shall comprise the administration and business generally of public services in connection with posts, telegraphs, and telephones, and all powers, duties and functions connected with the same, and shall include in particular the business powers, duties and functions of the branches and officers of the public services specified in the Eighth Part of the Schedule to this Act, and of which Department the head shall be, and shall be styled, an t-Aire Puist agus Telegrafa or (in English) the Minister for Posts and Telegraphs.

(*x*) The Department of Defence which shall comprise the administration and business of the raising, training, organisation, maintenance, equipment, management, discipline, regulation, and control according to law of the Military Defence Forces of Saorstát Éireann, and all powers, duties and functions connected with the same, and of which Department the head shall be, and shall be styled, an t-Aire Cosanta or (in English) the Minister for Defence, and shall be assisted by a Council of Defence as hereinafter provided.

(*xi*) The Department of External Affairs shall comprise the administration and business generally of public services in connection with communications and transactions between the Government of Saorstát Éireann and the Government of any other state or nation, diplomatic and consular representation of Saorstát Éireann in any country or place, international amenities, the granting of passports and of *visés* to passports, and all powers, duties and functions connected with the same, and of which Department the head shall be, and shall be styled, an t-Aire Gnóthaí Coigríche or (in English) the Minister for External Affairs.

MINISTERS

2.—(1) Each of the Ministers, heads of the respective Departments of State mentioned in Section 1 of this Act, shall be a corporation sole under his style or name aforesaid (which may be lawfully expressed with equal validity and effect whether in the Irish Language or in its English equivalent as set out in the preceding section), and shall have perpetual succession and an official seal (which shall be officially and judicially noticed), and may sue and (subject to the fiat of the Attorney-General having been in each case first granted) be sued under his style or name aforesaid, and may acquire, hold and dispose of land for the purposes of the functions, powers or duties of the Department of State of which he is head or of any branch thereof.

(2) The Executive Council shall on the recommendation of the Minister appoint the principal officer of each of the said Departments and each of the said Ministers may appoint such other officers and servants to serve in the Department of which he is the head, as such Minister may, with the sanction of the Minister for Finance, determine, but every appointment made under this sub-section shall be subject to the provisions of the Civil Service Regulation Act, 1923 (No. 35 or 1923) or of any Act for the time being in force replacing or amending that Act.

(3) The terms and conditions of appointment of all officers and servants appointed by any Minister shall be prescribed by the Minister for Finance and there shall be paid out of moneys provided by the Oireachtas, or if there be any fund properly applicable by law to such payment, then out of such fund to such officers and servants such salaries or remunerations as the Minister may from time to time determine.

(4) The expenses of each of the Departments of State established under this Act, to such amount as may be sanctioned by the Minister for Finance, shall be paid out of moneys provided by the Oireachtas.

ALLOCATION OF DEPARTMENTS AMONG MINISTERS

3.—(1) The President of the Executive Council for the time being shall so soon as may be after his appointment as such President determine and declare how many and which of the said Departments of State established by this Act shall be assigned to and administered by the members of the Executive Council to be appointed on his nomination pursuant to the Constitution.

(2) It shall be lawful to assign two or more of the said Departments of State to a single person who in such case shall be appointed to be the Minister head of each of such Departments. [*Ss. 4-6 omitted.*]

PARLIAMENTARY SECRETARIES

7.—(1) The Executive Council may from time to time, on the nomination of the President of the Council, appoint so many persons, being members of the Oireachtas and not exceeding seven in number as the Executive Council shall consider necessary, to be Parliamentary Secretaries to the Executive Council or to Executive Ministers, and may at any time remove any Parliamentary Secretary so appointed.

(2) Every person appointed under the next preceding sub-section to be a Parliamentary Secretary shall continue to hold office so long only as he continues to be a member of the Oireachtas and the President of the Executive Council by whom he was nominated continues to hold office. [*SSs. 3-7 and Ss. 8-11 omitted.*]

DISTRIBUTION OF PUBLIC SERVICES

12.—(1) It shall be lawful for the Executive Council from time to time by Order to prescribe the organisation of all or any of the said Departments of State and of the business and administration thereof in any manner which may seem to the Executive Council to be expedient or proper in the public interests and in particular to create units of administration to be called offices (divisions or branches) which may be wholly self-contained or not as may seem expedient and to make such Orders consequential on or necessary for giving effect to any such scheme of organisation as the Executive Council may consider expedient or proper: Provided, however, that in the case of any Department of State the Minister in charge of which is not for the time being a member of the Executive Council no such Order shall be made without the concurrence of such Minister first obtained.

(2) It shall be lawful for the Executive Council from time to time by Order to re-distribute all or any of the public services and officers, and the administration, jurisdiction, powers, duties and functions thereof amongst the several Ministers and Departments of State or any of them in any manner which may seem to the Executive Council to be expedient or proper in the public interests, and to make such Orders consequential on or necessary for giving effect to any such re-distribution as the Executive Council may consider expedient or proper. [*Remaining Sections omitted.*]

SCHEDULE
First Part
Particular Branches of Administration assigned to an Roinn Airgid (The Department of Finance)

The business and functions formerly administered and discharged by the British Treasury in Ireland.
The Revenue Commissioners.
The Paymaster General and Deputy Paymaster for Ireland.
The Government Actuary.
The Commissioners of Public Works in Ireland.
The Civil Service Commission.
The Commissioner of Valuation and Boundary Surveyor for Ireland.
The Ordnance Survey.
The Superintendent of the Teachers' Pension Office.
The Stationery Office.
The Old Age Pensions, save as regards appeals governed by Statute.
The Post Office Savings Bank (administered through the Minister for Posts and Telegraphs as agent).
The Registrar of Friendly Societies.

Second Part
Particular Branches of Administration assigned to an Roinn Dlí agus Cirt (The Department of Justice)

All Courts of Justice and the Offices thereof save in so far as the same are reserved to the Executive Council or are excepted from the authority of the Executive Council or of an Executive Minister.
Police.
The General Prisons Board for Ireland and all Prisons.
The Registrar of District Court Clerks.
The Public Record Office.
The Registry of Deeds.
The Land Registry.
The Commissioners of Charitable Donations and Bequests for Ireland.

Third Part
Particular Branches of Administration assigned to an Roinn Rialtais Aitiúla agus Sláinte Puiblí (The Department of Local Government and Public Health)

The Local Government Board for Ireland, including appeals under the Old Age Pensions Acts.
The Inspectors of Lunatic Asylums in Ireland.
National Health Insurance Commission.
The Registrar-General of Births, Deaths and Marriages in Ireland.
Roads Department (formerly Ministry of Transport).
Clerk of the Crown and Hanaper so far as concerned with Elections.
General Nursing Council and Central Midwives Board.

Fourth Part
Particular Branches of Administration assigned to an Roinn Oideachais (The Department of Education)

The Commissioners of National Education in Ireland.
The Intermediate Education Board for Ireland.
The Commissioners of Education in Ireland (Endowed Schools).

The Inspector of Reformatory and Industrial Schools.
The Department of Agriculture and Technical Instruction for Ireland (business and functions relating to Technical Instruction only).
The College of Science.
The Geological Survey in Ireland.
The National Museum of Science and Art.
The National Library of Ireland.
The National Gallery of Ireland.
The Metropolitan School of Art.
Meteorological Services.

Fifth Part

Particular Branches of Administration assigned to an Roinn Tailte agus Talmhaíochta (The Department of Lands and Agriculture)

The Irish Land Commission (including the late Congested District Board for Ireland—Agricultural and Land Branches).
The Department of Agriculture and Technical Instruction for Ireland (except the business and functions relating to Fisheries and Technical Instruction).
The Ministry of Agriculture and Fisheries except so far as concerned with the Ordnance Survey.
The Royal Veterinary College of Ireland.
The Public Trustee in Ireland.
The Forestry Commission.
Farm Institutes of or controlled by Government.
Royal Botanic Gardens.

Sixth Part

Particular Branches of Administration assigned to an Roinn Tionnscail agus Tráchtála (The Department of Industry and Commerce).

Ministry of Transport (excluding the Roads Department).
The Board of Trade.
Registrar of Companies.
Registrar of Business Names.
Registration of Shipping.
Minister for Labour.
Electricity Commissioners.
Chief and other Inspectors of Factories.

Seventh Part

Particular Branches o f Administration assigned to an Roinn Iascaigh (The Department of Fisheries)

Department of Agriculture and Technical Instruction for Ireland — Fisheries Branch.
Congested Districts Board for Ireland — Fisheries Branch, and Rural Industries Branch.
The Conservators of Fisheries.

Eighth Part

Particular Branches of Administration assigned to an Roinn Puist agus Telegrafa (The Department of Posts and Telegraphs)

Postmaster General.

[Ninth Part omitted.]

Tenth Part

Ministers named in former Acts	Corresponding Ministers under this Act
Minister for Finance	Aire Airgid (Minister for Finance)
Minister for Home Affairs	Aire Dlí agus Cirt (Minister for Justice)
Minister for Local Government	Aire Rialtais Aitiúla agus Sláinte Puiblí (Minister for Local Government and Public Health)
Minister for Education	Aire Oideachais (Minister for Education).
Minister for Agriculture	Aire Tailte agus Talmhaíochta (Minister for Lands and Agriculture)
Minister for Industry and Commerce	Aire Tionnscail agus Tráchtála (Minister for Industry and Commerce)
Minister for Fisheries	Aire Iascaigh (Minister for Fisheries)
Postmaster-General	Aire Puist agus Telegrafa (Minister for Posts and Telegraphs
Minister for Defence	Aire Cosanta (Minister for Defence)
Minister for External Affairs	Aire Gnóthaí Coigríche (Minister for External Affairs)

NOTE ON MAJOR ALTERATIONS AND ADDITIONS MADE SINCE 1924
(prepared by the Editor)

1928: Department of Lands and Agriculture became Department of Lands. Department of Fisheries became Department of Lands and Fisheries— Ministers and Secretaries (Amendment) Act, 1928 (No. 6).

1934: Fisheries Branch of the Department of Lands and Fisheries transferred to the Department of Agriculture and Department of Lands and Fisheries renamed Department of Lands — S.R. and O. 40/1934. (Subsequently Fisheries Branch was transferred to the Department of Lands by S.I. 67/1957.)

1937: Department of President of the Executive Council became Department of the Taoiseach—Constitution (Consequential Provisions) Act, 1937 (No. 40).

1939: Department of Supplies set up — Ministers and Secretaries (Amendment) Act, 1939 (No. 36).

1939: A Minister for the Coordination of Defensive Measures was appointed in 1939. His duties in this capacity were terminated in June, 1945.

1945: Department of Supplies wound up, its functions being transferred to the Department of Industry and Commerce — Department of Supplies (Transfer of Functions) Act, 1945, (No. 21).

1946: Department of Health established. Department of Social Welfare established — Ministers and Secretaries (Amendment) Act, 1946 (No. 38).

1947: Department of Local Government and Public Health became Department of Local Government — S.R. and O. 16/1947.

1956: Department of the Gaeltacht established — Ministers and Secretaries (Amendment) Act, 1956 (No. 21).

1959: Department of Transport and Power established — Ministers and Secretaries (Amendment) Act, 1959 (No. 17). Some functions previously carried out by the Department of Industry and Commerce transferred to it.

(c) MINISTERS WITHOUT PORTFOLIO

Document 4.9—Section 4 of Ministers and Secretaries (Amendment) Act, 1939 (No. 36).

4. — (1) Nothing in the Ministers and Secretaries Acts, 1924 and 1928, or this Act shall render it obligatory for every member of the Government to be a Minister having charge of a Department of State.

(2) A member of the Government who is not a Minister having charge of a Department of State shall be known as a Minister without portfolio.

(3) The Government may, whenever they think proper so to do, assign to any particular Minister without portfolio a specific style or title which shall be judicially and officially noticed.

7. THE ATTORNEY GENERAL

(a) *The Ministers and Secretaries Act*

Document 4.10—Extracts from Ministers and Secretaries Act, 1924 (No 16).

6.—(1) There shall be vested in the Attorney-General of Saorstát Éireann (who shall be styled in Irish Príomh-Atúrnae Shaorstáit Éireann and shall be appointed by the Governor-General on the nomination of the Executive Council) the business, powers, authorities, duties and functions formerly vested in or exercised by the Attorney-General for Ireland, the Solicitor-General for Ireland, the Attorney-General for Southern Ireland, the Solicitor-General for Southern Ireland, the Law Adviser to the Lord Lieutenant of Ireland and any or all of them respectively, and the administration and control of the business, powers, authorities, duties and functions of the branches and officers of the public services specified in the Ninth Part of the Schedule to this Act and also the administration and business generally of public services in connection with the representation of the Government of Saorstát Éireann and of the public in all legal proceedings for the enforcement of law, the punishment of offenders and the assertion or protection of public rights and all powers, duties and functions connected with the same respectively, together with the duty of advising the Executive Council and the several Ministers in matters of law and of legal opinion.

(2) The Attorney-General may be or become a member of Dáil Éireann, and if he is a member of Dáil Éireann at the time of his appointment he shall not be under any obligation to resign his seat or to submit himself for re-election. He shall hold office so long only as the President of the Executive Council by whom he was nominated continues to hold office.

Schedule—Ninth Part

Particular Services assigned to an Priomh-Atúrnae (The Attorney General)
Chief Crown Solicitor for Ireland.
Chief State Solicitor's Department and all local State Solicitors.
Treasury Solicitor for Ireland.
Parliamentary Draftsman.
Charities.
Estates of illegitimate deceased persons.

(b) *Bunreacht na hÉireann*

Document 4.11—Article 30 of Bunreacht na hÉireann (Constitution of Ireland).

Article 30.

1. There shall be an Attorney General who shall be the adviser of the Government in matters of law and legal opinion, and shall exercise and perform all such powers, functions and duties as are conferred or imposed on him by this Constitution or by law.

2. The Attorney General shall be appointed by the President on the nomination of the Taoiseach.

3. All crimes and offences prosecuted in any court constituted under Article 34 of this Constitution other than a court of summary jurisdiction shall be prosecuted in the name of the People and at the suit of the Attorney General or some other person authorised in accordance with law to act for that purpose.

4. The Attorney General shall not be a member of the Government.

5. 1° The Attorney General may at any time resign from office by placing his resignation in the hands of the Taoiseach for submission to the President.

2° The Taoiseach may, for reasons which to him seem sufficient, request the resignation of the Attorney General.

3° In the event of failure to comply with the request, the appointment of the Attorney General shall be terminated by the President if the Taoiseach so advises.

4° The Attorney General shall retire from office upon the resignation of the Taoiseach, but may continue to carry on his duties until the successor to the Taoiseach shall have been appointed.

6.   Subject to the foregoing provisions of this Article, the office of Attorney General, including the remuneration to be paid to the holder of the office, shall be regulated by law.

(c) *Permission to Engage in Private Practice.*
     Document 4.12—Extract from *Dáil Debates*, vol. 182, cols. 291-2
     (31 May 1960).

Dr. Browne asked the Taoiseach whether the Attorney General is permitted to carry on a private practice in addition to discharging his public office.

The Taoiseach: The Attorney General is at liberty to engage in such private practice as may be compatible with the full and proper discharge of the duties of his office.

Dr. Browne: Does the Taoiseach not agree that it is very difficult, if not impossible, for the Attorney General to discharge competently his public functions at the same time as he is running a private practice ? Does the Taoiseach not agree that the Attorney General's very costly and gross mishandling of the Singer case——

An Ceann Comhairle: The Deputy may not go into that.

The Taoiseach: With regard to the question which the Deputy relevantly asked, it was the practice, until 1948, to require the Attorney General not to engage in private practice but the Government of that day, of which I think the Deputy was a member, decided to reverse that practice and to require the Attorney General to engage in private practice. That decision was again reversed in 1951, when Mr. de Valera resumed office as Taoiseach, but again in 1954 it was reversed and the practice established in 1954 still persists.

8. ASSIGNMENT OF MINISTERS TO DEPARTMENTS
   (a) *The Taoiseach merely informs the Dáil.*
   Document 4.13—Extract from *Dáil Debates*, vol. 94, cols. 42-3 (9
   June, 1944).

The Taoiseach: I am proposing the following Deputies as Members of the Government:

Seán T. O Ceallaigh; Seán F. Lemass; Seán Mac an tSaoi; Séamus O Riain; Proinnsias Mac Aodhagáin; Tomás O Deirg; Gearóid O Beoláin; Oscar Mac Tréinfhir; Pádraig O Caoilte; Seán O Maoláin.

As I have said in Irish, they have worked well, both in their individual Departments and as a team. Individually, they are known to every member of the Dáil. They have been working for our country, most of them, from 1916 to the present time, and some of them also even further back. I do not think there is anything I could say that could possibly add to their reputation. It is known to every member of the House as it is to me. I have more than pleasure in proposing that they be again members of the Government.

General Mulcahy: I asked the Taoiseach before if he would state what particular Ministries are being assigned to the individual Deputies mentioned here ?

The Taoiseach: As the Deputy knows, according to the Constitution and the law, they are nominated and selected as members of the Government, and then it is the duty of the Taoiseach to assign Departments of State to them. When it is possible to indicate in advance the Departments to be assigned to the members of the Government it is perhaps well to do it, and I can indicate that I propose, at the moment anyhow, to assign to them the same Departments that they had just before the dissolution. I should also like to indicate that it is my intention to nominate Deputy Seán T. O Ceallaigh as Tánaiste, but, strictly speaking, that does not come before us immediately for consideration. The point is that they are being appointed really as members of the Government, and it is as such that the agreement of the Dáil is required to my nominations.

(b) *Taoiseach's power to assign and terminate made explicit.*
> Document 4.14—Section 4 of The Ministers and Secretaries (Amendment) Act, 1946 (No. 38).

4.—(1) The Taoiseach may from time to time assign a particular Department of State to a member of the Government and may assign more than one Department of State to the same person.

(2) The Taoiseach may at any time terminate the assignment of a particular Department of State to the member of the Government to whom that Department of State is then assigned.

9. NEW FUNCTIONS AND MACHINERY—ECONOMIC PLANNING
(a) *Economic Development*—A Study of National Development.
> Document 4.15—Extracts from *Economic Development*, Stationery Office, Dublin, 1958.

PREFACE

This study of national development problems and opportunities was prepared by the Secretary of the Department of Finance, with the cooperation of others in, or connected with, the public service. The views and recommendations it contains were considered by the Government in the formulation of its recently-issued Programme for Economic Expansion. The study is being published to make available the information assembled and coordinated in it and to stimulate interest in the subject of national development.

The study was completed in May, 1958, but in some instances it has been found possible to take into account developments subsequent to that date.

INTRODUCTION

1. How this study originated is shown in the documents reproduced as Appendix 1. It is well to reiterate here that the aim is not to draw up a detailed five or ten-year plan of national development. For a small country so exposed to the perpetual flux of world economic forces there would be little sense in trying to establish a rigid pattern of development. The aim is rather (a) to highlight the main deficiencies and potentialities of the economy and (b) to suggest the principles to be followed to correct the deficiencies and realise the opportunities, indicating a number of specific forms of productive development which appear to offer good long-term prospects. One must be prepared at all times for fluctuations and upsets. A readiness to adapt to changing conditions is a *sine qua non* of material progress. Nevertheless, one may reasonably hope to find some guiding principles which it would be advantageous to follow through thick and thin . . .

APPENDIX 1

Oifig an Aire Airgeadais,
16 Nollaig, 1957.

MEMORANDUM FOR THE INFORMATION OF THE GOVERNMENT
Economic Development

The Minister for Finance circulates, herewith, for the information of the Government, a copy of a minute dated 12th December, 1957, from the Secretary of his Department.

Minister,

1. This note records what I have said to you orally about the desirability of attempting to work out an integrated programme of national development for the next five or ten years, which I believe will be critical years for the country's survival as an economic entity.

2. I have not a "Plan" in mind. There would be little sense in trying to establish any rigid pattern of development for a small country so exposed to the perpetual flux of world economic forces. But I have thought for some time that it would be a useful national service to prepare a study embracing the following three elements: —

(i) as groundwork, a brief outline of the present state of the economy, concentrating on the main deficiencies and opportunities;

(ii) a statement of the principles to be followed in order most effectively to correct the defects and realise the opportunities; and

(iii) indications of the specific forms of productive development which appear to offer the best prospects.

3. Various Commissions have surveyed the Irish economy most thoroughly and it would be a waste of time and effort to cover the ground again. What is urgently necessary is *not* to know that more resources should be devoted to productive rather than non-productive purposes but rather to know what are the productive purposes to which resources should be applied and what unproductive, or relatively unproductive, activities can, with the minimum social disadvantage, be curtailed to set free resources for productive development.

4. This is urgent for at least five reasons : —

(i) the growing comment on the absence of a comprehensive and integrated programme is tending to deepen the all-too-prevalent mood of despondency about the country's future;

(ii) in the context of such a programme it would be easier to win acceptance for particular decisions of policy which, presented in isolation, might be strenuously opposed;

(iii) a slowing down in housing and other forms of social investment must be faced from now on because of the virtual satisfaction of needs over wide areas—and it is necessary to find productive investments which will prevent the unemployment problem from becoming very serious;

(iv) the favourable state of our balance of payments is, in part, the result of painful adjustments and could so easily be disturbed that it is most important to confine increases in national expenditure as far as possible to projects of a *productive* character;

(v) it is not enough to count on proposals being made by the World Bank Mission when it comes next May or June—we should be doing our own homework if for no other reason than to equip ourselves to make the most of the World Bank's expert assistance and advice.

5. While I deprecate planning in any rigid sense, I am convinced of the psychological value of setting up targets of national endeavour, provided they are reasonable and mutually consistent. There is probably a particular need in this country at present to harness the enthusiasm of the young and buttress the faith of the active members of the community in this way. But there is nothing to be gained by setting up fanciful targets. Failure to reach such targets would quickly produce disillusionment and renew the feeling of national despondency. Neither is there any use in suggesting that through some simple expedient, like reform of the banking system, rapid expansion of employment and living standards can be assured. Some improvements in the banking field are desirable but there is no solution to our difficulties in financial expedients. Greater output per head and increased saving (with corresponding restraint in consumption, both private and public) are essential conditions of economic improvement. Moreover, unless the individual members of the community have sufficient patriotism and realism to accept the standard

of living produced by their own exertions here—even if it should continue for some time to be lower than the standard available abroad—the basis for economic progress simply does not exist.

6. With all this in mind and feeling that the central position of the Department of Finance gives us a special responsibility for studying how economic progress can be promoted, I began some time ago the task of bringing together in an accessible form the information which seems most relevant to the determination of future policy in the economic sphere. I append the heads of the scheme on which, with the help of the Central Statistics Office, Mr. C. H. Murray and others, I have been working. It is intended to cover the three points indicated in paragraph 2 above.

7. This, I believe, is work that can best be done, as regards force, consistency and reasonableness, under one person's direction, provided that person has free access for information, advice and assistance to officers of the other Departments and State organisations concerned. What should be produced for consideration is a coherent and constructive document, bound by a realistic appraisal of the resources likely to be available rather than by Departmental allegiances; otherwise an official of the Department of Finance would find rather strange the rôle of advocate rather than critic of new forms of expenditure! Departments, as such, should I suggest remain officially uncommitted until the work is referred to them for critical examination prior to its formal consideration by the Government.

8. I would willingly—and as quickly as possible—complete the work in hands, on the basis outlined above, if it is felt that it serves a need and would be of assistance to the Government.

9. At some point consideration might perhaps be given to the question of inviting a wider range of views than those of Departments only but this is still some distance off.

T. K. Whitaker,
12th December, 1957.

SCHEME OF WORK

1. Introduction.
2. Economic position—general outline.
3. Development needs and resources.
4. Finance.
5. Agriculture—general.
6. Grasslands.
7. Cattle.
8. Milk and milk products.
9. Pigs and bacon.
10. Wheat and tillage generally.
11. Agricultural education—advisory services, etc.
12. State aid to agriculture.
13. Agricultural credit.
14. Agriculture—conclusions.

15. Fisheries.
16. Forestry.
17. Industry—general.
18. ⎫
19. ⎬ Particular industrial possibilities.
20. ⎭
21. Tourism.
22. Conclusions.

Roinn an Taoisigh,
Baile Átha Cliath.

S. 16066
An Rúnaí Príobháideach,
An tAire Airgeadais.

18 Nollaig, 1957.

I am to refer to the memorandum dated the 16th instant submitted by the Minister for Finance with a copy of a minute dated the 12th December, 1957, from the Secretary of his Department regarding the working-out of an integrated programme of national development and to inform you that, at a meeting of the Government held on the 17th instant, it was arranged : —

(1) that the Minister would approve the proposals, submitted to him in the minute, for the preparation of a study embracing : —

(a) as groundwork, a brief outline of the present state of the economy, concentrating on the main deficiencies and opportunities,

(b) a statement of the principles to be followed in order most effectively to correct the defects and realise the opportunities and

(c) indications of the specific forms of productive development which appear to offer the best prospects; and

(2) that, for the purposes of the study, the Secretary of the Department of Finance would have free access, for information, advice and assistance, to officers of the other Departments and State organizations concerned.

M. Ó Muimhneacháin,
Rúnaí an Rialtais.

(b) *The Committee on Industrial Organization*
Document 4.16—Official Announcement concerning the Committee on Industrial Organization, 30 August 1961 (Press release).

The Committee's terms of reference and functions are to make a critical appraisal of the measures that may require to be taken to adapt Irish industry to conditions of more intensive competition in home and export markets, to undertake an examination of the difficulties which may be created for particular industries and to formulate positive measures of adjustment and adaptation. The Committee will not regard itself as composed merely of representatives of particular interests, whether Departmental, business, or Trade Unions. It will carry out its task on the principle that searching, uninhibited and objective surveys of industries are the only kind worth undertaking as a serious preparation for adjustment to the realities of participation in the European Economic Community.

The industrial surveys will be carried out by working teams appointed by the Committee. The teams will comprise officers of the Department of Industry and Commerce and economists (drawn from the Department of Finance or from outside the public service) with the assistance of representatives of each industry or group of industries and, where necessary, of technical experts. A number of teams has already been formed. . . .

The reports prepared by the survey teams will not include information furnished in confidence about the private affairs of individual firms . . .

The Committee on Industrial Organisation will furnish views on the various reports, after such consultations as it may think necessary or desirable, before the reports are furnished to the Government, to the Federation of Irish Industries, to the individual manufacturers concerned, to the Federated Union of Employers, to the Irish Congress of Trade Unions and to other interested bodies. The Committee may also draw up general recommendations based on the reports as a whole.

(c) *The National Industrial Economic Council.*

Document 4.17—Extracts from *Address by Mr. Seán F. Lemass, Taoiseach, at Inaugural Meeting of National Industrial Economic Council,* 9 October, 1963 (Press release).

The Council is charged with the task of preparing reports from time to time on the principles which should be applied for the development of the national economy, and for the realisation and maintenance of full employment at adequate wages, with reasonable price stability and reasonable long-term equilibrium in the balance of external payments. In these reports the Council will have regard to the level and trend of incomes, from whatever source. The Council will not deal with agricultural matters. Some explanation may be expected for the decision to make a distinction between agriculture and the rest of the economy. The explanation lies in the fact that agricultural policy is determined to a large extent by external conditions, which we cannot hope to alter by decisions taken here. There would also be some practical difficulties in setting up a Council, which would be workable in size but fully representative in character, to deal with agriculture, industry and the rest of the economy. If, however, in the light of experience of the working of this Council, or for some other reason, it should appear to be beneficial to have this decision reconsidered, this could be done. . . .

The establishment of this Council and the tripartite nature of its membership mark an important step forward in the institution of formal machinery through which the advice of persons representing the main sectors of the community is made available to the Government. In recent years a number of bodies, on which both sides of industry are represented, have been set up under official sponsorship or with official encouragement. I refer to such bodies as the Irish National Productivity Committee, the National Employer/Labour Conference and the Committee on Industrial Organisation. The experience of these bodies gives ground for our belief that this form of co-operation can be utilized and developed with highly beneficial results to the whole community. . . . I hope that members of the Council will approach their task as individuals as well as representatives of the organisations which nominated them, and that each will play a full part in its deliberations. I can assure the Council that the Government will attach the utmost importance to the Council's recommendations, though they will, of course, retain ultimate responsibility to the Dáil and public for policy decisions involving Government action.

The Council is free to deal with and report on all matters coming within the ambit of its terms of reference as it thinks fit. In addition the Government may request it to prepare a general report or a report on a specific subject. The National Employer/Labour Conference may also request the Council to report on a specific subject. The first task the Government wish to entrust to the Council is to examine the Second Programme for Economic Expansion—other than the agricultural aspects— and to advise on how the objectives of the Programme can best be realised or, if possible, surpassed. The advice and assistance of the Council in regard to the Programme will be of great value in securing that the measures taken to implement it will have the full support of all sections of the Community.

The Council's terms of reference are, as I have already indicated, of very wide scope and the Government will be glad to see the Council undertake enquiries of a far-reaching nature. In many spheres the Council can contribute to the solution of problems facing the country and help it to choose the best road to future prosperity. The weight which the whole community will give to its views should be an important element in securing the proper relationship between incomes and national output without which it will be difficult to raise real living standards at a satisfactory rate and to realise the social progress which is the ultimate purpose of all economic activity. As members of the Council will know this is a matter which is now receiving urgent consideration in many democratic countries. . . .

(d) *The Second Programme.*

Document 4.18—Extracts from *Second Programme for Economic Expansion,* laid by the Government before each House of the Oireachtas, August, 1963, Stationery Office, Dublin, 1963.

AIMS AND ACHIEVEMENTS OF FIRST PROGRAMME

1. The Government's first programme for economic expansion was published in November, 1958. It outlined the objectives of economic policy in

agriculture, industry, tourism and the other main sectors of activity. It dealt specifically with the role of the State in promoting economic development, both directly through State investment and indirectly through the encouragement of private enterprise by grants, loans, tax incentives and other means. The programme was introduced at a time of concern about Ireland's capacity to progress economically at the rate needed to give all who want to live in Ireland an acceptable income. Its aim was to accelerate progress by strengthening public confidence, indicating the opportunities for development, and encouraging a progressive, expansionist outlook.

2. Economic growth is expressed in terms of Gross National Product (GNP) which is a measure of the money value of the goods and services which become available to the nation annually from economic activity. In 1958, after years of slow economic growth and deficits in external payments, to predict more than a 2 per cent per annum increase in GNP in real terms for the years immediately ahead seemed too hazardous. This 2 per cent growth rate was mentioned not as a target but as a deliberately modest forecast of what action on the lines of the programme might be relied upon to achieve. It was recognised that to achieve this forecast would be a welcome psychological tonic, as well as a materially advantageous achievement, whereas failure to reach a more ambitious target would risk re-creating a mood of despondency inimical to enterprise and effort.

3. We have reached the final year (1963) of the first programme a much better-off nation than in 1958. The rise in the community's standard of living during the four years to 1962 is expressed by the increase of about 18½ per cent in GNP measured at 1958 prices. This increase has been achieved in conditions of near-equilibrium in external payments. Over the period 1958-63, employment created in industries and services has come closer to offsetting the continuing and not unexpected movement of manpower from the land. During 1961-62 the long-established excess of emigration over the rate of natural increase of the population was reversed. The population is rising again, though slowly. . . .

MEANING OF A PROGRAMME

5. A programme is an attempt to apply to the management of the nation's economic affairs the same foresight, organisation and determination as a competent and prudent person applies to the management of his own household or business. In a democracy the national economic programme cannot be authoritarian. It proceeds on the assumption that there is widespread public agreement on making as much economic progress as possible and on the means by which such progress is to be achieved. Objectives and priorities are outlined but the programme does not in every instance specify how they are to be attained. Rather is it educative and indicative, combining help and guidance from the State for private enterprise with direct State action where this is needed to ensure full use of productive capacity. Targets may be set for the main sectors of the economy but it would be unrealistic to break these down into targets for individual enterprises. The penalty — and it is no

light one — involved by failure to reach a target is the slowing down both of individual and national progress.

6. Programming involves making the most reasonable estimate of the increase attainable in total production on certain assumptions about major factors such as population, individual output, exports, capacity to finance capital needs. At attempt must be made to foresee the relative contributions of agriculture, industry and services to overall expansion and to define the economic and financial policies needed to secure maximum output of competitive goods and services. It is only if these policies are effective, and internal and external conditions are favourable, that the desired growth rate can be achieved. A target is an indication of the progress the economy can make if certain assumptions and conditions are fulfilled; it is an aim, not a promise. . . .

BASIC PRINCIPLES OF SECOND PROGRAMME

21. Though the second programme is more comprehensive than the first and the economic and social environment will be different, the basic principles of the first programme, as set out in Part I of the 1958 White Paper, will remain fully applicable. It is still expected that the private sector, stimulated and guided by public policy and supplemented where necessary by State initiative, will be the principal source of new productive projects. The main emphasis in public activity will be on productive expenditure, which will increase the national output of goods and services capable of meeting competition in export markets. Earning and saving will continue to be encouraged by fiscal policy. Higher productivity and greater competitiveness remain the key to permanent improvements in employment and community welfare.

SUMMARY OF OBJECTIVES

22. The second programme will, therefore, be distinguished by the following principal characteristics :

(i) It will cover the period to the end of this decade.

(ii) It will have as its chief objective the raising of the real income of the community by 50 per cent in the 1960's, in line with the collective target of the OECD.

(iii) Its complementary aim will be to secure the progressive reduction of involuntary emigration so that by 1970 net yearly emigration will be reduced to 10,000 at most. The net increase in employment envisaged in the decade is 78,000.

(iv) Special attention will be given to education, training and other forms of " human investment ".

(v) The obligation of Ireland to give increased aid to less developed countries will be recognised.

(vi) The basic principles underlying the first programme will continue to be respected.

DEPARTMENT OF FINANCE, 1954

Minister

Secretary

Assistant Secretary — Assistant Secretary — Assistant Secretary — Assistant Secretary — Assistant Secretary

Establishments Division

Controls numbers of staff, recruitment, conditions of service (including remuneration), conciliation and arbitration.

Organization and Methods

Training

Controls expenditure of Department of Posts and Telegraphs including wireless broadcasting.

Finance Division

Taxation

Borrowing

Budget

Short-term economic forecasting

International trade and payments

Exchange control

O.E.E.C.

Banking and credit

Accounts

General financial and economic questions

State-sponsored bodies

Land Commission finances

Control of expenditure of Departments of Finance, Taoiseach, and of Land Commission

Social insurance

Supply Division

Controls expenditure of Departments of Agriculture, Defence, Education, External Affairs, Gaeltacht, Health, Industry and Commerce, Justice, Lands, Local Government, Social Welfare

State service pensions and superannuation

(Prepared from information supplied by The Department of Finance)

DEPARTMENT OF FINANCE, 1964

Minister

Secretary

Assistant Secretary	Assistant Secretary	Assistant Secretary	Assistant Secretary
Finance Division	*Development Division*	*Supply Division*	*Establishments Division*
Taxation	Controls expenditure of economic departments	Controls expenditure of Departments not dealt with by other Divisions	Controls numbers of staff, recruitment, conditions of service (including remuneration, conciliation and arbitration)
Borrowing			
Budget	Deals with state-sponsored bodies whose activities are economic in character	Deals with state-sponsored bodies associated with such departments	Organization and Methods
Short-term economic forecasting			
International trade and payments			Training
Exchange control	Long-term economic forecasting and programme for economic expansion	Controls various social service funds	
International institutions			Controls expenditure of Department of Posts and Telegraphs including Radio Eireann
Banking and credit		Civil Service pensions and superannuation	
Accounts			
Travelling and subsistence			

(Prepared from information supplied by The Department of Finance)

10. COALITION GOVERNMENT

(a) *Mr. Costello explains 'Inter-Party' Government.*

Document 4.19—Extracts from speech by the Taoiseach, Mr. J. A. Costello in *Dáil Debates,* vol. 110, cols. 67-9 (18 February, 1948).

A number of Parties in this country, after the General Election, came together, having put before the electors their varying and various policies and ideas. The various Parties who have formed this Government have sought to find, and have found, numbers of points on which they can completely agree. This Government has been formed on the basis of full agreement on all those points. Any points on which we have not agreed have been left in abeyance. . . .

I do not care whether Deputy Lemass calls this a coalition, an inter-Party Government, or anything else. He can call it what he likes. A group of Parties has come together and found agreement. That is an experiment, if you like. It shows this country, at all events, what Fianna Fáil tried to delude the country about, that it was not possible to form a Government from members of Parties with different policies and different ideas. We have at least shown this country that there can be some other Government instead of Fianna Fáil and that in itself is an achievement. . . . We have the idea of a group Government, if you like, an inter-Party Government if you like, but at the basis of all that is this, that there has been found amongst all those Parties common agreement and a common policy. We propose to do the best we can to implement that. . . .

Deputy Lemass wanted to know what was the policy of the Minister for Agriculture with regard to wheat, beet and the rest. He will hear that in due course. It will be the policy of the Government. Deputy Lemass wanted to know were we going to be a group Government or a Coalition Government. We are not evading our constitutional responsibilities. Deputy Lemass doubtless is aware that Article 28 of the Constitution makes it imperative for every Government to be such a Government as must meet and act with collective authority. No Government can be formed within the Constitution, or act within the Constitution, unless it meets and acts with collective authority. This Government will do that.

(b) *The Labour Party's decision to join a Coalition in 1954.*

Document 4.20—Extract from *The Labour Party: Report of the Administrative Council for the year 1953-4.*

49. In accordance with the decision of the Clonmel Conference i.e.,
" That in the event of no political party securing an over-all majority in

the next General Election, the Labour Party declares it is prepared to enter into discussions with another political party or group of parties on the question of the formation of a Government on the basis of the prior acceptance of an agreed programme, together with satisfactory assurances that the necessary legislative or administrative action will be taken by the future government to give effect to such programme. In its approach to the question of participation in a Government with other political parties, the Labour Party will be guided by the degree to which the points of policy which it considers essential are made the objectives of the new Government."

50. Arrangements were made for the summoning of the Conference for Sunday, 30th May, 1954.

51. Meantime, it being apparent that no single Party could form a Government, the Fine Gael Party approached the Labour Party. After protracted negotiations, agreement emerged in the following 12-point agreed programme: —

[Details of Programme omitted.]

52. There was also, as part of the agreement, an undertaking that the Party would receive four Ministerial posts and a Parliamentary Secretaryship. The Party insisted on the right to hold the post of Minister for Industry and Commerce.

53. The Parliamentary Labour Party met and approved the agreed Programme which was to be submitted to the Special Conference. The Conference met, as stated, on 30th May, 1954. It was attended by over 350 delegates from all parts of the country. The Party Leader (Deputy Norton) read and explained each section of the agreed programme. After full consideration and discussion of the document and the announcement of the fact that the Party would have certain Cabinet posts, the following resolution was passed unanimously and with acclamation: —

" This Conference authorises the participation of the Labour Party in inter-Party Government on the basis of the policy statement (12-point programme) submitted to this Conference."

(c) *The Labour Party chooses Ministers.*
Document 1.21—Extract from *Irish Times*, 2 June 1954.

. . . The Parliamentary Labour Party also held a meeting last night. . . No statement was made after the meeting but it was learned that the meeting was called to decide on its representatives in the new Government and on proposals for the position of Speaker of the Dáil. A number of proposals were made and it is likely that the names decided on included Mr. Norton, the Party's leader, Mr. M. Keyes, Mr. Everett and Mr. Corish for Cabinet posts, and Mr. T. A. Kyne and possibly one other for posts as Parliamentary Secretaries.

(d) *Collective responsibility and Ministers' speeches.*
Document 4.22—Extracts from *Dáil Debates,* vol. 113, cols. 309-11
(24 November 1948).

Mr. Lemass asked the Taoiseach if it is correct, as reported in the Press of November 16th, that in a speech at Washington, U.S.A., the Minister for Agriculture proposed a customs union between Britain, U.S.A., Canada, Australia and Ireland for ten years; whether such proposal was made with the authority and approval of the Government; and, if so, whether he will make a statement explaining the Government's policy in the matter.

The Taoiseach: I have seen Press reports of a statement made by the Minister for Agriculture on the subject referred to in the Deputy's question. The Minister clearly emphasised that he was expressing his own views and not those of the Government. Since he was speaking as an individual, and not for the Government, the question whether his views in this matter have the approval of the Government does not arise, nor does the question of Government policy. . . .

Mr. MacEntee asked the Taoiseach if his attention has been drawn to a speech delivered by the Minister for External Affairs at a recent debate in the Rathmines Town Hall. . . .

The Taoiseach: I have seen Press reports of the speech referred to in the Deputy's questions; these reports were, of necessity, abbreviated reports of the remarks made by the Minister, and the passages quoted must not be taken out of their context. The Minister made it perfectly clear at the outset that he was not speaking as a member of the Government, but was expressing his own personal views. I do not feel called upon, therefore, to make any further statement in the matter.

(c) *An 'Inter-Party' Government Minister's Views on Collective Responsibility.*
Document 4.23—Extracts from a speech by the Minister for Finance,
Mr. P. McGilligan, in *Dáil Debates,* vol. 119, col.
2521 (23 March 1950).

. . . Deputies on the other side of the House have anguished themselves with talk about the public embarrassment which there is over the fact that the Minister for External Affairs does not talk the same financial language as myself. I have yet to meet anybody outside the ranks of the professional politicians who is worried about that. Nobody is worried. Have we got to the stage in this country when, on a matter which may be an important point of policy when it is decided, we cannot have freedom of speech ? Have we got to the stage when men, just because they join the Government circle, must all, as one Deputy said, when they go out of the council chambers speak the same language ? . . .

(f)   *Resignation of a Minister*

(i)   Document 4.24—Letters published in *Irish Times,* 12 April 1951 (Also reprinted in *Southern Ireland, Church or State?,* Ulster Unionist Council, Belfast, n.d.).

Dear Dr. Browne,

Following upon your own declarations and the indications given by me, I had hoped that it would not have been necessary to write this letter. Unfortunately, by reason of the situation which has arisen, and for which I fear you are largely responsible, I have no alternative, as leader of Clann na Poblachta, but to request you to transmit, as soon as possible, your resignation as Minister for Health to the Taoiseach. . . .

S. MacBRIDE.

Dear Taoiseach,

I enclose a copy of a letter which I have sent by hand to-night to Dr. Browne, Minister for Health, requesting him to tender his resignation to you. . . .

S. MacBRIDE.

(ii)   Document 4.25—Extract from *Dáil Debates,* vol. 125, col. 779 (12 April, 1951).

The Taoiseach: I have received from Deputy Dr. Browne this letter yesterday afternoon : —

" Dear Taoiseach,

As demanded by Mr. MacBride, I hereby send you my resignation from the Government, to take effect as from to-morrow.

Yours faithfully,

NOEL C. BROWNE."

(iii)   Document 4.26—Extracts from a speech by The Taoiseach, Mr. J. A. Costello in *Dáil Debates,* vol. 125, cols. 777-8 (12 April 1951).

The Taoiseach: . . . The Minister for External Affairs told me he felt that as he had been responsible for introducing Deputy Dr. Browne as a member of the Government and as he felt he had not fulfilled the trust he had reposed in him, it was his duty to ask him to resign. That was not a matter for me, and I felt I ought not either to discuss, argue, persuade or dissuade my colleague in any action he though fit to take as Leader of his own political Party. . . .

The letter Deputy MacBride sent to Deputy Dr. Browne has appeared in the newspapers. I have no hesitation in saying in public here, pledging whatever reputation I have as a constitutional lawyer, that that action of Deputy MacBride was entirely in accordance with the Constitution and in accordance with democratic procedure. It is my function as Taoiseach to accept the resignations of my colleagues, if such arise: to ask for them if occasion requires. It is my function to appoint — where men are nominated in accordance with the Constitution — those people who shall fulfil ministerial posts. I see no reason why a member, even of my own Party, who thought one of his colleagues was not doing his duty, should not suggest that he ought to resign. It would be for that man to exercise his rights . . .

READING

B. Chubb: *The Government, an Introduction to the Cabinet System in Ireland,* Dublin, 1961.

D. E. Leon: *Advisory Bodies in Irish Government,* Institute of Public Administration, Dublin, 1963.

Chapter 5

THE CIVIL SERVICE

INTRODUCTION

The Irish Free State took over a comparatively efficient administration and a fully fledged civil service. Though the multiplicity of public offices was reduced to an ordered pattern, confirmed in the Ministers and Secretaries Act, 1924, there was, according to the Commission of Inquiry into the Civil Service (1935), 'no immediate disturbance of any fundamental kind in the daily work of the average civil servant' (Document 5.1). The masters had changed, but 'the same main tasks of administration continued to be performed by the same staffs on the same general lines of organization and procedure'. (Ibid). Some departments such as Agriculture, Education and Local Government, having previously been Dublin-centred, were virtually complete as they stood: others having been regional offices with London headquarters, required senior administrators and the 'top organization' to turn them into full ministerial departments: in only a few cases had virtually new organizations to be created. Where additions had to be made —and these were mainly of senior officers—ranks and jobs followed the existing British pattern.

As a result of this, and because Ireland has levels of education and administrative 'know how' comparable with those of the most advanced countries of the world, the new state did not face the appalling problem of an administrative vacuum which has beset so many new states recently. The proportion of the 21,000 transferred officers who took advantage of the terms offered by the Treaty to retire prematurely was fairly low, but the filling of these posts and of the rather high number of normal vacancies occurring in the twenties did, nevertheless, pose something of a problem. But though the Report of the Commission on the Civil Service remarked in 1935 on the large numbers of officers who in one way or another had entered without undergoing the usual tests, this was only a temporary phenomenon, for the Government quickly established a Civil

117

Service Commission on the British model and the traditional procedures of recruitment were resumed and have been continued. (Document 5.2).

Continuity was further strengthened by the legislation providing for the regulation of the Service. The main principles embodied in the Civil Service Regulation Act are those inherited from the British Service. (Document 5.3). And just as it is the Treasury which in Great Britain is charged with the regulation and control of the Civil Service, including such matters as classification, numbers, remuneration, the fixing of terms and conditions, and promotion, so in Ireland it is the Department of Finance. Hence it is that Department which is mainly concerned with negotiation and arbitration. Although at first the Government was inclined to reject 'Whitleyism' and to be less willing to negotiate with its servants by the processes of that system than was the British Government, negotiation and arbitration machinery and procedures satisfactory to both sides were gradually worked out and now operate. (Document 5.4).

The Civil Service has grown comparatively little in size. At first it did not grow at all, numbers being much the same in 1934 as they were in 1924. From the middle thirties to the middle fifties, it increased from about 20,000 to about 30,000 (of whom about one half were in the Post Office) and it is today still much about the same size. (Document 5.5).

These numbers are naturally very small as compared with Great Britain, and consequently it might be expected that not all the inheritance would be useful. Although it was over thirty years before action was deemed necessary, it seems that the British 'class' system, involving the rather complicated division of work into five categories each performed by officers recruited to have the appropriate ability to carry it out, was too elaborate a structure for business on the scale facing the Irish Administration. As it has happened also, the relative attraction of a civil service post (to all save graduates, it seems) has led to recruits to the various grades being of a higher calibre than envisaged and, therefore, potentially capable of doing more responsible work. In 1960, after consultation with staff associations, the Department of Finance announced the merging of the Writing Assistant, Shorthand Typist, and Typist grades into a new grade of 'Clerk-typist' with a wide range of duties, the suspension of recruiting for the clerical grade, and other changes heralding the eventual disappearance of that grade. (Document 5.6).

In another way, too, the Service has become rather different, for the number of entrants directly into the administrative grade from university has been small and the majority of the higher posts are filled by officers from the Executive grade. Increasingly, the character of the Service is influenced by the outlook and approach of these officers. Consequently, though the formal structure resembles the British closely and the Service has on the whole inherited and retained most of the admirable characteristics of the British Service, the different attitude of Irish civil servants is creating a new and distinctively Irish tradition, a tradition perhaps greatly influenced, as Mr. O Mathuna suggested in an important article some years ago, by the type of education provided by the Christian Brothers, which no less than three-quarters of the administrative, executive and clerical grades will have experienced. (See S. O Mathuna, 'The Christian Brothers and the Civil Service', *Administration*, vol. 3, no. 2-3, pp. 69-74).

The problem of the preparation and training of these officers who are destined to fill the key posts is one of increasing importance now that the role of the Civil Service in promoting and guiding the development of the community is so much greater than it was. Moreover, we have now reached a stage in the development of the social sciences (including economics) where it is possible and necessary for the social problems which it falls to the state to solve, to be tackled scientifically, using the ever-increasing variety of economic and sociological research techniques for acquiring precise knowledge and forecasting future trends and needs. This means both that civil servants must have been trained in one of the social sciences and that departments must organize themselves in a way that permits research and intelligence work to be done on a large scale. The implications of this, as also of the impact of modern management techniques, are now being absorbed by the Civil Service, and it is possible that we are on the eve of changes as important and far-reaching as those induced by the Northcote-Trevelyan Report. Certainly, the needs of the time seem to require them.

DOCUMENTS

1. THE ESTABLISHMENT AND ORGANIZATION OF AN IRISH CIVIL SERVICE
   Document 5.1—Extracts from *Final Report of the Commission of Inquiry into the Civil Service,* 1932-5.

RECENT CIVIL SERVICE HISTORY
(6) In order that the facts with which we have to deal may be observed in their proper setting it is advisable to indicate by a brief historical account the

main features of the transition from the former British régime to the Civil Service of Saorstát Éireann as we find it today.

The transfer of the administrative services from British to Saorstát control took place in general as from the 1st April, 1922, but was not fully effective for the Revenue Services and the Land Commission until the 1st April, 1923. Upon these transfers the officers engaged in Saorstát territory in the various services (together with some who had been engaged elsewhere in the United Kingdom) were transferred into the new Saorstát Civil Service. Such transferred officers carried with them into their new sphere of activity certain rights expressly conferred on them under the Treaty of the 6th December, 1921, whereby their future tenure and conditions of employment were protected in certain respects and provision was made for compensation in the event of retirement.

(7) The transferred Civil Servants numbered about 21,000 of whom 17,239 were classified as permanent and 3,176 as temporary, the remainder belonging to certain industrial classes. Besides these, there were incorporated into the Saorstát Civil Service between the 1st April, 1922, and the 1st October, 1923, a group of persons numbering 131 who had served under Dáil Éireann in the pre-Treaty period and 88 persons who had formerly been in the British Civil Service but had left it on political or similar grounds.

(8) The passing of the State services into the control of a native Government, however revolutionary it may have been as a step in the political development of the nation, entailed, broadly speaking, no immediate disturbance of any fundamental kind in the daily work of the average Civil Servant. Under changed masters the same main tasks of administration continued to be performed by the same staffs on the same general lines of organization and procedure. The chief new feature, so far as the Civil Service was concerned, was the constitution in relation to each of the Ministers of a fully organized department of State with adequate headquarters machinery. Such machinery was built up in the main from the personnel referred to in paragraph (7) above. The various new posts were graded and remunerated in rough conformity with existing standards, except that in the highest posts, for which usually no close analogy could be found in previous experience in Dublin, scales generally inferior to London standards were adopted.

(9) Under the British régime several branches of the Irish administration (e.g. Education, Agriculture and Local Government) had an effective headquarters in Dublin usually under the ministerial direction of the Chief Secretary. Other important services, however, (e.g. Revenue and Post-Office) were represented in Dublin only by local establishments depending upon a headquarters control in London. There were also a few services such as the Civil Service Commission which were operated almost entirely from London. The varying circumstances of these cases naturally affected the extent to which the headquarters staff of the departments of the different Saorstát Ministers was on the one hand taken over in effective working order or required on the other hand to be newly built up. In general the shifting of ministerial responsibility from London to Dublin created, on a scale not previously

experienced in the Irish Civil Service, a need for officers competent to undertake the highest advisory and administrative duties in relation to the functions of the several Ministers.

(10) From 1922 onwards transferred officers for various reasons took advantage of the special terms granted to them by the Treaty and resigned from the Civil Service before the normal retiring age. A table giving the numbers of such cases in each year is given in the Third Appendix to this report. Apart from these cases of special retirement many transferred officers have also retired in normal circumstances. The same Appendix includes a table which indicates the fall from time to time in the number of transferred officers still serving. The number of transferred officers still serving on the 1st January, 1934, was 9,823.

The premature retirement of transferred officers and the opportunities afforded through the building up of the new departments of State resulted as time went on in early and rapid promotion for many Civil Servants. This abnormal flow of promotion in the earlier years of the Saorstát has had reactions on the present problems of the Civil Service to which we shall refer in due course.

(11) Another transient and abnormal feature of the early days of the Saorstát Civil Service, the effects of which, however, still persist in certain respects, was the relatively high proportion of officials who had been recruited either temporarily or without undergoing the usual tests. This was in part a legacy from the previous administration, reflecting a consequence of the European War, but it arose also from the emergency conditions in which new recruitment had inevitably to be carried on in 1922-3 and from the need of providing staff for a large volume of work that was definitely of temporary character, in particular for dealing with compensation schemes in respect of both pre-Treaty and post-Treaty damage.

During the period from the 1st April, 1922, to the 1st October, 1923, apart from the special groups of ex-Dáil and reinstated officers mentioned in paragraph (7) above, 2,320 persons were recruited into the Civil Service, mostly on a temporary basis, of whom 676 were engaged in the Office of Public Works which was concerned largely with compensation problems and 468 were engaged in the Office of the Revenue Commissioners which amongst other new matters had to provide for the service of a Customs land frontier.

(12) The importance of an orderly regulation of the Civil Service was recognized from the beginning of the new régime. The control previously exercised by the Treasury was maintained with unbroken continuity by the Minister for Finance. There was, however, in 1922 no authority in the Saorstát which was in a position to perform the tasks that had previously fallen on the Civil Service Commission in London. To remedy this defect the Oireachtas enacted in 1923 the Civil Service Regulation Act, 1923, which provided for the appointment of Civil Service Commissioners to examine and certify the qualifications of entrants into the Civil Service. The details of this and of further legislation on the same subject in 1924 and 1926 will engage our attention later in this report.

(13) The Ministers and Secretaries Act, 1924, provides a statutory classification of the functions of government under the several departments of State. It thereby establishes the fundamental framework to which any organization of the Civil Service must conform.

The same Act contains, in Section 2, the following basic provisions affecting the Civil Service : —

"(2) The Executive Council shall on the recommendation of the Minister appoint the principal officer of each [Department of State] and each of the said Ministers may appoint such other officers and servants to serve in the department of which he is the head, as such Minister may, with the sanction of the Minister for Finance, determine, but every appointment made under this sub-section shall be subject to the provisions of the Civil Service Regulation Act, 1923 (No. 35 of 1923) or of any Act for the time being in force replacing or amending that Act.

"(3) The terms and conditions of appointment of all officers and servants appointed by any Minister shall be prescribed by the Minister for Finance and there shall be paid out of moneys provided by the Oireachtas, or if there be any fund properly applicable by law to such payment, then out of such fund to such officers and servants such salaries or remunerations as the Minister for Finance may from time to time determine."

(14) The Ministers and Secretaries Act, 1924, dealt also with another subject of particular interest in relation to our inquiry. One of the conspicuous features of the previous administration in Ireland was the extent to which use was made of Boards of Commissioners or similar authorities for the control, with varying degrees of discretion, of some of the public services. There was no uniformity in the administrative position of these bodies but the case of the Congested Districts Board may be taken as a convenient example to illustrate the factors which are of most importance from our standpoint. This Board was engaged in administering an extensive public service in a semi-independent fashion. The Chief Secretary, however, who was an *ex-officio* member, was responsible to Parliament for its proceedings and the Chancellor of the Exchequer had a modified control over its finances. Instead of being financed by the ordinary machinery of votes and being subjected to the limitations which such a procedure would entail, the Board had funds allotted to it from special sources by statute and enjoyed a large discretion in the application of them. The Board appointed its own officers and it is important to observe that these officers were in general not Civil Servants. It will be seen that the arrangement as a whole was an anomalous compromise between the regular method of administration through the Civil Service under full ministerial responsibility and a method of independent control by a body not answerable to Parliament. The one advantage which this system offered was that it provided some opportunity, which would otherwise not have existed, of placing the services affected under a semblance of Irish control.

The *raison d'être* for this type of administrative authority having disappeared with the Treaty, the Ministers and Secretaries Act made provision for enabling the Executive Council to abolish such bodies and their funds and to transfer their duties to the ordinary departments of State to be discharged in future on the lines applicable in the other public services. The Intermediate Education Board, Department of Agriculture and Technical Instruction and Petty Sessions Office were in due course dealt with in this manner and as part of the arrangement the staffs concerned became merged in the Civil Service. The case of the Congested Districts Board had already been similarly treated under the Land Law (Commission) Act, 1923, in priority to other cases. In this way a valuable step was taken towards eliminating unnecessary complexities in administrative organization.

(15) Another step of similar character was taken by the Court Officers Act, 1926, in regard to the staffs employed in connexion with the work of the Supreme Court, High Court and Circuit Courts. Under the former system members of these staffs differed from the ordinary Civil Service as regards mode of appointment and/or tenure. The effect of the Act in question was to impose Civil Service conditions as far as possible on such personnel and to place them for administrative purposes within the general ambit of the Department of Justice. [*Paragraphs* 16-30 *omitted.*]

ORGANIZATION

General

(31) The general scope of our task is affected by an important preliminary consideration on which it is necessary to make some comment. According to our interpretation of the terms of reference we are called upon not to frame *ab initio* an organization for the Civil Service but to inquire into an existing organization. The Civil Service as it exists is not a body assembled at haphazard which functions without reference to any accepted principle of co-ordination. It is, on the contrary, in a highly organized condition which has been developed gradually from one stage to another over a long period of time in the light of lessons derived from practical experience. In such circumstances we feel that our investigation must accept the established position as a starting point and that its subsequent direction must be determined chiefly by the extent to which we have evidence of definite shortcomings, especially as regards efficiency, which appear to demand some measure of reform.

(32) It is significant for this purpose that, as we have mentioned at the outset of this report, we have been offered no evidence from business circles or from any other section of the general community that they have experienced any practical need for reorganization of the Civil Service. In addition the official witnesses who have appeared before us from various departments of State have in no case suggested that any reform of major character appeared to be required. Staff witnesses appearing before us have in a number of instances advocated some reorganization but apart from some references to the system of financial control which will receive our special attention, the changes suggested are concerned with the somewhat limited, although important, problems of grading, remuneration and other conditions of service. Our report will, accordingly, be devoted largely to explanation and criticism of the existing system in the light of the evidence of official and staff witnesses.

(33) The Civil Service presents itself to us as a body of State employees distributed over eleven separate and well-defined departments of State. This framework is prescribed by the Ministers and Secretaries Act, 1924, but it is clear that apart from any enactment the different spheres of duty of the several Ministers would demand some such distribution of staff to enable the work of administration to be carried out conveniently. The question arises whether in reviewing or devising the organization of the Civil Service we are to treat each department of State as a unit in itself and consider its needs without reference to other departments, or to deal with the entire Civil Service as the fundamental unit in which the several departments find themselves associated by appropriate bonds of cohesion.

The necessity for treating the Civil Service in many respects as a unit is easily demonstrated. It arises particularly from the undivided constitutional responsibility of the Executive Council for the conduct of all branches of State administration. Although that responsibility is exercised through the several Ministers, it is evident that in the chief matters of policy affecting the terms and conditions of service of State employees coherent, if not uniform, practice must prevail in all departments. The absence of adequate co-ordination would lead to conflicting standards and methods in different branches of the State service and the Executive Council would as a consequence be hampered in its task of State administration.

The need for co-ordination is reflected in several of the features of the Civil Service system as it exists. For example, the Civil Service Regulation Acts and the functions of the Civil Service Commission thereby established apply indiscriminately, although subject to certain limitations, to the whole Civil Service. Admission to the Civil Service is thus controlled on a unified plan which extends also in some degree to transfers from one post to another after admission. Again, the Superannuation Acts apply a common pension system to all the main categories of the Civil Service. The most important provision, however, of a unifying character is that made by Section 9 of the Civil Service Regulation Act, 1924, which enacts as follows: —

"The Minister for Finance may from time to time make regulations for controlling the Civil Service of the Government of Saorstát Éireann and providing for the classification, remuneration and other conditions and terms of service of all persons employed therein whether permanently or temporarily; and may at any time revoke or vary any such regulation."

This enactment was later reinforced by provisions in the Ministers and Secretaries Act, 1924, which have been quoted in paragraph (13) above.

(34) The attribution to the Minister for Finance, under the Executive Council, of the responsibility for general control of the Civil Service is evidently due to the fact that most of the administrative problems which arise in relation to the terms of employment of Civil Servants have financial implications and that decisions upon them require always to be taken with due regard to, *inter alia,* the existing and future budgetary position. The situation in this respect has already been discussed in some of its aspects in our Majority report on Arbitration and other aspects of it will be considered later in the

present report. The point to which we wish especially to call attention here is that the exercise of this function of the Minister for Finance naturally entails the application of certain principles of uniformity in the staffing of the several departments. This result not only accords with the requirement that the policy of the Executive Council in regard to staff matters in all departments should be consistent but in addition reflects a special need of the Minister for Finance if his task in giving effect to this policy is to be performed with due efficiency. If every department were organized solely in the light of its own immediate work without conscious reference to the pay and classification of staff in other departments, the practical work of applying a proper measure of financial control would be prejudiced to an unnecessary degree. The Minister for Finance has to deal with all departments and in order that he may do so in an intelligible and orderly fashion he must treat like cases wherever found in a like manner. Any other course could only result in friction and disorder. The exercise by the Minister for Finance of the function of correlating standards and conditions between the several departments also entails advantages from standpoints other than the merely financial. It secures a flexibility and uniformity in respect of promotions and transfers which is of material value both to the State and the Civil Service.

The considerations which we have just mentioned are specially reflected in the existing organization of the Civil Service through the creation of " general service " classes, as they are called, whose members are normally employed on uniform scales and conditions throughout all departments, and are liable to transfer and eligible for promotion from one department to another.

(35) It has nevertheless to be recognized that the character of the work to be performed in any given case must be a leading consideration in deciding what class of Civil Servant should be assigned to it, and that in many cases the facts are such as to render the employment of officers of the general service unsuitable. It thus happens that we find numerous departmental classes throughout the Civil Service whose members are assigned exclusively to defined work in an individual department and are not graded alike with any bodies or officers in other departments. We shall have to consider later how far the use of departmental classes is necessary or desirable. At this point it suffices to mention that some resort to this arrangement is inevitable particularly for certain highly specialized types of work. This readiness to recognize the practical requirements of the situation is not, however, inconsistent with a general tendency to give a preference to organization on general service lines.

(36) Before we proceed to consider the details of classification and kindred topics it will be useful to examine the arrangements which prevail for the control and regulation of these matters and to deal with certain criticisms under this head which have been made in evidence before us. We shall deal first with the extensive jurisdiction in this respect of the Minister for Finance and then consider the more limited role assigned to the Civil Service Commissioners.

Control and Regulation

(i) *The Minister for Finance*

(37) We have seen that the effective responsibility for the general organization and regulation of the Civil Service is vested in the Minister for Finance. In order that the manner in which this responsibility is exercised may be clearly understood we propose to set out the essential features of the system somewhat fully.

The staff of each department of State is appointed formally by the Minister of that department. The number of officers, however, requires the sanction of the Minister for Finance and the terms and conditions of appointment are prescribed by him. All appointments, subject to limited categories of exceptions, are subject to the Civil Service Regulation Acts whereby the Civil Service Commissioners must certify that the entrant to the Civil Service is suitable in respect of age, health, character, knowledge and ability. The normal avenue of entrance is by open competitive examination but the Civil Service Commissioners have discretion to adopt an alternative procedure, for example, test by a selection board, where the circumstances seem to warrant it.

Where a vacancy is filled by promotion of an existing Civil Servant the appointment also rests formally with the Minister of the department of State in which the vacancy exists. In actual fact, the choice of the individual to be promoted will frequently have been determined by means of a selection board or by success in a competitive examination specially held for a group of Civil Servants from whose ranks the promotion falls to be made. As in the case of a new appointment the filling of a vacancy by promotion and the terms of appointment of the promoted officer are subject to sanction by the Minister for Finance.

The principal officer, or Secretary as he is called, of each department of State is appointed by the Executive Council on the recommendation of the Minister of the department. This ensures, *inter alia,* that the Minister for Finance, as a member of the Executive Council, has a voice in the appointment, a matter of importance in view of the fact that the Secretary is normally expected to act as Accounting Officer for the votes with which his Minister is concerned. The appointment of the principal officer is exempt from the restrictions of the Civil Service Regulation Acts.

(38) To provide for the discharge of the extensive duties imposed on him by this system the Minister for Finance has in his department a special Establishment Branch under the immediate control of an Assistant Secretary. This Branch is continuously engaged in the examination of proposals relating to the personnel of the Civil Service, the consideration of applications for sanctions in that connexion, the fixing of remuneration, the award of pensions, the preparation of legislation on these subjects, the scrutiny of proposed legislation of other departments which would have any bearing on staff matters, etc. In the other departments there is usually an Establishment Officer whose function it is, subject, of course, to the general control of the Secretary, to handle the staff matters which affect his own Minister including

the necessary correspondence with the Department of Finance and to maintain by personal contact a close relation with the Establishment Branch of the latter department. [*Paragraphs 39-46 omitted.*]

(ii) *The Civil Service Commissioners*

(47) The position and powers of the Civil Service Commissioners are regulated by the Civil Service Regulation Acts, 1924 and 1926. They are appointed by the Executive Council and hold office at the pleasure of that body. The Ceann Comhairle of Dáil Éireann for the time being has always heretofore been one of the Commissioners and of his two colleagues both of whom have been Civil Servants one is taken from the Establishment Branch of the Department of Finance. The Commissioners by law and custom act in close co-operation with that department.

(48) The functions of the Commissioners are concerned mainly with the admission of recruits into the Civil Service and they are empowered with the consent of the Minister for Finance to make regulations governing admission to either permanent or temporary employment therein. They issue certificates of qualification for all persons entering the permanent Civil Service; they conduct the competitive examinations which are the normal avenue of entry and in suitable cases they provide for appointment by selection according to a procedure which will engage our attention later.

(49) In certain cases the Commissioners have a discretion vested in them which on occasions might have considerable importance. Such discretion extends to dispensing with either examination or selection where the Executive Council is of opinion that a particular appointment ought to be made in the public interest. They also have a discretion to vary, either by addition or subtraction, the category of posts excluded altogether from the operation of the Civil Service Regulation Acts. [*Paragraphs 50-58 omitted.*]

General Service Classes

(59) The general service classes consist of the following main groups: —

(i) Administrative.

(ii) Executive (junior and higher).

(iii) Clerical (including Staff Officers).

(iv) Writing Assistants.

(v) Shorthand Typists.

(vi) Typists.

This classification is intended to reflect a corresponding analysis of a great part of the work that is required to be performed in Government offices. It is derived chiefly from the report of the British Reorganization Committee of 1920. . . . [*Paragraphs 60-67 omitted.*]

Departmental Classes

(68) Departmental classes find their most extensive use in the Post-Office and the Office of the Revenue Commissioners, each of which employs large numbers of the first type mentioned in paragraph (53). The only other department employing similar staff in any considerable number is the Department of Industry and Commerce where there are about nine hundred persons of this category engaged on the work of employment exchanges and unemployment assistance. In other departments, however, there are to be found various departmental classes of smaller numerical strength and it is these that appear to present the problems of most difficulty. [*Paragraphs 69-92 omitted.*]

RECRUITMENT

Written Competitive Examination

(93) The Civil Service is recruited in the main according to arrangements prescribed by or under the Civil Service Regulation Acts. The Acts contemplate as the normal course that recruitment should be effected by means of competitive examination conducted according to regulations made by the Civil Service Commissioners with the consent of the Minister for Finance. This is accordingly the usual procedure at the present time for obtaining recruits for the main branches of the Civil Service including the largest general service grades and the chief departmental classes. From the evidence we have heard we have formed the impression that the system is well administered, that it produces satisfactory results and that, in general, it has the confidence of the various interests concerned.

(94) The principal examinations, which are those for the general service grades, are devised so as to harmonize with the structure of the educational system and with the standards attained at the several educational stages. Thus the standard of the examination for Writing Assistants is the seventh standard of the primary schools, the standard of the clerical examination is the intermediate certificate course of the secondary school programme and the standard of the junior executive examination is the leaving certificate course of the secondary school programme. We have received evidence that notwithstanding this prescription of standards the successful candidates are frequently found to have attained a higher educational standard than that of the examination at which they competed. For example, out of 145 Writing Assistants appointed as the result of the examination of October, 1932, only 45 came direct from primary schools, the remaining 100 being candidates from secondary schools. Similarly a considerable proportion of the successful candidates at the clerical examination have obtained the leaving certificate. While these results are certainly contrary to the intention of the arrangements made for these examinations the feasibility of obviating them is doubtful. Reduction of age limit is perhaps an obvious remedy but it is one which may give rise to disadvantages in other directions. In the case of Writing Assistants in particular it seems to be undesirable to take any steps which would lower the average age at which such officers at present enter the Government service. An improvement in general economic conditions would,

no doubt, do much to bring about a remedy by diminishing the relative attractiveness which Government employment in recent years seems to possess. The matter is, however, one which we think should be kept under continuous observation by the authorities concerned as the employment of persons of superior educational attainment in inferior posts if carried to excess might easily become in course of time a fruitful cause of discontent. [*Paragraphs 95-105 omitted.*]

Selection Board

(106) While, as already explained, it is contemplated by the Civil Service Regulation Acts that the normal method of recruitment to the Civil Service should be by means of open competitive examination, provision is also made for the use of alternative methods where circumstances may so require. The main type of case requiring an alternative method is where the situation to be filled requires knowledge or experience wholly or in part professional or otherwise peculiar and not ordinarily to be acquired in the Civil Service. For dealing with such cases the Civil Service Commissioners have perfected in the course of years a regular procedure by means of selection boards. This procedure has now come to be of great importance and has enabled a great number of posts to be filled in a satisfactory manner which in former times were filled by the exercise of patronage. It is specially suited for filling posts of a technical or professional character where the candidates are above the normal age of entry to the Civil Service and will usually have already been engaged in outside practice. Evidence of experience and qualifications can readily be obtained in such cases and the testing of it by any form of Civil Service examination would not seem to serve a useful purpose.

The details of this system or procedure appear to have been carefully elaborated and they have been enforced with a strictness which has contributed towards establishing general confidence in the selection boards. The Commissioners take particular care to secure complete secrecy about the constitution of selection boards so that candidates for a particular position have no means of knowing the personnel of the board before which they will be called. Even the members of the selection board itself are not informed of the names of their colleagues until they meet to interview the candidates and the board is not made aware of the names and addresses of the candidates coming before it. [*Remainder omitted.*]

2. THE CIVIL SERVICE COMMISSION

Document 5.2—Extracts from Civil Service Commissioners Act, 1956 (No. 45).

DEFINITIONS

3.—(1) In this Act, "the appropriate authority" means—

(a) in relation to the position of member of the staff of the Houses of the Oireachtas—the Taoiseach,

(b) in relation to the position of an officer of the Attorney General—the Taoiseach,

(c) in relation to the position of member of the staff of the office of the Comptroller and Auditor General—the Minister,

(d) in relation to the position of member of the staff of the office of the Revenue Commissioners—the Minister, or

(e) in relation to any other position—the Minister of State by whom the power of appointment to that position is for the time being exercisable.

[*Remainder of S. 3 and Ss. 4-8 omitted.*]

THE COMMISSION

9.—(1) The Government shall from time to time as occasion requires appoint fit and proper persons to be Civil Service Commissioners to fulfil the functions assigned to them by this Act.

(2) The number of the Commissioners shall be three.

[*SSs. 3 and 4 omitted.*]

10.—(1) Each Commissioner shall hold office at the will and pleasure of the Government.

(2) A Commissioner may at any time resign his office by letter addressed to and sent to the Government.

(3) Each Commissioner shall receive such (if any) remuneration as the Minister may from time to time determine. [*SS. 4 omitted.*]

11.—(1) The Minister shall appoint to serve in positions on the staff of the Commissioners such and so many persons as he considers necessary. [*SS. 2 and S. 12 omitted.*]

APPOINTMENTS TO THE CIVIL SERVICE

13.—(1) No person shall be appointed to an established position unless the Commissioners, after holding a competition under section 15, have, under section 17, selected him for appointment to that position.

(2) Subsection (1) of this section does not apply to—

(a) the appointment of a person to an established position on promotion or transfer from another established position, or

(b) the appointment of a person to an established position under section 11 of the Regulation Act.

(3) Subsection (1) of this section does not apply to the appointment of a person to a particular established position where—

(a) the appropriate authority with, in case he is not the Minister, the consent of the Minister, recommends the appointment of that person to that established position, and

(b) the Government, having considered such recommendation, decide that such appointment would be in the public interest.

[*SS. 4 omitted.*]

14.—(1) No person shall be appointed to an unestablished position unless the Commissioners, after holding a competition under section 15, have, under section 17, selected him for appointment to that position.

(2) Subsection (1) of this section does not apply to—

(a) the appointment of a person to an unestablished position on promotion or transfer from another unestablished position, which is neither a position in a scheduled occupation nor an excluded position, or

(b) the appointment of a person to an unestablished position under section 11 of the Regulation Act,

(3) Subsection (1) of this section does not apply to the appointment of a person to a particular unestablished position where—

(a) the appropriate authority with, in case he is not the Minister, the consent of the Minister, recommends the appointment of that person to that unestablished position, and

(b) the Government, having considered such recommendation, decide that such appointment would be in the public interest.

COMPETITIONS

15.—(1) The Commissioners shall, subject to the consent of the Minister, hold such competitions as they consider necessary for the selection of persons for appointments to which either subsection (1) of section 13 or subsection (1) of section 14 applies.

(2) Where—

(a) it is proposed to make an appointment or appointments to a position or positions and either paragraph (a) of subsection (2) of section 13 or paragraph (a) of subsection (2) of section 14 applies to the appointment or appointments, and

(b) the Minister decides that it is proper that the person or persons to be appointed should be selected by means of competition, and requests the Commissioners to hold such a competition,

then, the Commissioners shall hold the competition.

(3) Every competition shall consist of such one or more of the following types of test as the Commissioners direct—

(a) a written examination,

(b) an oral examination,

(c) an interview,

(d) a practical examination,

(e) any other test or tests considered by the Commissioners to be appropriate.

(4) Where a competition consists of more than one of the types of test specified in subsection (3) of this section not more than one of the tests need be competitive.

(5) The Commissioners may make admission to any test conditional on a candidate's reaching such a standard as the Commissioners consider requisite.

16.—(1) Where it is proposed to hold a competition for appointment to one or more positions, the Commissioners shall make regulations which shall include provisions in relation to the following matters—

    (a) the type or types of test of which the competition shall consist,

    (b) where the competition is to be in whole or in part a written examination, the subject or subjects of the written examination,

    (c) the mode of application for admission to the competition,

(2) The Commissioners may, in making regulations under subsection (1) of this section in relation to a competition, provide, in addition to the matters specified in the said subsection (1), for all or any of the following matters—

    (a) the confining of the competition to citizens of Ireland,

    (b) the confining of the competition to a specified class of persons defined in such manner and by reference to such things (including service in the Civil Service, sex and physical characteristics) as the Commissioners think proper,

    (c) the requirement that, where females are not excluded from the competition, a female candidate to be eligible for selection shall be unmarried or a widow,

    (d) the age limits for candidates,

    (e) the fee to be paid for admission to the competition,

    (f) the expenditure (including fees for medical examination) to be met by candidates in satisfying the provisions of the regulations as to health,

    (g) such other matters (including qualifications) as the Commissioners think proper.

(3) The Commissioners may, in making regulations under subsection (1) of this section in relation to a competition for an appointment to an unestablished position, provide that the person appointed thereto may, in certain specified circumstances, be subsequently appointed to a specified established position.

(4) The Commissioners may make general regulations relating to all competitions or to competitions for appointments to positions of a particular class, description or grade, and may, in relation to a particular competition, do any of the following things by regulations made under subsection (1) of this section—

    (a) provide that all or any of the general regulations shall not apply,

    (b) modify all or any of the general regulations.

(5) Regulations under subsections (1), (2), (3) and (4) of this section shall not be made without the consent of the Minister.

SELECTION AFTER COMPETITION

17.—(1) For the purposes of this section, a person shall be accepted by the Commissioners as qualified for appointment to a position for which a competition is held if, but only if, the Commissioners are satisfied that—

(*a*) he possesses the requisite knowledge and ability to enter on the discharge of the duties of that position,

(*b*) he is within the age limits (if any) prescribed for that position by regulations made under section 16 and applicable to the competition,

(*d*) the manner in which the order of merit of the candidates is to be determined.

(*c*) he is in good health and free from any physical defect or disease which would be likely to interfere with the proper discharge of his duties in that position and possesses the physical characteristics (if any) prescribed for the position by the said regulations,

(*d*) he is suitable on grounds of character, and

(*e*) he is suitable in all other relevant respects for appointment to that position.

(2) Where a competition has been held under section 15, the Commissioners shall select for appointment from the competition such numbers of candidates as they think proper, subject however as follows—

(*a*) selection shall be made in accordance with the order of merit as determined under the regulations made under section 16 and applicable to the competition,

(*b*) only candidates who have been accepted by the Commissioners as qualified for appointment and have complied with the said regulations shall be so selected, and

(*c*) the filling of the positions for which the candidates are required has been approved by the Minister.

(3) If any question arises under this section as to whether a particular candidate is or is not qualified for appointment to a particular position or as to the place of a particular candidate in the order of merit the question shall be decided by the Commissioners whose decision shall be final.

NON-COMPETITIVE APPOINTMENTS

18.—(1) If any question arises under this Act as to whether the proposed appointment of a person to a position on promotion or transfer from another position is or is not in the customary course of promotion or transfer, as the case may be, the question shall be decided by the Commissioners.

(2) For the purposes of subsection (1) of this section the Commissioners may from time to time decide what classes of promotions or transfers are to be regarded as being in the customary course of promotion or transfer.

[*Ss. 19-25 omitted.*]

CERTIFICATES OF QUALIFICATION

26.—(1) Where a person (in this subsection referred to as the appointee), who is either (i) a person who has been selected for appointment to an established position under section 17 or (ii) a person to whose proposed appointment to an established position section 20, 21 or 22 applies, has been accepted by the Commissioners as qualified for appointment to the position (in this subsection referred to as the said position) for which he has been selected or to which it is proposed to appoint him (as the case may be)—

    (*a*)   the Commissioners shall as soon as may be thereafter, issue a certificate which shall state that the appointee has been accepted by them as qualified for appointment to the said position and the date of such acceptance,

    (*b*)   the certificate shall have effect as on and from that date.

(2) A certificate issued under subsection (1) of this section shall be called and known as a certificate of qualification.

(3) Where a certificate of qualification is required by subsection (1) of this section to be issued, the Commissioners may defer the issue thereof until the person in whose favour it is to be issued has taken up the duties of the position.

(4) The Commissioners may—

    (*a*)   cancel any certificate of qualification issued in error or as the result of fraud or deceit,

    (*b*)   correct errors in a certificate of qualification.

[*Ss. 27 and 28 omitted.*]

OTHER COMPETITIONS

29.—(1) The Commissioners shall hold—

    (*a*)   all competitions, examinations, interviews and tests which are for the time being required by law to be held by the Commissioners,

    (*b*)   such other competitions, examinations, interviews and tests as the Government or the Minister may from time to time direct.

(2) The Commissioners, with the consent of the Minister, may make regulations in relation to any competition, examination, interview or test held by them under this section, and may by such regulations fix the fee to be paid for admission to any such competition, examination, interview or test.

RULES GOVERNING CANDIDATES' CONDUCT

30.—(1) The Commissioners may make rules governing the conduct of candidates at competitions, examinations, interviews or tests held by them under this Act and providing for other matters in relation to the holding of such competitions, examinations, interviews or tests.

(2) The Commissioners may, in rules made under this section, provide for the disqualification or penalisation, at the discretion of the Commissioners, of candidates who fail to observe the rules under this section governing the conduct of candidates. [*Remainder omitted.*]

3. TERMS AND CONDITIONS OF EMPLOYMENT

Document 5.3—Extracts from Civil Service Regulation Act, 1956 (No. 46).

DEFINITIONS

2.—(1) In this Act, "appropriate authority" means—

(*a*) in relation to a civil servant holding a position to which he was appointed by the Government, the Government,

(*b*) in relation to a civil servant who is a member of the staff of the Houses of the Oireachtas or an officer of the Attorney General, the Taoiseach,

(*c*) in relation to a civil servant who is a member of the staff of the office of the Revenue Commissioners, the Minister, or

(*d*) in relation to any other civil servant, the Minister of State by whom the power of appointing a successor to him would for the time being be exercisable.

[Remainder of S. 2 omitted.]

3.—(1) In this Act, "suspending authority" means, in relation to a civil servant, each of the following—

(*a*) the appropriate authority in relation to that civil servant,

(*b*) a person who, by virtue of subsection (2) of this section, is for the time being a suspending authority in relation to that civil servant.

[Remainder of S. 3 and S. 4 omitted.]

TENURE

5.—Every established civil servant shall hold office at the will and pleasure of the Government.

6.—The appropriate authority may, subject to section 4 (where applicable), terminate the services of a civil servant who is not an established civil servant.

7.—[1]*[Where, in respect of a civil servant who has been appointed to an established position (in this section referred to as his probationary position) and who under his conditions of service is serving in a probationary capacity, the appropriate authority is, at any time during the civil servant's probationary period or such (if any) extension thereof as the appropriate authority may from time to time fix, satisfied that he has failed to fulfill the conditions of probation attaching to his probationary position]* then, subject to section 4 (where applicable), the following provisions shall have affect—

(*a*) the appropriate authority shall, notwithstanding section 5, terminate the services of the civil servant, unless, immediately prior to his appointment to his probationary position, he held another position in the Civil Service;

---

[1] Words in italics are an amendment made by Civil Service Regulation (Amendment) Act, 1958 (No. 34), Section 3.

(b) if the civil servant held, immediately prior to his appointment to his probationary position, an established position (in this paragraph referred to as his previous position), the appropriate authority shall terminate his appointment to his probationary position and, in that event, the civil servant may, if the Minister consents, forthwith be appointed to an established position (being a position which is, either, (i) in the same grade as that of his previous position, or (ii) in a grade or rank which, in the Minister's opinion, is equivalent to or lower than the grade of his previous position) to be designated by the Minister;

(c) where—
  (i) the civil servant is appointed to an established position under paragraph (b) of this section, and
  (ii) he held, immediately prior to his appointment to his probationary position, his previous position in a probationary capacity,
  then, the established position to which he is appointed shall have attached thereto such conditions of probation and such other conditions as the Minister may fix;

(d) if the civil servant held, immediately prior to his appointment to his probationary position, a position which is not an established position (in this paragraph referred to as his previous position), the appropriate authority shall terminate his appointment to his probationary position and, in that event, the civil servant may, if the Minister consents, forthwith be appointed to a position which is not an established position (being a position which is, either (i) in the same grade as that of his previous position or (ii) in a grade or rank which in the Minister's opinion is equivalent to or lower than the grade of his previous position) to be designated by the Minister.

RETIREMENT

8.—(1) In this section, "the retiring age" means—

(a) in relation to a civil servant who is an officer to whom the Act of 1919 applies, sixty years,

(b) in relation to any other civil servant, sixty-five years.

(2)(a) The appropriate authority may, notwithstanding section 5, require any civil servant who is an officer to whom the Act of 1919 applies, and who has attained the age of fifty-five years or any other civil servant who has attained the age of sixty years to retire, and such civil servant shall retire accordingly.

(b) Paragraph (a) of this subsection does not apply to a transferred officer who is an established civil servant.

(3) Every civil servant shall retire on attaining the retiring age.

(4) Notwithstanding anything in the preceding subsections of this section the appropriate authority may, with (provided the appropriate authority is not the Government or the Minister) the consent of the Minister (who may from time to time prescribe such conditions as he thinks fit governing the employment under this subsection of civil servants beyond the normal retiring age)—

(*a*) direct that the retiring age of an established civil servant may be raised by a period not exceeding three calendar months,

(*b*) direct that an established civil servant who reaches the retiring age may be retained in the Civil Service until he attains an age not exceeding, in case he is an officer to whom the Act of 1919 applies, sixty-five years or, in any other case, seventy years, and in that case any service rendered by him after the retiring age or, if his retiring age is raised under paragraph (*a*) of this subsection, his retiring age as so raised shall, notwithstanding anything contained in section 22 of the Superannuation Act, 1936 (No. 39 of 1936), not be reckoned as established service.

(*c*) direct that the retiring age of a civil servant who is not an established civil servant may be raised to any age not exceeding seventy-five years.

[SSs. 5 and 6 omitted.]

9.—(1) In this section "medical referee" means a registered medical practitioner appointed by the Minister to be a medical referee for the purpose of this section.

(2) Whenever—

(*a*) the appropriate authority is satisfied, on medical evidence, that an established civil servant has become, by reason of infirmity of mind or body, incapable of discharging the duties of his position and that such infirmity is likely to be permanent, and

(*b*) such civil servant has not tendered his resignation, and

(*c*) a notice has, at the instance of the appropriate authority, been served by registered post on such civil servant requesting him to resign from the Civil Service on or before a specified date, which said date (in this subsection hereinafter referred to as the appointed date) shall not be less than thirty days from the date on which the notice is posted, the following provisions shall, notwithstanding anything contained in section 5, have effect—

(i) if, before the appointed date, the appropriate authority receives such civil servant's resignation and the resignation is stated to have effect from a specified day, not later than the appointed date, his resignation shall take effect on the day so specified,

(ii) if, before the appointed date, the appropriate authority receives such civil servant's resignation and the resignation either specifies no effective day or a day which is later than the appointed date, his resignation shall take effect on the appointed date,

(iii) if the appropriate authority does not, before the appointed date, receive such civil servant's resignation or an application to have his case referred to a medical referee, he shall be deemed to have resigned from the Civil Service on the ground of ill-health on the appointed date,

(iv) if the appropriate authority, before the appointed date, receives from the civil servant an application to have his case referred to a medical referee and there is sent with the application such fee as may be fixed by the Minister—

(I) the appropriate authority shall refer his case to a medical referee for investigation,

(II) if it appears from the report of the medical referee that such infirmity is not likely to be permanent, the notice shall be deemed to be withdrawn and there shall be paid to the civil servant a sum equal to the said fee and also, if any expenses for travelling and maintenance were, in the opinion of the Minister, reasonably and properly incurred by such civil servant in connection with the reference, such sum in respect of those expenses as the Minister may determine,

(III) if it appears from the report of the medical referee that such infirmity is likely to be permanent the appropriate authority shall cause a notice (in this subsection referred to as the second notice) to be served by registered post on such civil servant stating the effect of the report and requiring him to tender his resignation within ten days after the date of posting of the second notice, and, in default of his so doing, such civil servant shall be deemed to have resigned from the Civil Service on the ground of ill-health on the appointed date or the tenth day after the posting of the second notice, whichever is the later.

(3) The preceding subsections of this section do not apply to (*a*) a civil servant serving on probation, unless immediately prior to his appointment to his probationary position he held an established position, or (*b*) a transferred officer who is an established civil servant.

(4) Nothing in this section shall be construed as affecting section 10 of the Act of 1859 or the said section 10 as applied by subsection (1) of section 1 of the Act of 1919, or subsection (2) of section 8.

RETIREMENT OF WOMEN ON MARRIAGE

10.—(1) Women holding positions in the Civil Service, other than positions which are declared excepted positions under subsection (2) of this section, are required to retire on marriage.

(2) The Minister may from time to time declare any particular positions (not being established positions) or class of positions (not being established positions) to be excepted positions for the purposes of subsection (1) of this section. [*S.* 11 (1) *omitted.*]

11.—(2) Where a widow to whom this section applies makes an application to the proper authority for re-admission to the Civil Service the following provisions shall, subject to subsection (3) of this section, have effect: —

(*a*) if her original position was an established position she may, before it is decided to grant or refuse her application, be required to serve on trial for such period and in such position (not being an established position) as the Minister may determine;

(*b*) if there is a suitable vacancy in a position which fulfils the conditions set out in paragraph (*d*) of this subsection and the proper authority would be the appropriate authority in relation to a civil servant holding that position then the proper authority may, if he thinks fit, appoint her to fill the vacancy in that position;

(*c*) if, in the absence of a vacancy in a position of the type referred to in paragraph (*b*) of this subsection, there is a suitable vacancy in another position which fulfils the conditions set out in paragraph (*d*) of this subsection the authority (not being the proper authority) who would be the appropriate authority in relation to a civil servant holding that position may, if he thinks fit, appoint her to fill the vacancy in that position;

(*d*) the following provisions shall apply in relation to the position to which a widow to whom this section applies may be appointed under paragraph (*b*) or (*c*) of this subsection—

(i) it shall be either—

(I) in the same grade as that of her original position, or

(II) in such grade or rank (being one which, in the opinion of the Minister, is equivalent to or lower than her original position) as the Minister may determine,

(ii) if her original position was an established position, it may be either an established position or a position which is not an established position,

(iii) if her original position was not an established position, it shall be a position which is not an established position.

[*SS.* 3 *and S.* 12 *omitted.*]

DISCIPLINARY MEASURES

13.—(1) A suspending authority may suspend a civil servant if—

(a) it appears to that suspending authority that the civil servant has been guilty of grave misconduct or of grave irregularity warranting disciplinary action, or

(b) it appears to that suspending authority that the public interest might be prejudiced by allowing the civil servant to remain on duty, or

(c) a charge of grave misconduct or grave irregularity is made against the civil servant and it appears to that suspending authority that the charge warrants investigation.

(2) A suspending authority may terminate the suspension of a civil servant suspended under subsection (1) of this section. [*S.* 14 *omitted.*]

15.—(1) (a) Where, in the opinion of the appropriate authority, a civil servant has, in relation to his official duties, been guilty of misconduct, irregularity, neglect or unsatisfactory behaviour, but a loss of public moneys or public funds has not resulted therefrom, the appropriate authority may, subject to subsection (5) of this section, do either or both of the following things—

(i) place the civil servant on a lower rate of remuneration,

(ii) reduce the civil servant to a specified lower grade or rank.

[*SSs.* 1 (*b*) *and* 1 (*c*) *omitted.*]

(2) (a) Where, in the opinion of the appropriate authority, a civil servant has, in relation to his official duties, been guilty of misconduct, irregularity, neglect or unsatisfactory behaviour and a loss of public moneys or public funds has resulted therefrom and the case is not one which, in accordance with arrangements made under subsection (2) of section 17, is to be referred to the Minister, the appropriate authority may, subject to subsection (5) of this section,

(i) place the civil servant on a lower rate of remuneration, or

(ii) reduce the civil servant to a specified lower grade or rank, or

(iii) place the civil servant on a lower rate of remuneration and also reduce him to a specified lower grade or rank.

[*SSs.* 2 (*b*) *and* 2 (*c*) *omitted.*]

(3) (a) Where, in the opinion of the Minister, a civil servant has, in relation to his official duties, been guilty of misconduct, irregularity, neglect or unsatisfactory behaviour and a loss of public moneys or public funds has resulted therefrom and the case is one which in accordance with arrangements made under subsection (2) of section 17 is to be referred to the Minister, the appropriate authority shall, subject to subsection (5) of this section, refer the case to the Minister and, if the Minister so directs and as may be so directed, shall—

(i) place the civil servant on a lower rate of remuneration, or

(ii) reduce the civil servant to a specified lower grade or rank, or

(iii) place the civil servant on a lower rate of remuneration and also reduce him to a specified lower grade or rank.

[*SSs. 3 (b), 3 (c) and 4 omitted.*]

(5) The civil servant concerned shall, before any action is taken under paragraph (*a*) of subsection (1) of this section or paragraph (*a*) of subsection (2) of this section or a reference is made to the Minister under paragraph (*a*) of subsection (3) of this section, be afforded an opportunity of making to the appropriate authority any representations he may wish to offer.

(6) The preceding subsections of this section do not apply to a civil servant holding a position to which he was appointed by the Government.

UNAUTHORISED ABSENCE

16.—(1) A civil servant shall not be paid remuneration in respect of any period of unauthorised absence from duty.

(2) If any question arises as to whether a particular period of absence from duty of a civil servant is a period of unauthorised absence from duty the question shall be determined by the appropriate authority.

MISCELLANEOUS POWERS OF MINISTER

17.—(1) The Minister shall be responsible for the following matters—

(*a*) the regulation and control of the Civil Service,

(*b*) the classification, re-classification, numbers and remuneration of civil servants,

(*c*) the fixing of—

(i) the terms and conditions of service of civil servants, and

(ii) the conditions governing the promotion of civil servants.

(2) The Minister may, for the purpose of subsection (1) of this section, make such arrangements as he thinks fit and may cancel or vary those arrangements. [*SS. 3 omitted.*]

REMUNERATION OF CIVIL SERVANTS

18.—The remuneration of every civil servant, as determined by the Minister, shall, subject to the provisions of any other enactment providing for the payment of his remuneration, be paid out of moneys provided by the Oireachtas.

STAFF OF HOUSES OF OIREACHTAS AND ATTORNEY GENERAL

19.—It is hereby declared that the power of appointing a person to be a member of the staff of the Houses of the Oireachtas or to be an officer of the Attorney General is vested in the Taoiseach and was, as respects any such appointment made before the coming into operation of the Constitution, vested in the President of the Executive Council and, as respects any such appointment made after the coming into operation of the Constitution and before the commencement of this Act, vested in the Taoiseach. [*Remainder omitted.*]

4. NEGOTIATING MACHINERY

Document 5.4 — Extracts from Department of Finance Circular 3/55
entitled *Conciliation and Arbitration Machinery for
the Civil Service.*

. . .   Agreement on a revised scheme of conciliation and arbitration for
the Civil Service to be established on a permanent basis has been reached
between the Minister for Finance on the one hand and the Post Office
Workers' Union, the Post Office Clerical Association, the Civil Service
Clerical Association, the Civil Service Alliance, the Institute of Professional
Civil Servants, the Irish Post Office Engineering Union, the Revenue group
of Departmental Associations and the Government Employees' Federation,
on the other hand.   A copy of the revised scheme is appended to this
Circular.   The scheme comes into operation on 1st April, 1955.   [*Paragraphs
2-10 omitted.*]

11.—(1) Industrial civil servants are wholly excluded from the scope of the
scheme.   Such employees fall into two categories : —

(*a*) Employees whose rates of pay are directly related to the rates paid
to workers in similar employment outside the Civil Service, and

(*b*) Employees who have no exact counterpart in outside employment
and whose rates of pay have hitherto been dealt with through the
medium of the Inter-Departmental Wages Advisory Committee
by reference to the rates paid to workers in comparable posts
outside the Civil Service.

(2) The position of industrial civil servants will continue to be regulated
by this Department's Circular 9/50 of 31st March, 1950.   The Chairman of
the Appeal Board referred to in the fourth paragraph of that Circular has
been the Deputy Chairman of the Labour Court and not the Chairman of the
Interdepartmental Wages Advisory Committee, as originally contemplated.
[*Paragraph 12 omitted.*]

SCHEME OF CONCILIATION AND ARBITRATION FOR THE CIVIL SERVICE
Part I: General

1.—The purpose of this scheme of conciliation and arbitration is to provide
means acceptable both to the State and to its employees for dealing with claims
and proposals relating to the conditions of service of civil servants and to
secure the fullest co-operation between the State, as employer, and civil
servants, as employees, for the better discharge of public business.

2.—The existence of this scheme does not imply that the Government have
surrendered or can surrender their liberty of action in the exercise of their
constitutional authority and the discharge of their responsibilities in the
public interest.

3.—The conditions governing the operation of the General Council, the
Departmental Councils and arbitration are set out in the succeeding Parts of
this scheme.

4.—(1) The following classes of civil servants are wholly excluded from the scope of the scheme : —

(*a*) civil servants, other than those indicated in sub-paragraph (2) following, serving in grades the maximum normal undifferentiated pay of which exceeds the maximum of the undifferentiated Higher Executive Officer scale.

(*b*) the Administrative Officer grade and the grades of Third Secretary and Second Secretary in the Department of External Affairs, and

(*c*) industrial civil servants.

[Remainder of paragraph 4 omitted.]

5.—(1) Before any staff association can be recognised for the purpose of the scheme it must make applications for recognition by the Minister for Finance. Only civil service staff associations recognised by the Minister for Finance for the purposes of conciliation and arbitration will be eligible to take part in the operation of the scheme. . . .

(2) Except as provided in sub-paragraph (3) following every application for recognition must be accompanied by a statement signed by the Chairman and the executive officers of the association concerned that the association is not affiliated to or associated in any way with any political organisation.

(3) Recognition will not be accorded to any staff association which is affiliated to, or associated in any way with, any political organisation unless such affiliation or association subsisted prior to 1st April, 1949. . . .

[Remainder of paragraph 5 omitted.]

6.—(1) Subject to the provisions of sub-paragraph (2) following, should a staff association, recognised for the purposes of this scheme, sponsor or resort to any form of public agitation as a means of furthering claims or seeking redress for grievances which are appropriate to be dealt with through the scheme, recognition may be withdrawn from such association, but the staff side of the General Council will be consulted before such withdrawal becomes effective.

(2) The provision of sub-paragraph (1) will not, in relation to (a) a non-arbitrable matter on which discussions at the General Council or at a Departmental Council have been concluded without agreement having been reached, or (b) a matter which has been the subject of a motion introduced in accordance with the provisions of paragraph 71 or paragraph 72 of the scheme and carried in Dáil Éireann, preclude staff associations — subject to the rules and regulations in force from time to time governing the conduct of civil servants — from publishing factual information or comment or holding public meetings of members of the Civil Service or officers of staff associations for the purpose of expressing their viewpoint. *[Paragraphs 7-9 omitted.]*

10.—Where a civil service staff association is associated with an outside organisation, it will not move the outside organisation to make representations on behalf of civil servants in respect of matters which could be dealt with through the scheme. Representations from outside organisations on behalf of civil servants will not accordingly be entertained.

11.—(1) An individual officer will continue to have the right to submit in writing through the normal channels any statement he may wish to make to the Head of his Department on any matter affecting his official position. Accordingly, claims affecting individual officers are excluded from the scope of the scheme. [*Remainder of paragraph* 11 *and paragraphs* 12 *and* 13 *omitted.*]

Part II: General Council

14.—The Council will consist of : —

    (*a*) a Chairman, nominated by the Minister for Finance, and not more than five other official representatives;

    (*b*) a principal staff representative and not more than five other staff representatives.

15.—(1) A panel of staff representatives will be formed to which representatives of each recognised association or group of associations will be appointed on the following basis:

    1 representative for each complete 500 members up to 2,000;

    1 representative thereafter for each further complete 2,000 members.

(2) The staff representatives to attend meetings of the Council will be selected by the members of the panel and may be varied from time to time.

16.—The Council will have two secretaries, both to be serving civil servants, one of whom will be nominated by the official representatives and one by the staff representatives.

17.—All members of the Council must be serving civil servants or staff association officials.

18.—The number of official and staff representatives may exceptionally be varied by agreement between both sides.

19.—Meetings will be held not less frequently than once every two months unless in any such period there is no subject for discussion, when by agreement between the official and staff side secretaries, it will be recorded that no meeting was required. Not more than one meeting will be held in any month except by agreement between the Chairman and the staff representatives. [*Paragraph* 20 *omitted.*]

21.—It will be open to the panel of staff representatives to request the placing of any matter which they believe to be within the province of the Council on the agenda for the next meeting of the Council. The question whether items so put forward come within the province of the Council will be a matter for the Chairman to decide. Before any item is excluded, the Council will be given an opportunity of expressing its views as to whether it should be included or excluded.

22.—The Minister for Finance may cause to be placed on the agenda of the General Council any matter on which he desires to obtain the views of the staff representatives provided the matter is among the subjects listed in paragraph 23 as appropriate for discussion by the Council, or, if it is not among the subjects so listed, that the Minister for Finance considers that it may appropriately be discussed by the Council.

23.—The subjects appropriate for discussion by the General Council will be: —

(a) Principles governing recruitment to general service classes and to professional, scientific and technical classes common to two or more Departments;

(b) Claims for increase or decrease of pay of the Civil Service as a whole;

(c) Claims relating to general service classes and to professional, scientific and technical classes common to two or more Departments in relation to (i) pay and allowances whether in the nature of pay or otherwise, (ii) overtime rates, (iii) subsistence allowances, (iv) travelling, lodging and disturbance allowances, (v) removal expenses;

(d) Principles governing remuneration and form of payment of additional remuneration, viz., whether by way of continuing allowance or periodic gratuity;

(e) Hours of weekly attendance of general service classes;

(f) Principles of promotion in the general service classes and in professional, scientific and technical classes which are common to two or more Departments;

(g) Principles governing discipline;

(h) Suggestions by the staff of general application for promoting efficiency in the Civil Service;

(i) General considerations in regard to the grading of general service classes and of professional, scientific and technical classes common to two or more Departments;

(j) Principles governing superannuation;

(k) Principles governing the grant of annual, sick and special leave;

(l) Claims relating to establishment of a proportion of unestablished general service and professional, scientific and technical classes common to two or more Departments;

(m) Questions of doubt or difficulty in relation to the subjects appropriate for discussion at Departmental Councils.

24.—The staff side may bring forward for discussion subjects not listed in paragraph 23 if the Minister for Finance agrees that they are appropriate for discussion by the Council. [*Paragraphs 25 and 26 omitted.*]

27.—The Minister for Finance will cause to be brought before the Council prior to decision any proposals for changes in the remuneration of civil servants generally or of general service classes or of professional, scientific and technical classes common to two or more Departments.

28.—The Minister for Finance will ascertain and give due weight to the views of the Council on proposals for legislation which, in the Minister's view, peculiarly affects the position of civil servants or any class of civil servants as distinct from the general public.

29.—It will not be within the competence of the Council to make agreements binding on the Minister for Finance but the Council may make agreed recommendations or may, at the request of either side, record disagreement.

30.—Agreed reports of all discussions which take place at meetings of the General Council will be submitted to the Minister for Finance and copies of each such report will be forwarded to the secretary of the staff side of the Council. [*Paragraphs 31-33 omitted.*]

Part III: Departmental Councils

34.—A Departmental Council will be set up in each Department and will consist of :—

(*a*) a Chairman, nominated by the Minister having charge of the Department, and not more than three other official representatives;

(*b*) a principal staff representative and not more than three other staff representatives.

35.—(1) The number of representatives of each recognised association (i.e., each association recognised for the purpose of departmental representation and representing staff employed in the Department) to be appointed to a panel of staff representatives will be settled by agreement among such associations or, failing agreement, by the panel of staff representatives attached to the General Council.

(2) The staff representatives to attend meetings of the Council will be selected by the members of the panel and may be varied from time to time. [*Paragraphs 36-42 omitted.*]

43.—The subjects appropriate for discussion by the Council will be :—
(*a*) Principles governing recruitment to departmental classes;
(*b*) Claims, relating to departmental classes only, in relation to (i) pay and allowances whether in the nature of pay or otherwise, (ii) overtime rates, (iii) subsistence allowances, (iv) travelling, lodging and disturbance allowances;
(*c*) Allowances and claims for allowances of purely departmental application payable to general service grades and professional, scientific or technical classes;
(*d*) Hours of weekly attendance of departmental classes and time-unit system of attendances;
(*e*) Principles governing promotion of members of departmental classes;
(*f*) Claims for grading of posts and blocks of work;
(*g*) Accommodation and working conditions affecting the health and safety of the staff;

(*h*) Annual leave of departmental classes;

(*i*) Suggestions by the staff for promoting efficiency in the Department;

(*j*) Acting appointments;

(*k*) Claims relating to establishment of a proportion of unestablished departmental classes;

(*l*) The application departmentally of general principles formulated at the General Council;

(*m*) Principles affecting existing departmental disciplinary codes.

[*Paragraphs 44-46 omitted.*]

47.—It will not be within the competence of the Council to make binding agreements but the Council may make agreed recommendations or may, at the request of either side, record disagreement.

48.—Agreed reports of all discussions which take place at a Departmental Council will be submitted to the Minister in charge of the Department, and through him to the Minister for Finance before a decision is announced, and copies of each such report will be forwarded to the secretary of the staff side of the Departmental Council.

49.—The decisions of the appropriate Minister or Ministers on matters discussed by the Council will be conveyed to the staff side secretary of the Council.

50.—The Minister for Finance will not reject the agreed recommendation of a Departmental Council without prior consultation on the part of representatives of his Department with the official side of the Departmental Council in question. [*Paragraph 51 omitted.*]

52.—The proceedings of the Council will be confidential and no statements concerning them will be issued except with the authority of the Council. Where an agreed report of a Departmental Council contains an agreed recommendation, the Council will not authorise any publication of the relevant proceedings until the decision of the appropriate Minister or Ministers has been conveyed on such agreed recommendation.

Part IV: Arbitration

53.—The Arbitration Board will consist of: —

(*a*) a Chairman;

(*b*) two members, being serving civil servants, to be nominated by the Minister for Finance for the hearing of each case;

(*c*) two members, being serving civil servants, to be nominated by the staff panel of the General Council for the hearing of each case.

54.—The Chairman will, on the nomination of the Minister for Finance in agreement with the staff side of the General Council, be appointed by the Government. He will hold office for such term as may be fixed by the Government at the time of his appointment. [*Paragraph 55 omitted.*]

56.—Members of the Oireachtas, persons serving in the Civil Service, and officials of Civil Service staff organisations will be ineligible for appointment as Chairman or Deputy Chairman. [*Paragraph 57 omitted.*]

58.—Only such staff claims as are made on behalf of a class or classes comprehended by the scheme and represented by a recognised staff association are appropriate for reference to the Arbitration Board. . .

59.—To be referable to the Arbitration Board a claim must (a) be arbitrable, (b) have been discussed at either the General Council or at a Departmental Council, as may be appropriate, and (c) have been the subject of either (i) recorded disagreement by the Council following such discussions or (ii) an agreed recommendation which has not been accepted by the Minister for Finance.

60.—(1) Subject to the provisions of sub-paragraph (2) hereunder, the following claims relating to classes of civil servants will be arbitrable, viz., claims for, or in regard to the rates or the amount of (i) pay and allowances in the nature of pay, (ii) overtime, (iii) total weekly hours of work, (iv) annual and sick leave, (v) subsistence allowances, (vi) travelling, lodging and disturbance allowances.

(2) Claims for the extension of children's allowances will not be arbitrable. [*Paragraph 61 omitted.*]

62.—(1) Where arbitration is requested by a civil service staff association, the staff association concerned will forward a statement of case, including proposed terms of reference, to the Secretary, Department of Finance.

(2) Where the arbitrability of the Claim is not disputed, the staff statement of case will be transmitted to the secretary to the Arbitration Board together with the official side's counter-statement and at the same time the secretary to the Arbitration Board will be informed whether the Minister for Finance agrees with the terms of reference proposed by the claimants. (Failing agreement, the respective statements of case together will, subject to the provisions of this scheme and to the rules of procedure of the Arbitration Board, constitute the terms of reference.) A copy of the official side's counter-statement will also be sent to the staff association making the claim.

(3) Where the arbitrability of the claim is disputed, the staff association making the claim will be so informed and the grounds on which arbitrability is disputed will be stated. The staff association may then request that the question of arbitrability be referred to the Arbitration Board for determination, in accordance with the provisions of paragraph 64 following, and will set out the grounds on which it claims that the matter comes within the category of arbitrable subjects. . . .

63.—(1) Where arbitration is requested by the Minister for Finance, he will cause to be transmitted to the secretary to the Arbitration Board and to the other party concerned, a statement of case, including proposed terms of reference. [*Sub-paragraph (2) omitted.*]

(3) Where the arbitrability of the claim is disputed, the Secretary, Department of Finance, will be so informed and the grounds on which arbitrability is disputed will be stated. The Minister for Finance may then request that the question of arbitrability be referred to the Arbitration Board for determination, in accordance with the provisions of paragraph 64 following, and will set out the grounds on which he claims that the matter comes within the category of arbitrable subjects. . . .

64.—Any dispute as to whether a particular claim comes within the category of arbitrable subjects will be determined by the Board whose decision will be final.

65.—Each party's statement of case will, as far as practicable, contain all submissions relied upon in relation to the claim.

66.—(1) Civil servants concerned in a claim referred to the Board may select not more than three advocates to present their claim to the Board. The persons so selected must be drawn from the following categories: (a) whole-time officials of staff associations concerned with the claim, or (b) serving civil servants of the class or classes concerned in the claim, or (c) subject to the consent in each case of the Head of the officer's Department, where it is proposed to take special leave, serving civil servants of another class.

(2) The Minister for Finance may select not more than three advocates to present the official case to the Board. The persons so selected must be serving civil servants.

67.—The Board may summon witnesses and request them to furnish evidence in writing or otherwise.

68.—Subject to the provisions of this scheme, the Board will settle its own procedure.

69.—The Chairman of the Board will submit to the Government through the Minister for Finance a report on every claim referred to the Board and such report shall be the report of the Board. This report will be signed by the Chairman only and no other report will be issued by the Board or by any member of it. The report will set out (a) the unanimous finding of the members of the Board or, if the members are not unanimous but a majority agrees on a certain finding, (b) the finding of such majority of the members of the Board or, if a majority of the Board is unable to agree, (c) the finding of the Chairman.

70.—Within three months of the receipt of a report from the Chairman of the Board the Government will present it to Dáil Éireann or, if at the expiration of three months the Dáil is not sitting, then on the first day of the next sitting. No such report will be published before presentation in Dáil Éireann.

71.—If the report of the Board does not concern a claim for a general revision of civil service pay, the Government will, as soon as may be after presenting the report to Dáil Éireann in accordance with paragraph 70 preceding, either authorise the implementation of the finding contained in the Board's report or will introduce a motion in Dáil Éireann recommending either the rejection of the finding or such modification therein as they think fit.

72.—(1) If the report of the Board concerns a claim for a general revision of civil service pay, the Government will when presenting the report to Dáil Éireann in accordance with paragraph 70 preceding adopt one of the following courses : —

(a) signify that they propose to give immediate effect to the finding of the Board in full;

(b) introduce a motion in Dáil Éireann
(i) proposing the rejection of the finding, or
(ii) proposing the modification of the finding, or
(iii) proposing (because they consider that it would not be possible, without imposing additional taxation, to give full effect to the finding within the current financial year) the deferment of a final decision on the report until the Budget for the next following financial year is being framed and indicating to what extent, if any, they propose in the interval, without prejudice to the final decision, to give effect to the finding, the extent of the payment in that event to be determined by the amount which can be met without imposing additional taxation.

(2) Should Dáil Éireann have approved of a motion presented to it in accordance with the terms of sub-paragraph (1)(b)(iii) preceding, the Government will, save in entirely exceptional circumstances, make full provision in the Budget for the following financial year for the annual charge appropriate to that financial year in respect of the report of the Arbitration Board and also for the amount necessary, as an addition to any amount already paid, to give full effect to the Board's finding from the date of operation recommended in the report to the end of the financial year in which the report was presented to Dáil Éireann. Where the Government do not so propose to give effect to the Board's finding, they will introduce a motion in Dáil Éireann indicating the action they propose to take and recommending such action to the House. [*Remainder omitted.*]

5. NUMBERS

Document 5.5 — Numbers in the Civil Service, 1963.

(Prepared from data supplied by Central Statistics Office)

These data exclude industrial staffs, sub-postmasters, branch managers of employment exchanges, Collectors of Taxes and a few casual and other employees. The term ' etc.' in each case means ' officers of equivalent status or salary '.

Grade	Numbers	
Group 1: Administrative and Executive		
Heads of Departments and chairmen of Boards of commissioners	18	
Deputy Secretaries etc.	22	
Assistant Secretaries etc.	59	
Principal Officers etc.	156	
Assistant Principals etc.	322	
Administrative Officers	53	
Higher Executive Officers	529	
Executive Officers	813	
Others including Inspectors and Assistant Inspectors of Taxes, Customs and Excise Staffs, Social Welfare Inspectors etc., Postmasters etc.	979	
Total — Group 1		2,951
Group 2: Staff and Clerical		
Staff Officers	545	
Clerical Officers	2,023	
Temporary clerks and clerical assistants	438	
Clerk Typists engaged on higher duties	2,561	
Others including Departmental grades	1,078	
Total — Group 2		6,645
Group 3: Typing		
Superintendents of Typists	26	
Clerk Typists	580	
Others	124	
Total — Group 3		730
Group 4: Professional, Scientific and Technical		
Architects	113	
Engineers	378	
Legal Officers	144	
Surveyors	38	
Teachers and Instructors	15	
Draughtsmen	111	
Medical Officers	29	
Others	1,563	
Total — Group 4		2,391
Group 5: Inspectorate — Total		1,086
Group 6: Supervisory, Minor and Manipulative		
Post Office	12,333	
Others, including Preventive Officers, Prison Officers, etc., Radio and other technical officers in the Department of Transport and Power	1,732	
Total — Group 6		14,065
Group 7: Messengers, Cleaners, etc.		
Messengers, Paper keepers, etc.	571	
Cleaners	771	
Others	518	
Total — Group 7		1,860
Grand Total		29,728

6. THE CLERK-TYPIST GRADE EXPERIMENT

Document 5.6 — Extracts from Department of Finance Circular 3/60 entitled *Reorganisation of Certain General Service Grades*.

A Dhuine Uasail,

1. I am directed by the Minister for Finance to refer to inter-departmental consultation on the subject of the reorganisation of certain general service grades and to inform you that the changes in contemplation were subsequently discussed by the General Council under the scheme of conciliation and arbitration for the Civil Service. Agreed recommendations in relation to certain grades have emerged from the Council's discussions and have been accepted by the Minister. I am to convey to all Departments instructions designed to give effect to these recommendations. The Minister wishes to stress that the objective of this reorganisation is to secure less dispersal of effort and thus to promote greater efficiency in the discharge of public business and, ultimately a reduction in numbers. He is confident of the ready co-operation of all concerned in achieving this aim.

2. Review

These arrangements will be reviewed in the light of experience when they have been in operation for four years. [*Paragraphs 3 and 4 omitted.*]

5. New Grade of Clerk-Typist

The present grades of Writing Assistant, Shorthand-Typist and Typist will be merged in a new female grade of Clerk-Typist in accordance with the arrangements set out in this Circular.

6. Duties

The duties of the grade of Clerk-Typist are set out in the appendix.

[*Paragraph 7 omitted.*]

8. Upper Duties Test

(1) A serving Writing Assistant or Typist or an officer recruited directly as Clerk-Typist may not preceed beyond the point 167s. 7d.—the present maximum of the Writing Assistant and Typist grades—unless she is certified by the Head of the Department as fully capable of discharging the highest duties of the grade of Clerk-Typist.

(2) A serving Shorthand-Typist may proceed to her present maximum of 184s. 8d. without the upper duties test.

(3) The upper duties test will be a searching one based normally on actual performance of the highest duties for at least six months. At the outset the special transition arrangements set out in later paragraphs will apply.

9. Assimilation

(1) Serving Shorthand-Typists and Writing Assistants will all be assimilated to the grade of Clerk-Typist as from the operative date.

[*Remainder of Paragraph and Paragraph 10 omitted.*]

11. *Serving Shorthand-Typists and Typists*

(1) Departments are requested to endeavour to combine shorthand-typing or typing with clerical duties where circumstances permit. The aim should be to ensure that, in sections where any large volume of work is at present done in longhand by Clerical Officers and Writing Assistants and then passed to the copying room for typing, the work—including typing—will be handled entirely in the section by the same Clerk-Typist and the longhand eliminated. It is recognised that the great bulk of typing will continue to be done in central typing pools. Where it is found possible to combine shorthand-typing or typing with clerical duties, a serving Shorthand-Typist or Typist on her maximum should be tested on the highest duties of Clerk-Typist.

[*Remainder of Paragraph* 11 *omitted.*]

12. *Clerical Officer Vacancies*

(1) It is intended (a) to suspend the open competitive examination for general service posts of Clerical Officer for at least three years commencing in 1961 and (b) to make a total of 120 appointments to such posts from limited general service and departmental competitions in the period from 1 July, 1960, to 30 June, 1964.

(2) Vacancies arising for Clerical Officers will, subject to (1), be filled by the assignment of Clerk-Typists . . .

13. *Staff Officer Grades*

(1) The grades of Staff Officer, Grades II and I, and Higher Staff Officer will be abolished.

(2) Staff Officers, Grade III, will in future be styled Staff Officers.

14. *Staff Officers, Grade II*

(1) Serving Staff Officers, Grade II, will be assimilated to the grade of Executive Officer as from the operative date. [*Remainder of Paragraph* 14 *omitted.*]

15. *Staff Officers, Grade I*

(1) Serving Staff Officers, Grade I, will be assimilated to the grade of Higher Executive Officer as from the operative date . . .

[*Remainder of Paragraph* 15 *omitted.*]

16. *Higher Staff Officers*

Serving Higher Staff Officers will be assimilated to the grade of Higher Executive Officer as from the operative date. Such officers will not, however, proceed beyond their present maxima, unless reassigned to a post with full Higher Executive duties.

17. *Filling of Posts of Executive Officer*

(1) Vacancies for Executive Officers arising during the four years commencing 1 July, 1960, will be filled as follows.

(2) Vacancies in each Department in former posts of Staff Officer, Grade II, which on the operative date were converted to Executive Officer will be filled by means of departmental selection boards from the Staff Officers serving in the Department. The Department of Finance will be represented on these selection boards to ensure a uniform standard.

(3) Apart from the posts referred to at (2), vacancies for Executive Officers will be filled in the proportion of one limited entrant to one open entrant from each of the open competitive examinations in the years 1960, 1961, 1962 and 1963. [*Sub-paragraph 4 omitted.*]

18. *Filling of Posts of Higher Executive Officer and Former Posts of Staff Officer, Grade I, and Higher Staff Officer*

(1) During the four years commencing 1 July, 1960, vacancies arising in posts of Higher Executive Officer will be filled as follows.

(2) (a) In making selections for posts of Higher Executive Officer, whether with or without restricted maxima, it is intended that present practice be continued.

(b) Higher Executive Officer posts other than regraded Higher Executive Officer posts will normally be filled by the promotion of Executive Officers; regraded Staff Officers, Grades I and II, and Higher Staff Officers will continue to be eligible as heretofore.

[*Remainder of Paragraph 18 and Paragraph 19 omitted.*]

20. *Queries and Suggestions*

Any difficulties arising out of the application of this circular should be listed and referred in writing to this Department. Departments are also invited to report from time to time on the operation of the scheme.

APPENDIX

Duties of Clerk-Typists

The range of duties will include those at present appropriate to Writing Assistants, Shorthand-Typists and Typists and in addition the following:—

Drafting letters, minutes, etc., asking for and giving factual information with no personal expression of judgment.

Checking or making arithmetical calculations (e.g., the calculation of interest).

Subject to any necessary departmental instructions, contacts (including telephone contacts) with other Departments and with the public confined to seeking, noting and giving factual information; interviews with members of the public where the business is straightforward.

Simple case work.

Making précis of and analysing material.

Preparation, scrutiny and verification of documents, statistics, records, etc., in conformity with official instructions.

Sorting and filing papers.

Compiling and maintaining indexes and writing transit cards.

Use of comptometers and calculating machines, etc.

This list illustrates rather than defines the appropriate duties; other duties of similar, but not higher, quality are not excluded.

READING

Final Report of the Committee of Inquiry into the Civil Service.

T. J. Barrington: 'The Structure of the Civil Service' in *Administration*, vol. 3.

T. J. Barrington: 'Selection in the Civil Service' in *Administration*, vol. 4.

T. J. Barrington: 'Cupidi Rerum Novarum' in *Administration*, vol. 8.

T. P. Linehan: 'The Growth of the Civil Service' in *Administration*, vol. 2.

M. D. McCarthy: ' The Structure of the Civil Service, Some Facts ' in *Administration*, vol. 3.

S. O Mathúna: 'The Christian Brothers and the Civil Service' in *Administration*, vol. 3.

In addition to the above, the volumes of *Administration* contain many other articles dealing with numerous aspects of the organization and working not only of the Civil Service but also of the various departments and services.

Chapter 6

THE HOUSES OF THE OIREACHTAS, 1—FUNCTIONS AND POWERS

INTRODUCTION

Strictly, the Oireachtas consists not only of two houses, a House of Representatives, Dáil Éireann, and a Senate, Seanad Éireann, but of the President also. It is defined in this way in the Constitution which also translates Oireachtas as 'National Parliament'. (Document 6.1). In practice, however, the word Oireachtas tends to be used to refer to the two houses alone, what in most countries would be called the Legislature or Parliament.

The first Parliament consisted of a single chamber, Dáil Éireann. However, the general belief in the usefulness of a second chamber and the promises made in order to safeguard the Southern Unionists, led to the provision in the Irish Free State Constitution of a 'Chamber of Deputies' and a 'Senate', and although that Senate had a chequered career culminating in its being abolished, provision for a new Senate, called Seanad Éireann, was made in Bunreacht na hÉireann.

In overall conception, the Oireachtas is based on the British Parliament. In general it resembles that body in its functions and powers, though its competence to enact legislation is limited by the Constitution, and also in its organization and procedures. This means that, in comparison with some other democratic countries, its role in government is modest. A Government backed by a majority in the Dáil is able to manage the conduct of business to suit itself and has a virtual monopoly of initiative in proposing bills and other motions. (Document 6.2). The Constitutional provisions relating to legislation (Document 6.3) do not rule out any member introducing bills or other business, except proposals involving expenditure which can only be passed on the recommendation of the Government (Article 17.2), but between 1958 and 1962, only thirteen bills were introduced by 'private members' of the Dáil and only one by a 'private member' of the Seanad. Also, the proportion of the Dáil's time spent on private members' business has been only between 3 per cent and 7 per cent.

Moreover, the ability of the Houses to enquire into the actions of the Government and officials, to extract information and to call the Government to account is limited by the inadequacy of their procedures and their facilities. For all its reputation as an important controlling device, the parliamentary question leaves much to be desired as a means of eliciting information and enquiring into matters in a systematic fashion. (Document 6.4). The procedures by which the Dáil decides on the adequacy of the Government's financial proposals, which task it is specifically assigned in the Constitution (Document 6.5), are increasingly recognized as being archaic in an era of high expenditure, far-reaching capital programmes, extensive subsidies, and long term planning for national economic and social development. And, although the machinery for dealing with the public accounts, involving the Comptroller and Auditor General and the Public Accounts Committee, is adequate so far as it goes, it increasingly fails to measure up to the needs of the times which require the use of modern methods and techniques for assessing the efficiency of the administration's operations and the quality of its management. (Documents 6.6 and 6.7). The use of such devices by powerful committees is essential to effective control, yet the Seanad's Committee on Statutory Instruments (See Document 12.3 below) and the Dáil's Public Accounts Committee are the only regular committees of any sort set up to investigate the conduct of public business. Furthermore, just as the Houses of the Oireachtas have never developed an effective committee system, so too they have failed to equip members with those secretarial and reference facilities and other aids which would permit them, if they so desired, to be more effective in scrutinizing the work of the administration.

It is understandable that Governments in power are not anxious to burden themselves with keen and effective critics, but what of the members generally and the Oireachtas as a body? Members have, it seems, accepted the comparatively passive role, so far as legislation and the scrutiny of the conduct of business are concerned, which has become such a feature of British parliamentary life in this age of disciplined parties and large-scale governmental operations.

Representatives are, however, far from indifferent to the detailed administration of business which affects their constituents' immediate interests or their local neighbourhood. There is evidence that, as in some other countries, including some Commonwealth countries, the Irish representative is primarily a local consumer representative, an advocate and expediter of affairs for his constituents and his locality. Certainly, many of them are heavily engaged in making representations to Ministers and officials on many matters of social welfare, housing, employment and local works and improvements. In the case of some country members, the burden of this work, which, because of the electoral system, is unavoidable, is very onerous (Documents 6.8 and 6.9). These services are no doubt valuable, but as was recently pointed out in the judgement in *O'Donovan v. the Attorney General*, they are not envisaged in the Constitution (Document 6.10). This case provides important evidence about the behaviour and attitudes of parliamentary representatives and brings out two conflicting views of their proper role.

DOCUMENTS

1. CONSTITUTION AND POWERS

Document 6.1—Article 15 of Bunreacht na hÉireann (Constitution of Ireland).

Article 15.

1.   1° The National Parliament shall be called and known, and is in this Constitution generally referred to, as the Oireachtas.

2° The Oireachtas shall consist of the President and two Houses, viz.: a House of Representatives to be called Dáil Éireann and a Senate to be called Seanad Éireann.

3° The Houses of the Oireachtas shall sit in or near the City of Dublin or in such other place as they may from time to time determine.

2.   1° The sole and exclusive power of making laws for the State is hereby vested in the Oireachtas; no other legislative authority has power to make laws for the State.

2° Provision may however be made by law for the creation or recognition of subordinate legislatures and for the powers and functions of these legislatures.

3.   1° The Oireachtas may provide for the establishment or recognition of functional or vocational councils representing branches of the social and economic life of the people.

2° A law establishing or recognising any such council shall determine its rights, powers and duties, and its relation to the Oireachtas and to the Government.

4.   1° The Oireachtas shall not enact any law which is in any respect repugnant to this Constitution or any provision thereof.

2° Every law enacted by the Oireachtas which is in any respect repugnant to this Constitution or to any provision thereof, shall, but to the extent only of such repugnancy, be invalid.

5.   The Oireachtas shall not declare acts to be infringements of the law which were not so at the date of their commission.

6.   1° The right to raise and maintain military or armed forces is vested exclusively in the Oireachtas.

    2° No military or armed force, other than a military or armed force raised and maintained by the Oireachtas, shall be raised or maintained for any purpose whatsoever.

7.   The Oireachtas shall hold at least one session every year.

8.   1° Sittings of each House of the Oireachtas shall be public.

    2° In cases of special emergency, however, either House may hold a private sitting with the assent of two-thirds of the members present.

9.   1° Each House of the Oireachtas shall elect from its members its own Chairman and Deputy Chairman, and shall prescribe their powers and duties.

    2° The remuneration of the Chairman and Deputy Chairman of each House shall be determined by law.

10.   Each House shall make its own rules and standing orders, with power to attach penalties for their infringement, and shall have power to ensure freedom of debate, to protect its official documents and the private papers of its members, and to protect itself and its members against any person or persons interfering with, molesting or attempting to corrupt its members in the exercise of their duties.

11.   1° All questions in each House shall, save as otherwise provided by this Constitution, be determined by a majority of the votes of the members present and voting other than the Chairman or presiding member.

    2° The Chairman or presiding member shall have and exercise a casting vote in the case of an equality of votes.

    3° The number of members necessary to constitute a meeting of either House for the exercise of its powers shall be determined by its standing orders.

12.   All official reports and publications of the Oireachtas or of either House thereof and utterances made in either House wherever published shall be privileged.

13.   The members of each House of the Oireachtas shall, except in case of treason as defined in this Constitution, felony or breach of the peace, be privileged from arrest in going to and returning from, and while within the precincts of, either House, and shall not, in respect of any utterance in either House, be amenable to any court or any authority other than the House itself.

14.   No person may be at the same time a member of both Houses of the Oireachtas, and, if any person who is already a member of either House

becomes a member of the other House, he shall forthwith be deemed to have vacated his first seat.

15.   The Oireachtas may make provision by law for the payment of allowances to the members of each House thereof in respect of their duties as public representatives and for the grant to them of free travelling and such other facilities (if any) in connection with those duties as the Oireachtas may determine.

2. SITTINGS AND BUSINESS

Document 6.2—Chapter 11 of J. C. Smyth, *The Houses of the Oireachtas*, 2nd edition, Institute of Public Administration, Dublin, 1964.

The Constitution (Article 15.7) provides that the Houses shall hold at least one session every year. Article 15.8 provides that the sittings of each House shall be public, but, in cases of special emergency, either House may hold a private sitting with the assent of two-thirds of the members present (no such private sitting has been held). The average sittings of the Houses over the ten years 1953-62 have been in the case of the Dáil 69 days per year, and in the case of the Seanad 23 days per year. The greater proportion of sitting days in each House is in the period preceding the Summer Recess which generally occurs about the end of July or the beginning of August.

DAIL

Under Standing Orders the Dáil, unless it otherwise resolves, meets every Tuesday and Wednesday, at 3 p.m. and every Thursday at 10.30 a.m. and adjourns not later than 11 p.m. on Tuesdays and Wednesdays and not later than 5.30 p.m. on Thursdays. The days and hours are subject, however, to variation depending on the state of business in the House.

Every sitting of the Dáil is governed by a printed Order Paper which is prepared under the direction of the Ceann Comhairle. The Taoiseach has the right to determine the order in which Government business shall appear on the Order Paper and he announces each day at the commencement of public business the order in which it is to be taken on that day.

On Tuesdays and Wednesdays questions are taken first in order normally at 3 p.m. On Thursdays questions are taken at 2.30 p.m. Second comes Private Business which relates to Private Bills and ancillary matters (to be distinguished from Private Members' Bills which are Public Bills introduced by Private Members, i.e. members other than Members of the Government). Then the House proceeds to deal with Public Business including motions relating to the introduction of Bills and Orders of the Day, i.e. business previously ordered by the House to be set down for that day.

On Tuesdays and Wednesdays, unless the House otherwise orders, Private Members' business is taken from 6 p.m. to 7.30 p.m. . . .

The following Table gives an indication of the principal business transacted by the Dáil over the past five years and the time devoted to financial business (i.e. Vote on Account, Estimates, Budget Debates and proposals for legislation consequential on them) and Private Members' motions.

TABLE III

Year	No. of Sittings of Dáil	Total No. of hours of Sitting	Parliamentary Questions		Financial Business	Private Members' Business
			Oral	Written		
	No.	Hours	No.	No.	Hours	Hours
1958	72	516	2,401	232	265	38 (i)
1959	72	508	1,874	243	205	16
1960	76	559	2,483	270	237	31½ (ii)
1961	75	562	2,944	187	214	32 (iii)
1962	77	581	5,055	357	298	29½ (iv)

(i) Includes 12½ hours devoted to "no confidence" motion spread over two days, and 5 hours of Government time.
(ii) Includes 11 hours of Government time.
(iii) Includes 18½ hours of Government time.
(iv) Includes 8 hours of Government time.

SEANAD

Under its Standing Orders the Seanad, unless it otherwise resolves, meets on Wednesdays and Thursdays at 3 p.m. and on Fridays at 10.30 a.m. The sittings, however, are largely dependent on the volume of business sent to it from the Dáil. While the Dáil is discussing the Estimates very little legislation is passed by it, and the Seanad has no occasion to meet. The disparity in sittings is explained first by the difference in number of members and, secondly, by the fact that debates similar to those in the Dáil on the Budget and the Estimates do not take place in the Seanad.

Every sitting is governed by an Order Paper which is prepared under the direction of the Cathaoirleach. Government Bills take precedence over all other business except Private Business.

The order of precedence of Government Bills which form the greatest proportion of the work of the Seanad is decided by the Leader of the House after consultation with other interested parties. (The Leader of the House is a member of the House who supports the Government and who moves, on behalf of the Government, motions for resolutions, bills, etc.; non-members of the House, as members of the Government and Parliamentary Secretaries normally are, may not move motions in the House.) It may be noted, however, that, under Standing Orders, Bills coming from the Dáil, other than Money Bills and Bills the time for the consideration of which by the Seanad shall have been abridged, cannot be considered, unless the Seanad otherwise orders, before the expiration of three clear days after receipt from the Dáil.

The following Table sets out the number and total hours of sittings of the Seanad in the five years 1958-62. Approximately 90-95 per cent of the work consisted of the consideration of legislation sent to it by the Dáil.

TABLE IV

Year	No. of Sittings of Seanad	Total Number of Hours of Sittings
1958	18	116
1959	28	174
1960	28	188
1961	30	189
1962	18	113

3. LEGISLATION

Document 6.3—Extracts from Bunreacht na hÉireann (Constitution of Ireland).

Article 20.
1. Every Bill initiated in and passed by Dáil Éireann shall be sent to Seanad Éireann and may, unless it be a Money Bill, be amended in Seanad Éireann and Dáil Éireann shall consider any such amendment.
2. 1° A Bill other than a Money Bill may be initiated in Seanad Éireann, and if passed by Seanad Éireann, shall be introduced in Dáil Éireann.
2° A Bill initiated in Seanad Éireann if amended by Dáil Éireann shall be considered as a Bill initiated in Dáil Éireann.
3. A Bill passed by either House and accepted by the other House shall be deemed to have been passed by both Houses.

Money Bills

Article 21.
1. 1° Money Bills shall be initiated in Dáil Éireann only.
2° Every Money Bill passed by Dáil Éireann shall be sent to Seanad Éireann for its recommendations.
2. 1° Every Money Bill sent to Seanad Éireann for its recommendations shall, at the expiration of a period not longer than twenty-one days after it shall have been sent to Seanad Éireann, be returned to Dáil Éireann, which may accept or reject all or any of the recommendations of Seanad Éireann.

2° If such Money Bill is not returned by Seanad Éireann to Dáil Éireann within such twenty-one days or is returned within such twenty-one days with recommendations which Dáil Éireann does not accept, it shall be deemed to have been passed by both Houses at the expiration of the said twenty-one days. [*Article 22 omitted.*]

Time for Consideration of Bills

Article 23.

1. This Article applies to every Bill passed by Dáil Éireann and sent to Seanad Éireann other than a Money Bill or a Bill the time for the consideration of which by Seanad Éireann shall have been abridged under Article 24 of this Constitution.

1° Whenever a Bill to which this Article applies is within the stated period defined in the next following sub-section either rejected by Seanad Éireann or passed by Seanad Éireann with amendments to which Dáil Éireann does not agree or is neither passed (with or without amendment) nor rejected by Seanad Éireann within the stated period, the Bill shall, if Dáil Éireann so resolves within one hundred and eighty days after the expiration of the stated period be deemed to have been passed by both Houses of the Oireachtas on the day on which the resolution is passed.

2° The stated period is the period of ninety days commencing on the day on which the Bill is first sent by Dáil Éireann to Seanad Éireann or any longer period agreed upon in respect of the Bill by both Houses of the Oireachtas. [*Remainder of Article 23 omitted.*]

Article 24.

1. If and whenever on the passage by Dáil Éireann of any Bill, other than a Bill expressed to be a Bill containing a proposal to amend the Constitution, the Taoiseach certifies by messages in writing addressed to the President and to the Chairman of each House of the Oireachtas that, in the opinion of the Government, the Bill is urgent and immediately necessary for the preservation of the public peace and security, or by reason of the existence of a public emergency, whether domestic or international, the time for the consideration of such Bill by Seanad Éireann shall, if Dáil Éireann so resolves and if the President, after consultation with the Council of State, concurs, be abridged to such period as shall be specified in the resolution.

2. Where a Bill, the time for the consideration of which by Seanad Éireann has been abridged under this Article,

(*a*) is, in the case of a Bill which is not a Money Bill, rejected by Seanad Éireann or passed by Seanad Éireann with amendments to which Dáil Éireann does not agree or neither passed nor rejected by Seanad Éireann, or

(b) is, in the case of a Money Bill, either returned by Seanad Éireann to Dáil Éireann with recommendations which Dáil Éireann does not accept or is not returned by Seanad Éireann to Dáil Éireann,

within the period specified in the resolution, the Bill shall be deemed to have been passed by both Houses of the Oireachtas at the expiration of that period.

3.   When a Bill the time for the consideration of which by Seanad Éireann has been abridged under this Article becomes law it shall remain in force for a period of ninety days from the date of its enactment and no longer unless, before the expiration of that period, both Houses shall have agreed that such law shall remain in force for a longer period and the longer period so agreed upon shall have been specified in resolutions passed by both Houses.

Signing and Promulgation of Laws

Article 25.

1.   As soon as any Bill, other than a Bill expressed to be a Bill containing a proposal for the amendment of this Constitution, shall have been passed or deemed to have been passed by both Houses of the Oireachtas, the Taoiseach shall present it to the President for his signature and for promulgation by him as a law in accordance with the provisions of this Article.

2.   1° Save as otherwise provided by this Constitution, every Bill so presented to the President for his signature and for promulgation by him as a law shall be signed by the President not earlier than the fifth and not later than the seventh day after the date on which the Bill shall have been presented to him. [*Remainder of S. 2 and Ss. 3 and 4.1° omitted.*]

4.   2° Every Bill signed by the President under this Constitution shall be promulgated by him as a law by the publication by his direction of a notice in the *Iris Oifigiúil,* stating that the Bill has become law.

3° Every Bill shall be signed by the President in the text in which it was passed or deemed to have been passed by both Houses of the Oireachtas, and if a Bill is so passed or deemed to have been passed in both the official languages, the President shall sign the text of the Bill in each of those languages.

4° Where the President signs the text of a Bill in one only of the official languages, an official translation shall be issued in the other official language.

6° In case of conflict between the texts of a law enrolled under this section in both the official languages, the text in the national language shall prevail.

4. PARLIAMENTARY QUESTIONS

Document 6.4—Extracts from T. Troy, 'Some Aspects of Parliamentary Questions' in *Administration*, vol. 7.

The distinctive feature of the Parliamentary Question (in the limited sense with which we are concerned here) is that it is put down by a member who is not at the time speaking to a motion before the House. The Standing Orders of Dáil Éireann regulate Parliamentary Questions in some detail and a practice based on precedents has been built up. Due notice must normally be given, the question must be in writing, it must relate to public affairs connected with the Department of the Minister concerned, or to matters of administration for which he is officially responsible. The purpose of the question, which must be as brief as possible and contain no argument or personal imputation, must be to elicit information upon or to elucidate matters of fact or policy. In certain circumstances, the reply may be in writing but there is no obligation on the Minister to answer at all. A deputy may ask supplementary questions and may, in certain circumstances and with the permission of the Chair, raise the matter on the adjournment of the House if he is not satisfied with the Minister's reply.

Questions are taken at a fixed time of the day and any questions not dealt with within the time allotted are held over. The rules set out above facilitate the speedy taking of questions. A further practice dispenses with the reading out of the actual question, the number of the question on the Order Paper being called out instead by the Chair. The rule that notice must be given of questions and that supplementary questions must be relevant, enable each Minister to be briefed in advance by his Department which provides material for reply to the actual question and to any likely supplementary questions.

Parliamentary Questions are a simple, convenient and speedy routine, one of a number of instruments available to deputies for getting information from the Government. . . .

From October, 1956, to July, 1957, a period which covers part of the term of office of two Governments, approximately 1,800 Parliamentary Questions were tabled by Deputies of Dáil Éireann, 390 being put down by members of the Party or Parties forming the Government. Sixteen per cent of the questions from the Government side led to supplementary questions (not all directed at actions of the Government of the day) and 33⅓ per cent of those from other deputies. There were 13 adjournment debates owing to the unsatisfactory nature of the reply.

Classifying questions according to their subject matter we find that 608 questions were asked about economic matters such as unemployment, prices, finance and trade; of these, about 100 were of a purely local nature. At the other extreme there was a total of 203 questions regarding land division, arterial drainage and building of schools, nearly all these questions being of purely local interest. 497 questions were put down about local authorities and public corporations and 189 about matters which may be loosely described as relating to "administration." The remaining questions were of a miscellaneous nature. . . .

Our submission is that the parliamentary question is primarily an instrument of political debate aimed at influencing public opinion (in fact, one of a number of such instruments available to the individual deputy) and only indirectly, by means of this influence, for affecting Government action (the effect on Government action may not always be really desired, especially if it is likely to make the Government more popular!). This is most obvious in the case of questions regarding present and future policy which account for about half of all questions. The aim of questions need not necessarily be political in a party sense; the deputy may simply desire to demonstrate his personal interest in the problems of his constituents. It sometimes happens in regard to local issues that more deputies than one from the same constituency put down questions on the same subject on the same day. Questions are used in the same way to support sectional interests. It is submitted that the parliamentary question is not a very effective instrument in present circumstances. The number of questions dealt with on a typical day shows that the usual time allowed for an individual question is from one to two minutes, and the Chair will normally find it necessary to restrict the number of supplementary questions that may be asked. Any assertion made by the deputy will be printed (if they are printed) side by side with the Minister's counter assertion. The Minister usually appears to be better briefed (as one might expect) and is moreover in a superior position psychologically — he is the person deemed to have the information and can assert categorically while the deputy must put his statements in interrogative form. The Minister does not have to actively persuade, as no vote is taken — it will be sufficient if he can demonstrate *some* tenable basis for his action. Finally there is no guarantee that the necessary publicity will be forthcoming and without publicity the question has little value.

5. FINANCIAL CONTROL

(a) *The Estimates*

Document 6.5—Extracts from Bunreacht na hÉireann (Constitution of Ireland).

Article 28.

4.   3° The Government shall prepare Estimates of the Receipts and Estimates of the Expenditure of the State for each financial year, and shall present them to Dáil Éireann for consideration.

Article 17.

1.   1° As soon as possible after the presentation to Dáil Éireann under Article 28 of this Constitution of the Estimates of Receipts and the Estimates of expenditure of the State for any financial year, Dáil Éireann shall consider such Estimates.

2° Save in so far as may be provided by specific enactment in each case, the legislation required to give effect to the Financial Resolutions of each year shall be enacted within that year.

2.   Dáil Éireann shall not pass any vote or resolution, and no law shall be enacted, for the appropriation of revenue or other public moneys unless the purpose of the appropriation shall have been recommended to Dáil Éireann by a message from the Government signed by the Taoiseach.

(b) *The Comptroller and Auditor General*

Document 6.6—Extracts from Article 33 of Bunreacht na hÉireann (Constitution of Ireland).

Article 33.

1.   There shall be a Comptroller and Auditor General to control on behalf of the State all disbursements and to audit all accounts of moneys administered by or under the authority of the Oireachtas.

2.   The Comptroller and Auditor General shall be appointed by the President on the nomination of Dáil Éireann.

3.   The Comptroller and Auditor General shall not be a member of either House of the Oireachtas and shall not hold any other office or position of emolument.

4.   The Comptroller and Auditor General shall report to Dáil Éireann at stated periods as determined by law.

5.   1° The Comptroller and Auditor General shall not be removed from office except for stated misbehaviour or incapacity, and then only upon resolutions passed by Dáil Éireann and by Seanad Éireann calling for his removal. [*Remainder of S. 5 omitted.*]

6.   Subject to the foregoing, the terms and conditions of the office of Comptroller and Auditor General shall be determined by law.

(c) *The Committee of Public Accounts*

Document 6.7—Extracts from Interim and Final Reports of the Committee of Public Accounts (Appropriation Accounts, 1959-60).

1. ORDERS OF REFERENCE

22nd June, 1960:—*Ordered,* That, in pursuance of Standing Order No. 123, the Committee of Public Accounts be appointed, and that the members of the Committee be nominated by the Committee of Selection;

That the Committee have power to send for persons, papers and records;

That the Appropriation Accounts, with the Report of the Comptroller and Auditor General for the year ended 31st March, 1960, be referred to the Committee for examination and report [*Parliamentary Secretary to the Taoiseach*].

19th July, 1960:—Committee accordingly nominated consisting of Deputies Booth, Seán Browne, Carty, Cosgrave, Cunningham, Desmond, Geoghegan, Jones, Thaddeus Lynch, Moloney, O'Toole and Sheldon.

2. EXTRACT FROM FINAL REPORT

1958-59 Accounts.

Defence.

5. The Committee notes that the report of the agreement concluded at a conference in the Department in 1947 which was signed by the Chairman of the Company and the Secretary of the Department was regarded as constituting a formal agreement; but it observes that the Department obtained legal advice in 1950 that the Company could not legally be held liable for the payment of compensation to the Department in respect of its outlay on the jetty. In the circumstances the Committee must regard the initial procedure followed as unsatisfactory.

6. The Committee is perturbed to learn that the regulations relating to fire protection at all barracks and posts are considered inadequate. It trusts that a complete revision will be carried out without further delay.

Public Works and Buildings.

7. The Committee attaches importance to the maintenance and check of inventories of furniture in Embassies and Legations abroad and it notes the progress made towards this end since it commented on the subject. It expects to be informed at an early date of the completion of all the inventories.

Health.

8. The Committee notes the views of the Minister for Finance regarding the control of expenditure from voted moneys on the health services. It recognises that some latitude must be allowed to local authorities which are responsible for the administration of these services but it is concerned to ensure that the substantial sums made available by the Oireachtas are administered wisely and with due regard to economy. It welcomes the Minister's comment that the operation of recent health legislation and the administrative action which is being taken to remedy deficiencies in services should tend to produce a more uniform pattern of expenditure throughout the country.

In order that the Committee may be able to observe future trends it would like to be furnished annually with a statement of expenditure by health authorities on lines similar to those made available in Appendix XVII to its report dated 6th April, 1960. . . . [*Paragraphs 9-12 omitted.*]

1959-60 Accounts

Public Works and Buildings.

13. Two tenders for the supply of plant and equipment which were accepted on behalf of the Commissioners of Public Works were subsequently withdrawn and cancelled because the successful tenderer failed to supply the items at the quoted prices. The Commissioners were advised that the acceptance of the tenders did not constitute enforceable contracts as they were not under seal or under the hand of an authorised officer appointed under section 23 of the State Property Act, 1954. The contracts for supply were later awarded to the next lowest tenderers at an additional cost of £730. The

Committee is perturbed to learn of such haphazard procedure relating to contractual work. It notes that the defect in this instance has been remedied, but it was stated in evidence that there were many different practices and methods to be investigated and that this would be a long term process which could only be done in stages. The Committee cannot but express its dissatisfaction with the manner in which this matter is being dealt with. It would have expected that from the Commissioners' experience and the experience of other Departments a well defined procedure for the enforcement of Government contracts would have already been established and it trusts that this question will receive immediate attention.

14. Stores control and accounting records at the Central Engineering Workshops, Inchicore, have been subject to discussion and comment by the Committee in earlier reports.

In the year under review the Comptroller and Auditor General stated that a system of material control had been set up in 1954 for the compilation of limits for maximum and minimum stocks of spare parts but that it did not prove fully effective due to staffing difficulties. A survey had disclosed that spare parts to an approximate value of £50,600 were no longer required and further items valued at £45,000 were surplus to immediate requirements. It is stated that these parts were bought on the best technical advice available to the Commissioners at the time and that pending the completion of an investigation purchases are being confined to essential current and short-time requirements.

The Committee was informed that of the spare parts valued at £50,600 items valued at £5,000 were retained for transfer to other Government Departments and the balance was sold by public auction realising about 10 per cent of the book value. It notes that the organisation of the Workshops is again under investigation and that it is hoped as a result to have an effective system of stores control.

Before commenting on the circumstances in which the surplus spare parts were acquired the Committee will await the further report promised by the Accounting Officer on this matter. It is, however, gravely concerned that after nearly ten years of operation the difficulties of the earlier years have not yet been solved nor has a proper system of control been devised.

6. THE ROLE OF MEMBERS OF THE OIREACHTAS

(a) *Senator Hayes describes the situation.*

Document 6.8—Extract from a speech by Senator Michael Hayes in *Seanad Debates*, vol. 55, cols. 1685-88 (19 December 1962).

Professor Hayes: I support this Bill but the Minister did not really deal with the things that are behind the Bill. I would like to deal with them, if I may, in an objective way. The matters concerned in the Bill came within my purview when I was Ceann Comhairle of the Dáil and my sympathies always lay with Deputies who had enormous correspondence but we failed to find any remedy for the situation. The Minister has found a scheme which is really only a matter of trial and error.

The thing the public should know about this is that the expenses of the members of the Dáil arise from a complete change in the nature of the functions which now fall to the lot of a parliamentary representative. If a member of the Oireachtas had only to attend and legislate, it would be a very desirable thing but, in fact, members of the Oireachtas have an entirely different and much more onerous and less useful function. My purpose is to ask the Minister whether, in consultation with members of other Parties, he could not find some method of remedying that situation. The power of the State has increased steadily since its foundation and the social services have extended enormously. The result is that members of the Dáil are treated rather as intermediaries or messengers between their constituents and the State itself, the Civil Service and the various State bodies.

That has increased enormously the duties of Deputies and it is, to my mind, creating an onerous and extremely expensive situation, not only for Deputies themselves but also for the State. Many people first try a Fianna Fáil Deputy to get something for them if a Fianna Fáil Government is in office and, if not successful, they try a Fine Gael Deputy and, if there is an odd Labour Deputy knocking around, they try him. There is a certain amount of competition between the Parties in this matter and there is also competition between members of the same Party in the same constituency. The constituent who fails to get something from AB will then go to CD in the hope of getting something on the promise of a No. 1 vote at the next election.

I cannot see why, if Patrick Murphy is entitled to certain benefits from the State, he cannot get them in his own right and in a reasonable time, without requiring a Deputy or Senator to speak for him. I would like to see that situation brought about and I am sure the Minister would be glad to bring it about. It would save a great deal of money to the State and of labour to the members of the Dáil in particular. It would improve immeasurably the work done by both Dáil and Seanad by way of legislation.

There is a fixed notion that cannot be got out of people's heads that Deputies can get you something that you cannot get from anybody else. Deputies whose Party are in office say that the Minister is precluded from doing so and so by the statute and they get a letter from the Minister to that effect. When these Deputies are in Opposition, they say they cannot get the Minister to do what is needed. They say: "We have tried the Minister but this Minister, Ryan, above all, will not do it". That is the position and everybody here knows it. It goes even further than that. Deputies are not above saying that a man in their own Party will not do it but that they themselves will try.

The point of view held by the public about this is quite wrong. Most Deputies will tell you that they rarely get a letter which contains all the truth. The correspondent will tell only the part that suits himself and will leave out anything against him. Even as a Senator, I have had some experience of that. People put things from their own point of view and do not mention anything which is likely to take from their chances. The more experienced a public representative is, the less he is inclined to help. When a man comes to me and tells me that his daughter is up for an examination for writing assistants, as Chairman of the Civil Service Commissioners for ten years, I know that I cannot do anything for him, that the Civil Service Commissioners will deal with the matter; but there are people who will get a letter from a Department and will send it on to the constituent who will say to himself: " This fellow is doing his best for me."

I know of a Minister who went to open a golf club in his constituency on a Sunday afternoon. On the steps of the club, he met a constituent who began to tell him a long story. The Minister listened as politely as he could and then the constituent asked him: " Have you not got a piece of paper and a pencil to take down the particulars ? " He wanted the Minister to take down the particulars of his case on a Sunday afternoon on the steps of a golf club. I suggest that all this procedure is wasteful and expensive and that is one of the reasons why Deputies find the burden so great that they want postage and telephone facilities.

A Deputy has to write to his constituents and then to the Department concerned on behalf of his constituents. The Department writes back to him and, as most of us are aware, most of the Departments send out their replies with carbon copies. The Deputy sends the carbon copy to the constituent and very often the constituent starts off again with another representative, thereby repeating the whole process. I wonder whether it would be possible for the Minister, in consultation with his officials or with members of other Parties, to devise some means of restricting the number of letters and interviews, thereby lightening the burden which is being placed on members of the Dáil and Seanad.

People often comment that the seats in the Dáil are empty. Of course they are. The people who should be in them and who should be dealing with legislation are going about persecuting civil servants, telling them things the civil servants already know themselves. Some of the things are not quite true, a fact which the Deputy finds out only when he is told by the civil servants. Deputies, instead of being in the Dáil are in the Library writing piles of letters to their constituents. I have some knowledge of this but I have an objective view of it because I have been privileged never to have had this burden imposed on me. The Minister would help the economy of the State by devising some method which would reduce the number of letters and interviews Deputies have to deal with. The system is open to abuse. It is alleged at the present moment that a particular Parliamentary Secretary is using his position entirely for the benefit of his own Party. I do not know and, in a way, I do not care, but from the point of view that such a thing could be done, it is a very bad system.

(b) *The Evidence of Deputies Themselves*

Document 6.9—Extracts from evidence given by Ministers and Deputies in the case of *O'Donovan v. The Attorney General* (as reported in the *Irish Times*, 12-25 January, 1961)[1].

(i) Evidence of Minister for Local Government

Mr. MacBride — would you not agree that there is a strong body of opinion that thinks that it is undesirable that deputies should intervene in departmental affairs otherwise than through representations in the Dáil.

The Minister agreed that there was that opinion, but commented that whether that opinion was well-founded was another matter. He thought it was in the very nature of a deputy's work to interview departmental officials on behalf of constituents. By his very familiarity with legislation a deputy was in a special position to put the facts of a case, and this knowledge applied especially to borderline cases where the constituent concerned might not himself be able to place the full facts before the department, or put them to the best advantage.

When asked by Mr. MacBride what was the general view about deputies being members of county councils and other local bodies, the Minister said he did not know what the general view was, but his own view was, and he was fairly strong on it, that it would be well if deputies should be members of their own local bodies. He agreed that there was also another viewpoint. He also said that it was his experience that since he ceased being a member of the Donegal County Council his constituency work was not less.

The Minister agreed that a fair number of deputies — possibly there were 20 such — did not reside in their constituencies, and that one of the Donegal deputies resided in Dublin and had done so for a number of years. He did not agree that that showed that these deputies were well able to represent their constituencies without doing the amount of travelling he had mentioned. These deputies travelled fairly frequently to their constituencies.

By and large, he said, these deputies who do not reside in their constituencies were the older, long-established deputies who came in at a particular phase, some of whom were accepted from outside the counties that elected them. They had never resided in their constituencies and were elected possibly due to their efforts in the struggle for freedom and had been accepted

1. This was a case in which the constitutionality of the Electoral (Amendment) Act, 1959, the twelve yearly revision of constituencies demanded by the Constitution, was challenged. The appellant's claim that the ratios of members to population infringed the Constitution, by favouring rural areas as against Dublin, elicited much evidence about the work of the Deputies. Some sections of the Act were, in fact, found to be repugnant to the Constitution.—Editor.

as national figures, but that did not say that deputies elected to-day would be tolerated to live outside their constituencies — certainly not for long.

(ii) Deputy Carty's evidence

Asked about what his work for his constituents, apart from his work in the Dáil, consisted of, he said that on each Monday he had a meeting of constituents in Loughrea, where he lived. In addition to that he had meetings with his constituents on each Sunday. The meeting on the Mondays might go on from about 10 o'clock in the morning until, perhaps, eight or nine o'clock at night and on the Sunday he would be meeting constituents from about noon until about two o'clock. On the Mondays he would interview about 100 constituents and on the Sunday he would interview from 10 to 20.

On weekdays when the Dáil was not sitting he might also see from 20 to 30 people. All these constituents would call in regard to problems affecting them in one way or another. These problems might include something in regard to the Health Act; land project grants, housing grants and matters of that kind, and all these calls would entail further activities on his behalf. He would have to get in touch, either by writing or calling, with the Government department concerned or with the County Council, or, if he was in Dublin, he would have to telephone the department concerned or call to the office.

Mr. Carty said that there were 67 branches of his organisation in his constituency and he had to attend at least the annual meeting of each branch. It was of vital importance that a deputy should keep in touch with his constituents.

Mr. Butler—For what reason ?—If he wants to keep his seat; and, secondly, to hear the views of his constituents.

Mr. Carty referred to the period when part of South Galway was in the Clare constituency and said that it was almost impossible to get the people of that part of Galway to take an interest in the elections. That, he said, was true of all parties.

He did not think, he said in reply to further questions, that it would be satisfactory to combine South Galway and North Galway in one constituency. He would find a conflict of interest because of the difference in the economies of the two areas. This would be particularly so in regard to land division. The complaint in South Galway when a big farm was divided was that migrants were brought in from North Galway.

(iii) Deputy Haughey's evidence

Charles Haughey, Parliamentary Secretary to the Minister for Justice, stated, in reply to Mr. Butler, that he was one of the deputies representing the constituency of Dublin North-East, which is a five-seat constituency, and which was proposed to be a five-seat constituency under the 1959 Electoral Act. In his constituency there was a central headquarters at Amiens street, where he attended every Sunday between 12.30 p.m. and 1.30 p.m., when he was available for anyone who wanted to see him. Most of the people who wanted to see him came there, but others called to see him at Leinster House.

The number of callers on Sunday mornings would be about 12, and those at Leinster House would be about three or four a night, but the numbers varied. Apart from these calls, he would also have correspondence on behalf of his constituents. There was a number of reasons for the large disparity between the work of a city and country deputy. The Electoral Act, 1959, provided for 31 deputies for the city and county of Dublin. Under the 1947 Act, the number was 30.

From his knowledge and experience, the work of a rural deputy was three or four times at least as great as the work undertaken by a Dublin deputy. The Dublin deputy got to his work far more easily than the rural deputy, and when the Dáil was in session the Dublin deputy was right beside his constituency, whereas the country deputy was out of his constituency two or three days a week. While doing everything that he should do, and all that was expected of him, and doing it well, the Dublin deputy was not doing anything like the amount of work done by the country deputy, nor would the work be so onerous. Most Dublin deputies had full-time occupations which they could carry on. There might, of course, be the exception; but it was true of the most of them. But there were very few country deputies who could carry on a full-time occupation. It was easier for the Dublin deputy to represent his constituents, as they were organised in trade unions or other groups.

Mr. Haughey said that the Dublin deputy was able to get from these organisations the requirements of his constituents, and he was also able to obtain from them the views and outlook of his constituents in regard to various matters. This was something which the country deputy would have to find out from his constituents themselves.

Asked about disparity between country and city constituencies, he said if there was any disparity it was fully justified. The whole circumstances were such that a Dublin deputy could more easily represent a far greater number of constituents, and do it adequately, than a country deputy.

Cross-examined by Mr. McGilligan, he said that he had three years' experience as an ordinary deputy before his appointment as Parliamentary Secretary. He said that on average he had two dozen calls and wrote from 30 to 50 letters a week on behalf of constituents.

(c) *The Court interprets the Constitution*

Document 6.10—Extracts from the Judgment of Mr Justice Budd in *O'Donovan v. The Attorney General* [1961] I.R. 114.

The second conflict between the parties on the question of the construction of sub-clause 2, 3° [of Article 16], has now to be resolved. It is, perhaps, the most crucial point in the case. A principle is laid down: the ratio specified of members to population throughout the country is to be the same but with the qualification, "so far as it is practicable." The sense in which the word, "practicable," is used may be ambiguous. As to what is "practicable" depends upon the relevant circumstances. It is on the question as to what are the relevant circumstances that ambiguity may arise. In order to discover what is practicable in the circumstances thus involves determining what difficulties there are that should properly be taken into consideration having regard to that which is enjoined to be done. Having discovered what the difficulties are that exist to which legitimate regard may be had, one will then be in a position to say how far and to what extent they justify a departure from what is directed to be done. Any departure from what can properly be justified amounts to a failure to observe the principle laid down. It is on the question as to what circumstances or difficulties may legitimately be taken into consideration that the parties differ. The plaintiff says that the only difficulties that may legitimately be considered in arriving at a conclusion as to what is practicable are those relating to what may be described as the electoral system, that is to say, those involved in the administrative machinery of elections, to which I have referred in some detail when dealing with the provisions of the Electoral Acts. The defendant, on the other hand, while agreeing that these difficulties should properly be taken into consideration, says that other difficulties involving the working of the parliamentary system should also be considered in deciding what may or may not be practicable. His contention was that these matters justified a markedly greater departure from the principle of parity than mere administrative difficulties would justify. In practice, this contention meant that the exigencies of the parliamentary system demanded that some constituencies should have a greater proportion of deputies per head of the population than would be permissible if the stipulated ratio were to be strictly observed.

Having regard to what appeared to be the *prima facie* meaning of the phrase, " in so far as it is practicable," a difficult question arose as to the admissibility of evidence with regard to these matters relating to the working of the parliamentary system. Refusing to hear it would have involved deciding a most crucial point, the meaning of the qualification, against the defendant in the middle of the case. At the stage when the evidence was tendered it was difficult to say what precise bearing it might have on the case. If it could be shown that the adoption of a plan involving a close parity of ratio would make the operation of the parliamentary system unworkable, that might well be something that should be carefully reviewed when considering what was " practicable." I therefore decided, with some hesitation, to allow the evidence to be adduced.

Evidence was accordingly given on behalf of the defendant by a number of Parliamentary representatives, including a Minister and a Parliamentary Secretary, who told me of the difficulties they saw of working on any other basis than that provided by the Act of 1959, in so far as achieving a proper working of the Parliamentary system was concerned. As I believed that the plaintiff was taken by surprise by the contentions of the defendant in the matter I allowed rebutting evidence to be called by the plaintiff. A further group of deputies, including an ex-Minister, then gave evidence tending to show that an alteration in the present plan in the Act aimed at a greater degree of parity of ratio would be quite workable in their view. All these witnesses on both sides gave me every assistance in their power.

As counsel for the Attorney General said, it is not easy to summarise the difficulties arising in the working of the Parliamentary system stated in the evidence or which he submitted were relevant to consider, but briefly as I understood them they are these. It was suggested that it was part of the duties of deputies to keep continuous touch with their constituents in order to hear their views and thus be able to reflect those views and represent them properly in the Legislature and also to assist them in their everyday problems. The latter function, it was said, would involve helping them in connection with securing their legitimate rights in such matters as loans and grants to which they might be entitled and seeing that they secured the full benefit from Government schemes with regard to such matters as health, housing and agriculture. For this purpose it was often necessary, it was said, for deputies to visit Government departments in their constituents' legitimate interests. Deputies were also expected to forward the interests of their constituents with local authorities in connection with matters of interest to them administered by such authorities. It was pointed out that on the western seaboard particularly the indented coastline, large sparsely-populated areas, mountains and other geographical considerations gave rise to difficulties of communication and thus made it hard for constituents to see their deputies and for deputies to serve their constituents properly. Furthermore, deputies for these areas had to spend much time in travelling to and from Dublin where the Dáil sits. These difficulties, it was suggested, did not affect the deputies and their constituents in the Dublin area in the same way because of the ease of communication and high density of population. Moreover, it was suggested that the population in Dublin did not have occasion to make such great demands on their deputies as people in the west of the country and the loss of time in travelling did not occur. It was submitted that in order to make the parliamentary system operate properly and effectively, it was necessary to have a higher ratio of members to population on the western seaboard in order to achieve a fair equality. That is to say, it was necessary to have more deputies in these areas in relation to the population than elsewhere so that they could adequately perform their functions having regard to the difficulties that faced them.

These considerations, it was said, justified any apparent discrepancy in the ratio of members to population which might appear to exist as between the west part of the country and Dublin, such discrepancy as might exist being merely statistical and not in any way real in the practical operation of the parliamentary system. Such considerations, it was submitted, should be given careful consideration by the Court, which should appreciate that the Legislature, consisting of deputies from all over the country, was a body eminently suited to decide what was practicable and a Court should only intervene if it was clearly shown that such matters could not properly be taken into consideration by the Legislature.

It was further suggested on the part of the Attorney General that any alteration in the areas of existing constituencies, especially in the West, aimed at securing parity of ratio in the country, generally, would be impracticable as it would involve deputies in having to represent people with adverse economic interests, a different mode of life and different social outlook. It was also suggested that it was impracticable for various geographical reasons affecting communications; any changes involving taking portions of a county and adding them to another were also said to be impracticable in the parliamentary system because the population of the area added to another constituency were then deprived of the assistance of the deputies of their own county, while the deputies of their then constituency would not be in touch with the local government administration in the original county. People in " fragmented " areas, it was also alleged, lost interest in political matters.

A problem thus arises. I must determine whether or not the alleged difficulties of working the parliamentary system are relevant to consider in determining what is " practicable."

There is, it is to be observed, no direction whatsoever contained in the Constitution that these matters of difficulties of communications, differing economic interests, differing modes of life or the convenience of constituents or the difficulties of deputies or any of the other matters relied on by the defendant, should be taken into consideration when the Legislature is performing its functions in enacting the electoral laws. All of these are, in their own sphere, important matters, and if those who enacted the Constitution had intended them to be taken into consideration when the Legislature was enacting the electoral laws, pursuant to sub-clause 2 of Article 16, it is scarcely credible that they would not have said so. Most important functions are positively assigned to deputies by the Constitution, the paramount duty being that of making laws for the country. It is also for them to nominate the Taoiseach and approve the members of the Government. It will be found again, however, that the Constitution does not anywhere in the Articles relating to the functions of deputies recognise or sanction their intervention in administrative affairs. Furthermore, the indications in the Constitution are that the representation of vocational interests is a matter for the Senate, while the Dáil is to represent the entire population. No justification can thus be found in any Articles of the Constitution for regarding any of these matters as being relevant to consider when the Legislature is engaged in the legislative function of forming the constituencies with the required ratios of members to population. . . .

READING

B. Chubb: ' Going about Persecuting Civil Servants: the Role of the Irish Parliamentary Representative' in *Political Studies,* vol. 11.

B. Chubb: ' The Independent Member in Ireland ' in *Political Studies,* vol. 5.

W. J. McCracken: *Representative Government in Ireland, Dáil Eireann* 1919-1948, London, 1958.

J. C. Smyth: *The Houses of the Oireachtas,* 2nd edition, Dublin, 1964.

Chapter 7

THE OIREACHTAS, 2—MEMBERSHIP AND ELECTIONS

INTRODUCTION

Article 16 of Bunreacht na hÉireann provides for the apparatus of democratic representation in Ireland. (Document 7.1.) It covers the franchise, the composition of the Dáil, the ratio between the number of members and the population, constituency revision, the electoral system, meetings of the Dáil and the maximum duration of the Dáil. The provisions it contains follow closely those of the Irish Free State Constitution (mainly Articles 26-28) and subsequent legislation.

In one respect the system established in 1922, and continued since, was unusual — members of the Dáil are elected on 'the system of proportional representation by means of the single transferable vote' in multi-member constituencies, which is almost, if not entirely, unique so far as a national assembly is concerned. The single transferable vote system is used also for Seanad elections and for local authority elections.

The adoption of P.R. in 1922 was due to three main reasons. First, at that period, it was widely believed in Europe, where many new constitutions were being drafted, that P.R. was more advanced, indeed, more democratic, than the simple majority system. Second, as a result of the activities of the Proportional Representation Society, one particular form of P.R., the single transferable vote system, had been much publicized. It found favour with the Sinn Féin movement, and Arthur Griffith himself was a founder member of the Proportional Representation Society of Ireland. On the other side, the influential Protestant minority saw its advantage to them also. The 1914 Home Rule Act included a provision for its use in a few constituencies and, though that Act, of course, never operated, later legislation provided for its use, first for the town of Sligo, later for local authority elections generally, and, finally, under the Government of Ireland Act, 1920, for parliamentary elections. With the coming of independence, the safeguard offered by such a system became a matter of primary importance to the Unionists who sought and obtained a guarantee of proper representation including the use of P.R. The system was thus entrenched in the Irish political system where it offers an important case study in electoral methods and their effects upon political life and behaviour, all too often ignored.

To many continental students of politics, the single transferable vote system is not at all well-known. To many English and English-speaking students it appears complicated, and besides condemning it because they say it makes for unstable government and a multi-party system (not wholly borne out by Irish experience by any means), they argue that it is too difficult for the average voter. However, the arrangements in force in Ireland (Documents 7.2 to 7.4) do not in practice seem to bear out this charge either. Irish electors do not find their task, that of marking the candidates named on the ballot paper in the order of their choice, too difficult, as is shown by the fact that the number of spoiled votes is less than 1 per cent. Nor are the principles which govern the counting of the votes and ascertaining who has been elected unduly complex — they certainly seem as simple as some European systems which involve such devices as *panachage* and *apparentement*.

Nevertheless, the single transferable vote system has not found favour universally in Ireland itself. Perhaps mainly because it does not distort the proportion of seats to votes gained, does not give a substantial bonus of seats to the party which gets the most votes, and does not, of itself, much prejudice the position of small parties, it is held by some to militate against good government. In 1958 the Fianna Fáil Government proposed a constitutional amendment to replace the existing system by a simple majority system and single member constituencies. It was, as we have seen (p. 47 above), rejected at the referendum. The long debates that preceded the referendum covered all possible arguments for and against (and included many that were irrelevant). Perhaps the major arguments were among those made in the Dáil debates by the respective leaders of both sides. (Document 7.5.)

If the use of P.R. is a noteworthy feature of Irish politics, the composition of the Seanad is certainly unique. The Irish Free State Senate, as we have remarked, had a chequered career. The problems of its composition and a suitable election system were never successfully solved, and its powers to hamper a Government's measures, when they were used, proved to be its undoing. In proposing its abolition, Mr de Valera declared himself doubtful about the usefulness of second chambers in general, but since there appeared to be much opinion in favour of bi-cameralism, the Government appointed a Commission to consider the functions, powers and composition of a second House.

The difficulties of devising a satisfactory scheme for a senate in a democracy were certainly experienced by this body and in no matter were they in greater disagreement than in respect of the method of selection. One of the ideas put forward by some members (Document 7.6) was for selection of Senators on the basis of vocations, a principle at that time enjoying a particular vogue among Catholic social theorists, following upon it having been advocated by Pope Pius XI in his Encyclical *Quadragesimo Anno*. Mr de Valera, who was at the time preparing Bunreacht na hÉireann, adopted the principle in respect of the majority of his proposed Seanad. (Documents 7.7 and 7.9). His speeches (Document 7.8) make it clear that he regarded his proposals only as a step in the right direction, and indeed he provided in the Constitution for more direct vocational participation should circumstances make it possible. Certainly the composition of the panels, which separate labour from management, and the dilution of direct representation of organizations in an effort to make the system more democratic, resulted in arrangements that were far from amounting to vocational representation and, from the beginning, the predominance of party politics over vocational representation has been a feature. (Document 7.10). Curiously, the university representatives, included to compensate the universities for having lost their representation in the Dáil in 1936, might be thought to approximate more nearly to the vocational type, for they represent the universities' interests, the professional classes generally, and, in a rough way, some specific vocations—particularly the law, medicine and the church (Document 7.11).

DOCUMENTS

(1) THE DAIL

(a) *Constitutional Provisions*

Document 7.1 — Article 16 of Bunreacht na hÉireann (Constitution of Ireland).

Article 16.

1.   1° Every citizen without distinction of sex who has reached the age of twenty-one years, and who is not placed under disability or incapacity by this Constitution or by law, shall be eligible for membership of Dáil Éireann.

2° Every citizen without distinction of sex who has reached the age of twenty-one years who is not disqualified by law and complies with the provisions of the law relating to the election of members of Dáil Éireann, shall have the right to vote at an election for members of Dáil Éireann.

3° No law shall be enacted placing any citizen under disability or incapacity for membership of Dáil Éireann on the ground of sex or disqualifying any citizen from voting at an election for members of Dáil Éireann on that ground.

4° No voter may exercise more than one vote at an election for Dáil Éireann, and the voting shall be by secret ballot.

2.   1° Dáil Éireann shall be composed of members who represent constituencies determined by law.

2° The number of members shall from time to time be fixed by law, but the total number of members of Dáil Éireann shall not be fixed at less than one member for each thirty thousand of the population, or at more than one member for each twenty thousand of the population.

3° The ratio between the number of members to be elected at any time for each constituency and the population of each constituency, as ascertained at the last preceding census, shall, as far as it is practicable, be the same throughout the country.

4° The Oireachtas shall revise the constituencies at least once in every twelve years, with due regard to changes in distribution of the population, but any alterations in the constituencies shall not take effect during the life of Dáil Éireann sitting when such revision is made.

5° The members shall be elected on the system of proportional representation by means of the single transferable vote.

6° No law shall be enacted whereby the number of members to be returned for any constituency shall be less than three.

3.   1° Dáil Éireann shall be summoned and dissolved as provided by section 2 of Article 13 of this Constitution.

2° A general election for members of Dáil Éireann shall take place not later than thirty days after a dissolution of Dáil Éireann.

4.   1° Polling at every general election for Dáil Éireann shall as far as practicable take place on the same day throughout the country.

2° Dáil Éireann shall meet within thirty days from that polling day.

5.   The same Dáil Éireann shall not continue for a longer period than seven years from the date of its first meeting: a shorter period may be fixed by law.

6.   Provision shall be made by law to enable the member of Dáil Éireann who is the Chairman immediately before a dissolution of Dáil Éireann to be deemed without any actual election to be elected a member of Dáil Éireann at the ensuing general election.

7.   Subject to the foregoing provisions of this Article, elections for membership of Dáil Éireann, including the filling of casual vacancies, shall be regulated in accordance with law.

(b) *The Election System.*

Document 7.2 — Extracts from Electoral Act, 1963 (No. 19).

FRANCHISE

5.—(1) A person shall be entitled to be registered as a Dáil elector in a constituency if he has reached the age of twenty-one years and he was, on the qualifying date—

    (*a*) a citizen of Ireland, and

    (*b*) ordinarily resident in that constituency.

(2) (*a*) A person shall be entitled to be registered as a local government elector in a local electoral area if he has reached the age of twenty-one years and—

        (i) he was, on the qualifying date, ordinarily resident in that area, or

        (ii) he has, during the whole of the period of six months ending on the qualifying date, occupied, as owner or tenant, any land or premises in that area.

        [*Remaining Sub-sections omitted.*]

REGISTRATION OF ELECTORS

6.—(1) A register by reference to registration areas consisting of administrative counties and county boroughs shall be prepared and published in every year of persons who were entitled to be registered as electors on the qualifying date and, in so far as it relates to Dáil electors, the register shall be the register of Dáil electors and, in so far as it relates to persons entitled to vote at local elections, it shall be the register of local government electors. [*SSs. 2 and 3 omitted.*]

7.—(1) It shall be the duty of each council of a county and corporation of a county borough to prepare and publish the register of electors in accordance with regulations made by the Minister, after consultation with the Minister for Justice, and references in this Part of this Act to the registration authority shall be construed accordingly. [*Remaining Sub-sections omitted.*]

8.—(1) An appeal shall lie to the Circuit Court from any decision on any claim or objection which has been considered under the regulations under section 7 of this Act. [*Remaining Sub-sections and S. 9 omitted.*]

DURATION OF DAIL

10.—The same Dáil shall not continue for a longer period than five years from the date of its first meeting.

RETURNING OFFICERS

11.—(1) The returning officer for a constituency shall be—

    (*a*) in case the whole of the constituency is situate in a county or county borough for which there is a sheriff—the sheriff, (*b*) in case part of the constituency is situate in a county borough and part in a county and there is a sheriff for the county borough and a sheriff for the county—such one of the sheriffs as the Minister appoints from time to time,

(*c*) in any other case—the county registrar or, where part of the constituency has one county registrar and part another county registrar or parts other county registrars, such one of the county registrars as the Minister appoints from time to time.

[*Remaining Sub-sections omitted.*]

WRITS

12.—(1) Where the Dáil is dissolved, the Clerk of Dáil Éireann shall, immediately upon the issue of the Proclamation dissolving the Dáil, issue a writ to each returning officer for a constituency directing him to cause an election to be held of the full number of members of the Dáil to serve in the Dáil for that constituency.

(2) Where a vacancy occurs in the membership of the Dáil by a person ceasing to be a member otherwise than in consequence of a dissolution, the Chairman of Dáil Éireann (or, where he is unable through illness, absence or other cause, to fulfil his duties, the Deputy Chairman of Dáil Éireann) shall, as soon as he is directed by the Dáil to do so, direct the Clerk of Dáil Éireann to issue a writ to the returning office for the constituency in the representation of which the vacancy has occurred directing the returning officer to cause an election to be held of a member of the Dáil to fill the vacancy mentioned in the writ. [*Remaining Sub-sections omitted.*]

REGISTRAR OF POLITICAL PARTIES

13.—(1) (*a*) The person who for the time being holds the office of Clerk of Dáil Éireann shall be the Registrar of Political Parties for the purposes of this section.

(*b*) If and so long as the office of Clerk of Dáil Éireann is vacant or the holder of that office is unable through illness, absence or other cause to fulfil his duties, the Clerk-Assistant of Dáil Éireann shall act as Registrar of Political Parties for the purposes of this section.

(*c*) In the subsequent subsection of this section, "the Registrar" means the Registrar of Political Parties for the purposes of this section or the Clerk Assistant of Dáil Éireann acting as such Registrar (as may be appropriate).

(2) The Registrar shall prepare and maintain a register (to be known as the Register of Political Parties) in which, subject to the subsequent provisions of this section, he shall register any political party—

(*a*) which applies to him for registration, and

(*b*) which is in his opinion,—

(i) a genuine political party, and

(ii) is organised to contest a Dáil election or a local election.

(3) The following particulars shall be entered in the Register of Political Parties in respect of a political party registered therein:

    (*a*) the name of the party,

    (*b*) the address of the party's headquarters,

    (*c*) the name or names of the officer or officers of the party authorised to sign certificates authenticating the candidature of candidates of the party at elections.

(4) Immediately on setting up the Register of Political Parties, the Registrar shall register therein the parties then represented in the Dáil by the names by which they are commonly known and shall complete each such registration by inserting the particulars referred to in paragraphs (*b*) and (*c*) of subsection (3) of this section on being informed thereof.

(5) A political party shall not be registered in the Register of Political Parties if its name—

    (*a*) is identical with the name of any party already registered in the Register of Political Parties or, in the opinion of the Registrar, so nearly resembles such name as to be calculated to mislead, confuse or deceive,

    (*b*) is, in the opinion of the Registrar, unnecessarily long, or

    (*c*) in the case of a party operating in relation to a particular part only of the State, does not include such reference to that part as, in the opinion of the Registrar, distinguishes the party as so operating.

(6) A political party registered in the Register of Political Parties shall from time to time keep the Registrar informed as to the name or names of the officer or officers referred to in paragraph (*c*) of subsection (3) of this section.

(7) The Registrar shall, with respect to each party registered in the Register of Political Parties, enquire at least once in each year, by letter sent by post to an officer of the party referred to in paragraph (*c*) of subsection (3) of this section, whether the party desires to remain registered and, unless he receives an affirmative reply to such an enquiry within twenty-one days from the date of the posting of the letter containing the enquiry, he shall cancel the registration of the party concerned.

(8) (*a*) Any doubt, dispute or question which may arise in connection with the Register of Political Parties shall be decided by an appeal board.

    (*b*) The appeal board shall consist of a Judge of the High Court (to be nominated by the President of the High Court), who shall be chairman, the Chairman of Dáil Éireann (or, where he is unable, through illness, absence or other cause to fulfil his duties, the Deputy Chairman of Dáil Éireann) and the Chairman of Seanad Éireann, (or, where he is unable, through illness, absence or other cause to fulfill his duties, the Deputy Chairman of Seanad Éireann).

    (*c*) A decision of the appeal board shall be complied with by the Registrar.

RE-ELECTION OF OUTGOING CHAIRMAN OF DAIL EIREANN

14.—(1) Where the Dáil is dissolved and the outgoing Chairman of Dáil Éireann has not announced to the Dáil before the dissolution that he does not desire to become a member of the Dáil at the general election consequent on the dissolution, he shall be deemed without any actual election to be elected at such general election as a member of the Dáil for—

(a) the constituency for which he was a member of the Dáil immediately before the dissolution, or

(b) if a revision of constituencies takes effect on the dissolution, the constituency declared on the revision to correspond to the constituency mentioned in the foregoing paragraph.

(2) Where an outgoing Chairman of Dáil Éireann is deemed by virtue of this section to be elected at a general election as a member of the Dáil for a particular constituency, the number of members actually elected at that general election for that constituency shall be one less than would otherwise be required.

(3) In this section " outgoing Chairman of Dáil Éireann " means a person who, immediately before the dissolution of the Dáil in relation to which the expression is used, was the Chairman of Dáil Éireann. [*S. 15 omitted.*]

BALLOT PAPER

16.—(1) The following section is hereby substituted for section 26 of the Principal Act:

" 26. Votes at a Dáil election shall be given by ballot, and the ballot of each voter shall consist of a paper (in this Act called a ballot paper) in form 5A in Part III of the Fifth Schedule to this Act."

(2) The form and directions set out in Part II of the Second Schedule to this Act are hereby inserted in Part III of the Fifth Schedule to the Principal Act after form 5, and the returning officer shall comply with such directions. [*S. 17 omitted.*]

NOMINATIONS

18.—At a Dáil election the last day for receiving nominations shall be the last day of the period which consists of the nine days (disregarding any excluded day) next following the day on which the writ or writs for the election is or are issued. [*S. 19 omitted.*]

DEPOSITS BY CANDIDATES

20.—The following section is hereby substituted for section 20 of the Principal Act:

" 20—(1) A candidate at a Dáil election, or someone on his behalf, shall deposit with the returning officer before the expiration of the time appointed for receiving nominations the sum of one hundred pounds, and, if he fails to do so, his candidature shall be deemed to be withdrawn." [*S. 21 omitted.*]

POLLING DISTRICTS AND PLACES

22.—(1) The council of a county or corporation of a county borough may, after consultation with the returning officer for Dáil elections in respect of the county or county borough and in accordance with regulations made by the Minister, make a scheme dividing the county or county borough into polling districts for the purpose of Dáil elections and elections of members of local authorities within the meaning of Part VI of this Act and appointing a polling place for each polling district. [*Remaining Sub-sections omitted.*]

POLLING CARDS

23.—(1) Where a poll is to be taken at a Dáil election in a constituency, the returning officer shall send to every elector whose name is on the register of Dáil electors for the constituency and is not on the postal voters list a card (in this section referred to as a polling card) in the form specified by regulations made by the Minister informing him of his number (including polling district letter) on the register of Dáil electors and of the place at which he will be entitled to vote. [*Remaining Sub-sections omitted.*]

TIMES OF POLL

24.—(1) A poll at a Dáil election—

    (*a*) shall be taken on such day as shall be appointed by the Minister by order, being a day during the period which consists of the nine days (disregarding any excluded day) next following the period which consists of the seven days (disregarding any excluded day) next following the last day for receiving nominations, and

    (*b*) shall continue for such period, not being less than twelve hours, between the hours of 8.30 a.m. and 10.30 p.m. as may be fixed by the Minister by order, subject to the restriction that, in the case of a general election, he shall fix the same period for all constituencies.

    [*Remaining Sub-sections and Ss. 25-33 omitted.*]

ADVANCE POLLING ON ISLANDS

34.—(1) This section applies where—

    (*a*) a poll is to be taken at a Dáil election in a constituency, and

    (*b*) the returning officer is of opinion that, in the case of a polling station situate on an island, it is probable that, owing to stress of weather or transport difficulties, either

        (i) the poll could not be taken on the polling day appointed by the Minister, or

        (ii) If the poll were taken on that day, the ballot boxes could not reach the place for the counting of the votes at or before the hour of 9 a.m. on the day next after the polling day.

(2) Where this section applies, the returning officer shall give public notice in the polling district stating that he will take the poll at the polling station on the island on a specified day, being a day earlier than the polling day

appointed by the Minister and later than the sixth day before the said polling day, and the following provisions shall, notwithstanding anything contained in the Principal Act, have effect:

(a) the returning officer may take the poll at the polling station on the island on the day specified in the notices or, where he is of opinion that, owing to stress of weather, the poll cannot be taken on that day, on the first day after that day on which in his opinion transport between the island and the mainland is reasonably safe.

(b) where owing to transport difficulties the poll cannot begin at the hour fixed by the Minister for the commencement of the poll, it shall begin as soon as possible after that hour,

(c) where, after the polling has continued for not less than four hours, the presiding officer is of opinion that, if the poll were further continued, the ballot boxes could not reach the place for the counting of the votes at or before the hour of 9 a.m. on the day next after the polling day appointed by the Minister, he may then close the poll.

[*Remaining Sub-sections and S. 35 omitted.*]

THE COUNT

36.—(1) The following Rule is hereby substituted for Rule 2 of the Third Schedule to the Principal Act:

"2. Any ballot paper—

(a) which does not bear the official mark, or

(b) on which the figure 1 standing alone is not placed at all or is not so placed as to indicate a first preference for some candidate, or

(c) on which the figure 1 standing alone indicating a first preference is set opposite the name of more than one candidate, or

(d) on which anything except the number on the back is written or marked by which the voter can be identified.

shall be invalid and not counted, but the ballot paper shall not be invalid by reference only to carrying the words 'one', 'two', 'three' (and so on) or a mark such as 'X' which, in the opinion of the returning officer, clearly indicates a preference or preferences."

[*Remaining Sub-sections and Ss. 37-40 omitted.*]

41.—(1) The following Rules are hereby substituted for Rules 29 to 33 of Part I of the Fifth Schedule to the Principal Act:

" 29. The candidates may respectively appoint agents to attend the counting of the votes and the name and address of every agent so appointed shall be transmitted to the returning officer two clear days at least before the polling day. Not more than five agents shall be appointed by a candidate unless the returning officer otherwise permits.

30. (1) The returning officer shall provide suitable accommodation and all equipment necessary for counting the votes and shall count the votes at a place within the constituency but—

(*a*) in case the constituency consists of a part which is part of a county borough and a part which is outside that borough, the returning officer may provide the accommodation and equipment and count the votes—

    (i) at a place within the other part of that borough, or

    (ii) with the consent of the Minister, at a place outside that borough and outside, but convenient to, the constituency,

(*b*) in any other case, the returning officer may, with the consent of the Minister, provide the accommodation and equipment and count the votes at a place outside, but convenient to, the constituency.

(2) One clear day at least before the day fixed for the commencement of the poll the returning officer shall give to the election agent of each candidate notice in writing of the place at which he will count the votes. He shall give the agents of candidates all such reasonable facilities for overseeing the proceedings at the count (including, in particular, facilities for satisfying themselves that the ballot papers are correctly sorted), and all such information with respect thereto, as he can give them consistently with the orderly conduct of the proceedings and the performance of his functions.

31. The returning officer, his assistants and clerks, members of the Garda Síochána on duty, and the agents of the candidates whose names and addresses have been given to the returning officer under Rule 29 hereof, and no other person, except with the permission of the returning officer, may be present at the counting of the votes.

32. At the hour of 9 a.m. on the day after the close of the poll and at the place for the counting of the votes, the returning officer shall, in the presence of the agents of the candidates, open the ballot boxes, count and record the number of ballot papers therein and proceed to verify the ballot paper account accompanying each ballot box. He shall then mix together the whole of the ballot papers contained in the ballot boxes. The returning officer, while counting and recording the number of ballot papers, shall keep the ballot papers with their faces upwards and shall take all proper precautions for preventing any person from seeing the numbers printed on the backs of such papers.

33. After compliance with Rule 32 hereof the returning officer shall forthwith begin to count the votes and shall, so far as practicable, proceed continuously with the counting of the votes allowing only time for refreshment, and excluding (except so far as he and the candidates otherwise agree) the hours between 11 p.m. and 9 a.m. on the succeeding morning. During the excluded time the returning officer shall place the ballot boxes and documents relating to the election under his own seal and shall take proper precautions for the security of such boxes and documents."

[*Remaining Sections omitted.*]

SECOND SCHEDULE

PART II

5A

FORM OF BALLOT PAPER

(*Front of Paper*)

Counterfoil No................	Marcáil ord do rogha sna spáis seo síos.	
	Mark order of preference in spaces below.	Marc Oifigiúil. Official Mark. →
		DOYLE—WORKERS PARTY. (James Doyle, of 10 High Street, Builder).
Voter's No. on register.		LYNCH—DEMOCRATS. (Jane Ellen Lynch, of 12 Main Street. Grocer.)
Letter. | No.		O'BRIAIN—CUMANN NA SAORANACH (Séamus O'Briain, ó 10 An tSráid Ard, Oide Scoile.)
		O'BRIEN, EAMON (Barrister)—NON-PARTY. (Eamon O'Brien, of 22 Wellclose Place, Barrister.)
		O'BRIEN, EAMON (Solicitor)—YOUNG IRELAND. (Eamon O'Brien, of 102 Eaton Brae, Ranelagh, Solicitor.)
		O'CONNOR—NATIONAL LEAGUE. (Charles O'Connor, of 7 Green Street, Gentleman.)
		THOMPSON—FARMERS PARTY. (William Henry Thompson, of Dereen Park, Farmer.)

TREORACHA

I. Féach chuige go bhfuil an marc oifigiúil ar an bpáipéar.
II. Scríobh an figiúr 1 le hais ainm an chéad iarrthóra is rogha leat, an figiúr 2 le hais do dhara rogha, agus mar sin de.
III. Fill an páipéar ionas nach bhfeicfear do vóta. Taispeáin *cúl an pháipéir* don oifigeach ceannais, agus cuir sa bhosca ballóide é.

INSTRUCTIONS

I. See that the official mark is on the paper.
II. Write 1 beside the name of the candidate of your first choice 2 beside your second choice, and so on.
III. Fold the paper to conceal your vote. Show *the back of the paper* to the presiding officer and put it in the ballot box.

(*Back of Paper*)

No. ....

Election for Constituency of ....

(c) *The Counting of Votes*

Document 7.3—Extract from Michael Lawless, 'The Dáil Electoral System' in *Administration*, vol 5.

The returning officer must, before he begins the counting, give notice to the agents of the candidates of the time and place at which he will carry out the count. The returning officer, his assistants and clerks, and the candidates and their agents and no other person, except with the sanction of the returning officer, are entitled to be present at the counting of the votes. The idea of this is to prevent any disturbance during the process of counting. The returning officer commences the work of counting by assembling the ballot boxes, breaking the seal on each and checking the number of ballot papers in it with the returns of ballot papers furnished by the presiding officers in charge of the polling stations. The ballot papers are mixed together thoroughly and any invalid papers rejected. The ballot papers are arranged in parcels according to the first preference recorded for each candidate and counted. The returning officer records on a result sheet the number of first preferences for each candidate and the total number of valid votes. The next step is to ascertain what is known as the quota. The quota is the smallest number of votes which will, for a certainty, secure the election of a candidate and it is the key to the whole system of counting.

The quota is got by dividing the total number of valid votes by a number equal to the number of vacancies to be filled plus one and then adding one to the result of this division—any fractional remainder being disregarded. At first sight it might appear that the quota should be got by dividing the total number of votes by the number of vacancies and not by the number of vacancies plus one. In fact, in the early days of proportional representation this was the practice. If there is only one vacancy to be filled it is obvious that a candidate who obtains just over half the votes should be elected. It would be absurd to require him to have any greater support than a majority of the electorate. Suppose, to take another example, there were three seats to be filled and that the total poll was 100. It may seem that in this case a candidate has to get 34 votes to be elected but 34 is more than enough. The result obtained by dividing 100 by one more than the number of seats to be filled, that is, by dividing 100 by 4, and then adding one to the result is 26. If 3 candidates each get 26 votes they will have in all 78 votes. This leaves 22 to be shared by all the other candidates. Therefore, if each of 3 candidates gets 26 then they each get more than any other candidate could get even if he got all the remaining votes. We can see from this that the maximum number of candidates who can get the quota is equal to the number of seats to be filled.

Having ascertained the quota and entered it on the result sheet the returning officer then examines the number of first preferences received by each candidate. Any candidate who has received a number of votes equal to or greater than the quota is declared elected. Let us assume first, that say 2 candidates, A and B, have received more than the quota. The first and obvious step is to transfer the surplus votes of A and B. By surplus votes is meant the number of votes by which the total number of votes credited to a candidate exceeds the quota. If A has a greater surplus than B then A's surplus is transferred first. In transferring A's surplus the returning officer has to see that it is transferred proportionately to the candidates for whom a second preference is given. To achieve this the returning officer goes through all A's papers and arranges them in the order of the second preferences indicated on them. He makes a separate parcel of non-transferable papers, that is, papers on which a second preference for a candidate still in the running is not recorded. If on some of A's papers a second preference is recorded for B this preference is ignored because B is already elected and the next available preference is taken into account. The votes of A which are to be transferred are taken from the parcels of transferable votes. The total number to be transferred is equal to the surplus and the number of votes to be taken from each parcel of transferable votes is got by the formula: —

$$\frac{\text{surplus}}{\text{No of transferable votes}} \times \text{No of papers in the parcel}$$

It follows that the number of votes to be left behind in the parcels of transferable votes plus the number of non-transferable votes must equal the quota. A holds on to this quota throughout the counting. We have seen how the number of votes to be taken from each parcel is calculated. The actual votes to be taken and transferred are taken from the top of each parcel. If, say, on 100 of A's first preference votes there is a second preference for C and if, say, 20 votes are to be transferred to C under the formula, then the top 20 votes on C's parcel are selected. There is an element of chance here because the distribution of the third and later preferences in the 20 votes selected may not be the same as in the whole of the parcel. This element of chance is largely theoretical because when the number of votes concerned is large, as happens generally, and when the votes prior to counting have been thoroughly mixed, it is safe to assume that the votes selected from the top of a parcel will be characteristic of the whole parcel.

This disposes of A's surplus. B's surplus is similarly dealt with. It will be remembered that A's surplus was greater than B's and that A's surplus was transferred before B's. We can see the reason for this now. Let us suppose, to take a simple case, that all A's supporters gave their second preferences to C and that all B's supporters gave their second preferences to D and suppose that C and D were within a few votes of election. Now the instructions given by the voters were that their votes were to be used for the election of the candidate to whom they gave their No 1 vote but that in the event of his already having received sufficient votes or having so few that he had no chance of election, these votes were to be transferred to the candidates indicated by the No 2 preferences. Now obviously A's votes must be transferred to C before B's can be transferred to D because C's supporters are greater in number and, therefore, carry more weight.

If when the surplus of A and B is transferred both C and D have reached the quota, the next step is to transfer the surplus of C and D.

In transferring the votes of C and D the original votes they received, that is, their own first preferences are not touched. The surplus is transferred from the parcel which they received from A or B. Suppose, say, C received 1,000 first preference votes and that he got 300 more from A and that the quota was 1,100. Then 200 votes must be transferred from the parcel of 300 votes which C received from A. C will retain his original 1,000 votes and 100 out of 300 votes he received from A.

If the returning officer reaches a stage when he can make no further transfers of surpluses then he must transfer the votes of the lowest candidate to the next available preference recorded on the papers. In transferring these votes a preference for a candidate already elected is ignored and account is taken of the next preference.

It is not necessary for every candidate to obtain the quota in order to be elected. A common case which arises in practice is in a five-member constituency where, say, four candidates get the quota with two still in the running. The returning officer declares the higher of these two candidates elected and this completes the counting.

(d) *Number of members and constituencies*

Document 7.4—Table taken from J. C. Smyth, *Houses of the Oireachtas*, Institute of Public Administration, Dublin, 1964 (Some additions made by Editor).

Electoral Act	No. of Constitu- encies	Constituencies returning							Total No. of members
		9	8	7	6	5	4	3	
1923	30	1	3	5	–	9	4	8	153
1935	34	–	–	3		8	8	15	138
1947	40	–	–	–	–	9	9	22	147
1959[1]	*39*	–	–	–	·	*9*	*9*	*21*	*144*
1961	38	–	–	–	–	9	12	17	144

1. Some sections of this Act were held to be repugnant to the Constitution and it never operated. The scheme it envisaged was replaced by that laid out in the 1961 Act. — Editor.

(e) *The Proposal to Replace the P.R. System*

Document 7.5—Extracts from the Debate on The Third Amendment to the Constitution Bill, 1958, in *Dáil Debates,* vol. 171, cols. 994-1018 (22 November, 1958).

Mr de Valera: . . . The position is that P.R. has not, in my opinion, in recent times worked out well. As has been pointed out more than once, and as the Leader of the Opposition pointed out when this matter of the Constitution was being discussed, it worked very well for a time, because there were issues so large in the public eye that they dominated all other issues and, therefore, the people voted on one side or the other because these issues were there. That continued fairly well up to 1938. A year afterwards we had the war, and during the war the main aim of trying to maintain the neutrality of this country was in the people's minds. But, even during the war, it needed two elections to get the stability which was required. Some of this stability was acquired rather in spite of the system.

Fianna Fáil came into office in 1932. It was by far the biggest Party. It had not an overall majority. It got the support of another Party up to a certain time, but then a time came when the other Party tried to use its position for pressure. This was going to mean that it was not the policy of the major Party that was going to be the policy of the country but a policy dictated by a smaller Party. Such being the position, we felt that the people should decide the matter and we had an election in 1933 which did give the overall majority — but the overall majority was got only after two elections.

A similar position arose in 1937. We had a general election in that year and, again, although Fianna Fáil was returned by far the largest Party, it did not have an over-all majority and, again, in order to get the strength and the stability to carry out our programme, we had to go to the people a second time. In 1943 and 1944, the same was the position. We went to the country in 1943. We did not get an over-all majority, but we were returned by far the largest Party. In order to get the stability and the power to carry out our policy, we had to go to the electorate a second time, and in 1944 we got the majority.

In 1948, we were returned again by far the largest Party. My recollection is that Fianna Fáil at that time had more members returned than all the other organised Parties put together, but the other groups, no doubt, thought — I suppose there was a certain amount of fair ground for their thinking — that if we carried on as a Government and if again we found that we were unable to do our work, to carry out our programme, because of an insufficient number, we would again appeal to the electorate. I have no doubt whatever that, had we been in and had there been a second election in 1948, we would again have got the power, but we required in each case two elections to secure it.

The whole effect of the present system of P.R. has been to cause multiplicity of Parties. I will give the Leader of the Opposition praise for having sufficient foresight at the time when he was opposing putting the single transferable vote into the Constitution. He said much as I have said up to the present, that is, that we should not assume that, because it had worked during the years up to that time, it would work out in that way in future when no dominant issue would be before the people. He said, very rightly, that it leads to the multiplicity of Parties and it would do so here and instanced the type of Parties that might grow up. . . .

When we go to an election, what do we go to the people for ? As anybody who has read or made any speeches knows, the main question before the people at the time of an election is what sort of Government they will have for the succeeding five years, what sort of policy they will have. As I have said already, one of the chief features of this system is that it leads to multiplicity of Parties. With the present system, there is multiplicity of Parties, each little group trying to get some support, knowing full well that they have not the slightest chance, independently, of being the Government. Yet, they can go out and promise, for that very reason, knowing that it will get them some votes.

They have not the responsibility that a Party would have that felt they would have to implement the policy which they put before the people. They can promise anything they choose. They can get some votes for it — the extreme right on one side and the extreme left on the other — and then, although they have been preaching quite contradictory policies, when the elections are over and the people can no longer be spoken to, they can come in and unite. Under the system of straight voting, they will have to unite beforehand, not after. They will have to unite in front of the people.

This does not cut off the possibility of Parties. You can have Parties all right. Sectional interests, of course, can organise and can put themselves in the strongest position to make an impression upon the various constituencies, but, when they do that, if they want to get a majority, they must try to think of the central, common good and not their own sectional interests, because their sectional interests may be small. If they want to join with other people, they can do so. They can form a combined group before an election. During the time the Coalition were here, I suggested they should do that beforehand, and put their combined policy to the people, so that the people would know the alternatives they would have to face. That was not done. It was much better, in their opinion, to wait until each one promised the most contradictory things, the right getting the most support from the most conservative section and the left getting its support from the most radical section, if I may use that word, and the two of them combining afterwards to make a certain bargain behind the backs of the people.

The system of straight voting compels that bargaining to be done in front of the people. There must be a candidate chosen who will be acceptable to all the groups and, therefore, the people, when they are voting, will know better what the candidates stand for, for whom they are voting. That system makes for two groups, the Government and the Opposition, and in the Opposition the people can see an alternative to a Government, if they are dissatisfied with the existing one.   The rival policies of each will have to be aimed at the common good so far as those policies are to appeal to the majority of the people, and each will have to have regard not merely to sectional interests.   It is easy, of course, to talk about the advantages of the representation of minorities, but a great deal of that is illusory.   It is all right on paper, but when it comes to the practical working out of politics, we all know that that does not work at all. . . .

Speaking of the Protestant minorities in the country, I suppose they are scattered and, if you were prepared to give P.R. to them, you would have to take the whole country as one constituency, but, wherever they happen to be in a majority, they will undoubtedly get representation.   It is far better, I would suggest, and it has shown itself here, that groups like that should be represented in the individual Parties rather than to put themselves apart as a separate and distinct element in the community.

As I have said, the main feature of the straight vote is that it is an integrating influence, whereas the other is a disintegrating influence. We have reason enough, goodness knows, for forming groups and Parties without, so to speak, being encouraged by our fundamental system to do so. I have great pleasure, therefore, in asking for a Second Reading of this Bill.

Mr. J. A. Costello: I move the amendment standing in the names of myself and Deputy Mulcahy: —

2. To delete all words after the word "That" and substitute therefor the words: —

Dáil Éireann, believing that the abolition of the system of Proportional Representation

1. will interfere with the legitimate rights of minorities,
2. is contrary to our democratic traditions,
3. is likely to lead to unrepresentative parliaments and to arrogant government,
4. will make more difficult the ending of Partition,
5. has not been demanded by public opinion, and,
6. therefore, in present world conditions and in our economic circumstances will impair rather than assist the solution of our national problems,

refuses to give a Second Reading to the Bill; and recommends instead that for the purpose of informing public opinion an expert commission be established to examine and report on the present electoral system. . . . .

We have had experience in this country for 36 years of the present system of voting. It is due to the people to say that their political education has advanced to such a point that they fully understand the working of this electoral system and have, on the whole, very intelligently made their wishes known through the instrumentality of that system. At least, we have had experience of 36 years of its working. In the course of his remarks today, the Taoiseach said that such a system leads to a multiplicity of Parties and to bargaining between Parties. He says that the electorate do not know what political groups or Parties may come together to form a Government—as they did on two occasions in recent years—that their policy should be put before the people, that the people should know it and have it out in public.

Whatever may be said about the formation of the first inter-Party Government—and very little, if anything, can be said—there can be no doubt whatever that, in the 1954 election, the people were told that we, as Fine Gael, were going to combine with any Party that would combine with us to form a Government, and even the Taoiseach recognised, immediately the result was declared, that what the electorate at that time had declared for and wanted was an inter-Party Government and that they had given a sufficient majority to enable it to be carried out. Here was an intelligent electorate, having it put before them that there was likely to be an inter-Party Government with, as the Taoiseach said, some of the Parties going around putting forward their own particular policies: but at all events, the electorate, knowing that was going to happen, made it very clear, as the Taoiseach admitted at the time, that what they wanted at that time, after the experience of the Fianna Fáil Government from 1948 to 1951 [sic][1], was an inter-Party Government.

When the electorate wanted to give the Fianna Fáil Party a majority, they did so. They gave Mr. W. T. Cosgrave an overall majority for ten years. They changed when they thought conditions permitted them to change and they let Fianna Fáil in. They gave the Fianna Fáil Party an overall majority on several occasions when they wanted to do so. I think we are entitled to say —and the people are entitled to get credit for it—that the electorate are sufficiently educated politically and intelligent enough to be able to work this system in the way they want to work it and wish to have it worked. . . .

We are in existence as a State for only 36 years. We have not had the time—and the conditions under which the institutions of this State have been built up and developed since 1922 have been such that we have not been able—to create, form and foster those political traditions which are of such inestimable value in maintaining public respect and veneration for the public institutions of the State. We have formed some traditions and those we must foster, keep, and safeguard. One of the few traditions we have is that of dealing fairly with minorities and, when I say dealing fairly with minorities, I do not confine that phrase merely to religious minorities. I mean minorities of every kind. Our tradition is to give them full representation in the Parliament of the Irish people. These are our traditions.

Mr. Dillon: Hear, hear!

Mr. J. A. Costello: We should hold on fast to that tradition. If this Bill is passed and if it be—as I believe it will not be—sanctioned by the referendum, then we are throwing away one of those valuable traditions which have been of inestimable value to us, which have made this country a headline outside, as a democratic country dealing fairly, not merely with minorities in the sense of religious minorities, but with minorities of all kinds and all sections. If we are to change this system, or if we are to amend it—and it is capable of improvement and adjustment, and has, in fact, evolved in some way: I suppose

---

[1] Deputy Costello presumably meant to say 'from 1951 to 1954'.

the Taoiseach would at least say it has given additional strength and stability to Government formed under it—there are ways of dealing with this matter. There are ways of improving the system and, perhaps, giving additional methods by means of which strengthened Government can be achieved, not-withstanding all the fears uttered by the Taoiseach in the course of his remarks today and other times; but why go to the radical extremes that this Bill does?

We should, if we wish to change the electoral system—and subsequently I shall have to point out one method by which that can be done—if it is to be done at least we should make the change in accordance with our traditions and within the system itself. . . .

Now because Fianna Fáil have been beaten twice under the system, they want to try, if they can, to ensure that they will never be beaten again and incidentally, the net result may be, though I do not say it will be—Deputies have to consider the possible results as well as the probable results—the end of political democracy as we know it in this country because the results of the operations of this particular electoral system advocated by the Government will almost certainly, in existing conditions, have the effect of doing away with all except a very small section of parliamentary opposition.

Parliamentary democracy cannot work without an Opposition and not just an Opposition that is allowed to talk merely when the Government thinks right, but an Opposition that is effective, that can make its will known and make its voice heard throughout the country and that can stop corruption, in-justice and inefficiency. Unless you have an Opposition capable of doing that job—and it is not capable of doing its job, unless it can form an alternative Government—then we will have nothing but arrogant Government tending to dictatorship. I am quite well aware that it is probably highly likely, even under the system proposed, that the electorate will be so disgusted with Fianna Fáil that there will be such an election as will root Fianna Fáil out of office.

As I said on Sunday in Carlow, even though that may be to the political advantage of Fine Gael, and even though it may be that Fine Gael would get, sooner than people expect, an overall majority as a Government, nevertheless we stand by our traditions and by the example of those who founded our Party. We wish that all minorities should get their proper representation in this Parliament because we are convinced that the true interests of the Irish people lie in such an arrangement. . . .

2. THE SEANAD

(a) *The Principle of Vocational Representation*
    Document 7.6 — Extracts from *Report of the Second House of the Oireachtas Commission, 1936.*

20. It was in regard to the method of selecting the members of the Second House that the greatest diversity of opinion prevailed. While the proposals

made to the Commission—with one exception—included nomination as a method for obtaining a part of the membership of the Second House, the proposals differed as to the number to be so obtained, and, principally, as to the method by which the remaining members were to be selected. The main proposals for constituting the House—other than the proposals embodied in this Report—may be summarised as follows: — [*Proposals (i)-(iii) omitted.*]

(iv) That it should be, in part, nominated, and, in part, elected by a system of Vocational Election; . . .

27. A proposal which recommended itself to some members of the Commission was, that a proportion of the Second House be selected on the basis of vocations or occupations, but these members did not reach a scheme which satisfied a majority of the Commission to recommend to you.

It is to be noted, however, that a selection of members of the Second House on a basis of vocations or occupations was not contemplated for the purpose of making the Second House a body to represent such vocations or occupations in the discharge of the functions and powers of the Second House, but rather that it might be possible by selecting for a Panel persons who had attained positions of responsibility and distinction in their own particular vocations or occupations to afford a wide choice of persons certainly qualified by their ability, character, knowledge and experience for membership of the House, and that the selection of members might not be made on a political party basis. It is realised that the Second House is not to be contemplated as consisting of individual specialists in their own particular business, whose function would be in the nature of giving expert advice on their own particular subjects, but it is repeated, that it is suggested for the purpose of securing the selection of generally eligible persons to constitute the Second House who should be competent to deal with all its business whatever it may be. . . .

EXTRACT FROM A MINORITY REPORT BY DR. D. A. BINCHY AND OTHERS

12. Selection upon a functional basis seems to us to be the most desirable method of composing a Second Chamber. Apart from its advantages as an adjunct to geographical democracy, this method would provide a diversification of type and a variety of expert knowledge which, it is generally agreed, should characterise a Second Chamber. Even those who do not approve of the general principle of organised functional democracy might agree to accept our recommendations as providing a method of selection which would minimise party conflicts and secure the services of persons who would normally remain out of public life, although exceptionally fitted for the task of criticising and improving particular types of legislation.

13. If all or any of the "Functional and Vocational Councils representing branches of the social and economic life of the nation" had already been established by the Oireachtas, as envisaged in Article 45 of the Constitution,

we would favour direct election to the Second Chamber by such Councils; and in the event of any of them being established in the future, we recommend that this method of selection be adopted. In present circumstances we recommend that, where substantially representative vocational organisations exist, they should be given a direct voice in the selection of candidates for membership of the Second Chamber according to the procedure suggested in paragraph 16 below. We realise, however, that important branches of the social and economic life of the nation are at present either unorganised or insufficiently organised, and that complete functional representation cannot be obtained on the basis of existing vocational organisations alone.

(b) *Constitutional Provisions*

Document 7.7 — Articles 18 and 19 of Bunreacht na hÉireann (Constitution of Ireland).

Article 18.

1. Seanad Éireann shall be composed of sixty members, of whom eleven shall be nominated members and forty-nine shall be elected members.

2. A person to be eligible for membership of Seanad Éireann must be eligible to become a member of Dáil Éireann.

3. The nominated members of Seanad Éireann shall be nominated, with their prior consent, by the Taoiseach who is appointed next after the re-assembly of Dáil Éireann following the dissolution thereof which occasions the nomination of the said members.

4. The elected members of Seanad Éireann shall be elected as follows : —
   i. Three shall be elected by the National University of Ireland.
   ii. Three shall be elected by the University of Dublin.
   iii. Forty-three shall be elected from panels of candidates constituted as hereinafter provided.

5. Every election of the elected members of Seanad Éireann shall be held on the system of proportional representation by means of the single transferable vote, and by secret postal ballot.

6. The members of Seanad Éireann to be elected by the Universities shall be elected on a franchise and in the manner to be provided by law.

7. 1° Before each general election of the members of Seanad Éireann to be elected from panels of candidates, five panels of candidates shall be formed in the manner provided by law containing respectively the names of persons having knowledge and practical experience of the following interests and services, namely : —
   i. National Language and Culture, Literature, Art, Education and such professional interests as may be defined by law for the purpose of this panel;

    ii. Agriculture and allied interests, and Fisheries;

    iii. Labour, whether organised or unorganised;

    iv. Industry and Commerce, including banking, finance, accountancy, engineering and architecture;

    v. Public Administration and social services, including voluntary social activities.

    2° Not more than eleven and, subject to the provisions of Article 19 hereof, not less than five members of Seanad Éireann shall be elected from any one panel.

8.   A general election for Seanad Éireann shall take place not later than ninety days after a dissolution of Dáil Éireann, and the first meeting of Seanad Éireann after the general election shall take place on a day to be fixed by the President on the advice of the Taoiseach.

9.   Every member of Seanad Éireann shall, unless he previously dies, resigns, or becomes disqualified, continue to hold office until the day before the polling day of the general election for Seanad Éireann next held after his election or nomination.

10.   1° Subject to the foregoing provisions of this Article elections of the elected members of Seanad Éireann shall be regulated by law.

    2° Casual vacancies in the number of the nominated members of Seanad Éireann shall be filled by nomination by the Taoiseach with the prior consent of persons so nominated.

    3° Casual vacancies in the number of the elected members of Seanad Éireann shall be filled in the manner provided by law.

Article 19.

    Provision may be made by law for the direct election by any functional or vocational group or association or council of so many members of Seanad Éireann as may be fixed by such law in substitution for an equal number of the members to be elected from the corresponding panels of candidates constituted under Article 18 of this Constitution.

(c) *Mr de Valera's views on the Senate*
Document 7.8 — Extracts from Dáil Debates, vol. 69, cols. 1607-21
(2 December 1937).

The President (Mr. de Valera): . . . Much of this discussion, which has ranged over two or three years, in reference to the constitution of a Second Chamber confirms me largely in the view that I held at the beginning. I stated it on one or two occasions, and it was this, that it would pass the wit of man to devise a really satisfactory Second Chamber. Any quotations that have been brought up here today or at any other time will prove that that was my view. Most of my arguments against the old Seanad were adduced to show up the fallacies and the line of reasoning of those who thought that you could get a Second Chamber which was going to be a check on the First Chamber and so relieve democracy of all its weaknesses. I tried to prove that was not so. I will admit a great deal of my argument was of an abstract type, but I always had a reserve behind it which I described in more than one speech as a hankering—I could hardly justify it on the ground of abstract reasoning, but I had a certain hankering after a Second House, provided that we could constitute it on any reasonable basis and that it was not going to be a mere reflection of the First House or that it would be so constituted as to impede the natural work which the First House had to do.

That has been the basis of my attitude towards the Second House all the time. I will say this, that in the constitutional circumstances in which we were, with the national objectives which we had in front of us, I wanted to get rid of a Second House, and particularly I wanted to get rid of the previous Second House whilst a certain piece of constitutional work was being done. Fortunately for the country, it was not there at the time that a certain piece of important constitutional work had to be done. I sympathise with people who may say to themselves: "Very well, then, there may be some other occasion also in which, from the national point of view and from the point of view of the good of the people, there may be a conservative Second House which may try to do something like what was done by the old House when they tried to stand against the will of the people by refusing to implement the judgment of the people, say, on the removal of the Oath." I can quite understand why people who have that point of view might be against the constitution of a Second House, and I would be against the constitution of a Second House if it had powers such as the old House had to do such a thing.

One of my first cares in dealing with the Constitution was to see that the Second House in future would have no such resisting power and would not be capable of doing the damage the old Seanad tried to do at a very critical time when we were dealing with another country on important matters. I challenged the Opposition at the time, and I said to them: "Will you show us how to constitute a Second Chamber?" I myself had given a certain amount of thought to this whole question of a Second Chamber in the scheme of representative institutions. I tried to get some satisfactory scheme for a Second Chamber and I had failed. I challenged the Opposition in the way I have mentioned when they were talking about Seanads in a very different strain from the strain in which they are talking about Seanads now. Then they were dilating on the false ideas people had on the efficacy of a Second Chamber. On that background they were painting a certain picture and trying to get people to believe that a Second House would cure all the ills of democracy. We pointed out that it was not going to cure all the ills of democracy and that if a Seanad was going to be established which could do that, it could also do a great deal of damage at the same time. I said to them: "Since you are talking about a Seanad as if an ideal Seanad were possible, show us how to constitute one." They did not do that.

We asked them to participate in a committee of all parties to examine this question of a Second Chamber and to consider what should be its powers and constitution, on the understanding that we were not committing ourselves in advance to the setting up of a Second Chamber unless we were satisfied that any proposals that came from that Committee would really make for the improvement of our political institutions. We set up that committee. Look at the names of the members. I defy anybody to maintain that that committee was set up on a Party basis. It is true that the Opposition did not support us by consenting to representation on the committee, but we went outside and tried to pick people of standing, politically associated with them but not members of their Party, who had shown an interest in this matter. We invited them to act on the committee and, with commendable public spirit, they did act on it. We did not give them a very long time, I admit, to consider the matter. Perhaps we hurried them too much. I had hoped to get the constitutional work done much earlier than it was found possible to do it. However, we gave them a certain time, the Chief Justice presided and the result of their work is here. If anybody is interested, he can read the report and see the diversity of view exhibited there as to the way in which a Seanad could be constituted. I studied the report carefully, and I think the majority of that body had arrived at the same sort of view I individually had arrived at— that was, that certain limited powers might be given to a Second House and that as long as they were limited and the Second House could not be much more than a revising Chamber—taking up measures, criticising them from an independent standpoint and with as great a variety of viewpoint as possible —a Second House might be of some value. I worked on the basis of a remark made by either Deputy Rowlette or Deputy Alton. That was "Even if we cannot get an ideal Seanad, then a bad Seanad is better than no Seanad."

Having secured that the Seanad, so far as I could see, could not do harm, I said: "All right, we will give way to those who think there is some virtue in a Second House. If a Second House can do some good, we will try to give them a Second House with these limited powers." A Second House can do a great deal of work in the way of revision of legislation. Even if we did not have a Second House, I recognised that we should have to set up some revising Committee of the Dáil for this purpose. I tried to have the smallest number possible on the Seanad, as I explained when the Constitution was going through. The reason the Seanad consists of 60 and not of 45 was in order to give reasonable representation to the small Parties. . . .

The view I have of vocational organisations is that, in certain industries, the employers and the employed would get together and would have power, so far as it was given to them to do it and so far as it was at all possible to permit it with safeguards for the interests of other sections of the community, to settle a number of things that we try to settle here and do not settle as well as they who know their own business would settle them. I admit that we have not begun seriously to work on that line here. If a start is made, there may be difficulties in the way of doing it, but that at any rate is the type of organisation I had in mind. It is to the governing bodies of such an association, and not to individual members, that I would give the power of electing to the Seanad. . . .

The important thing in a Second Chamber is that you should have people who will know the effects of legislation on certain groups, and who on that account will be able to point out defects and suggest remedies in legislation that, from the general point of view of national policy, has passed through the First House. I believe that we can get through this agency of outside nominating bodies some people anyhow who otherwise would not perhaps get into political matters at all. When I say political I hope I will be understood. I said it would be nonsense to talk of the Seanad as non-political. We are using the word "politics" in a peculiar double sense. It must be admitted that anyone dealing with affairs of this sort is dealing with politics. He is dealing with fundamental political matters. If you define a politician as one who is dealing with politics, then anybody who has to deal with these fundamental political matters is inevitably a politician.

I never had a dream of having a Second House which would not be political in that sense, but political in the sense of being a member of a pledge-bound Party is quite a different matter. I try to distinguish between the two classes of people. As regards the first class, it would be well if, by a method such as this, we could get their brains and interests in affairs working in criticising legislation. Under the Constitution they cannot prevent the really representative House from having its way, and, therefore, the will of the people as a whole being given expression to. But they can put forward constructive criticism.

Mr. Dillon: Is the President going to elaborate his own scheme now?

The President: The other schemes have been elaborated.

Mr. Dillon: On a point of procedure, I would like to know if the President is going to elaborate his scheme now.

The President: To tell the truth, what I am hoping to do is to avoid the necessity of any more speeches on the general principles. If we can get a decision on these proposals, I will do my best, in the rest of the debate, to confine myself rigidly to Committee treatment of the Bill. As I was saying, there is nomination from outside and nomination from inside. What harm is there in giving that type of body the opportunity to express itself in the Second House? The Dáil and the county councils will be able to pass judgment as between the various people who are put forward as to which of them are the best. We are insisting that 21 of those outside people, nominated in this particular way, are going into the Seanad. We put the figures 21 and 22 for the Dáil. One reason for doing that is that I am doubtful at the present time whether we should throw the fate, so to speak, of the Second House altogether on the outside bodies. I do not think that we have arrived at the stage at which we could do that with safety, and that is why we have restricted them to 21. If conditions were otherwise, I would prefer to say at least 21, and not to restrict them to 21 and 22.

There are members of this House who think that the Dáil itself is a better nominating body and a better electorate for the choosing of the Seanad. That point of view is met to the extent of half, over half, so that this proposal is a compromise, and it is necessary, in my opinion, in our present state of development. It is a compromise with the Labour proposal which would allow the Dáil to nominate and elect, and with the idea of having a completely vocational Seanad. I would like to have that if our conditions were such as would warrant it. This, of course, is like most compromises, that it can be attacked by both Parties whose points of view it is hoped to meet. We get by this proposal a Seanad of 43 members, 22 from nominees put up by the Dáil, and 21 members from nominees put up by outside bodies. In addition, you will have the six members elected by the universities, and then the 11 nominated by the Taoiseach. It so happens that I am here at this moment. Goodness knows who will be here when the second election comes on, or who will be here even when the first election comes on. Therefore, I am not such a fool as to put forward this proposal on the basis that it is I who will be nominating the 11. At the outside I suggested that a good approach to the consideration of this whole question of the Seanad would be this: If the Opposition would only imagine themselves, for the time being, as the Government, and if the Government would imagine themselves, for the time being, as the Opposition.

(d) *The Panel Members*
> Document 7.9 — Extracts from J. C. Smyth, *The Houses of the Oireachtas*, 2nd edition, Institute of Public Administration, Dublin, 1964.

Section 44 of the Seanad Electoral (Panel Members) Act, 1947, provides that the electorate for the forty-three members of the Seanad elected from panels of candidates shall consist of:

(a) the members of the Dáil (elected at the Dáil election consequent on the dissolution of the Dáil which occasioned such Seanad general election),

(b) the members of the Seanad, and

(c) the members of every council of a county or county borough.

Where a person is a member of the electorate by virtue of more than one qualification his name is entered once only in the electoral roll.

The electorate for bye-elections for casual vacancies among the panel members consists only of the members of the Dáil and the members of the Seanad who at a date prior to polling day are then entitled to sit and vote in their respective Houses (section 69 of the Seanad Electoral (Panel Members) Act, 1947). . . . Every election of the elected members of the Seanad is held on the system of proportional representation by means of the single transferable vote and by secret postal ballot (Article 18.5 of the Constitution). There is a separate election in respect of each panel. . . .

At an election for panel members a candidate may be nominated either by—

(i) four members of the Houses of the Oireachtas (section 25 of the Seanad Electoral (Panel Members) Act, 1947), or

(ii) a registered nominating body (section 26 of the Seanad Electoral (Panel Members) Act, 1947).

The names of the candidates nominated by members of the Houses to a panel ultimately comprise the Oireachtas sub-panel of that panel, and lists of the nominations by the nominating bodies to it ultimately comprise the nominating bodies sub-panel.

A member of either House may not join in the nomination of more than one person. Registered nominating bodies in respect of a particular panel are entitled to propose for nomination such number of persons as is provided for by section 26 of the Seanad Electoral (Panel Members) Act, 1947, as amended by the Act of 1954.

At bye-elections for casual vacancies among the panel members a candidate may be nominated either by

(i) nine members of the Houses of the Oireachtas (section 67 of the Seanad Electoral (Panel Members) Act, 1947), or

(ii) a registered nominating body (section 59 of the Seanad Electoral (Panel Members) Act, 1947 as amended by the Act of 1954).

according as the vacancy has occurred among Senators elected from the Oireachtas sub-panel, or from the nominating bodies sub-panel of the particular panel.

REGISTER OF NOMINATING BODIES

Register of Nominating Bodies entitled to nominate persons to the panels of candidates for the purpose of every Seanad general election revised at the annual revision and signed by the Seanad Returning Officer in pursuance of section 19 of the Seanad Electoral (Panel Members) Act, 1947, as amended by the Seanad Electoral (Panel Members) Act, 1954 (as revised on 16th March, 1963).

Cultural and Educational Panel

Name of Body	Address
Royal Irish Academy	19 Dawson Street, Dublin 2.
Cumann Leabharlann na hEireann (The Library Association of Ireland)	18 Ely Place, Dublin 2.
Irish National Teachers' Organisation	9 Gardiner's Place, Dublin 1.
Association of Secondary Teachers, Ireland	36 St. Stephen's Green, Dublin 2.
An Cumann Gairm-Oideachais i n-Eirinn ... ... (The Irish Vocational Education Association)	Central Technical Institute, Waterford.
The Incorporated Law Society of Ireland	Solicitors' Buildings, Four Courts, Dublin 7.
Cumann Dochtúirí na hEireann ... (The Irish Medical Association)	10 Fitzwilliam Place, Dublin 2.
Royal College of Surgeons in Ireland	123 St. Stephen's Green, Dublin 2.
Dental Board	57 Merrion Square, Dublin 2.
Veterinary Council	53 Lansdowne Road, Ballsbridge.
The Pharmaceutical Society of Ireland	18 Shrewsbury Road, Ballsbridge, Dublin 4.
The General Council of the Bar of Ireland	Law Library, Four Courts, Dublin 7.
Bantracht na Tuatha ... ... (Irish Countrywomen's Association)	23 St. Stephen's Green, Dublin 2.
Royal Society of Antiquaries of Ireland	63 Merrion Square, Dublin 2.
Muintir na Gaeltachta	"Uí Máine," Ceanannus Mór, Co. Na Midhe.
The Royal Irish Academy of Music ...	36-38 Westland Row, Dublin 2.
Irish Dental Association	23 Harcourt Street, Dublin 2.

Agricultural Panel

Name of Body	Address
Royal Dublin Society	Ballsbridge, Dublin 4.
The Irish Agricultural Organisation Society, Limited	84 Merrion Square, Dublin 2.
National Executive of the Irish Live Stock Trade	Prosperity Chambers, 5, 6 & 7 Upr. O'Connell Street, Dublin 1.
The Bloodstock Breeders' and Horse Owners' Association of Ireland ...	9 Merrion Square, Dublin 2.
The Irish Sugar Beet Growers' Association, Limited	Athy Road, Carlow.
The Irish Creamery Managers' Association	32 Kildare Street, Dublin 2.
Munster Agricultural Society ...	21 Cook Street, Cork.

Labour Panel

Name of Body	Address
Irish Congress of Trade Unions ...	Merrion Building, Lower Merrion Street, Dublin 2.
The Irish Conference of Professional and Service Associations	31 Fitzwilliam Place, Dublin 2.

Administrative Panel

Name of Body	Address
Irish County Councils General Council	1-2 Cavendish Row, Dublin 1.
The Association of Municipal Author- ities of Ireland	Town Hall, Mallow, Co. Cork.
Central Remedial Clinic	Prospect Hall, Goatstown, Co. Dublin 14.
National Association for Cerebral Palsy (Ireland) Limited	St. Brendan's, Sandymount Avenue, Sandymount, Dublin 4.

(e) *The Verdict of the Vocational Organization Commission*
   Document 7.10 — Extract from the *Report of the Commission on
   Vocational Organization*, 1943, p. 310.

The remaining forty-three members are selected from five panels of candidates, nominated as set out in the Constitution and the Panel Members Act. The nominations are made partly by members of Dáil Éireann and partly by Nominating Bodies. With regard to the latter, we have received much evidence to indicate that they are not fully representative of the organised vocations and that owing to the method of selection followed they tend to nominate not those who are most eminent in their professions or callings but those who are most likely to be acceptable to the political parties. Though candidates nominated by Dáil members must belong to one or other of the five functional panels, the Constitution only requires that they " have knowledge or practical experience," with the result that persons on the perimeter of vocational activity rather than at the centre find themselves placed on the cultural or other panels. Finally, there is the most important stage of all, the election itself. The electoral body is not composed of vocational representatives but of members of the Dáil and seven delegates from each County Council and County Borough.[1] This body elects twenty-two from the

1. In 1947 the electorate was extended and now includes, besides the members of the Dáil (1) all members of county and county borough councils and (2) the outgoing members of the Seanad. See Document 7.9 above.—Editor.

nominations made by the Dáil and twenty-one from those made by the nominating bodies. The deciding principle in the election is, therefore, a political one, and this naturally affects every preceding step leading to the poll. The evidence which we have received from vocational bodies reflects the realisation of the predominant position of political rivalry in the contest. Some have stated that from the professional standpoint the atmosphere of the election is obnoxious to them. They hold that the degree to which it has succeeded in introducing vocationalism into politics is considerably less than that to which it has introduced politics into vocational bodies. On the subject of the Seanad, therefore, our conclusion is that the existing system of election is only partially determined by vocational principles; candidates are not elected directly by vocational bodies, they are not even entirely nominated by them.

(f) *University Members*

Document 7.11 — Extracts from Seanad Electoral (University Members) Act, 1937 (no. 30).

CONSTITUENCIES AND ELECTORS

6.—(1) At every Seanad election—

(a) the National University of Ireland shall be a constituency (in this Act referred to as the National University constituency) for the election of three members of Seanad Eireann, and

(b) the University of Dublin shall be a constituency (in this Act referred to as the Dublin University constituency) for the election of three members of Seanad Eireann, and

(c) every person who is for the time being registered as an elector in the register of electors for the National University constituency shall be entitled to vote in that constituency, and

(d) every person who is for the time being registered as an elector in the register of electors for the Dublin University constituency shall be entitled to vote in that constituency.

(2) No person shall be entitled to vote at an election in a university constituency unless he is registered as an elector in the register of electors for that constituency.

(3) Nothing in this section shall entitle any person to vote at an election in a university constituency while he is prohibited by law from so voting, nor shall anything in this section relieve any person from any penalties to which he may be liable for so voting.

(4) The National University constituency and the Dublin University constituency are in this Act referred to as university constituencies and the expression "university constituency" shall in this Act be construed accordingly.

7.—(1) Every person who is a citizen of Ireland and has received a degree (other than an honorary degree) in the National University of Ireland and has attained the age of twenty-one years shall be entitled to be registered as an elector in the register of electors for the National University constituency.

(2) Every person who is a citizen of Ireland and has received a degree (other than an honorary degree) in the University of Dublin or has obtained a foundation scholarship in that University or, if a woman, has obtained a non-foundation scholarship in the said University and (in any case) has attained the age of twenty-one years shall be entitled to be registered as an elector in the register of electors for the Dublin University constituency. [*Ss.* 8-15 *omitted.*]

NOMINATION

16.—(1) Every candidate at an election in a university constituency shall be nominated in writing on a nomination paper subscribed by two registered electors of the constituency as proposer and seconder respectively and by eight other registered electors of the constituency as assenting to the nomination.

(2) No person who is for the time being disqualified from or incapable of being elected as a member of Dáil Éireann shall be a candidate at an election in a university constituency.

(3) An elector may subscribe (whether as proposer, seconder, or assenting elector) as many nomination papers as there are vacancies to be filled and no more.

(4) Every candidate shall be described in the nomination paper by his name, address and description, in such manner as, in the opinion of the returning officer, is calculated sufficiently to identify such candidate.

(5) Every nomination paper shall be in the prescribed form, and the returning officer shall supply to any registered elector of the constituency such number of forms of nomination paper as he shall reasonably require. [*Ss.* 17-20 *omitted.*]

METHOD OF VOTING

21.—(1) On the day appointed for the issue of ballot papers at an election in a university constituency the returning officer at such election shall send by post to each person whose name is on the register of electors for such constituency a ballot paper together with a form of declaration of identity.

(2) Every declaration of identity shall be in the prescribed form.

(3) The returning officer at an election in a university constituency in sending out, receiving, and otherwise dealing with the ballot papers at such election shall observe the rules contained in the Second Schedule to this Act.

22.—(1) Every person entitled to vote at an election in a university constituency shall be entitled to vote at that election in the following and no other manner, that is to say, by marking and returning by post to the returning officer at such election a ballot paper sent to him under this Act together with the form of declaration of identity similarly sent to him therewith duly made and completed by him.

(2) An elector in giving his vote at an election in a university constituency must place on his ballot paper the figure 1 opposite the name of the candidate for whom he votes and may in addition place on his ballot paper the figures 2 and 3, or 2, 3, and 4, and so on opposite the names of other candidates in the order of his preference.

(3) Any ballot paper—

(*a*) which does not bear the official mark, or

(*b*) on which the figure 1 standing alone is not placed at all or is not so placed as to indicate a first preference for some candidate, or

(*c*) on which the figure 1 standing alone indicating a first preference is set opposite the name of more than one candidate, or

(*d*) on which the figure 1 standing alone indicating a first preference and some other number is set opposite the name of the same candidate, or

(*e*) on which anything except the number on the back is written or marked by which the voter can be identified,

shall be invalid and not counted. [*Remainder omitted.*]

READING

D. E. Butler (editor) et al.: *Elections Abroad*, London, 1959. (Chapter 3 entitled ' Ireland 1957 ' is an account of the general election of 1957 by Basil Chubb.)

Basil Chubb: ' Vocational Representation and the Irish Senate ' in *Political Studies*, vol. 2.

James Hogan: *Election and Representation*, Oxford, 1945.

Michael Lawless: 'The Dáil Electoral System' in *Administration*, vol. 5.

J. L. McCracken: *Representative Government in Ireland, Dáil Eireann 1919-1948*, London, 1958.

J. F. S. Ross: *The Irish Election System, what it is and how it works*, London, 1959.

J. C. Smyth: *The Houses of the Oireachtas*, Dublin, 1964.

Chapter 8

POLITICAL PARTIES

INTRODUCTION

No collection made up mainly of formal documents can hope to give an adequate picture of a working political system. The bare constitutional provisions in respect of, for example, the Government might well mislead almost as much as they illuminate. The electoral Acts, to take another example, do not even begin to tell us anything about the voters. Indeed, even the record of their votes, i.e. election results, does not go far towards providing us with information about what they think and feel. To find out what their votes signify, public opinion polls, surveys, and the techniques of political sociology are necessary. In no case is this more true than of political parties which are by their very nature 'informal' political institutions. A bridge between the formal organs of the state and the community which the state serves, parties are, significantly, not mentioned in the Constitution, and it was not until 1963 that the law authorized the printing of the party affiliations of candidates on the ballot paper. Even the available domestic documents of the parties do not give an adequate picture of party life and activity and no sociological studies yet exist. The documents included in this chapter inevitably therefore cover only such matters as formal organization, the advice and ideas of the two major parties on how to organize a successful election campaign, and some important points from current policy programmes.

Just as Ireland adopted the parliamentary tradition, so too, like the white Commonwealth states in general, she developed a party system in which, although there existed three or more parties, the two or three biggest of them took up attitudes of responsibility for the government of the country, whether they were in power or in opposition. Each was concerned to win enough popular support to form a government, if possible composed solely of its own leaders. The existence of such parties tended to create a stable

211

Government on the one side and a stable opposition on the other—if not a two party system, at least a two party group system. The loyalty and consistent behaviour of the supporters of both sides in the Dáil usually gave the two groups a stability and a coherence sufficient to enable electors to recognize that they had a choice between two possible prime ministers whose names they knew in advance and two possible governments whose outlook and composition they also knew in a general way at least.

Fianna Fáil and Fine Gael developed as parties of this sort, and though it might look as though the latter's chances of actually winning an absolute majority are not at present great, the important thing is that it has often behaved as though it might, while, in 1948 and after, it was the major partner in a stable and responsible coalition. Labour for its part, though it has not the possibility of winning an electoral majority, did at first carry the burden of parliamentary opposition (before Mr de Valera led Fianna Fáil back into the parliamentary arena) and, when the opportunity offered, entered a coalition which it played its part in maintaining.

The consequence of these attitudes has been that Irish politics has exhibited many of the characteristics which are often associated with the two party system—two stable groups alternating between power and opposition with the swing of the electoral pendulum, and a clear choice offered to the voters between two known alternative leaders and governments. So far, only once, in 1948, was this pattern clearly broken.

The existence of large nation-wide parties and the establishment of an 'ins and outs' pattern, combined with a cabinet system on the British pattern, would of itself make the resemblance between Ireland and some Commonwealth countries obvious enough. The internal organization of the major parties and the distribution of power within them will further heighten the resemblance. The constitutions and rules of the three major parties reveal only the formal structure, of course, but this is markedly similar to the British parties (Documents 8.1 to 8.3). As in Britain, the branches and constituency organizations are primarily vote getting agencies manned by local politicians and voluntary and unpaid enthusiasts. To a large extent dormant, sometimes almost moribund, between elections, these local organizations spring to life at election time. While they receive guidance and advice from the centre (Documents 8.4 and 8.5), as well as some material help, they must rely to a large extent on their own efforts and resources. As *Córas Bua*, Fianna Fáil's election handbook, says, 'the assistance which can be given any individual constituency . . . is very limited', and success or failure depends much more upon the position and efforts of local candidates and their supporters than on any other factor.

The role of local organizations in influencing policy is not at all accurately portrayed by the formal rules, and in this, too, Irish parties resemble the British. As in Britain, local branches elect representatives to attend the annual party meeting (Árd Fheis) which according to the rule books is the supreme authority in the party, but which in practice, despite some lip-service to the proposition, is nothing of the sort. The resolutions of these conferences are no more than guides to party opinion for the attention of the real policy and decision makers who are in fact the leaders of the parliamentary group in the party (the parliamentary party), perhaps reinforced with a few members of the central executive committee not in the Oireachtas. It is with these people, and above all, if he so wishes, with the leader of the party that initiative in devising and proposing policy rests. There is nothing wrong in this—indeed it is inevitable that policy should be proposed by a few at the centre—it is only that the rules do not give this impression. On the contrary, with varying degrees of emphasis, they suggest something different.

The principal cause of the polarization of Irish politics and the emergence of large nation-wide parties, to which we have referred above, was the split of Sinn Féin over the Treaty. This opened up a gulf which divided people clearly and unequivocally for a quarter of a century. On one side stood Mr de Valera and Fianna Fáil; on the other, those who were to become Fine Gael. And if the existence of the Labour Party, the oldest party in the state, indicated that there were some who gave more weight to social and economic issues, the inability of Labour ever to attract the support of more than about a tenth of the electorate reveals how complete and deep was the basic division. Though the issue is now dead and the wound healed over, the parties that were born of it are well established, each with a tradition and a traditional following of its own. Political aims and ideals have to be pursued to a large extent through them (or possibly Labour) and so, too, does a political career or political power.

What has lent stability to this situation, until recently at least, and at the same time has emphasized the polarity of Irish politics, has been the fact that Fianna Fáil has always attracted the support, if not of a majority of the voters, of something tantalizingly close to it. Consequently, the party, as Dr David Thornley has said, 'has tended to explain electoral defeat as a manifestation of popular folly and ingratitude much as Jehovah endured the periodic deviation of the Israelites . . . it is only necessary to wait and the day of retribution will dawn' (*Irish Times*, 20 August 1963).

With the issue of the Treaty now otiose and in the absence of any great divisive principle, religious, ideological or any other, it might have been expected that differences of emphasis or of pace in dealing with economic or social welfare issues would have arisen to produce a clear basis for a new party division. Some differences of this sort there certainly have been, and still are, but they are far from clear cut (Documents 8.6-8.15). Differences óf opinion between the conservative and radical elements of Fianna Fáil probably parallel to a considerable extent those to be found in Fine Gael, though the comparative weights of each element may differ markedly. Nor is the policy of the Labour Party any longer basically distinctive, some elements of it having been espoused both by Fianna Fáil and, perhaps more hesitantly, by Fine Gael. However, this phenomenon is by no means peculiar to Ireland, for it is to be seen also in a number of European countries today. With the wholesale acceptance by whole communities of the state's role as the principal architect of economic and social development and of massive state intervention to attain this end, the traditional division into left and right is becoming increasingly obsolete and even the concept of left and right is beginning to lose its usefulness.

Concentration on the big parties, which has led us to remark upon the similarities with Great Britain, should not blind us to the existence of smaller parties whose birth is at least not hindered by the election system. Though Clann na Poblachta (with one member of the Dáil) and Clann na Talmhan (with two members) seem today to be barely recognizable as political parties at all, it should be remembered that there have always been small parties of one sort or another, that they have not infrequently held the key to power, and that the striking rise of Clann na Poblachta in 1947-8 illustrates 'that the Irish electorate can respond to a novel summons' (David Thornley, *ibid*). Going further, the opportunities offered by the election system to a people who habitually give considerable weight in choosing a representative to personal and local considerations, allow not only for small parties but for Independents. Independent members of the Dáil are a permanent feature of the political landscape and, like the small parties (which are sometimes indeed little more than parliamentary alliances of two or more like-minded Independent T.D.s), Independents have sometimes held the key to political power in Ireland (Document 8.16).

1. AIMS AND ORGANIZATION

(a) *Fianna Fáil*

Document 8.1—Extracts from *Córú agus Rialacha* (*Constitution and Rules*), Approved by 24th Árd Fheis, 1953.

CONSTITUTION OF FIANNA FAIL

The aims of Fianna Fáil shall be: —

1. To secure the Unity and Independence of Ireland as a Republic.
2. To restore the Irish Language as the spoken language of the people and to develop a distinctive national life in accordance with Irish traditions and ideals.
3. To make the resources and wealth of Ireland subservient to the needs and welfare of all the people of Ireland.
4. To make Ireland, as far as possible, economically self-contained and self-sufficing.
5. To establish as many families as practicable on the land.
6. By suitable distribution of power to promote the ruralisation of industries essential to the lives of the people as opposed to their concentration in cities.
7. To carry out the Democratic Programme of the First Dáil.

RULES

1. The Organisation shall include the Árd-Fheis; the National Executive elected at the Annual Árd-Fheis; Cómhairlí Dáilcheanntair (or County Executives); Cómhairlí Ceanntair; and Cumainn.

Membership

2.—Membership of the Organisation is open to all persons of Irish birth, parentage, or residence, who accept the Córú of Fianna Fáil.

3.—Membership is obtainable through a Cumann only. A person becomes a member of Fianna Fáil when he or she is elected a member of a Cumann and signs a written declaration of acceptance of the Córú. A person to whom membership of a Cumann has been refused shall have the right to appeal to the Cómhairle Ceanntair and Cómhairle Dáil-cheanntair. [*Sections 4-7 omitted.*]

Associate Membership

8.—A person, who for private or business reasons, is unable to become an active member of the Organisation, may be enrolled as an associate member of the Cumann of the district in which he or she resides, on election as such by the members of the Cumann, and on signing a written declaration of acceptance of the Córú.

9.—Associate members shall pay a regular contribution to the funds of the Cumann and assist actively when called upon. [*Ss.* 10-11 *omitted.*]

Registration Fee

12.—Each Cumann shall pay a minimum Registration Fee of Ten Shillings (10/-) yearly to the Honorary Treasurers of the National Executive on or before the First Day of January.

13.—A National Public Collection shall be taken up annually throughout the country on a Sunday or Sundays, to be fixed by the National Executive, and it shall be the duty of each Cumann to organise this Collection and to forward the gross proceeds thereof to the Honorary Treasurers of the National Executive, with an account duly signed by the officers of the Cumann. For certain areas a special method of National Collection may be sanctioned by the National Executive. [*S.* 14 *omitted.*]

The Cumainn

15.—Branches of the Organisation, which shall be known as Cumainn, shall be formed in the manner hereinafter set out, and shall consist of not less than ten members.

(*a*) *In Rural Areas*—The basis of the Cumann will be the Church area or Polling Station area.

(*b*) *In Urban Areas and City Boroughs*—The basis of the Cumann will be the urban area, or ward, or such other area as may be directed, in particular cases, by the Cómhairle Ceanntair, Cómhairle Dáil-cheanntair or National Executive.

(*c*) *In Foreign Countries*—In such manner as may be directed, in particular areas, by the National Executive.

[*Ss.* 16-18 *omitted.*]

Duties of Cumainn and Cumainn Officers

19.—It shall be the duty of a Cumann and of the members thereof, to: —

(*a*) Abide by the spirit of the Córú of the Organisation.

(*b*) Promote the interests of the Organisation in its areas, and to secure public support for its programme.

(*c*) Endeavour to increase its membership to include all supporters of Fianna Fáil in its area.

(*d*) Carry out loyally such specific instructions as are from time to time transmitted to it from the bodies with authority to do so.

[*Ss.* 20-22 *omitted.*]

23.—The National Executive shall have power to expel from membership of the Organisation, or to remove from any office he may hold therein, or from membership of the National Executive, a Cómhairle Dáilcheanntair, a Cómhairle Ceanntair, or a Cumann, any member who has supported any candidate contesting a Dáil or Local Government Election in opposition to a Fianna Fáil candidate, or who, in the opinion of the National Executive shall have been otherwise guilty of conduct unbecoming a member of the Organisation. Cómhairlí Dáilcheanntair, Cómhairlí Ceanntair and Cumainn shall have like power in respect of their members, subject to the right of appeal to the superior bodies in each case. Provided always that expulsion or removal as aforesaid shall not be valid or effective unless at a specially convened meeting of the body concerned two-thirds of the members present and voting so decide.

Cómhairlí Ceanntair

24.—A Cómhairle Ceanntair shall be set up in each County Electoral Area or in such other area as may be directed by the National Executive, in view of local administration.

25.—The Cómhairle Ceanntair shall consist of delegates from the Registered Cumainn in its area, as set out hereunder : —

(*a*) The Secretary and one delegate from each Registered Cumann.

(*b*) Not more than three co-opted members, each co-option to take place at the discretion of the Cómhairle Ceanntair.

[*Ss. 26 and 27 omitted.*]

28.—The Teachtaí Dála and the Delegate to the National Executive shall have the right to attend and speak at all meetings of the Cómhairlí Ceanntair in the Constituency, but shall not have the right to vote, provided that where a Cómhairle Ceanntair is, in accordance with the Rules, exercising the powers and functions of a Cómhairle Dáilcheanntair, the Teachtaí Dála and Delegate to the National Executive shall have the right to vote. [*Ss. 29 and 30 omitted.*]

31.—It shall be the duty of the Cómhairle Ceanntair to:

(*a*) Supervise, direct and advise the Registered Cumainn in its area.

(*b*) Arrange for the formation of new Cumainn in districts where none exist.

(*c*) Arrange public meetings, conduct propaganda, and collect funds, in accordance with the instructions of the Cómhairle Dáilcheanntair or National Executive, and at the end of the year to forward a statement of accounts to the Cómhairle Dáilcheanntair.

(*d*) Carry out loyally any specific instructions issued to it from the bodies in authority over it.

(*e*) Arrange conventions for the selection of candidates for election to Local Government Boards, in accordance with the instructions of the National Executive and control all local elections in its area (Rule 54).

The proportion of the total membership which shall constitute a quorum shall be fixed by the Cómhairle Ceanntair. [*Ss. 32 and 33 omitted.*]

Cómhairlí Dáilcheanntair

34.—A Cómhairle Dáilcheanntair shall be set up in each constituency. It shall consist of the Honorary Secretary and two delegates from each Cómhairle Ceanntair in the constituency, the elected Fianna Fáil Teachtaí for the constituency, the Constituency Delegate to the National Executive, and not more than three co-opted members. In the case where two counties are comprised in the one constituency, the number of delegates from each Cómhairle Ceanntair shall be so arranged as to ensure equal representation from each county. Fianna Fáil County and Borough Councillors shall have the right to attend and speak at all meetings of the Cómhairle Dáilcheanntair for the area they represent. [*Ss. 35-37 omitted.*]

38.—It shall be the duty of the Cómhairle Dáilcheanntair to:—

(*a*) Direct the organisation of the constituency with a view to contesting elections.

(*b*) Summon Conventions for the selection of candidates for Dáil Elections, in accordance with the instructions of the National Executive.

(*c*) Collect funds for election purposes, and be responsible for the discharge of liabilities incurred by contesting Dáil Elections.

(*d*) Arrange public meetings, conduct propaganda, and supervise and direct similar activities on the part of the Cómhairlí Ceanntair.

(*e*) Carry out such other specific instructions as may, from time to time, be transmitted to it by the National Executive.

[*Ss. 39 and 40 omitted.*]

Conventions

41.—In the case of a General Election for Dáil Éireann, the National Executive shall determine the number of candidates to be selected for each constituency by the respective Constituency Conventions, and the Chairman of the Convention shall announce the number so decided.

42.—Conventions for the selection of candidates at Dáil elections shall be convened by the Honorary Secretaries of Cómhairlí Dáilcheanntair, or in such other manner as may be directed by the National Executive, and shall consist of:

(*a*) A Chairman (without a vote), appointed by the National Executive.

(*b*) Two delegates from the Cómhairle Dáilcheanntair and two from each Cómhairle Ceanntair in the constituency.

(*c*) Three delegates from each Registered Cumann of at least three months' standing in the constituency and which has made the National Collection.

(*d*) Nominees for selection as candidates for Dáil Elections shall not be eligible to act as delegates to the Convention nor, until after the candidates have been selected be permitted to be present thereat.

43.—Where in the opinion of the National Executive the circumstances existing prior to a General Election or By-Election so permit, the following conditions shall apply to the selection of candidates by Conventions:

(*a*) Each Registered Cumann shall have the right to put forward, in writing, to the Honorary Secretaries, before a date to be fixed by them, the names of suggested candidates, not exceeding the number of candidates to be selected.

(*b*) Each such name shall be accompanied by the signed pledge and written consent of the suggested candidate, together with a written declaration signed by the Chairman and Honorary Secretary of the Cumann, to the effect that the decision to suggest the person concerned as a candidate was made at a special meeting of the Cumann held for the purpose and properly convened after due notice.

(*c*) A list of all persons suggested as candidates by Cumainn, from whom signed pledges and consents have been received by the Honorary Secretaries, shall be prepared and submitted to the National Executive, and that body having considered it, shall have the right to add a name or names to the list.

(*d*) A copy of the list of suggested candidates, as determined by the National Executive in accordance with Section (*c*) of this Rule, shall be circulated to all Cumainn prior to the summoning of the Convention.

(*e*) No person whose name is not on the list of suggested candidates circulated by the National Executive shall be eligible to be selected by the Convention.

(*f*) Conventions, in selecting candidates, and the National Executive in deciding ratifications, will be expected to give preference to Irish-speaking nominees, provided they are otherwise properly qualified. This shall be especially so in dealing with Gaeltacht constituencies, and it shall be the duty of the Presiding Officer at any Convention for the selection of candidates to explain and emphasise this policy to the Convention before selection.

[*Ss. 44 and 45 omitted.*]

46.—All voting for the selection of candidates at Conventions shall be by ballot, and if there be more than two names for ballot, and none secure more than half of the valid votes cast, a further ballot or ballots shall be taken, the name or names standing lowest on the list being eliminated in each case, until a candidate has secured more than half of the valid votes cast. When more than one candidate is to be elected, separate ballots shall be held for each place on the panel, unless the Chairman, with the consent of the Convention, decides otherwise.

47.—The names of those recommended for nomination as candidates by the Convention shall be submitted to the National Executive, which shall consider whether the person or persons thus recommended are suitable to contest the election in the constituency, and if so satisfied shall ratify their selection.

48.—In any constituency in which the National Executive is satisfied that such action is necessary in the best interests of the Organisation, it may add a name or names to the panel of candidates to be nominated at a General Election [*S. 49 omitted.*]

50.—Where the National Executive so decides, the name of an outgoing Deputy shall not be considered for nomination by any Convention. [*S. 51 omitted.*]

52.—In the event of a By-Election, the National Executive, after consultation with the Cómhairle Dáilcheanntair, may decide to summon a Convention or may select a candidate.

53.—The pledge to be signed by each candidate for the Dáil is:

I, ... do hereby signify my consent to stand if selected as a candidate for the Constituency of .... and pledge myself, if elected, to work to the best of my ability for the aims and objects of Fianna Fáil as stated in the Córú, and to abide at all times by majority decisions of the Party or resign my seat as Teachta Dála. I further promise that if called upon by the National Executive, by a two-thirds ($\frac{2}{3}$) majority of the members present, and voting, at a meeting specially convened for the purpose, to resign my seat as Teachta Dála, I will do so.

Local Government Elections

54.—(1) Conventions to select candidates for election or co-option to County Councils shall be summoned in each County Electoral Area by the Honorary Secretary of the Cómhairle Ceanntair of the area concerned, and shall consist of:

(*a*) A Chairman, without a vote, appointed by the Cómhairle Dáilcheanntair;

(*b*) Two delegates from the Cómhairle Ceanntair;

(*c*) Three delegates from each Registered Cumann in the area of at least three months' standing and which has made the National Collection.

(2) Where more than one Cómhairle Ceanntair operates in the Electoral Area the Cómhairle Dáilcheanntair shall decide the number of candidates to be selected by each Convention in that Electoral Area.

55.—The names of the Candidates selected shall be submitted to the Cómhairle Dáilcheanntair for ratification. When, in the opinion of the Cómhairle Dáilcheanntair, the best interests of the Organisation would be served by such action, the Cómhairle Dáilcheanntair may add a name or names to the list and such list shall be the final one for nomination for the area concerned. [*S. 56 omitted*]

57.—The Cómhairle Dáilcheanntair may decide that all elections to Urban Councils and Town Commissioners, or any particular election to such bodies, shall not be contested by Fianna Fáil as a Party and such decision shall be binding on the Organisation in its area.

58.—Convention to select candidates for election or co-option to Urban Councils or Town Commissioners shall be held in such manner as the Cómhairle Dáilcheanntair shall direct. In the case of an Urban District or Town where there is more than one Cumann the Convention shall be summoned by the Honorary Secretary of the Cómhairle Ceanntair for the area concerned and shall consist of: —

(*a*) A Chairman appointed by the Cómhairle Dáilcheanntair;

(*b*) Three delegates from each Registered Cumann of at least three months' standing in the Urban District or Town and which has made the National Collection.

59. Candidates for Municipal Elections shall be selected by the Registered Cumainn in their respective areas at a Convention duly convened, and separate Conventions shall be held for each electoral area subject to control by the National Executive.

60. Fianna Fáil Councillors shall be summoned following an election, and annually thereafter, to appoint a Chairman and Secretary, the duties of the latter shall include the calling of regular meetings of the group to consider the Council Agenda and to ensure united action in matters of national policy.

61. The pledge to be signed by each candidate for a Local Government Body is:

"I, ..., hereby pledge myself if elected to the position of .... on the .... to support the policy of Fianna Fáil in all matters, and particularly in its Local Government Programme, and I also pledge myself to act in conjunction with the other members of the above Council nominated by the Fianna Fáil Organisation, and to carry out any specific instructions issued from time to time by the National Executive. I further promise if called upon by the National Executive, by a two-thirds ($\frac{2}{3}$) majority of the members present and voting at a meeting specially convened for the purpose, to resign the position, I will do so."

Árd-Fheis

62. The supreme governing and legislative body of the Organisation shall be the Árd-Fheis, which shall be convened annually by the National Executive and shall consist of : —

(a) Two delegates from each Registered Cumann of at least three months' standing.

(b) One delegate from each Cómhairle Ceanntair and Cómhairle Dáilcheanntair.

(c) The elected Fianna Fáil Teachtaí.

(d) The members of the National Executive.

[Section 63 omitted.]

64. The Árd-Fheis shall assemble ordinarily in the month of October. The place and date of the meeting, together with the rules governing procedure, shall be decided by the National Executive. Admission cards, clár and list of nominees for election to the National Executive shall be sent to each delegate at least seven days in advance.

[Ss. 65-69 omitted.]

National Executive

70.—When the Árd-Fheis is not in session, the National Executive shall be the supreme governing body of the Organisation, but save in exceptional or unforeseen circumstances, shall not have power to alter, or amend, or ignore any decision of the Árd-Fheis. A proposal for the amendment of the Rules may be submitted to a special meeting of the National Executive, seven days' notice of which shall have been given to all members thereof. And if adopted, by a two-thirds ($\frac{2}{3}$) majority of those present and voting shall be valid and effective until the next following Árd-Fheis, when, if not approved by that Árd-Fheis, it shall lapse. The National Executive shall be empowered to deal with and determine all matters and questions not otherwise expressly provided for in these Rules.

71.—The National Executive shall consist of the following, who shall take office immediately on election :

(a) A President, two Vice-Presidents, two Honorary Secretaries, and two Honorary Treasurers;

(b) A Committee consisting of fifteen members of the Organisation available for weekly meetings in Dublin, elected by the Ard-Fheis, of whom not more than five shall be Teachtaí and Seanadóirí.

(c) One delegate from each Dáil constituency resident in that constituency, elected by ballot of the Cumainn in the constituency; each Cumann having the right to record its vote by post in the manner hereinafter specified: Where two counties are comprised in the one constituency there shall be one delegate from each county, similarly elected. In the case of Dublin metropolitan constituencies the delegate shall reside within the city boundaries and be a member of a Cumann in the constituency for which he or she is nominated. Teachtaí Dála shall not be eligible for election as Constituency or County Delegates.

(d) Five co-opted members, of whom not more than two shall be Teachtaí and Seanadóirí.

[*Ss. 72-75 omitted.*]

76.—The National Executive shall hold office for one year, or until the next following annual Árd-Fheis assembles.

[*S. 77 omitted.*]

78.—The National Executive shall, in general, meet weekly in Dublin, but at least once each month. Special meetings shall be held at the discretion of the President, or, in his absence, of either of the Vice-Presidents, or on a requisition of seven of the members. A quorum shall consist of seven members, provided that not more than three of the seven be Teachtaí and Seanadóirí.

(b) *Fine Gael.*

Document 8.2 — Extracts from *Constitution and Rules,* by authority of National Council, November 1963.

CONSTITUTION

WHAT FINE GAEL STANDS FOR:

To secure for all our people in a United Ireland a decent standard of living with equal opportunity for all—whether they live in town, city or country—to earn a secure livelihood in their own land and to use their talents for the betterment of themselves and our common country.

SCHEME OF ORGANISATION

RULES

The Organisation of Fine Gael (United Ireland) shall be constituted and controlled in general accordance with the following rules: —

1.—*Membership*:
Membership shall be open to any person who accepts the programme of Fine Gael and who agrees to abide by its rules.

2.—The units of the Organisation shall be: —

(a) Branch.

(b) District Executive (except where dispensed with by Constituency Executive).

(c) Constituency or County Executive (whichever is the more convenient).

(d) Oireachtas Party.

(e) National Council and its Sub-Committees.

(f) Ard Fheis.

BRANCH

3.—(i) A BRANCH shall normally consist of the members of the Organisation ordinarily resident or working in the Polling District round which the Branch is organised. The area of Branch activities may, where necessary, be defined by the Constituency Executive.

(ii) The Branch shall, subject to the Constituency or County Executive, organise Party supporters within its area into Polling Booth groups under a Polling Booth Director to fight elections. The Branch, by taking an active interest in local affairs, by holding regular meetings and organising social activities and by other propaganda methods, shall seek to increase the strength and effectiveness of Fine Gael. In special circumstances, with the approval of the National Council, branches may be formed which need not be based on any electoral area.

4.—The minimum annual subscription for Branch members shall be two shillings. Each Branch shall be registered at National Headquarters on 1st January each year on payment of an annual affiliation fee of £1 0s. 0d.

5.—The Officers and Committee of the Branch shall be elected at the Annual General Meeting and shall consist of a Chairman, Vice-Chairman, Secretary, Treasurer and such additional members as shall be decided upon by the Branch, any of whom may be appointed to act jointly as Secretary or Treasurer. The Branch must hold an Annual General Meeting, which shall be summoned by the Branch Chairman, Secretary or other person authorised by the Committee. Such General Meeting shall be held between 1st November and 14th December in every year. At the Annual General Meeting, reports from the outgoing officers shall be received and considered, and delegates shall be elected to represent the Branch on superior executives and at the Árd Fheis. [*Ss. 6-8 omitted.*]

DISTRICT EXECUTIVE

9.—(i) The area under the DISTRICT EXECUTIVE shall be defined by the County or Constituency Executive. The District Executive shall consist of the County or Urban Councillors and Town Commissioners representative of the district, and at least 3 delegates from each branch within the District area (of whom one at least must be a member of the Branch Committee). Where it is unnecessary or inconvenient for effective organisation to form a District Executive, same may be dispensed with by the Constituency Executive.

(ii) The District Executive shall co-ordinate and stimulate activity among the Branches in its district, and shall promote and form Branches.

[*Ss.* 10-12 *omitted.*]

CONSTITUENCY EXECUTIVE

13.—(i) A CONSTITUENCY EXECUTIVE shall be established in each constituency. It shall consist of the Deputies, Senators, County or Urban Councillors representative of or ordinarily resident in the constituency, together with at least 3 representatives from each District Executive in the constituency (one at least of whom shall be either the District Executive Chairman or Secretary), or their duly appointed deputies. The number of District representatives may be varied by the Constituency Executive. Alternatively, if the Constituency Executive so decides and with the consent of the National Council, the Constituency Executive shall consist of an equal number of representatives from each Branch. The Constituency Executive shall have power to co-opt not more than three additional members. It shall appoint Directors of Elections, Transport, Publicity, etc. who shall, during their period of office, be members of the Constituency Executive.

(ii) The Constituency Executive shall, subject to the control of the National Council, have full responsibilty for the Fine Gael Organisation in the constituency.

[*S.* 14 *omitted.*]

15.—The Constituency Executive shall meet quarterly and whenever it is thought necessary by the Chairman, Secretary or National Council.

16.—The Constituency Executive shall, after consultation with National Headquarters, call a Constituency Convention at least once a year to review the work of the Organisation in the constituency during the previous year and to plan for the future. A Convention shall also be convened when required to select candidates for Dáil Éireann and to ratify candidates for Local Authorities, or to take decisions on a constituency basis or for any purpose that the National Council may direct.

17.—The Constituency Convention shall consist of the members of the Constituency (or County) Executive, and not less than two and not more than five delegates from each Branch in the constituency and any persons who are nominated by the National Council. [*S.* 18 *omitted.*]

NATIONAL COUNCIL

19.—THE NATIONAL COUNCIL shall consist of : —

(i) The President, Vice-Presidents, Hon. Trustees, Hon. Secretaries and General Secretary (ex officio).

(ii) Two representatives (neither being a member of the Oireachtas) nominated by each County or Constituency Executive, whichever is the smaller.

(iii) Ten members nominated by the President.

20.—(a) Subject to the authority of the Annual Árd Fheis, the management, control, government and administration of the Organisation shall be vested in and exercised by the National Council, whose Secretariat shall be known as National Headquarters. The National Council may approve and sanction the affiliation of Branches, convene the annual Árd Fheis or a special Árd Fheis and Conventions and special meetings of any unit of the Party.

(b) In connection with a General Election to Dáil Éireann, the National Council shall determine the number of candidates to be selected for each constituency and shall authorize the appointment of the Chairman for such Conventions.

(c) The National Council shall fix the date, method and allocation of the Annual National Collection and fix the target for Constituency or County contributions to National Headquarters.

(d) There shall be not less than two Trustees in whom the property and assets of the Party shall be vested and who shall be permanent members of the National Council. The Trustees shall be appointed by the Árd Fheis and shall continue in office until death, resignation, or removal by the National Council. [*Sub-paragraph (e) omitted.*]

21.—The National Council may deprive a person of his membership of Fine Gael or may order the dissolution of a Constituency or District Executive or of a Branch, or direct a new election of officers in such Executive or Branch, but shall not order the dissolution of a Branch or District Executive until it has consulted the Constituency Executive.

22.—(i) The National Council shall meet quarterly, or if necessary at more frequent intervals, and a quorum shall be eleven members. The National Council may delegate all or any of its powers and functions to a Standing Committee, a Finance Committee or other Sub-Committee whose members need not be members of the National Council.

(ii) Vacancies on the National Council created by death, resignation or otherwise, shall be filled in the case of a Constituency or County representative, by the Executive concerned, and otherwise by nomination of the President.

23.—The Standing Committee on behalf of the National Council shall ratify or reject candidates nominated for Oireachtas or Local Elections, and shall also have power to vary the number of candidates.

ARD FHEIS

24.—The Árd Fheis shall be held annually at a date to be fixed by the National Council and shall be the supreme governing body of Fine Gael.

25.—The Árd Fheis shall consist of : —
(a) The outgoing members of the National Council.
(b) The members of each Constituency and District Executive.
(c) Two delegates at least from each Branch.
(d) The Fine Gael members of the Oireachtas.
(e) Such other persons as may be invited by the National Council to attend.

26.—The business of the Árd Fheis shall be : —
(a) Election of Chairman.
(b) The regulation of its procedure.
(c) Report of Hon. Secretaries.
(d) Statement by outgoing President.
(e) Election of President.
(f) Election of not more than four Vice-Presidents.
(g) Election of Honorary Secretaries.
(h) Notices of Motion.
(i) Any other business.

[Paragraphs 27-31 omitted.]

32.—The National Council or Standing Committee may waive or vary any of the foregoing in so far as may be necessary for the betterment of the Fine Gael Organisation.

(c) *The Labour Party.*

Document 8.3 — Extracts from *Constitution,* as approved by the National Conference, 18th April 1952, and as subsequently amended (stencilled).

II.—PRINCIPLES AND OBJECTS

1.—The Labour Party is a distinctive, independent, political Party and representing the interests of the workers by hand and by brain, it seeks to secure adequate control of the machinery of the State in order to establish in all Ireland a democratic Republic based upon the social teachings of its founder — JAMES CONNOLLY.

2.—The Labour Party affirms that the national territory consists of the whole island of Ireland, its islands and territorial seas; and it accepts as part of its immediate programme the work of securing social justice and equal opportunities for all citizens in accordance with the declaration of Democratic Principles embodied in the Proclamation of Easter, 1916.

3.—The Labour Party believes in a system of Government which, while recognising the rights of private property, shall ensure that when the common good requires, essential industries and services shall be brought under public ownership and democratic control.

4.—The Labour Party believes that the Nation should be an ordered community in which every individual will be guaranteed an opportunity to obtain a decent livelihood and to this end the State shall utilise its powers, when and where necessary, to provide employment by the expansion of industrial and agricultural production and generally by the fullest development of the Nation's resources.

5.—The State, in addition to ensuring economic security, must also provide to all its members the fullest opportunity for educational and cultural development, for the maintenance of physical well-being and, by the promotion and development of the arts, crafts and literature of the Nation, to provide wider opportunities for all citizens to participate in general cultural activities.

6.—The Labour Party insists that the material and cultural possibilities of the Nation must be organised and fostered, in order to maintain and enhance the dignity of Ireland as a nation among the nations of the world. The Irish people must also co-operate, on the basis of equal rights and opportunities, with the peoples of other countries for the purpose of building up an international community on the same principles of peace, justice and order as must inspire the national community.

7.—The Labour Party believes that banking and the control of credit are of paramount importance to the well-being of the people and that the proper use of the community's credit can bring about a substantial improvement in the standard of living of the people. The Labour Party will, therefore, seek to bring banking and the control of credit under public ownership through a Board operating under the authority and supervision of the Government and subject to Parliamentary control.

In accordance with the foregoing principles, the Labour Party will seek: —

(a) to establish in the entire national territory a Republican form of government founded on the principles of social justice, sustained by democratic institutions and guaranteeing civil and religious liberty and equal opportunities to achieve happiness to all citizens;

(b) to secure the political union of Ireland in conformity with the principles set out above in paragraph (a) and pending the realization of this objective to foster friendly co-operation between the two parts of the country;

(c) to provide the widest possible measure of Social Security for all classes in the community;

(d) to provide on an insurance basis and without any means test, a comprehensive scheme of medical services for all citizens so as to make available to them the best possible services in all branches;

(e) to ensure the fullest utilisation of the natural resources of the country so as to provide greater wealth for the Nation and a rising standard of living for the people;

(f) to bring under public ownership such industries and services, including banking, as will promote the common good by the provision of better services for the community;

(g) to provide the best possible conditions of employment with special regard to wages, hours of work, annual holidays and factory and office accommodation in conformity with modern standards;

(h) to secure for organised workers the right of participation in the management of industries and public utilities;

(i) to expand agricultural production by providing credit facilities to farmers to purchase stock, equipment, fertilisers, to protect the home market for Irish agricultural produce, to guarantee fair prices for main agricultural commodities and by breaking up ranch lands, to settle as many persons as possible on adequate holdings with facilities for stocking and working the land;

(j) to establish the rights and accept the obligations of Ireland as a Sovereign State in relation to the other states of the world, to increase its activity and influence in international affairs and to cultivate friendly relations with other States;

(k) to co-operate with the Irish Trade Union Movement in matters of common concern;

(l) generally, to secure that the legislative, financial and administrative powers of the State shall be used to the fullest extent for the benefit of the whole community;

(m) to encourage and foster the national language by all reasonable means and by the provision of schemes designed to inculcate a love of the language in the people, to induce them to speak their native tongue.

III.—MEMBERSHIP

1.—Any person who subscribes to the Principles and Objects of the Party, accepts its Constitution and is not a member of any other political party or of an organisation subsidiary or ancillary thereto, may be accepted as an individual member of the Party.

2.—An individual member must sign a declaration of adherence to the Principles and Objects and of submission to the Constitution and Standing Orders of the Party and either

(a) be accepted into membership by a Branch of the Party in the Dáil Constituency in which he or she resides, or for which he or she is registered as a Dáil elector, or

(b) be accepted as an individual subscribing member by the Administrative Council.

[Ss. 3-7 omitted.]

8.—Trade Unions, professional associations, co-operative societies and other organisations the objects and activities of which are recognised by the Administrative Council as consistent with those of the Party may be admitted as corporate members of the Party. A Branch of such an organisation may be admitted as a corporate member if the organisation as a body is not a member.

IV.—BRANCH AND CONSTITUENCY ORGANIZATION

1.—A Branch of the Party may be formed in any district with the approval of the Administrative Council, which shall, if necessary, define the functional area of the Branch. *[Ss. 2 and 3 omitted.]*

4.—Each Branch shall hold an annual meeting for the purpose of considering the state of the organisation within its functional area, of electing Branch Officers and Committee and transacting any other relevant business. It shall, in addition, hold a minimum of four business meetings during the year.

5.—A Constituency Council may be formed in any Dáil Constituency with the approval of the Administrative Council and upon its formation every Branch in the Constituency shall be obliged to affiliate to the Constituency Council. *[Ss. 6 and 7 omitted.]*

8.—Wherever the Administrative Council consider it necessary to do so, they may sub-divide the area of any Constituency for the purpose of establishing two or more Divisional Councils. In every such case they shall define the functional area and the duties of the Divisional Council. *[Ss. 9-11 omitted.]*

12.—With the approval of the Administrative Council two or more Constituency Councils, covering adjacent functional areas, may jointly form a Regional Council to co-ordinate their work. *[Ss. 13-19 omitted.]*

20.—The records of a Branch, Divisional Council, Constituency Council or Regional Council shall be forwarded for inspection if required by the Administrative Council, or shall be made available at all reasonable times for inspection by the Administrative Council or a member of the Administrative Council appointed for that purpose. *[Remaining Sections of IV omitted.]*

V.—NATIONAL CONFERENCE

1.—The ultimate control of the Labour Party shall be exercised by the National Conference.

2.—The National Conference shall meet annually at such time and place as shall be decided by the Administrative Council. It may be summoned to meet specially at any time by decision of the Administrative Council.

3.—The National Conference shall consist of : —

(a) Delegates appointed by each Branch in accordance with the following scale : —
Membership not exceeding 50, 2 delegates.
Membership exceeding 50 but not exceeding 100, 3 delegates.
Membership exceeding 100 but not exceeding 150, 4 delegates.
And for every complete 50 members additional, 2 additional delegates.

(b) Delegates appointed by corporate members in accordance with the following scale : —
Membership not exceeding 500, 2 delegates.
Membership exceeding 500 but not exceeding 1,000, 3 delegates.
Membership exceeding 1,000 but not exceeding 1,500, 4 delegates.
Membership exceeding 1,500 but not exceeding 2,000, 5 delegates.
Membership exceeding 2,000 but not exceeding 3,000, 6 delegates.
Membership exceeding 3,000 but not exceeding 5,000, 7 delegates.
And for every complete 2,000 members additional after the first 5,000, 1 additional delegate.

(c) Delegates appointed by Constituency Councils, 1 for each Council.

(d) Delegates appointed by Divisional Councils, 1 for each Council.

(e) Delegates appointed by Regional Councils, 1 for each Council.

(f) Members of the Administrative Council who shall have the right to speak, but not to vote as such.

4.—Members of the Labour Party in the Oireachtas shall have the right to attend and speak at the National Conference but not to vote unless attending as delegates. [*Remaining Sections of V omitted.*]

VI.—THE ADMINISTRATIVE COUNCIL

1.—In the interval between National Conferences the control of the organisation and the administrative affairs of the Party shall be carried out by the Administrative Council which shall be elected at the annual meeting of the National Conference.

2.—The Administrative Council shall consist of a Chairman, Vice-Chairman, Financial Secretary, the Leader and Deputy Leader of the Labour Party in Dáil Éireann, six members of the Labour Party in the Oireachtas elected by that Party and seventeen ordinary members elected by the National Conference.

VII.—NATIONAL OFFICERS

1.—The Party Officers shall be (1) the Chairman of the Administrative Council, (2) the Vice-Chairman, (3) the Secretary, (4) the Financial Secretary and Leader and Deputy Leader of the Labour Party in Dáil Éireann.

2.—The Leader and Deputy Leader of the Labour Party in Dáil Éireann shall be chosen by the members of the Party in that House.

3.—The Party Secretary shall be appointed by the Administrative Council upon such conditions as to remuneration and tenure of office as may be determined by the Council.

4.—The Chairman, Vice-Chairman and Financial Secretary shall be elected annually by the National Conference from among persons nominated by Branches or other organisations entitled to make nominations.

[Part VIII omitted.]

IX.—PARTY PROGRAMME

1.—The Party Programme of specific measures of legislative, administrative and financial action shall be determined from time to time by the National Conference.

2.—The Administrative Council may from time to time issue and publish proposals or statements of policy in regard to specific items of legislation or administration whether national or local.

3.—The Administrative Council, in consultation with the Labour Party in Dáil Éireann, shall prepare for publication the Election Programme which shall be issued by the Administrative Council prior to every General Election and define the attitude of the Party towards the principal issues raised in the Election, which are not covered by the Election Programme.

X.—SELECTION OF CANDIDATES

(a) *Dáil, Senate and Local Authorities*

The Administrative Council shall prescribe the procedure to be adopted for the selection of the Party's candidates to Dáil and Seanad Éireann and Local Authorities. A copy of the procedure so prescribed shall be submitted to the Annual Conference. All corporate bodies, Branches and individual members must comply with the procedure so prescribed. *[Remainder omitted.]*

2. THE CONDUCT OF ELECTION CAMPAIGNS

(a) *Fianna Fáil.*

Document 8.4 — Extracts from *Córas Bua.* (This is a 52-page pamphlet on election organization and tactics, first issued in 1957.)

FOREWORD

The Scheme of Election Organisation in this Handbook, *Córas Bua* should be adhered to as closely as possible in each constituency and there should be no departure from it in any essential detail except with the approval of the Cómhairle Dáilcheantair. . . .

The assistance which can be given any individual constituency, however, is very limited, and it is, therefore, of vital importance that the local organisation should appreciate the scope of its duties and responsibilities and be prepared to make the fullest possible use of its own resources under every head.

The Constituency Director of Election is appointed by the Cómhairle Dáilcheantair. In the case of a By-Election the appointment is made by the National Executive.

The Cómhairle Dáilcheantair should prepare the data (listed on Page 6[1]) that will be required by the Constituency Director of Election on appointment, and every detail of it should be checked and brought up to date at each Annual Meeting of the CDC to ensure that the Scheme can be put into operation at the shortest notice. . . .

SECTION I
THE ELECTION STAFF

Constituency

The Constituency Director will be fully responsible for the conduct of the election campaign and will appoint his staff as follows:

(1) Director of Finance
(2) Director of Transport
(3) Director of Canvass
(4) Director of Publicity
(5) Election Agent.

Comhairle Ceantair

The Constituency Director will also appoint an Area Director for each Comhairle Ceantair directly responsible to him for the conduct of the campaign in the area. This Area Director will appoint the following staff:

(1) Area Director of Finance
(2) Area Director of Transport
(3) Area Director of Canvass
(4) Area Director of Publicity.

---

[1]Data required by Constituency Director.

The Director must have at his disposal in the office:
(1) A map of the constituency showing the Registration Units.
(2) Two full copies of the current Register of Electors.
(3) Complete List of Polling Stations with the name of the Cumann responsible for each station.
(4) An accurate list of Churches with times of Masses and evening devotions, and name of Cumann in whose area they are located.
(5) A copy of the Electoral Act, and of the Prevention of Electoral Abuses Act.
(6) List of halls and schools available for meetings.
(7) Names and full postal addresses of Cumainn and Comhairlí Ceantair Officers.
(8) Names and addresses of members and friends of the Organisation who have cars.
(9) List of approved speakers resident in the constituency.
Whenever space permits, the Director should reserve a room at Headquarters for his personal use and to ensure privacy for meetings of his election staff.

Cumann

This organisation should be repeated in each polling area in large towns and cities. In rural districts the Polling Area Director will be responsible for getting all the work of the election done in the area covered by the polling stations under his control.

SECTION II
THE CONSTITITUENCY DIRECTOR OF ELECTION
[*' Summary of Duties' omitted.*]

Line of Action

As soon as possible after his appointment the Constituency Director should call a meeting of his staff (including the Area Director for each Comhairle Ceantair) and the Candidates, to discuss arrangements for the campaign, with particular reference to the following matters of major concern:

(1) State of the Organisation and action required to remedy defects.

(2) Election Fund Campaign.

(3) Printing of local publicity material.

(4) Polling Day transport.

(5) Area Committee Rooms.

(6) Start of the Canvass.

(7) Public meetings.

(8) Personation Agents and Sub-Agents.

(9) Nomination of Candidates.

(10) Insurance of workers, premises, transport.

All the work before the campaign proper begins is covered under one to five of these heads. The Constituency Director should carefully consider each item and have his plans prepared before the meeting. Numbers six to ten must be tackled immediately the election is declared. . . .

The Key-stone

The key-stone of the election organisation is the Cumann in charge of each polling station, and wherever an active Cumann does not exist immediate action must be taken to remedy the defect. The primary concern of the Director of Election on his appointment is, therefore, to have a Cumann or Group formed in all such areas since it is clear that no Scheme of Election Staff Organisation can produce satisfactory results unless the actual workers are available in *every* polling area.

Early selection of a Polling Area Director for each polling station is vital to the efficient operation of the election scheme, and the Constituency Director should make it his special business to ensure that this is done — paying as much attention to the most remote districts as to those near his Headquarters.

Teamwork

The Director must do everything possible to see that there is one hundred per cent co-operation and harmony between the election staff and the Candidates.

He must insist that the Candidates work as a team for the team, and that they carry out his instructions in all matters relating to the conduct of the campaign. Absence of this team-spirit in some areas in the past resulted in bad transfers of preference votes and was responsible in a few cases for the loss of seats. The Director should be tactful in his approach to any departure from the spirit of teamwork, but firm in his decision to deal with it.

He should not, in any circumstances, countenance the division of the constituency into spheres of influence among the Candidates, each of whom should be free, subject to the Director's arrangements, to speak or canvass anywhere in the constituency. Allocation of preferences between the Fianna Fáil Candidates is a matter for the individual voter who, if a known supporter, must be allowed to exercise his own choice without any pressure from the Organisation.

General

Public meetings are the responsibility of the Constituency Director of Election and a special section of *Córas Bua* is designed to give him guidance on all aspects of the matter.

In rural areas it should be the aim to hold at least one after Mass meeting in every parish, but the Director should guard against the illusion that such meetings, no matter how enthusiastic or well attended, are any substitute for a canvass which enables our workers to concentrate on the individual voter who may not be politically minded, who may never listen to speeches or read election leaflets—but who, nevertheless, will decide the result of the election. . . .

SECTION III

THE CONSTITUENCY DIRECTOR OF FINANCE

Summary of Duties

The Director of Finance is responsible for the collection and the economical expenditure of the Election Fund. He must aim at getting in enough money to fight the campaign on as large a scale as possible. He should receive all contributions to the Election Fund, authorise all payments, and pay all accounts.

Since funds must be available before they can be spent, he should, immediately on his appointment, take steps to raise them, bearing in mind that each constituency is responsible for financing its own campaign.

Fund Raising

Experience has shown that it is easier to get money for election purposes before the election than after it, no matter what the result.

A Fund Raising Drive should, therefore, be organised on a systematic basis as soon as possible. In this connection it must be emphasised that Press and circular appeals for subscriptions, without the personal follow-up, rarely bring in enough to meet their cost. Card drives, carnivals, céilithe, dances and sweeps give much more satisfactory returns. In addition, however, the Director must arrange for a collection from house-to-house and at the Church gates in every parish. . . .

[*Section IV omitted.*]

SECTION V
CONSTITUENCY DIRECTOR OF CANVASS

Duties

A systematic canvass of every street, village and townland is the key to victory in the election.

The Constituency Director is responsible for seeing that it is well organised and thoroughly carried out in every polling district in the constituency. . . .

SECTION VI
CONSTITUENCY DIRECTOR OF PUBLICITY

Duties

The Constituency Director is responsible for production of local election publicity under all heads, and for the speedy and efficient distribution of material supplied by National Headquarters.

He must establish and maintain close contact with his Area Director in each Comhairle Ceantair so that he will be in a position to cater for any special needs of a particular town or district that may arise during the campaign. He must ensure that every area gets its proportionate share of the material available and that it is used to the best effect.

The Director should regularly check on distribution and display of posters and leaflets throughout the constituency, and take immediate action to remedy any defects he may find in the arrangements.

Above all, he should remember that the main purpose of all publicity is to keep the names of the Candidates so constantly before the minds of the voters that they cannot forget them.

First Essential

The Director of Publicity must appreciate the fact that having been at school and having learned to read and write does not make a person literate.

A great number of people read with difficulty because they have never acquired the reading habit. For election purposes it must be accepted that a vital ten per cent of the electorate is illiterate and the constant repetition of the Candidates' names in speech and print is, therefore, a first essential of election publicity. Their names (and, of course, the name of the Party) must appear on every piece of printed matter issued locally, and must be referred to by every speaker at public meetings during the campaign.

There is little use in asking people to "Vote Fianna Fáil" unless they know the names of its standard-bearers. . . .

[*Section VII omitted.*]

SECTION VIII

[*Portion omitted.*]

General

The Polling Area Director should arrange for meals for the Personation Agent and booth workers who cannot get home during the day. Intoxicants should not be supplied.

He should have as many influential supporters as possible outside the booth during the Poll (and especially between six and nine in the evening) to make a last minute canvass and to give every voter a Card or Specimen Ballot Paper.

He should keep a check on the Poll and see that his Transport Officer is supplied with lists of those who have not voted.

He should arrange to have posters with the names of our Candidates pasted on sheets of wood or cardboard and prominently displayed at the approaches to the booth. . . . [*Remainder omitted.*]

(d) *Fine Gael.*

Document 8.5 — 'Organize for Victory Now' by Senator T. J. Fitzpatrick and Councillor A. J. O'Brien in *Fine Gael Digest*, vol 12, no 1, pp. 21-23 (February, 1962).

ORGANISE FOR VICTORY — NOW

Elections are not won merely by activity on polling day — or even on the days between nomination and polling. Long before the election the groundwork must be done in every constituency and the seeds sown that will bear fruit on polling day. This article by Senator T. J. Fitzpatrick and Councillor A. J. O'Brien of Cavan shows how the task should be handled in a typical constituency.

To a great extent the success of a Political Party depends on Constituency Organisation, intelligent and persistent publicity and careful attention to the Register of Electors.

CONSTITUENCY ORGANISATION

It should be the aim of every Constituency Executive to have a Unit or Branch for every polling place in the constituency. This Unit need not necessarily be numerically strong but it must be active, thorough and well-informed. The Secretary, in particular, should be a live-wire — young, energetic and enthusiastic. Officers and members of each Branch should know their duties and responsibilities with regard to the Register, canvassing,

Polling day activities, transport of voters etc. The Branch should aim at having enough funds to fight the election in its own area — to pay for transport and to look after election day workers.

A thorough canvass of the electors in the Branch area is one of the most important duties of the Branch. The canvassers should be intelligent and be thoroughly informed on all aspects of Party Policy — especially on those which have a strong appeal in the area. Canvassers should leave an Election Card in each house bearing the names of all the Fine Gael Candidates for the Constituency and in the case of Local Government Elections the names of all the Party Candidates for that Electoral Division. The necessity of voting 1, 2, 3 etc. for the Fine Gael candidates must be impressed on the electors.

The Church gate collection is another important responsibility of the Branch. Such collections apart altogether from their value as fund-raising activities have tremendous prestige value. To leave the collection to two or three persons damages the Party prestige.

Each Local Electoral Area should have a *District Executive* on which all Branches in the Area are represented. The District Executive should meet regularly and its meetings should be attended by Deputies and Senators of the Constituency and County Councillors for that area. In Local Government Elections the District Executive is the controlling unit of organisation for the Electoral area on all matters pertaining to Election Day Organisation. The value of emphasising the names of all Party candidates for that Area cannot be over stressed. *The Constituency Executive* should meet quarterly and public representatives for the Constituency should attend. It is the duty of Constituency Executive officers to see to it that the Fine Gael Party line on current topics is made known at Executive Meetings. Matters of interest to the Party on a constituency level should be discussed.

PUBLICITY

It is often said that Fine Gael has fallen down on publicity. To be effective publicity must be intelligent and persistent and not left over to the eve of the election. In other words it must be kept up from election to election. We have no national newspapers at our command and we must adopt other means of getting the Fine Gael viewpoint across to the voters.

Fine Gael members of *Local Bodies,* County Councils, Corporations, Urban Councils, Committees of Agriculture, Vocational Committees should know exactly what the Fine Gael Policy is on the various matters that come up for discussion and should state that policy clearly and fearlessly. Reports of these meetings are given full coverage in local newspapers—papers which are read by over 80% of our people.

Local newspapers too afford space to *letter writers* who have a case to make and many provincial papers will also publish short news items concerning local Branch Meetings or District Executive Meetings, names of Officers elected or Resolutions passed, etc., if a concise report is submitted by the local secretary or press officer in good time. Such opportunities for publicity should be availed of on every possible occasion.

Election Literature sent out by Headquarters is admirable but of necessity it is done to win National support. The local Director of Elections or his publicity agent should carefully study all such literature from Head Office and where necessary adapt it to meet local conditions and to strengthen local appeal.

Public meetings may not, in these days of Radio and Television, have the value they once had but they cannot yet be discarded. The publicity value of a successful meeting is still very great and a "flop" meeting is a disaster. The entire constituency organisation should go into action when a public meeting is to be addressed by the Party Leader or a front-bench speaker, a suitable platform, a good microphone should be provided and care should be taken in ensuring that the platform party is respected and representative.

On the question of National Publicity we must prepare ourselves for the new medium of *Television*. We believe that Fine Gael can afford to welcome Television because we have the material to meet and beat all opposition on the TV screen.

THE REGISTER

Elections are won and lost on the Register. The work done in checking the Register is not spectacular but it is of vital importance particularly to us because the Voters' List, the basis of the Register, is compiled by Rate Collectors most of whom are active Fianna Fáil workers in their areas. The Voters' List can be effectively checked only by the Branch or Polling District Unit of the Organisation—a Branch that neglects this work is falling down on the job.

Those entitled to go on the *Electors List* are those who have reached the age of twenty-one and were resident at the qualifying address on September 15th. *Objections* must be lodged with the Registration Officer not later than December 14th and claims not later than December 22nd. Every Branch Secretary should be supplied with a copy of the Voters' List for his Polling District. It is his duty to see that it is checked, that an objection is lodged with the Registration Officer against anyone whose name wrongly appears and that *claims* are lodged on behalf of supporters whose names have been omitted within the proper time. Only by attention to the Voters' List can we ensure that all our supporters are entitled to vote on Election Day. We must repeat: the Electors' list can be effectively checked only at local level.

Neither our policy however sound nor our Headquarters however efficient can win Elections without wholehearted and consistent attention to organisation, publicity and the Voters' List in each and every constituency. An all-out effort all the way from Branch level to National Council level will win—and win decisively the next Election.

3. POLICIES

(a) *Fianna Fáil*

(i) Social and Economic Policy

Document 8.6 — Extracts from Address by Mr Seán F Lemass, Taoiseach, to Comh-Chomhairle Átha Cliath of Fianna Fáil, 7 October 1963 (Stencilled press release).

The directive principles of social policy set out in the Irish Constitution, which guide the Oireachtas in the enactment of the nation's laws, are not nowadays mentioned very frequently in Dáil debates. They do not need to be because they are not in dispute. The assessment of the merits of measures proposed for enactment in the light of these principles is instinctive with all our elected representatives. . . .

These directive principles of social policy were framed in the light of Catholic social teaching which has in recent times been elaborated and clarified in the great Encyclicals of Pope John XXIII. They are, however, in no sense sectarian, because they do not conflict with the social doctrine proclaimed by all Christian Churches, and indeed beyond the limits of Christianity.

For all men, in all countries, who have responsibility as members of Governments to seek to put these principles into effect, the Encyclicals of Pope John are of enormous help, because they remove doubts and uncertainties, and give to all mankind the benefit of a clear guiding light. In these modern days, no nation can operate in isolation, and social progress anywhere depends in some degree on progress everywhere. It is therefore true that the universal understanding and application of the social teachings of Pope John can help every nation, including Ireland, in their effective application. For the Irish Government, I can say that Ministers keep these Encyclicals at hand for constant inspiration and reference when working out their plans to accelerate the application of the social policy which we are seeking to develop. . . . .

This is a good time to stress the significance of the progress of our thinking since the drafting of the First Dáil's Democratic Programme, in view of the fact that we are now in the process of settling our Programme for Expansion until 1970. A Programme, in our modern thinking, is something very much more precise than the members of the First Dáil had conceived of or indeed were, in the circumstances of their times, capable of formulating. Our knowledge of the problems of economic growth, our information about our national circumstances, and about the international conditions which bear on our development policies, are all vastly greater than they were at any previous period.

. . . The first real attempt at the systematic planning of national development was in the 1958 Programme and we have learned much even since then, both as to our potential for development, as well as to the methods by which it may be achieved. Indeed, the public attitude has changed in some degree also. While the publication of the First Programme was welcomed, generally and almost uncritically, as a breath of fresh air blowing into our nearly moribund economy, the very growth of public confidence which it inspired, and the expectation which it aroused that our progress would assuredly be maintained has gathered a more selective attitude to the Second Programme. This we expected and it is something which all who look for signs of developing maturity in our community can only welcome.

I think it is true to say that everybody now understands that the improvement of living standards and social conditions depends on the success of measures to make the nation as a whole better off by reason of an increase of the total production of its farms and factories. There is no source of material wealth except human labour applied intelligently to natural resources. A Programme for Economic Expansion—for stimulating and organising the production of more wealth—is an essential foundation for the realisation of social objectives. Economic progress and social progress march together. As the aim of economic policy is to promote the expansion of productive activities to enable the people generally to become wealthier, so also the aims of social policy, in many important spheres, must be directed to enhancing the nation's capacity for production. We have no aim of facilitating men and women of normal health and age to live without working: rather it is our purpose, by reason of their better education, training, health, housing and general sense of security to enhance their capacity to work productively. . . .

It is, of course, the function of leadership at every level—in the Government, and in the organisations which operate for major economic interests— to help the community to get organised, to generate the right response amongst their members, and to lead them away from courses of action which can be prejudicial to success. This is the process in which we have now to engage. It would be foolish to think that it is going to prove easy. There are still too many people, and organisations, which have not yet begun to regard themselves as integral parts of the nation, who are still standing aloof from the national effort, thinking in terms of how much more they can extract from the growing pool of national resources instead of what they can contribute to it, and who seem sometimes even willing to consider, in the pursuit of narrow sectional interests, policies which can defeat the nation.

If the targets set in the Second Programme are realised, we can visualise the country, and every one of its citizens individually, becoming better off, in terms of a real improvement of their living standards, at an average annual rate of about 4%. . . .

One of the requirements of national economic and social progress which is emerging in all democratic countries as a factor of major importance, is what is usually described as an incomes policy—some arrangement or agreement, or climate of opinion which would operate to relate expectations of increased incomes of any kind—salaries, wages, profits, rents and so on—to the rate of growth of total national resources and to the requirements of social justice. I do not think it is any exaggeration to say that the effectiveness of Democracy, in the spheres of economic and social planning, will be called in question unless some method of meeting this requirement can be devised—a method conforming with the basic concepts of democratic freedom. It is a crucial test of the superiority of the democratic over the totalitarian method of national administration. For this country also, this is likely to prove an essential requirement of continued progress.

An incomes policy is linked in the minds of many workers with the concept of "restraint" which they do not like, and which they tend to interpret as meaning that they should voluntarily forego for somebody else's benefit possibilities of wage increases, even when improving national circumstances and their own higher productivity would justify increases. In fact a sound incomes policy should better be related to such a term as "income assurance" because this is what it should mean—assurance to all workers that their wages and salaries will rise steadily and continuously as national resources expand, that the increases they will obtain will represent a real improvement of their buying capacity and not be offset or nullified by rising prices, and that all workers, and not only those whose key positions in the national economy give them bargaining power, will benefit when increases are possible, and particularly those whose remuneration lags behind the national average.

Our own experience and that of other countries have shown that this kind of income assurance cannot be left to haphazard methods. If every worker is to become progressively better off we must work out some method of organising ourselves to secure this result in a regular and orderly manner. In this day and age the danger of social injustice, and of widening inequalities in our community, is far less to be feared from the old-fashioned type of capitalist mentality than the undue exploitation of their economic power by sections of workers—in key posts on which the employment of many other workers depend—seeking more than their due share of the increase of national resources and thereby making it impossible for other workers to get any share at all, or even, by causing unemployment, to deprive them of the incomes they have. . . .

In this connection, it is vital to remember that this country lives by its export trade to a relatively greater extent than most others. In 1960, 38% of all we produced was disposed of in export markets and our Development Programme visualises an increase to just under 45% in 1970.

. . . Any courses of action which tend to make our export prices uncompetitive, due to higher material or labour costs, or dearer transportation, or power, or anything else, places the employment of these Irish workers in jeopardy and could condemn them to a total loss of income and to emigration. These men are in the vulnerable front line of the national advance, whereas others may have safe and secure "base" posts, and it is their interests which should be the touchstone by which we must judge the soundness of any course of action which may be suggested.

Improvements in general living conditions are not expressed only in terms of increases in pay, because in a modern society many of the services and facilities which make for better living can only be provided by public authority. The extension of the education service, better housing conditions, including the provision where still required of water and sewage services, the strengthening of security against undeserved poverty by the extension of social welfare arrangements, better health services, better roads, and footpaths and parks, and the improvement of many of the other, if less costly, facilities now provided by the Government or local authorities, also represent the fulfilment of the operation of translating an increase of total national resources into social progress and better living. Some part of the additional resources gained by economic expansion must be set aside to meet the higher cost of improving these social services, and there will be some years when this may necessitate an adjustment of taxation rates. . . .

At this time, there will be few to question that investment in education is entitled to a very high priority, and the Second Programme contemplates very substantial developments during the next seven years, particularly in the post-primary fields. . . .

For those for whom social housing is a necessity—that is people who must receive help from public sources to secure dwellings of proper modern standards within their means—there are some categories which have not yet been brought fully within the scope of housing policy and the extension of the social housing programme to include them will now become possible.

It is certain that the Select Committee of the Dáil which is at present reviewing the Health Services will have many changes to propose, and it is equally certain they will involve increased expenditure on these services. . . .

It is a fact that the wealthier countries of Europe expend on community social activities of this kind a higher proportion of their national incomes than in this country. This is understandable because when the basic requirements of comfortable living have been made secure, the people of every country have shown that they wish to see an extension of public activities in these social spheres. It is certain that the Irish public will react to expanding national wealth in exactly the same way as other peoples.

(ii) Foreign Policy

Document 8.7—Extracts from 'Ireland in the New Europe', Speech by Mr Lemass to the 33rd Árd Fheis, 1962, in *Irish Press*, 21 November, 1962.

My remarks will reveal to you the extent to which all political action and every decision is now influenced by the existence of the European Economic Community and the likelihood of this country's participation in it. When I addressed the Árd Fheis at its meeting in January last, it was on the eve of my departure, with the Minister for Industry and Commerce, to make the first formal submission in Brussels in support of our application for membership. On that occasion, the Árd Fheis adopted, with unanimity and enthusiasm, a resolution approving of the course on which we had decided.

Everything that has happened since has confirmed us in our belief in the soundness of that decision, and in our expectation that the participation of this country—small and limited in resources though it may be—in the movement for European integration would be welcomed by the member states.

Since then we have, with all persistence, pushed ahead with our preparations, in the expectation that our wish to acquire membership of the Community will, in due time, be realised.

Every national plan for economic and social advancement has now to be adjusted to the new circumstances which have emerged in Western Europe. Although preparing the country to meet the impact of these circumstances involves nothing which would not be worth doing for the benefits which it would confer in better organisation of the nation's whole economy, we would, in different circumstances, have undertaken it at a more leisurely pace.

Now we are working under the compulsion of a time-table which is not of our own devising. We do not regret this. Wide though may be the scope of our adjustments—and difficult and costly in some sectors—all human experience supports the view that a nation—and this is I believe especially true of the Irish nation—will respond more whole-heartedly to the urgent demands of a grand design than to the slower fulfilment of a piecemeal programme. . . .

Now for the first time there has emerged the prospect of replacing . . . bilateral trade agreements with our European neighbours, including Britain, by the permanent and impartial rules of an international community of which we will be a member on equal terms with all the other members.

Although the adaptation of our economy to the new system will not be easy, it is not surprising that we welcomed the opportunity, now presented to us, to escape from the restrictions and uncertainties of our present circumstances and from the disadvantages of our limited bargaining power—that we saw in the European Community a door opening to new economic opportunities not previously available to us and the prospect of a much more secure foundation for our future prosperity.

For a party with our philosophy and national background no other course was possible. The alternative course would condemn us in perpetuity to a position of economic inferiority, leave us a beggar amongst the nations, seeking to maintain a dying economy on the crumbs of charity from our wealthier neighbours.

That the creation of an economic union by the nations of Western Europe is only a first step on a path which leads to political confederation, at some time and in some form, is no deterrent to our taking that course. From the very outset we foresaw the inevitability—and the logic—of the economic union developing a political character, even if others are now pretending to be surprised that it should be so. For our part we welcomed the prospect of the negotiation of an agreement for European political integration—not solely because of its inevitability, nor because it was necessary to make the economic union work, nor because we recognised that the economic and political affairs of nations could not be maintained in water-tight compartments, but because we saw in this prospect a new source of national strength, an extension of our freedom, and a better opportunity of fulfilling our cultural, economic and social aims. . . .

It is inevitable that this movement to unify and strengthen Western Europe should provoke the hostility of the leaders of international Communism. . . .

In our case, the issue which is being given prominence is that of neutrality, and this may be causing some confused thinking, perhaps even amongst people who would not knowingly take inspiration from any Communist source. In the world of today there exists a situation unprecedented in history in which many old concepts and definitions have little meaning. International diplomacy is not now concerned with problems of the equilibrium of power, between states whose basic philosophies and systems do not greatly differ, and for which the concept of neutrality had a precise legalistic as well as a political significance. . . .

The Communist purpose is to impose their materialistic philosophy on a world in which no pockets of individual freedom will be allowed to survive. The nations are dividing into two camps—in one the Communistic states and their satellites, and in the other the free nations which, whatever their deficiencies, adhere to the age-old principles which we respect.

Can we pretend to be indifferent to this situation—careless whether the democratic or the Communist philosophy should dominate the world? If this is what is meant by being neutral, then that is not our position—it never was and never will be. Rather do we wish to proclaim that we are on the side of those nations which accept the democratic principles which we have enshrined in our own Constitution. . . .

Although, in this respect, we have stated our position, beyond possibility of misinterpretation, it may, nevertheless, be necessary to make our position equally clear in another respect also. We are not a party to any international agreement involving commitments of a military character, other than those arising from the Charter of the United Nations. It is understandable that we should have asked ourselves whether this fact was likely to have any bearing on our application for membership of the European Economic Community. We are now satisfied, from our discussions with the Governments of the member states, that it is not a factor in its consideration, nor have we been asked to accept any obligations of that kind as a condition of our entry. . . .

There is no question of sinking our national identity in some new conception of European citizenship. We do not intend this, and there are none in Europe who ask for it. Everywhere in Europe I found full recognition of the fact that the Irish Nation is a separate entity. . . .

Because some people, who have always been indifferent, if not openly antagonistic, to the national policy of reviving the Irish language and developing other aspects of our national culture, may seek to use this new situation to urge the abandonment of these aims, the duty devolves on Fianna Fáil of encouraging right thinking in this regard. The bringing of the language into everyday use within our community remains a dominant feature of our policy and closer ties with our European neighbours will not affect this policy in the least degree.

(iii) Partition

Document 8.8 — Extracts from speech by Seán F. Lemass, Taoiseach, at Tralee, Monday, 29th July, 1963 (Stencilled press release).

We have never failed to recognise the genuineness of the fears which have influenced the religious minority in the North, or to understand that the assurances which have been given in this respect, down the years, by all national leaders, or the evidence of tolerance and non-discrimination elsewhere in the country, are not regarded as sufficient, and that more positive and binding safeguards would for a time—probably quite a long time—be needed before full confidence would be established. We have in effect said to our separated countrymen: "What safeguards do you need in a reunited Ireland? Whatever you may in reason ask we are prepared to give." . . .

The efforts which appeared to be developing spontaneously for contact and discussion are now being countered by a new gimmick called "constitutional recognition". That this is just a gimmick—an excuse for inaction—is, I am sure, recognised by those who use it. What it means is never made very clear. Sometimes it is presented as meaning that the six north-eastern Irish counties are a part of Britain which is an absurdity. Sometimes it seems to mean some formal abandonment of our hopes for Irish unity which is an impossibility.

We recognise that the Government and Parliament there exist with the support of the majority in the Six-County area—artificial though that area is. We see it functioning within its powers, and we are prepared to stand over the proposal made by the united Republican Cabinet of 1921 that they should continue to function with these powers, within an all-Ireland constitution, for so long as it is desired to have them. Recognition of the realities of the situation has never been a difficulty with us.

We believe that it is foolish in the extreme that in this island, and amongst people of the same race, there should persist a desire to avoid contacts even in respect of matters where concerted action is clearly seen to be beneficial. We would hope that from the extension of useful contacts at every level of activity, a new situation would develop which would permit of wider possibilities in accord with our desires. Whether this hope would prove to be justified only time would tell, but it seems timorous in the extreme for leaders of the dissentient minority to want to avoid contacts for fear that they might result in their being convinced that something more permanent and extensive would be a good thing. . . .

The solution of the problem of Partition is one to be found in Ireland by Irishmen, and as we move towards it we can be sure that there is no power or influence anywhere which can prevent its implementation when the barriers of misunderstanding and suspicion which have sustained it are whittled away. . . .

(b) *Fine Gael*

Document 8.9 — Extracts from 'Mr Dillon outlines Fine Gael Policy to the Árd Fheis' in *Fine Gael Bulletin,* no 2, June 1963.

SOCIAL AND ECONOMIC POLICY

. . . The recent announcement that the countries of the European Free Trade Association propose to abolish all tariffs between them by 1966 must have significant consequences for our export trade, and may result in serious adjustment in our industrial life for which effective provision should be made now. Plans are being formulated to help industrialists to adapt their business to the new situation, but there can be little doubt that the jobs of a great many people will be put in jeopardy by this new development, and there is no more urgent task than that of making provision now to help people whose employment is interfered with, to meet this new situation.

I want to say emphatically that I do not consider that any Government has done its duty in this regard unless it is prepared to say that our resources will be mobilised, and the first charge upon them before there are any loans, grants, or anything else, is the assurance to the working man with a family to support, that if as a result of changes in world conditions which make high protection no longer practical, he is thrown out of work, we will do either of two things—we will either give him a pension appropriate to his age and circumstances, or we will provide a period of adjustment of a year or two, in which he will have to retrain himself at an inconvenience which we are prepared to acknowledge, and which will be shared by industrialists and farmers. . . .

It is vitally important in the time that lies ahead for successful industrial expansion that we should secure the enthusiastic co-operation of all those engaged in industry—workers and employers— to feel that they are in this campaign of expansion together, and that the burdens and the benefits will be equitably shared. An incomes policy for the maintenance of stability must be fair to everybody if it is to have any prospect of success. If there is to be restraint in regard to wages and salaries, there must be restraint in regard to dividends and profits as well. . . .

We fully appreciate the vital importance of industrial development and expansion, and *Fine Gael undertakes to safeguard and protect the interests of industrial workers and of those who have invested their money in Irish industry.* Fine Gael will encourage private enterprise by tax and fiscal policies appropriate to modern conditions, and will intensify the efforts to establish home industries, especially those based on Irish raw materials which are prepared to cater for export markets. Fine Gael, believing in the right of Irish men and women to earn their livelihood in Ireland, will strive to provide employment for all and will make arrangements for the granting of loans at a specially low rate of interest for approved projects which will provide permanent employment at good wages for our people in their own country.

Nothing is more important to the realisation of this objective than the maintenance of good industrial relations, and *we accept it as a basic fact that such good relations are best achieved through direct negotiations conducted in a spirit of mutual confidence between the trade unions and employers.* A free and responsible trades union movement is as vital an element in a free society as parliament itself.

If we are to meet effectively competition of the new era of free trade, it is manifest that we must undertake some measure of economic planning in this country. Without abridging the freedom of capital investment by private enterprise, some co-ordination between the investment of the Government itself, of State sponsored bodies, Local Authorities and private enterprise, is urgently necessary if waste of capital and effort is to be avoided. Just as technologists are necessary for the development of science and industry, so in economic planning the advice of economists, scientists, and technologists must be mobilised, and to do this effectively, the Government requires a Department of Economic Planning to advise the Government on the one hand, and industry on the other, as to how best our available resources can be most efficiently deployed in the interest of the economy as a whole.

Far from withdrawing through increased Corporation Profits Tax the resources necessary for the modernising of our industrial equipment, we should encourage industry to plough back into expansion and modernisation a larger share of their annual earnings. Every tax incentive or concession calculated to expand domestic investment in Irish industry should be availed of. . . .

While it is true that an increased capital formation is desirable in every productive direction it is a disastrous illusion to allow the urgent need for such fixed capital formation in housing and schools to be postponed, as it has been postponed by the present Government during the last seven years.

FOREIGN POLICY

. . . Our foreign policy must be based on the defence of freedom at home and abroad, against the materialist aggression of Atheistic International Communism, and our aim should be to multiply the number of our friends among the free nations of the world.

We have not the power to intimidate enemies, but we could have influence to persuade friends, and the more of them we have, the more we shall be able to do to promote in the world the fundamental political beliefs which our people hold dear. It is a commonly held illusion that recent disagreements between Peking and Moscow mean that the fundamental threat of Communist aggression is receding, but it is important to remember that these Communist Powers may differ amongst themselves as to the best means of destroying freedom and democracy in the world, but they share a common aim to effect its destruction, and if they ever believe that there is a prospect of achieving that aim of world conquest for Communism, they will gladly combine to share the spoils of conquest. *The only way to prevent the success of their hopes is to make it clear that no Communist conspiracy will ever be strong enough to overcome the combined resources of freedom.* That was the objective of President Kennedy's proposal for an Atlantic Partnership, and though for the present that grand design may be postponed, ultimately it will provide the sure guarantee of the survival of freedom in the world.

PARTITION

Foreign policy for Ireland must always have regard to the bitter fact of the partition of our country, and Fine Gael believes that a united Ireland can and will ultimately be achieved on the basis of full respect for the rights of all sections of our community irrespective of their political or religious beliefs. Partition was established by a British Act of Parliament, for which no Irish vote—Orange or Green—was ever cast, and our people have never acknowledged, and never will acknowledge, the right of any authority to partition the Irish Nation, nor the *de jure* existence of any boundary dividing a part of Ulster from the Province or the Nation to which it rightly belongs. . . .

AGRICULTURE

Great as must be the contribution of industry to our future development, it remains true that the greatest national asset we have is twelve million acres of arable land, and the people who live and get their living on it. The more one thinks of the future potential of the agricultural industry of this country, the clearer it is that the most urgent development necessary for the expansion of economic agricultural production, is the provision of a National Agricultural Advisory Service. There are thousands of acres of land in this country which are not producing more than half of what they could be made to produce, and it is not for the want of hard work on the part of those who own them, it is for the want of technical know-how and adequate credit facilities to operate up-to-date methods of production.

We accordingly propose to establish *an adequate Agricultural Advisory Service* based on Parish Agents and the Advisory Services of the County Committees of Agriculture, working in close collaboration with the Agricultural Institute, which we established when we were last in Office. . . .

There is no use providing advice for the farmer if he cannot afford to act upon it, and therefore, we should provide *interest-free loans to farmers* of sums up to £1,000 for schemes for increased production planned in conjunction with the Advisory Services. . . .

Unless we have the right type of livestock it is impossible for us to keep our place in the export markets of the world, and therefore the *progeny testing of livestock* is urgently necessary. We established a Progeny Testing Station for pigs in Cork when we were last in Office, and had plans for the establishment of another. We still have only one Progeny Testing Station, and we ought to have four. It will be our intention to see that this is done.

We also believe that an *adequate Veterinary Advisory Service* should be provided in association with the Artificial Insemination Service for cattle, to eliminate the present excessive incidence of infertility in cattle.

The present Government stopped *Part B. of the Land Project,* and thus with-held from a great many farmers the credit facilities without which they cannot avail of the Land Project. We believe that this was a mistaken decision, and we shall restore these credit facilities.

The *Local Authorities Works Act* must be re-established to facilitate the effective drainage of the land and to carry out other essential works in rural Ireland, which are now being neglected as a result of the Fianna Fáil decision to wind up activities under that Act.

. . . We are convinced that it is time that farmers should be helped to improve their own housing accommodation, and to this end *we propose to inaugurate a scheme under which farmers will be enabled to build their own houses,* and having received the appropriate grant from the Government and the Local Authority, to add the balance of the cost to their land annuity to be paid off over the next 30 or 40 years, through a Land Commission Annuity.

EDUCATION

. . . Without adequate educational facilities for Primary, Secondary, Technical and University, no community can prosper and expand. This country can no longer afford to allow its children to be denied the opportunity of developing the gifts God gave them, because of the financial circumstances of the families into which they happen to be born. The best that we can provide in primary, secondary, technical and university education should be available to every boy and girl who can benefit from it, without regard to their economic circumstances, and a comprehensive system of scholarships should be made available to open these educational opportunities for all young people.

No effort should be spared to preserve the Irish Language, but it would be infinitely preferable if our efforts to that end were emphatically dissociated from the present system of compulsion, which is promoting opposition and dislike of the language itself. *The task of promoting knowledge of Irish and love of the language itself, would be infinitely simplified if it were based on voluntary effort and enthusiasm such as is manifest in voluntary organisations like Gael Linn, and kindred Movements, stimulated and supported by every support and encouragement which the Government could give them;* . . .

Nothing is more certain than the fact that the Irish Language cannot be revived unless the majority of our people want to revive it. We believe that the present methods of compulsion are building up opposition to the revival of Irish, and we propose to do something about it.

(1) *We believe that the teaching of infants in the National Schools through Irish should be stopped, and that they should be taught through the language of their home.*

(2) *We believe that Irish should be taught like any other subject in the schools, but that teaching mathematics or history or any other subject through the medium of Irish where Irish is not the language of the home should be put an end to. Where a group of parents, however, want a school where Irish shall be the medium of instruction, because they have made Irish the language of the home, in Dublin or anywhere else, we believe that such facilities should be made available wherever possible.*

(3) *We believe that the Leaving Certificate should not be withheld from any child who has passed or got honours in other subjects but who has failed in Irish.*

(4) *We believe that promotion in the Public Services for technical posts should no longer be made subject to a test in Irish.*

(5) *And, we would hope to establish a scheme of scholarships leading to secondary, vocational and university education, for children who showed a special aptitude for Irish, which we believe would foster and develop a growing love of the language, and which would produce in time a growing body of highly educated men and women, the hallmark of whose higher education would be proficiency in Irish. . . .*

HEALTH AND SOCIAL WELFARE

Next to Education, we regard the promotion of the health of our people as vital to the whole future of the nation, and we therefore are resolved to carry out a complete re-organisation of the Health Services and introduce a new comprehensive Health Service based on insurance. The new comprehensive Health Service will have the following main features:

(1) *The present vexatious Means Test and the Blue Card system will be abolished.*

(2) *Those unable to provide for themselves, for example, Old Age Pensioners, persons receiving Widows' Pensions, Unemployment Benefit, or Unemployment Assistance, Home Assistance, small farmers and such like, will be provided with all services, medical, surgical and hospital, and drugs and medicines free of charge and without contribution.*

(3) *A free medical service based on the family doctor will be extended to all persons within the scheme. A free choice of doctor, free of charge, will, where possible, be provided.*

(4) *Free hospital and specialist services will be provided for all patients within the scheme.*

(5) *Drugs and medicines, at substantially reduced prices, will be provided for those who do not get them free.*

. . . We believe that it should be possible to improve the circumstances of pensioners, and intend to expand the existing social welfare benefits as our resources will allow, and for those persons in categories not catered for by the existing schemes for old age, widows and orphans, we believe that a new scheme could be provided along the lines of the Voluntary Health Insurance Scheme, which would be open to persons wishing to supplement any incomes which they might be entitled to, but which at present render them ineligible for pensions under the existing Pensions Code.

LOCAL GOVERNMENT

The burden of *Rates* has now reached unprecedented dimensions and is becoming intolerable. We believe they should be reduced (1) by the *reorganisation of the present Health Services* which we propose, and (2) by giving the County Councils and Corporations a *wider discretion to use the Road Funds* in the way they think best in the interests of the rate-payers. There are many roads in the country which could be taken over by the Local Authority for maintenance, but they cannot do it because they cannot afford to take them over in their present state. We believe that grants should be provided to bring these roads up to a condition in which the County Council could accept responsibility for them. Rates have become so formidable a burden- that we believe many people are deterred from repairing or improving their premises by the prospect of having their valuation increased, and we therefore propose to introduce legislation to provide *exemption from rates for seven years* in respect of such improvements.

GROUND RENTS

On the subject of Ground Rents, we intend to introduce legislation to enable all persons paying Ground Rents to buy them from their landlords on terms fair to themselves and to the landlord. [*Remainder omitted.*]

(c) *The Labour Party*
    (i) Policy on Coalition
    Document 8.10 — Paragraphs 28 and 29 of *Report of the Administrative Council and the Parliamentary Labour Party for the Years 1960-61 and 1961-62.*

28. The Party contested the General Election as an independent political Party, with its own Policy and Programme.

29. On 13th September, 1961, in a broadcast during the election campaign, Mr. Brendan Corish, the Party Leader, made the following statement:

"*Labour is an independent Party with a distinctive policy. Whatever the result of this Election, Labour will pursue an independent policy in the next Dáil and will not take part in a Government.*

"*Whatever the composition of the next government, we will strive to have our Labour Policy adopted by the Dáil and, as in the past, we will support proposals and measures that are consistent with our policy and oppose those which we believe are detrimental to the interests of the people.*"

(ii) Social and Economic Policy

Document 8.11 — Extracts from speech by Deputy Brendan Corish at Labour Party Annual Conference, June 1963 (Press release).

Labour has always stood for positive economic planning—and this is not the same thing as the Government's so-called plans for economic expansion which do little more than attempt to forecast what will happen to the economy. The basic need today is to develop our economy so as to increase employment and raise living standards. Our economy must be planned so that none of our resources are left idle or wasted. Economic planning can ensure that by a combination of public enterprise, co-operative effort, and private initiative all our productive potentialities are fully developed.

Co-ordination and planning for the various forms of economic activity must be under public direction but the various economic groups and trade organisation such as the trade unions should be consulted where decisions concerning the broad lines of economic policy are involved. To assist in the direction of the economy and the planning of the full utilisation of all our resources Labour proposes that a planning body of independent experts should be set up. This body would assist in working out a flexible national economic plan and an annual economic budget which the Government would implement through its control of investment, credit and taxation policies. The body would also assist private industry in working out their expansion plans after consultation with both sides of industry through Development Councils for the different industries. The functions of the planning body would also include the preparation of a programme for an increased rate of investment in productive projects, the co-ordination of the level of public and private investment so as to maintain a steady rate of increase in overall investment, the co-ordination of the work of the various State bodies and Government departments concerned with productive projects particularly with a view to the development of new projects, and making available information concerning expansion plans and new developments so that full advantage would be taken of them.

Labour believes firmly that there should be a greater emphasis on the expansion of public enterprise in our economy. In the past, public enterprise has advanced Irish economic development, and improved the general welfare of the community. Its full potential has not yet been fully appreciated, much less put into practice. The dynamic possibilities of public enterprise must be exploited as far as possible if our human and material resources are to be employed fully and effectively.

We recognise also that private enterprise should be assisted in those fields in which it proves able to combine efficiency with responsibility to consumers, employees, and the community. It should be recognised however that cases do arise in which private industrialists or employers fail to fulfil their obligations either to the workers or to the public at large. We have seen examples of industries which have been allowed to decay and die through the lack of public conscience of their private owners. In such cases some form of Government action must be taken to prevent large-scale redundancy and economic decay.

While, as I have said, Labour is prepared to welcome any real conversion of the present Government to Labour policies of economic planning and public enterprise, we must remember that the real evidence which we have of Government economic policy is the Pay Pause and the Turnover Tax. It is difficult to see how either of these policies—the one a determined effort to prevent wage increases without any corresponding control on prices and profits, and the other a tax on the very necessities of life—could be interpreted as a 'move to the left'.

(iii) Agriculture

Document 8.12 — Extracts from *Address to Labour Party Annual Conference by the Chairman, Mr James Tully, June 1963* (Press release).

We in the Labour Party realise the need for investment in agricultural aid and improvement. We know that in practically every European country, and in many other countries throughout the world, Governments have found it necessary to encourage and support agriculture by subsidy and other means. What we question is whether the present Government expenditure on agriculture is directed in the best possible way—whether it helps those who need help, whether it makes a real contribution to progress in agriculture. The fault which we have found with the present Government measures of support for agriculture is that they have an overall tendency to give the most help to the largest farmer, who is least in need. Many grants and loans are available only where the farmer already has a considerable amount of capital which he can freely spend himself. The small or medium-sized farmer cannot benefit, because he has not the necessary initial capital. Labour considers that our investment in agriculture should be channelled towards those who are most in need of aid—the small and medium-sized farmer, and the agricultural labourer who wishes to acquire land and stock, in order to start farming on his own behalf.

The present plight of the agricultural labourer is nothing less than disgraceful. His wages and conditions are far below those of other workers; what he can earn would barely serve to keep a single man alive, let alone enable a man to support a wife and family.

(iv) Health

Document 8.13 — Extracts from *Labour's Policy for a New Health Service,* revised edition, May 1963 (Stencilled).

1. All citizens, irrespective of their means, should be entitled to the best medical care and attention available. Need, not means, should be the only test of eligibility for whatever medical treatment any member of the community may require. [*Paragraphs 2 and 3 omitted.*]

4. There is widespread dissatisfaction with the existing health services not only among the poorer sections but also among the so-called middle income group. Whatever hopes may have been entertained when the Health Act of 1953 was introduced, the experience of the last ten years has been a great disappointment. In particular, the manner in which the means test for the lower income group has operated has been most unsatisfactory, the great majority of wage and salary earners having been excluded from the free health services such as they are. The continuation of the dispensary system, the absence of any choice of doctor for the lower income group and the charges for hospital treatment are among the other unsatisfactory features of the existing services.

5. We are convinced that the best solution for these difficulties lies not in any further amendment of the Health Acts but in the provision of a new health service that would give to all citizens equal opportunities for availing of whatever medical attention they might require including diagnosis and treatment.

6. Briefly we propose that a new health scheme should be introduced which would cover general practitioner services, hospital treatment, specialist services, dental services, ophthalmic (eye) services and pharmaceutical services. There would be no direct charge for the general practitioner service, hospital treatment or specialist services. There would be partial charge to some persons for the remaining services (dental, eye and pharmaceutical) but these services would be without direct charge to certain categories of persons. The dispensary system in its present form would be abolished and all persons covered by the scheme would have a free choice of doctor. The present charges for hospital treatment would be abolished.

7. The new health scheme would be on a contributory basis so that all persons covered, including their dependents, would be entitled as of right to the benefits provided by the scheme.

[*Paragraph 8 omitted.*]

9. There are administrative difficulties in bringing in literally everybody within a contributory scheme. The Labour scheme would, however, embrace the vast majority of the community. It would cover all employees irrespective of income, as well as farmers and certain other self-employed persons. Old Age Pensioners and others in receipt of social welfare benefits would be automatically regarded as contributors for the purpose of the scheme. Contributions would be compulsory for all employees and for farmers with holdings

having valuations from £15 to, say, £100. It would also be compulsory for other self-employed persons below a specified income limit, say £1,500.

10. The scheme would cover not only the contributor but his dependents as well. In the case of farmers it would also cover members of the family assisting on the farm.

11. Employees' contributions to the scheme would be collected by means of a weekly stamp through a link with the existing social insurance scheme which would be amended so as to bring in all employees irrespective of income. (At present there is a £800 limit for non-manual employees.) Farmers' contributions would be collected twice yearly in conjunction with the local rates. The contributions of other self-employed persons would be on a stamp basis.

[*Remainder omitted.*]

(v) Education
Document 8.14 — *Challenge and Change in Education*, Policy Document issued by the Labour Party, 1963.

Introduction

Labour's policy on education is firmly based on certain broad principles. Firstly, the criterion for the further education of any child must be the ability of the child to benefit rather than the ability of the child's parents to pay for such education. Education in Ireland today, despite the undoubted fact that increasing numbers of children are receiving post-primary education of one sort or another, remains essentially a part of a structure of social and financial class privileges which serve to prevent the full utilisation of the human resources of the community and which are in complete opposition to Labour's concept of a good society. Labour believes that post-primary education should be free to all children and that the opportunity to receive university and other forms of education should be made available to all those with ability to benefit from it. . . .

Labour also believes that a better educational system and a more efficient method of selecting the type of education suited to each child is not only desirable on social or moral grounds, but is a basic economic investment. In the next few years this country is going to face enormous economic problems, problems which may indeed put our survival as an independent nation in question. It is, therefore, essential that planning in education should be an inherent part of our economic planning. Already shortages of certain types of skill are becoming felt in our economy, and at the same time there is a surplus of other skills, resulting in under-employment and emigration. We also need a coordinated and continuous research programme.

National Planning of Education

The Labour Party believes that one of the prime necessities for the improvement of the educational system is an end to the present method of regarding education as being divided into four water-tight compartments—primary, secondary, vocational and university—and an integration and coordination of our whole educational system. We have also drawn repeated attention to the need for rational educational forecasting, planning and research.

To achieve these ends, the Labour Party recommends the setting up of a National Planning Branch in the Department of Education, which would undertake the task of this co-operation, integration, and planning. This Planning body should not, however, be a purely Civil Service centralised body, or consist of administrators without any practical experience of education. While the planning body would need to have at its disposal the services of full-time officials, Labour recommends that the planning branch should consist of representatives of the Department of Education, the Local Authorities, the Churches, managers', headmasters' and teachers' organisations, and other representative bodies. Such a board would undertake the continuous planning and development of our educational system. The planning branch would also consult the local education authorities, and we point out elsewhere the necessity for local authorities and education committees to play a greater part in our educational system.

The first task of this planning branch would be to continue the survey of our educational system. In this task they would be helped by the present two-year investigation by the OECD Survey Team. We recommend that local area committees be set up under the aegis of the local public and educational bodies, which would report on the position and needs of their areas to the local authority. The local committees and teachers should also have easy access to the planning branch to discuss any urgent difficulties which arise at other times. . . .

Within the Department of Education itself, the planning branch would take steps to integrate the present widely separated branches of the Department, and ensure that the officials of each branch appreciate the aims and problems of the education system as a whole.

We have logically recommended that the planning branch be part of the Department of Education. In doing so, we are conscious of the present deficiencies within that Department, particularly in respect of its unduly conservative outlook and beliefs. A radical change in the approach of the Department is hoped for by the Labour Party.

(vi) Foreign Policy

Document 8.15 — Extracts from *Address to Labour Party Annual Conference by the Chairman, Mr James Tully, June 1963* (Press release).

Labour's foreign policy remains consistent, as it has been approved by several successive Annual Conferences. Labour stands for the further support and strengthening of the United Nations Organisation as the foundation for a system of world government and world peace, and believes that this country should not become involved in military alliances which are likely to lead only to an increase in world tension and the danger of war. . . .

4. THE INDEPENDENTS

Document 8.16 — Extracts from Basil Chubb, 'The Independent Member in Ireland', in *Political Studies*, vol 5 (1957).

Notwithstanding cabinet government on the British model and well-organized political parties, there have been enough Independent members in Dáil Éireann . . . to make them important in political life and, occasionally, to give them as a group a key position. In the House they have a recognized status and, though they may be by no means agreed, they are treated for procedural purposes as though they are a party group. When their numbers and the political circumstances have warranted it, they have even received ministerial office. Though they number only five today, which is fewer than ever before. . . not so long since, fourteen strong, they were in the very centre of the political stage and on that occasion five votes were decisive. The Independent is, then, a political phenomenon of importance in Ireland and by no means a curious rarity or unusual survival well out of the main stream of political life.

The term 'Independent' calls for definition. For purposes of this article an Independent may be said to be 'a person independent of the party machines'. He does not necessarily call himself an 'Independent'. He may not be a 'true' or 'pure' Independent who fights his own election battle and, possibly, fights it largely on his own money. He may not even be a 'temperamental Independent', one who belongs from time to time to a party, but cannot stay in it; or a dissident, one who has left or been expelled from his party. He may, indeed, be a virtual camp-follower of one of the parties, always supporting it, tolerated by it, perhaps not even seriously opposed by it in his constituency. Or he may even sit and vote with other like-minded 'Independents' in a loose, though informal, group. Or, however labelled, he may have the support of a small or localized organization with a title and political objects, such as a county farmers' association, and he might in fact obey his 'Executive'. The important characteristics of the Independent as defined here are, first, that he does not have behind him at election time the resources of any political party worth the name; and, second, that he does not take a party whip in the House.

The Independent member in Dáil Éireann owes his existence to the operation of proportional representation in a situation where personal and local factors have great weight in politics. . . . This system gives scope to electors to combine in groups which do not coincide with party divisions and behind candidates who are not necessarily party first choices, or even party choices at all. Until 1935 no less than eighteen out of thirty constituencies returned five or more members and thus gave considerable scope for minority groups. Successive revisions of constituencies have however, substantially altered this position and, theoretically, lessened the chances of minority and, hence, Independent representation. That the potentialities of P.R. are actually realized is due to the fact that personal and local considerations loom large in Irish political life. Although the major parties are organized on a national scale and one or two national issues have been the principal governors of political allegiance, the party label is by no means all that the electors look for. A parliamentary representative is usually a well-known and active local man with a great web of local and county connections and great influence in local social and political life. He will normally be a county councillor or must soon become one. A man with 'a national record' (i.e. in the struggle for independence), a man with a family name, or a well-known Gaelic football player, will get votes for these attributes. Once returned, a member can do more to ensure retaining his seat by working for his constituents personally and as a group than in any other way. Except for the sophisticated city type, members regard themselves, and are regarded, more as contact men for their constituents in political and administrative circles, than as legislators. They may be, and their constituents certainly are, less concerned with broad, general issues than with immediate local affairs and personal interests. The Deputy who works hard to forward the personal interests of his constituents and to get, or seem to get, as much public money as possible for his area is virtually assured of re-election. He does not *have* to be a party man to do this. In circumstances such as these, Independent members might be returned and, once in, continue to be returned regularly.

The numbers of Independent candidates (under whatever name they stood) and of successful candidates have on the whole remained very constant, as the accompanying table shows.

Candidates and Members Returned at Elections to Dáil Éireann[1]

	Candidates		Members returned	
Election	Total no. of candidates	Independent candidates	Total no. of members	Independent members
1923 . . .	375	70–75*	153	16
1927 (June) .	376	57	153	16
1927 (Sept.) .	263	33	153	13
1932 . . .	279	38	153	14
1933 . . .	245	13	153	9
1937 . . .	254	36	138	8
1938 . . .	214	11	138	7
1943 . . .	355	34*	138	10
1944 . . .	251	24	138	11
1948 . . .	406	32	147	12
1951 . . .	296	31	147	14
1954 . . .	302	31	147	5
1957 . . .	288	26	147	9
1961 . . .	300	28	144	6

* On these occasions it is not possible from the evidence to classify all candidates exactly.

[1.] Table brought up to date.

. . . In the parliamentary battle between the parties, the numbers and comparative homogeneity of the Independents in the past often made them important, and might seem to have assured them generally of a strong bargaining position, parliamentary majorities being so small. In fact, until recently, this has not been so. Statistically, Mr. Cosgrave may be said to have relied on them from 1927 to 1932, and undoubtedly he had to take their views into account. When he did not, in 1930, some of them helped to inflict on him one of the rare parliamentary defeats a government has suffered in Ireland. But quasi-party that they were, they in their turn depended on him. They might defeat his bills, but they would not willingly see him replaced by Mr. de Valera, whom they disliked and feared. From 1932 to 1948 Mr. de Valera never needed their support: with only the odd exception he would not have got it if he had. Thus it was not until 1948, when the political situation had altered and the Independents were a mixed and diverse group, that they began to assume a key role and a strong bargaining position. When, in that year, a broad-based 'Inter-party Government' was being formed to replace Fianna Fáil, those Independents who were likely to support such a Government were numerous enough if reckoned as a group to be entitled to a minister in the share-out of offices which was proceeding on mathematical lines. What is more, their support was essential, and, following on discussions with them as if they were a party, one of their number did in fact receive a portfolio. In 1951 Independents who had usually voted for the 'Inter-party Government' forced the Taoiseach (Prime Minister) to dissolve by threatening him with defeat in the House. After the ensuing election, which was a straight fight between Fianna Fáil and all other parties, Mr. de Valera found himself five, and Mr. Costello (his rival) ten, short of a majority in a House containing fourteen Independents, some of whom were uncommitted. Whatever one may think of post-election bargaining between political parties, it is hard to deny the undesirability of situations such as this, in which great power is put into the hands of men who may not have declared their sympathies, and great responsibilities are imposed on men who, for one reason or another, may have chosen not to commit themselves in the struggle for power between responsible parties seeking the electorate's approval.

READING

Fianna Fáil: *The Story of Fianna Fáil: First Phase*, Dublin, 1960.

J. L. McCracken: *Representative Government in Ireland; Dáil Eireann*, 1919-48, London, 1957.

D. Thornley: 'The Development of the Irish Labour Movement' in *Christus Rex*, vol. XVIII, no. 1, January-March, 1964.

Chapter 9

LOCAL GOVERNMENT

INTRODUCTION

The considerable continuity in governmental institutions and procedures after independence, which we have already mentioned in preceding chapters, is nowhere more clearly to be seen than in local government. The major local authorities were created in Victorian times. (Documents 9.1 to 9.5.) British legislation tended to be applied to Ireland with only necessary minor modifications and, accordingly, there occurred the same swing, first, towards a number of specialized authorities and, then, after 1888 in Britain and 1898 in Ireland, towards the county (including the county borough) as the major local government unit. This trend has, in fact, been even more pronounced in Ireland than in Great Britain. The parishes, the bottom tier of the Victorian 'grass roots' system, were never constituted as local authorities in Ireland; in 1925 the rural districts were incorporated in the County Boards of Health and Public Assistance, and these in turn were absorbed into the counties in 1942. With these and other changes, local government has become to a great extent county government.

Modern needs, and particularly developments in medicine, have led, however, to a growing use of the 'joint body' device. Originally a Victorian creation, it is a flexible instrument for coping with the need to provide certain services for an area larger than a county, without plunging into full-scale regional government or having to remove the functions concerned from local government altogether. (Documents 9.6 to 9.8.)

On the fringes of local government are other authorities on a county basis, the Vocational Education Committees and the County Committees of Agriculture. (Documents 9.9 to 9.10.) Though these are not local authorities for the purposes of the main body of local government law, County Councils appoint members to them and they exhibit many of the essentials of local government bodies. Indeed, with the increasing load of planning, policy development and advisory services pressing ever more heavily upon central departments, it might be advantageous to devolve the administration of more public services on to county authorities. On the other hand, however, the scientific and technical advances in medicine, which have made bigger planning and 'catchment areas' necessary in health and so have led to the creation of the Health Authorities, perhaps suggest the need to remove such functions from local government altogether and transfer them to single purpose statutory authorities like the Regional Hospital Boards and local Executive Committees of the British National Health Service.

At the historical centre of the system of local government lies the provision of basic environmental services such as roads and 'public health' or 'sanitary' services. These, together with the personal health services, public assistance, and housing, provide citizens with most of the essential help which they are likely to need, literally, 'from the womb to the tomb'. (Document 9.11.) That levels of public knowledge and interest are so low (though not as low as in Great Britain) is perhaps partly explained by a fact not widely appreciated, that on the whole these services are well performed and with a certainty and regularity that makes us take them for granted.

The efficiency of local government is partly at least due to the success of the manager system, which is perhaps Ireland's major invention in the field of government. Arising out of the needs of the nineteen-twenties and pressed for by some business elements who were influenced by American manager systems, an indigenous system was introduced for Cork City in 1929. It was extended to the other county boroughs in the thirties, and, largely because the members of the County Boards of Health and Public Assistance could no longer cope with the volume of business facing them, was applied to the counties in 1942 when the functions of the Boards were taken over by the counties. (Documents 9.12 and 9.13). By this time, though, local government in an independent Ireland had become settled in its ways, and there was some hostility to the introduction of a professional general manager intended to replace committee administration to a great extent.

This hostility has now largely disappeared, although the system does not operate as one might envisage it reading the acts, and especially the County Management Act, 1940. That measure, following the City Management Acts, enunciated the principle of 'reserved' and 'executive' functions and gave the impression of a fairly clear-cut division of functions, authority and responsibility. Following controversy about where the line should be drawn, the City and County Management (Amendment) Act, 1955 affected to move it in favour of the Council (Document 9.14). In some ways this debate was otiose for, in practice, the Manager has almost inevitably become the major initiator of policy. This is because the springs of new policy are often to be found to a large extent in the administration of existing services. The Council, it is true, approves the estimates and votes the rates, but it is the Manager who prepares the budget. On the Manager lies the onus to produce workable schemes and adequate solutions to problems: on the Council rests the final authority, except in respect of certain staff matters and decisions about entitlement to benefit; and on the Council rests the onus of bringing to bear the preferences, and of mentioning the grievances, of the consumers, their constituents. These respective roles are increasingly obvious and are now well understood.

The officers of local authorities have gradually been welded into one service with standard conditions and, consequently, have the opportunity for transfer and promotion from authority to authority, as have civil servants from department to department in theory (though rather little in practice). Because all administrative and professional posts are advertised and filled by open competition by the Local Appointments Commission, who nominate their choice for formal appointment by the authority, local government officers do, in fact, usually expect to find advancement by appointment to vacant posts in other authorities. The welding of local authority staffs into one service has indeed been largely effected by a combination of the Local Appointments Commission system and the activities of the Department of Local Government which has wide powers in respect of local authority staff matters. (Documents 9.15 to 9.17.)

Considerable central control has, of course, always been a feature of local government. It manifests itself particularly in financial matters where the growing inadequacy of the rates and the growing proportion of central government grants as services increase (Document 9.18) have perpetuated controls devised in Victorian days. Many think that we are long past the time when local authorities needed to be closely scrutinized to ensure high levels of administrative, financial, and technical performance, and that the detailed type of control so well symbolized by the local government audit system, is now no longer justified (Documents 9.19 and 9.20). But staff and financial controls by no means exhaust the Minister's powers. In addition, other ministers, and particularly the Minister for Health, have powers in respect of the functions with which they are concerned. All these add up to a truly formidable array. (Documents 9.21 to 9.23.)

Yet to concentrate upon controls perhaps leads one to miss the other, and increasingly important, role of the Department of Local Government and other Departments as providers of common services and advice, and as stimulators and even partners. That the development of new and less frustrating relationships is contemplated is clear from a recent article by the Secretary of the Department of Local Government. When referring to ' the ever-present tendency in supervising authorities to concentrate on controls as being easier to operate than to curtail, involving no fresh thinking', Mr Garvin added:

> but I hope to show that the general trend, in spite of these, has been in the direction of cutting out particular controls, of generalizing sanctions, and of freeing local authorities to operate within reasonably wide limits of autonomy. I should like to see this trend emphasized even more, so that the time and energy of the Department could be directed to a greater degree into positive, constructive thinking and action. The future relationship — partly realized already — between central and local authorities, as I see it, will not be of leader and led, still less of controller and controlled, but a partnership in which Department and local authorities will work together in planning the course of development for both, and in concerting measures for realizing the objectives so planned. (*Administration,* vol. 11, p. 226.)

DOCUMENTS

Note.—Many Acts relating to local government have been much amended and the state of the law is sometimes rather complicated — at least to the layman. Mr H. A. Street, in *The Law Relating to Local Government*, Dublin, Stationery Office, 1955, attempted to provide a guide to the law as it stood when he wrote and in the case of most of the statutes printed below, his version has been reproduced. Where necessary, his version has been brought up to date by inserting the recent amendments. In his work Mr Street annotated the statutes in great detail. Most of his notes have been omitted. Those included are ascribed to him in the appropriate footnote.

1. GENERAL DEFINITION AND DESCRIPTION

   (a) *Statutory Definition*

   Document 9.1 — Extract from Local Government Act, 1941 (No. 23), in H. A. Street, *The Law Relating to Local Government*, pp. 249-50.

(2) Each of the following bodies (whether corporate or unincorporated) shall be a local authority for the purposes of this Act and the Acts which may be collectively cited with this Act, that is to say: —

    (*a*) a council of a county, a corporation of a county or other borough, a council of an urban district, a public assistance authority, commissioners of a town, a *port sanitary authority*[1], and

    (*b*) a committee or joint committee or board or joint board (whether corporate or unincorporated) appointed by or under statute to perform the functions or any of the functions of any of the bodies mentioned in the immediately preceding paragraph of this subsection, and

    (*c*) a committee or joint committee or board or joint board (whether corporate or unincorporated), other than a vocational education committee or a committee of agriculture of or appointed by one or more of the bodies mentioned in paragraph (*a*) of this sub-section.

(b) *Short description*
    Document 9.2 — Extract from *Returns of Local Taxation for the Year ended 31 March 1961*, Dublin, Stationery Office.

LOCAL AUTHORITIES

The elected local authorities are—

County councils (27)	County borough corporations (4)
Borough corporations (7)	Urban district councils (49)
Town commissioners (28)	

The members of these authorities are elected on a system of proportional representation. Elections were held in the years 1955 and 1960 and are due to be held every five years thereafter. All qualified persons registered as local government electors are entitled to vote. In general every person who is twenty-one years of age or over on the date when the register comes into force (i.e. 15th April) is entitled to be registered for the local electoral area in which he or she is ordinarily resident. Non-resident occupiers of premises are also entitled to be registered in certain circumstances. An elector may not vote more than once in the election of a local authority.

County councils have a membership of from twenty to forty-six and county borough councils from fifteen to forty-five. Borough councils usually have

---

[1]These authorities were abolished by orders made under Act 28 of 1947, s. 107 —Street.

twelve members and urban district councils and town commissioners nine members. To be eligible for election as a county councillor a person must be registered as an elector for the county electoral area for which he is a candidate or be the owner of property in that area. To be eligible for election to a borough or urban district council or as a town commissioner, a person must be a local government elector for the urban area or town, or own property or have lived in the area for the twelve preceding months. In the county boroughs no such qualifications are necessary.

2. THE PRINCIPAL AUTHORITIES

(a) *The Boroughs*

Document 9.3 — Extract from Municipal Corporations (Ireland) Act, 1840 (3 and 4 Vict. c. 108) in Street, *op. cit.*, pp. 532-562.

WHEREAS divers bodies corporate at sundry times have been constituted within the cities, towns, counties of cities, counties of towns, and boroughs of Ireland, to the intent that the same might for ever be and remain well-regulated and quietly governed; and it is expedient that the charters by which several of the said bodies corporate are constituted should be altered in the manner hereinafter mentioned: Be it therefore enacted etc.

1.—So much of all laws, statutes, and usages, and so much of all royal and other charters, grants, and letters patent, rules, orders, and directions, now in force relating to the several boroughs named in the schedules (A), (B) and (I,) to this Act annexed, or to the inhabitants thereof, or to the several bodies or reputed or late bodies corporate named in the said schedules, or any of them, as is inconsistent with or contrary to the provisions of this Act, shall be repealed and annulled, from the time when this Act shall come into operation in each of such boroughs respectively. [*Ss. 2 to 11 repealed or omitted.*]

12.—And whereas it is expedient that the boroughs named in the schedule (A.) to this Act annexed should continue to be towns corporate: And whereas it may be expedient that some of the boroughs named in the schedule (B.) to this Act annexed, which now are towns corporate, and also sundry other towns in Ireland not named in the schedules to this Act annexed, in some of which the corporations have been extinct, and others of which never have been towns corporate, should receive charters of incorporation under this Act: And whereas it is also expedient to make provision for the administration of the corporate funds of those boroughs named in the said schedule (B.) to which charters of incorporation under this Act shall not be granted, pursuant to the provisions herein-after contained; be it enacted, that after the first election of councillors under this Act in any borough named in the said schedule (A.) the body or reputed body corporate named in the said schedule in connexion with such borough shall take and bear the name of the mayor, aldermen, and burgesses of such boroughs, except the Corporation of Dublin,[1] which shall bear the name of the Right Honourable the Lord Mayor, Aldermen, and Burgesses of Dublin, and by those names shall have perpetual succession, and shall be capable in law, by the council herein-after mentioned of such borough, to do and suffer all acts which such bodies corporate lawfully may do and suffer, and shall be entitled to, invested with, and possessed of all the lawful franchises, rights, trusts, powers, authorities, properties, and estates now or of late legally vested in or belonging, or which of right ought to belong, to such boroughs, or bodies corporate respectively, solely or jointly with any other person or body corporate, save only those in respect of which other provisions are herein contained, but subject to such mortgages, charges, debts, and incumbrances, rents, contracts, covenants, and conditions as the same respectively now are subject or liable to; and the mayor of each of the said boroughs shall be capable in law to do and suffer all acts which the chief officer of such borough might or may lawfully do and suffer, so far as such powers, rights, trusts, and privileges respectively are not altered or annulled by the provisions of this Act. [*S. 13 omitted.*]

14.—If a petition to grant a charter of incorporation under this Act to the inhabitants of any borough named in the schedule (B.) to this Act annexed, or to the inhabitants of any other town in Ireland, in which the population according to the census or abstract then last laid before both Houses of the Oireachtas as by law required, shall exceed the number of three thousand, signed by a majority of the local government electors thereof shall be presented to the Government; it shall be lawful for the Government, by any such charter, to extend to the inhabitants of any such borough or town, within the district to be set forth in such charter, the powers and provisions in this Act contained; provided that notice of every such petition, and of the time when it shall please the Government to order that the same be taken into consideration shall be published in the *Iris Oifigiúil* one calendar month at least before such petition shall be so considered: provided also, that, within six weeks after the commencement of each session of the Oireachtas a return of all the towns in Ireland from which petitions shall have been presented for charters of incorporation, in pursuance of the provisions hereinbefore contained, shall be laid by the Minister for Local Government before both Houses of the Oireachtas[2]. [*Remainder of Act still in force omitted.*]

---

1. Cork has a Lord Mayor under a patent of 1900—Street.
2. Only the borough of Wexford obtained such charter (1846). The boroughs of Dun Laoghaire and Galway have been incorporated by statute.—Street.

SCHEDULES

(Omitting references to Northern Ireland)

SCHEDULE A.

Borough	Wards	Aldermen	Councillors	Style of corporate body
Clonmel ...	2	6	18	The Mayor, Free Burgesses, and Commonalty of the town of Clonmel.
Cork ...	8	16	48	The Mayor, Sheriffs and Commonalty of the city of Cork.
Drogheda ...	3	6	18	The Mayor, Sheriffs, Burgesses and Commonalty of the county of the town of Drogheda.
Dublin ...	15	15	45	The Right Honourable the Lord Mayor, Sheriffs, Commons and Citizens of the city of Dublin.
Kilkenny ...	2	6	18	The Mayor and Citizens of the city of Kilkenny. The Portreeve, Burgesses, and Commons of the borough or town of Irishtown.
Limerick ...	5	10	30	The Mayor, Sheriffs and Citizens of the city of Limerick.
Sligo ...	3	6	18	The Provost, Free Burgesses and Commonalty of the borough of Sligo.
Waterford ...	5	10	30	The Mayor, Sheriffs and Citizens of the County of the City of Waterford in the Kingdom of Ireland.

SCHEDULE B.

Borough	Style of Corporate Body
Ardee ...	The Portreeve, Burgesses, and Commons of the Corporation of Atherdee.
Athlone ...	The Sovereign, Bailiffs, Burgesses, and Freemen of the Town of Athlone.
Athy ...	The Sovereign, Bailiffs, Free Burgesses, and Commonalty of the Borough of Athy.
Bandon ...	The Provost, Free Burgesses, and Commonalty of the Borough of Bandon Bridge.
Boyle ...	The Borough Master, Free Burgesses, and Commonalty of the Borough of Boyle.
Callan ...	The Sovereign, Burgesses, and Freemen of Callan.
Carlow ...	The Sovereign, Free Burgesses, and Commonalty of the Borough of Catherlagh.
Cashel ...	The Mayor, Aldermen, Bailiffs, Citizens, and Commons of the City of Cashel.
Charleville ...	The Sovereign, Bailiffs, and Burgesses of the Borough of Charleville.
Cloghnakilty ...	The Sovereign, Free Burgesses, and Commonalty of the Borough of Cloghnakilty.
Dingle ...	The Sovereign, Burgesses, and Commonalty of the Town of Dingle-i-couch.
Dundalk ...	The Bailiff, Burgesses, and Commonalty of the Borough of Dundalk.
Ennis ...	The Provost, Free Burgesses, and Commonalty of the Town of Ennis.
Enniscorthy ...	The Portreeve, Free Burgesses, and Commonalty of the Borough of Enniscorthy.
Fethard ...	The Sovereign, Chief Burgesses, Portreeve, and Freemen of the Town of Fethard.
Galway ...	The Mayor, Sheriffs, Free Burgesses, and Commonalty of the Town and County of the Town of Galway.

Borough	Style of Corporate Body
Gorey ...	The Sovereign, Burgesses, and Free Commons of the Borough and Town of Newborough.
Kells ...	The Sovereign, Provost, Burgesses, and Commonalty of the Borough of Kells.
Kinsale ...	The Sovereign, Burgesses, and Commonalty of the Town of Kinsale.
Longford ...	The Sovereign, Bailiffs, and Burgesses of the Borough of Longford.
Maryborough ...	The Burgomaster, Bailiffs, Burgesses, and Commonalty of Maryborough.
Monaghan ...	The Provost, Free Burgesses, and Commonalty of the Borough of Monaghan.
Naas ...	The Sovereign, Provost, Burgesses, and Commonalty of Naas.
Navan ...	The Portreeve, Burgesses, and Freemen of the Town or Borough of Navan.
New Ross ...	The Sovereign and Burgesses of New Ross.
Portarlington ...	The Sovereign, Bailiffs, and Burgesses of the Borough and Town of Portarlington.
Tralee ...	The Provost, Free Burgesses, and Commonalty of the Borough of Tralee.
Trim ...	The Portreeve, Burgesses, and Freemen of Trim.
Tuam ...	The Sovereign, Free Burgesses, and Commonalty of the Borough of Tuam.
Wexford ...	The Mayor, Bailiffs, Free Burgesses, and Commonalty of the Town or Borough of Wexford.
Wicklow ...	The Portreeve, Free Burgesses, and Commonalty of the Town of Wicklow.
Youghal ...	The Mayor, Bailiffs, Burgesses, and Commonalty of the Town of Youghal.

(b) *The Towns*

Document 9.4 — Extracts from Towns Improvement (Ireland) Act, 1854 (17 and 18 Vict. c. 103) in Street, *op. cit.,* pp. 613-15.

4.—Upon the application of twenty-one or more householders of any city or town in Ireland applying that this Act or that specific portion thereof described as hereinbefore provided) may be carried into execution in such city or town, which application shall specify the boundaries proposed for the purposes of this Act, and a copy of which application shall be inserted in the *Iris Oifigiúil,* and in one or more newspaper or newspapers published in such city or town, and if none be therein published, then in one or more newspaper or newspapers published nearest to such city or town, it shall be lawful for the Minister for Local Government, one month after receipt of such application, and if he shall approve of such proposed boundaries, to order and direct that the mayor or other chief magistrate of such town (being a corporate town), or the county manager for the county in which the town is situate, shall convene a meeting for the purpose of considering the carrying of this Act into execution, and one of them shall preside thereat, such orders and directions to be signified by the Minister for Local Government, and a copy of such orders and directions, with the names of the parties signing the application for the same, and the boundaries so approved of, shall be inserted, under the direction of the Minister for Local Government, in such *Iris Oifigiúil* and newspaper or newspapers as aforesaid. [*Ss. 5 and 6 omitted.*]

7.—At any such meeting convened as aforesaid the local government electors registered in respect of qualifications within the town shall be admitted and entitled to vote and no other person whatsoever.

[*Remainder of Act in force omitted.*]

(c) *The Counties, County Boroughs and Urban Districts*

Document 9.5 — Extracts from Local Government (Ireland) Act, 1898 (61 and 62 Vict. c. 37) in Street, *op. cit.,* pp. 5-31.

1.—A council shall be established in every administrative county, and be entrusted with the management of the administrative and financial business of that county, and shall consist of a chairman and councillors.

2.—(1) The councillors of a county shall be elected by the local government electors for the county. [*S. 3 omitted.*]

4.—(1) Subject to the provisions of this Act, there shall be transferred to the council of each county all the business of the grand jury not excepted by this section, and all the business of the county at large presentment sessions[1]; and the county council for the purpose of such business shall, save that any fiat or other sanction of a judge shall not be required, have the powers and duties of the grand jury and the said presentment sessions in connection with the said business, and also such further powers and duties as are conferred on them by or in pursuance of this Act, or as may be necessary for conducting, as an administrative body, the business hereby transferred.

(2) Nothing in this Act shall transfer to a county council or a member thereof—

(a) any business relating to bills of indictment or any business of the grand jury at common law relating to crime[2]; or

(b) any business by this Act transferred to the county court[3]; or

(c) any power to appoint a visiting committee for a prison.[4]

[*S. 5 omitted.*]

6.—There shall be transferred to the council of each county—

(a) the business of the guardians with respect to making, levying, collecting, and recovering the poor rate in so much of the county as is not comprised in an urban county district[5];

(b) the business of the guardians as local authority under the Diseases of Animals Act, 1894, and the Destructive Insects Act, 1877; and

(c) the business of the justices in petty sessions under the Explosives Act, 1875, except the power to appoint any officer, which power shall cease.

[*Those parts of Ss. 7-20 still in force omitted.*]

---

1. The business transacted by the grand jury may be divided into (1) administrative, (2) criminal, and (3) financial—Street.
2. The criminal duties of the grand jury were abolished by Act 10 of 1924, s. 27—Street.
3. Now the Circuit Court.—Editor.
4. Visiting committees are now appointed by the Minister for Justice, Act 11 of 1925, s. 2.—Street.
5. The guardians previously levied poor rate as the poor law authority under 1 & 2 Vict. c.56 s.61 and as rural sanitary authority under 41 & 42 Vict. c.52 ss.232 and 233. Under s.51(1) of the 1898 Act the council was to pay the expenses of the guardians and of the rural district council on demand. The county council now (Act 24 of 1946, s.12(1)) recovers the poor rate as "county rate".—Street.

21.—(1) Each of the boroughs mentioned in the Second Schedule to this Act[1] shall be an administrative county of itself, and be called a county borough.

(2) The mayor, aldermen, and burgesses of each county borough acting by the council[2] shall, subject as in this Act mentioned, have the powers and duties of a county council under this Act and the powers of baronial present-ment sessions in so far as they have not the same already, and the provisions of this Act with respect to administrative counties shall, so far as circum-stances admit, apply in the case of every such borough with the necessary modifications, . . .

[*Remainder of S. 21 omitted.*]

22.—(1) All urban sanitary authorities[3] shall be called urban district councils and their districts shall be called urban districts, but nothing in this section shall alter the style or title of the corporation or council of a borough.

[*Ss. 23-26 still in force omitted.*]

27.—(1) Subject to the provisions of this Act there shall be transferred—

[*Sub-paragraph (a) omitted.*]

(b) to the district council of every urban county district, so far as respects their district, the business of the grand jury of the

1. Dublin, Cork, Limerick and Waterford—Street.
2. The county borough council is known as the "city council" in Dublin (Act 27 of 1930 s.1), Limerick (Act 35 of 1934, s.1) and Waterford (Act 25 of 1939, s.1). Cork retains a "borough council" under Act 1 of 1929, s.1—Street.
3. Existing urban sanitary authorities may be divided into:
(1) Boroughs, including the county boroughs, which became urban sanitary districts under s. 4 of the Public Health Act, 1878, viz. Dublin, Cork, Limerick, Waterford, Clonmel, Drogheda, Kilkenny, Sligo and Wexford.
(2) Towns with a population of over 6,000 which fell within the same section in 1878, viz. Athlone, Carlow, Carrick-on-Suir, Cobh, Dundalk, Dungarvan, Ennis, Fermoy, Kinsale, New Ross and Tralee. Under 37 & 38 Vict., c. 93 Bandon was by mistake included (see 1877 report of Local Government Commission p. 128).
(3) Towns having commissioners under a local Act within the same section, viz. Bray (29 & 30 Vict. c. cclxi.).
(4) Towns which petitioned under s. 7 of the Act of 1878 and were constituted as urban districts by provisional order confirmed by Parliament, viz. Athlone, Baile na h-Uaimhe (Navan), Ballinasloe, Birr, Cashel, Ceanannus Mór (Kells), Clonakilty, Clones, Enniscorthy, Killarney, Kilrush, Letterkenny, Listowel, Mallow, Monaghan, Skibbereen, Templemore, Thurles, Trim, Westport, Wicklow and Youghal.
(5) Towns which petitioned under the said section 7 and by virtue of s. 42 *infra* were constituted as urban districts without confirmation of order by Parliament, viz., Athy, Ballina, Buncrana, Bundoran, Carrickmacross, Castlebar, Castleblayney, Cavan, Longford, Macroom, Midleton, Nas na Riogh (Naas), Nenagh, Tipperary and Tullamore.
(6) New Boroughs which have the powers of an urban district by statute, viz. Dún Laoghaire (absorbing the previously existing urban districts of Kingstown, Blackrock, Dalkey and Killiney and Ballybrack, Act 27 of 1930 ss. 3 and 42) and Galway (Act 3 (private) of 1937 s. 13).
As to loss of urban status see s. 74 of Act 5 of 1925 — Street.

county in relation to public works, the expense of the maintenance of which is not wholly or partly leviable off the county at large[1]; but the said transfer shall only operate so far as the business is not already the business of the district council.

42.—(1) Where a town has a population exceeding one thousand five hundred according to the last published census for the time being, but is not an urban sanitary district, any order of the Minister for Local Government constituting such town an urban sanitary district shall, unless within three months after the order is published the Minister receives a petition against it, from at least one-fourth of the local government electors within the town, take effect without the authority of the Oireachtas; and a certificate of the Minister that no such petition has been received, and that the order has taken effect, shall be conclusive evidence of those facts.

[Remainder omitted.]

(d) *Joint Bodies*
(i) Document 9.6 — Section 38 of The Local Government (Application of Enactments) Order, 1898 (22 December 1898) in Street, *op. cit.*, pp. 116-17.

38.—(1) Any county councils, including councils of county boroughs, may from time to time join in appointing out of their respective bodies a joint committee for any purpose in respect of which they are jointly interested.

(2) Any council taking part in the appointment of any joint committee under this Article may from time to time delegate to the committee any power which such council might exercise for the purpose for which the committee is appointed.

(3) Provided that nothing in this Article shall authorise a council to delegate to a committee any power of making a rate or borrowing any money.

(4) Subject to the terms of delegation, any such joint committee shall, in respect of any matter delegated to it, have the same power in all respects as the councils appointing it, or any of them, as the case may be.

(5) The members of a joint committee appointed under the Act shall be appointed at such times and in such manner as may be from time to time fixed by the councils who appointed them, and shall hold office for such time as may be fixed by those councils, so that such committee do not continue for more than three months after any triennial election of councillors of those councils.

---

1. The works here described were confined to roads now urban roads within s.24 of Act 5 of 1925—Street.

(6) The cost of a joint committee shall be defrayed by the councils by whom its members were appointed, in the proportion agreed to by them; and the accounts of such joint committee and their officers shall, for the purposes of the provisions of the Act, be deemed to be accounts of the county councils and their officers.

(7) In the case of a joint committee the councils appointing the joint committee shall jointly have the powers given by this Order to each council in respect of a committee appointed by that council.

(8) This Article shall apply to district councils *inter se* in like manner as to county councils.

(ii) Document 9.7—Extracts from Section 45 of Health Act, 1953 (no. 26).

45.—(1) The Minister may by order provide for and authorise joint action by two or more health authorities in the performance of any of their functions either as respects the whole or part of their functional area.

(2) An order under this section may provide for the manner in which the expenses incurred in carrying out the joint action are to be met.

(3) An order under this section may provide for the establishment of a joint board for the purposes of the order.

(4) The following provisions shall have effect in relation to a joint board established by order under this section:
  (*a*) the board shall be a body corporate with perpetual succession by the name given to them by the order,
  (*b*) the board shall have power to sue and be sued in their corporate name,
  (*c*) the board shall have power to hold and dispose of land,
  (*d*) the board shall provide and have a common seal and such seal shall be authenticated by the signature of the chairman or some other member authorised to act in that behalf and the signature of an officer of the board authorised to act in that behalf,
  (*e*) all courts of justice shall take judicial notice of the seal of the board and every document purporting to be an order or other instrument made by them and to be sealed with their seal (purporting to be authenticated in accordance with the foregoing paragraph) shall be received in evidence and be deemed to be such order or instrument without further proof unless the contrary is shown,
  (*f*) the board shall be a joint body within the meaning and for the purposes of the County Management Acts, 1940 and 1942,
  (*g*) the board shall be a joint authority within the meaning and for the purposes of the Health Services (Financial Provisions) Act, 1947 (No. 47 of 1947),

(*h*) the Minister may by order apply to the board any provisions of the Principal Act or this Act or of any regulations thereunder and may so apply such provisions with any specified modifications or limitations.

[*Remainder omitted.*]

(e) *Health Authorities*

Document 9.8 — Extracts from Health Authorities Act, 1960 (no. 9).

2.—(1) There is hereby established a body which shall be known as the Dublin Health Authority.

(2) The Dublin Health Authority shall consist of nine members appointed by the council of the county of Dublin, fifteen members appointed by Dublin Corporation and three members appointed by the Dún Laoghaire Corporation.

(3) The Minister may by regulations substitute different numbers for all or any of the numbers specified in subsection (2) of this section and, while any such regulations are in force, that subsection shall have effect accordingly.

(4) The functional area of the Dublin Health Authority shall consist of the county borough of Dublin and the administrative county of Dublin, together with, with respect to functions related to the operation of services under the Mental Treatment Acts, 1945 to 1958, the administrative county of Wicklow[1].

(5) (*a*) Three members of the council of the county of Wicklow shall be appointed by resolution by that council for the purposes of this subsection.

[*Remainder of S. 2 and Ss. 3-6 omitted.*]

7.—(1) A health authority established by this Act shall perform all the functions which, immediately before such establishment were performed by the relevant local authorities under, in relation to the operation of services provided under, or in connection with the administration of, the following enactments:

(*a*) the Health Acts, 1947 to 1958,

(*b*) the Mental Treatment Acts, 1945 to 1958,

(*c*) the Public Assistance Act, 1939,

(*d*) the Births and Deaths Registration Acts, 1863 to 1952,

(*e*) the Notification of Births Acts, 1907 and 1915,

(*f*) the Acts relating to the registration of marriages,

(*g*) the Sale of Food and Drugs Acts, 1875 to 1936,

(*h*) Part I of the Children Act, 1908, and sections 2 and 3 of the Children (Amendment) Act, 1957,

(*i*) the Rats and Mice (Destruction) Act, 1919,

(*j*) the Blind Persons Act, 1920,

(*k*) the State Lands (Workhouses) Act, 1930,

---

[1]. Unified Health Authorities on this pattern were also established for the county boroughs of Cork, Limerick and Waterford and the adjoining counties.

    (*l*) the Registration of Maternity Homes Act, 1934,

    (*m*) the Midwives Act, 1944, as amended by the Nurses Act, 1950, and section 60 of the Nurses Act, 1950,

    (*n*) section 3 of the Housing (Amendment) Act, 1946,

    (*o*) the Adoption Act, 1952.

3. STATUTORY AUTHORITIES CLOSELY CONNECTED WITH LOCAL GOVERNMENT

(a) *County Committees of Agriculture*

Document 9.9 — Extracts from Agricultural Act, 1931 (no. 8).

13.—There shall be in every county a committee, to be called a committee of agriculture, to fulfil in respect of such county the functions assigned to committees of agriculture by this Part of this Act. [*S. 14 omitted.*]

15.—Subject to the provisions of this Act constituting a committee appointed under section 14 of the Act of 1899 to be a committee of agriculture for the purposes of this Act, the committee of agriculture for a county shall be appointed by the council of that county and the provisions contained in the Second Schedule to this Act shall apply to and regulate the appointment and membership of every such committee. [*Remaining Sections omitted.*]

SCHEDULE 2

[*Paragraph 1 omitted.*]

2. Every committee of agriculture shall be composed at the discretion of the council either wholly of persons who are members of the council or partly of persons who are and partly of persons who are not members of the council.

3. The following provisions shall have effect in relation to the constitution of every committee of agriculture for a country, that is to say:

    (*a*) the number of members of such committee to be appointed in an election year at the annual meeting of the council held in that year shall not be less than three times nor more than four times the number of county electoral areas in the county at the date of such annual meeting;

    (*b*) subject to the provisions of the foregoing sub-paragraph, the number of members of such committee to be appointed in an election year at the annual meeting of the council held in that year shall be such number as the council think fit, and such committee shall, notwithstanding any change in the number of electoral areas in such county in the meantime, until the annual meeting of the council held in the next following election year, consist of such last mentioned number of members.

4. The members of a committee of agriculture shall include in respect of each county electoral area in the county at least one person who is resident in such county electoral area.

5. No person shall be appointed to be a member of a committee of agriculture unless he either has a practical, commercial or technical knowledge of land or has an estate or interest in some agricultural land in the county or has special local knowledge of agricultural matters.

6. The members of the committee of agriculture (other than a member appointed to fill a casual vacancy) shall be appointed in every election year at the annual meeting of the council held in that year and the appointment of such members of such committee shall be part of the first business to be transacted at every such annual meeting. [*Remainder omitted.*]

(b) *Vocational Education Committees*

Document 9.10 — Extracts from Vocational Education Act, 1930 (no. 29).

6.—(1) Every county borough shall be a borough vocational education area for the purposes of this Act.

(2) Every scheduled urban district shall be an urban district vocational education area for the purposes of this Act.

(3) Every county (excluding so much, if any, thereof as is for the time being included in a scheduled urban district) shall be a county vocational education area for the purposes of this Act.

(4) In this Act the expression "vocational education area" includes a borough vocational education area, an urban district vocational education area, and a county vocational education area.

7.—(1) There shall be a committee (in this Act referred to as a vocational education committee) in and for every vocational education area to fulfil in respect of such area the duties assigned to vocational education committees by this Act. [*SSs. 2 and 3 omitted.*]

8.—(1) The vocational education committee for a borough vocational education area shall consist of fourteen members elected by the council of the county borough which is such borough vocational education area, of whom not less than five nor more than eight shall be persons who are members of such council.

(2) The vocational education committee for an urban district vocational education area shall consist of fourteen members elected by the council of the urban district which is such urban district vocational education area, of whom not less than five nor more than eight shall be persons who are members of such council.

(3) The vocational education committee for a county vocational education area shall consist of—

(a) fourteen members elected by the council of the county which is or includes such county vocational education area, of whom not less than five nor more than eight shall be persons who are members of such council; and

(b) where such vocational education area contains one or more urban districts which are not scheduled urban districts—

(i) if the number of such urban districts does not exceed four, two members elected by the council of each of such urban districts, each of whom may at the discretion of such council be a person who is or a person who is not a member of such council, or

(ii) if the number of such urban districts exceeds four, one member elected by the council of each such urban district who in every case may at the discretion of such council be a person who is or a person who is not a member of such council.

(4) A local authority electing under this section persons to be members of a vocational education committee shall have regard to the interest and experience in education of the person proposed to be so elected and to any recommendations made by bodies (including associations or bodies of employers or of employees) interested in manufacturers or trades in the area of such committee and shall, where it appears desirable and circumstances permit, so make such election as to provide for the representation of such bodies on such committee. [*Remaining Sections omitted.*]

FIRST SCHEDULE
THE SCHEDULED URBAN DISTRICTS

The Urban District of Bray
The Borough of Drogheda.
The Borough of Dun Laoghaire.
The Urban District of Galway.
The Borough of Sligo.
The Urban District of Tralee.
The Borough of Wexford.

4. FUNCTIONS

Document 9.11 — Extract from *Returns of Local Taxation for the Year ended 31 March, 1961,* Dublin, Stationery Office.

The functions of county councils can conveniently be classified under seven main headings as follows: — Roads, Public Assistance, Mental Health, Health, Sanitary Services, Housing and General Purposes.

Roads—Roads for which local authorities have responsibilities may be regarded as falling into three categories—main, county and urban. Main roads are roads declared to be such by order of the Minister for Local Government and county councils are responsible with minor exceptions for their construction and maintenance. County roads are the other public roads in a county and they are also the responsibility of the county councils. Urban roads, which are the public roads in an urban district or a borough, excluding the main roads, are normally the responsibility of the urban authority.

Public Assistance, Health and Mental Health—Public assistance covers the provision of the necessaries of life for poor persons unable to provide these necessaries for themselves or for the persons whom they are liable to maintain.

As health authorities, county councils provide a general hospital service, operate the dispensary medical service, deal with food hygiene, maternity, school health and child welfare services, dental services for children, tuberculosis hospital services, general hospital services in extern hospitals, certain specialist services, the control of infectious disease and other services including the maintenance of tuberculosis and fever hospitals.

As health authorities, county councils also provide accommodation, staff, equipment and other facilities for the treatment of mental ill-health. This service is administered by a joint body in certain counties.

Prior to 1st July, 1960, in every administrative county except Dublin, Cork, and Waterford, the county council was the public assistance authority and the health authority. Dublin County Borough and the portion of Dublin County adjoining the city, were comprised in the Dublin Public Assistance District the authority for which was the Dublin Board of Assistance. The remainder of Dublin County was divided into two public assistance districts the authorities for which were the Rathdown Board of Assistance and the Balrothery Board of Assistance. An area consisting of Cork County Borough and portion of Cork County was comprised in the South Cork Public Assistance District which was administered by the South Cork Board of Public Assistance. (The Cork County Council was the public assistance authority for the remainder of the county.) The area consisting of Waterford County and Waterford County Borough formed one public assistance district, the public assistance authority for which was the Waterford Board of Public Assistance. These joint bodies also administered certain of the health services in their areas of jurisdiction.

As from the 1st July, 1960, under the Health Authorities Act, 1960, the Cork, Dublin, Limerick and Waterford Health Authorities were established to perform the health functions formerly performed by the County Councils and the County Borough Corporations of Cork, Dublin and Waterford, the health and public assistance functions performed by Limerick County Council and Limerick Corporation, the public assistance functions performed by Cork County Council and all the functions of the Dublin, Balrothery, Rathdown, and Waterford Boards of Assistance, the South Cork Board of Public Assistance, the Dublin Fever Hospital Board, the Cork Santoria Board and the Grangegorman, Cork, Limerick and Waterford Mental Hospital Boards. (All the boards in question were abolished). . . .

Prior to 1st July, 1960, the mental hospital services were administered by the county councils as mental hospital authorities but since that date are administered by the county councils as health authorities. Under the Health Authorities Act, 1960, these services were styled mental health services and the administration of them was merged with that of the general health services.

The Western Health Institutions Board which is comprised of two representatives from each of the 5 Connacht County Councils controls and manages the Sanatorium at Merlin Park, Galway, and such other institutions as the constituent councils jointly provide.

Sanitary Services—Under this heading county councils deal mainly with water supply, sewerage schemes, public lighting and burial grounds.

Housing—As housing authorities, county councils can, in addition to providing houses, make loans under the Small Dwellings Acquisition Acts to persons providing houses for themselves.

General Purposes—This includes the provision of scholarships to universities and secondary and vocational schools, fire brigades, public libraries, the sale or guaranteeing the sale of fertilizers and certain seeds, meeting the cost of preparation of franchise and jurors' lists (part of which is recouped by the State grant), the provision and maintenance of courthouses, the cost of rate collection, and also the making of contributions to certain other bodies such as vocational education committee.

The functions of county borough corporations are much the same as those of county councils and are classified under the same main headings. The functions of borough corporations and urban district councils are classified under the headings, *Roads, Sanitary Services, Housing and General Purposes.* For convenience the seven borough corporations (Clonmel, Drogheda, Dun Laoghaire, Galway, Kilkenny, Sligo and Wexford) are dealt with in these Returns as urban district councils. Town commissioners have functions of a more limited nature.[1]

5. THE MANAGEMENT SYSTEM

(The manager system was first introduced into Cork City in 1929 (Act. no. 1 of 1929). In 1930 it was extended to Dublin (Act. no. 27 of 1930); in 1934, to Limerick (Act. no. 35 of 1934); and in 1939, to Waterford (Act. no. 25 of 1939). In general, the system in the cities is the same as in the counties and only the principal County Management Act is reproduced in this section.—Editor).

(a) *Description*

Document 9.12 — Extract from *Returns of Local Taxation for the Year ended 31st March, 1961.*

All of the local authorities dealt with in these Returns (except An Chomhairle Leabharlanna) comprise two elements, the elected members and a

---

1. These include housing, allotments, fairs and markets.—Editor.

manager. In the four county borough corporations the manager is an officer of the corporation. In the counties the manager is an officer of the county council. The county manager as well as being manager for the county council, is manager for every borough corporation, urban district council, board of town commissioners, and every joint body whose functional area is wholly within the county. He is paid by the county council such salary as the Minister for Local Government directs. The county council recovers part of the salary from the other bodies concerned.

The functions of the local authorities under management are divided into two classes known as reserved functions and executive functions. The reserved functions are performed directly by the elected members of the local authority. They comprise mainly decisions on major matters of policy and principle, and include the making of rates, borrowing of money and making, amending or revoking of bye-laws, the bringing into force of enactments and the nomination of persons to act on other public bodies. Every function which is not a reserved function is an executive function, which is performable directly by the manager. The executive functions include matters such as the employment of staff, the acceptance of tenders, the management of the local authority's property, the collection of rates and rents and generally the day to day administration of the affairs of the authority.

It is the duty of the county manager to advise and assist the county council and every other local authority for which he is manager in regard to the exercise by them of their reserved functions and also in regard to any particular matter on which the local authority requests his advice or assistance. A local authority may appoint from amongst its members an estimates committee to prepare the annual estimate of expenses. The manager must give this committee whatever assistance they require and, if the committee fail to prepare the estimate or where no such committee has been appointed, he must prepare the estimate himself. The local authority is, however, not bound to accept the estimate of expenses as prepared either by the estimates committee or the manager. The manager is bound by the decisions of the elected members on the provision made by them in the annual estimates and, save with their consent, he cannot exceed the amount provided by them for any particular purpose. He has the right to attend meetings and to take part in discussions as if he were a member of the local authority but he is not entitled to vote. He must, whenever requested by the chairman or the elected members, furnish all information in his possession or procurement concerning any business of the authority. The elected members have the power, subject to certain restrictions, to require the manager to inform them of his proposals before performing any specified executive function and to require him to act in accordance with their wishes in any particular matter. The manager must as a matter of course inform the elected members before undertaking any new works other than works of maintenance and repair, and before he commits the local authority to any expenditure in connection with them. The local authority may prohibit the undertaking of any such works thus brought to their notice, provided they are not works which the local authority are required by law to undertake. The manager cannot submit any proposal to increase or decrease the number of permanent offices nor can he fix an increased or decreased rate of remuneration applicable to any class, description or grade of officers or servants without the consent of the elected members.

(b) *The Principal Act*

Document 9.13 — Extracts from County Management Act, 1940 (no. 12).

OFFICE OF MANAGER AND TENURE

3.—(1) There shall be in every county a county manager for such county who shall be called and known as the .... County Manager (with the name of the county prefixed).

(2) The several counties (in this Act referred to as grouped counties) mentioned in the First Schedule to this Act shall, for the purposes of this Act, be grouped in the manner set forth in that Schedule and, in the case of each such group, one and the same person shall be the county manager for each of the counties included in such group.

(3) The office of the Dublin City Manager and the office of Dublin County Manager shall always be held by one and the same person.

(4) The county manager for a county shall be an officer of the council of that county. [*S. 4 omitted.*]

5.—(1) Every person appointed to be the county manager for a county shall hold office until he dies, resigns, or is removed from office.

(2) Every county manager for a county (other than the county of Dublin) shall be paid by the council of that county such remuneration as the Minister shall from time to time direct, and the moneys required for the payment of such remuneration shall be raised by such council as a county-at-large charge. [*SSs. 3 and 4 omitted.*]

6.—(1) The county manager for a county shall not be removed by the council of that county without the sanction of the Minister.

(2) The county manager for a county shall not be suspended or removed by the council of that county save by a resolution passed by such council for the purpose of such suspension or such removal and for the passing of which not less than two-thirds of the members of such council voted and of the intention to propose which not less than seven days' notice was given to every person who was a member of such council when such notice was given.

COUNTY MANAGER TO BE MANAGER FOR OTHER AUTHORITIES

7.—The county manager for a county shall, by virtue of his office, be the manager for every elective body of which the functional area is wholly within such county.

8.—(1) Where the functional area of a joint body extends into two or more counties, the county manager for that one of those counties which the Minister shall by order appoint shall be also the manager for such joint body. [*Remainder of S. 8 and Ss. 9-15 omitted.*]

RESERVED FUNCTIONS

16.—(1) Neither the council of a county nor any elective body shall directly exercise or perform any power (other than a power which is vested by law (including this Act) in such council of body and is by this Act expressly made exercisable by resolution of such council or body), function, or duty of such council or body in relation to the officers or servants of such council or body, or the control, supervision, service, remuneration, privileges, or superannuation of such officers or servants or any of them.

(2) Subject to the provisions of the next preceding sub-section of this section, every council of a county and every elective body shall directly exercise and perform the powers, functions, and duties (if any) of such council or body in relation to each of the several matters mentioned in the Second Schedule to this Act.

(3) Save as is otherwise provided by this section, the Minister, whenever he so thinks proper, may by order direct that the powers, functions, and duties of every or of any particular council of a county or of every elective body of a specified class or of any particular elective body in relation to any matter specified in such order (not being a matter mentioned in the Second Schedule to this Act) shall be exercised and performed directly by such council or such body, as the case may be.

(4) The Minister, whenever he so thinks proper, may revoke or amend any order made by him under the next preceding subsection of this section or any order (made under this sub-section) amending any such order.

(5) Whenever and so long as an order made by the Minister under this section is in force, the powers, functions, and duties specified in such order shall be exercised directly by the council or councils or the elective body or bodies in respect of which such order is made.

(6) No order made by the Minister under this section shall extend or apply to any power, function, or duty to which the first sub-section of this section applies.

(7) Every appointment by the council of a county of a rate collector for a rate collection district lawfully established in such county shall be made by such council directly by resolution, but no such appointment shall have effect unless or until approved of by the Minister.

(8) Every power, function, or duty of the council of a county or of an elective body which is required by this section to be exercised directly by such council or body shall, for the purposes of this Act, be a reserved function of such council or body, and the expression "reserved function" shall in this Act be construed and have effect accordingly.

EXECUTIVE FUNCTIONS

17.—(1) Every power, function, or duty of the council of a county or of an elective body which is not a reserved function shall, for the purposes of this Act, be an executive function of such council or body, and the expression "executive function" shall in this Act (including this section) be construed and have effect accordingly.

(2) Every county manager shall exercise and perform for the council of his county all the executive functions of such council and, in particular, all powers (other than a power which is vested by law (including this Act) in such council and is by this Act expressly made exercisable by resolution of such council), functions, and duties of such council in relation to the officers and servants of such council and the control, supervision, service, remuneration, privileges, and superannuation, of such officers and servants.

(3) Every county manager shall exercise, for the several elective bodies for which he is the manager, the executive functions of such elective bodies respectively and, in particular, all powers, functions, and duties of any such elective body in relation to the officers and servants of such body and the control, supervision, service, remuneration, privileges, and superannuation of such officers and servants.

(4) All such matters and things, including the making of contracts and the affixing of the official seal, as are necessary for or incidental to the exercise or performance of the executive functions of the council of a county or of an elective body shall, subject to the provisions of this Act, be done (as the case may be) by the county manager for such county or the manager for such elective body.

(5) A county manager shall not affix the official seal of the council of a county or of an elective body to any document save in the presence of the chairman of such council or body or, in the presence of a member or any of a number of members of such council or body nominated in that behalf by such council or body. [*S.* 18 *omitted.*]

19.—(1) Every act or thing done or decision taken by a county manager for the council of his county or an elective body which, if done or taken by such council or elective body would be required by law (other than this Act) to be done or taken by resolution of such council or elective body, shall be done or taken by such county manager by an order in writing signed by him and containing a statement of the time at which it was so signed. [*Remainder of S.* 19 *omitted.*]

20.—(1) The officers and servants of the council of a county or of an elective body shall perform their duties as such officers and servants in accordance with such directions as the county manager for such county or the manager for such elective body (as the case may be) may from time to time give either generally or in regard to the performance of any particular duty or any particular class or classes of duties or in regard to the performance of any such duty by any particular officer or servant, and such county manager shall have and exercise control and full supervision of and over such officers and servants and any and every act or thing done or to be done by them in their capacity as officers and servants of such council or body, as the case may be.

(2) Subject to any orders or regulations made by the Minister under any Act and for the time being in force in relation to the service, remuneration, privileges, or superannuation (as the case may be) of the officers and servants of a local authority, the county manager for a county or the manager for an elective body shall consider and decide all such questions as may from time to time arise in relation to the service, remuneration, privileges and super-annuation of the officers and servants of the council of such county or of such elective body, as the case may be. [*Ss. 21-26 omitted.*]

MANAGER TO GIVE INFORMATION TO ELECTED COUNCILS

27.—Every county manager shall whenever requested by the council of his county or by an elective body for which he is the manager or by the chairman of such council or of any such body so to do, afford to such council, body, or chairman (as the case may require) all such information as may be in the possession or procurement of such county manager in regard to any act, matter, or thing appertaining to or concerning any business or transaction of such council or body (as the case may be) which is mentioned in such request. [*Ss. 28 and 29 omitted.*]

ATTENDANCE OF MANAGER AT MEETINGS

30.—(1) Every county manager shall have the right to attend meetings of the council of his county and of every elective body for which he is manager, and to take part in discussions at such meetings as if he were a member of such council or body, but he shall not be entitled to vote on any question which is decided by a vote of the members of such council or body.

(2) A county manager shall, so far as is not inconsistent with the due performance of his duties, attend—

(*a*) any meeting of the council of his county which he is requested by such council to attend, and

(*b*) any meeting of a committee of such council which he is requested by such council to attend, and

(*c*) any meeting of an elective body for which he is manager which he is requested by such body to attend, and

(*d*) any meeting of a committee of such elective body which he is requested by such body to attend.

(3) Whenever a county manager attends a meeting of the council of a county or of an elective body or of a committee in pursuance of the next preceding sub-section of this section, he shall give to such council, body, or committee (as the case may be) such advice and assistance as shall reasonably be required of him by such council, body, or committee, and shall for that

purpose arrange for the attendance at such meeting of such of the officers of such council or body as may be necessary having regard to the business to be transacted at such meeting. [*SS. 4 omitted.*]

DUTY OF MANAGER TO ADVISE AND ASSIST COUNCIL

31.—(1) It shall be the duty of every county manager to advise and assist the council of his county and also every elective body for which he is manager in regard generally to the exercise or performance by them of their reserved functions and also in regard to any particular matter or thing in relation to such exercise or performance on or in respect of which such council or body requests the advice or assistance of such county manager.

(2) It shall be the duty of every county manager to carry into effect all lawful orders of the council of his county and also of every elective body for which he is manager in relation to the exercise and performance of the reserved functions of such council or body, as the case may be.

MANAGER TO ACT IN LEGAL PROCEEDINGS

32.—(1) In every action or other legal proceeding, whether civil or criminal, instituted in any court of law or equity by or against the council of a county, the county manager for that county shall act for and on behalf of such council and may do all such acts, matters, and things as he may consider necessary for the preparation and prosecution or defence of such action or other proceeding in the same manner in all respects as if (as the case may require) he were the plaintiff or prosecutor or the defendant therein, and, where such action or other proceeding relates to the exercise or performance by such council of a reserved function of such council, such county manager shall, in the doing of any such act, matter, or thing as aforesaid, act with the express authority of such council, and such authority shall be deemed to have been given unless or until the contrary is shown.

(2) In every action or other legal proceeding, whether civil or criminal instituted in any court of law or equity by or against an elective body, the manager for such elective body shall act for and on behalf of such elective body and may do all such acts, matters, and things as he may consider necessary for the preparation and prosecution or defence of such action or other proceeding in the same manner in all respects as if (as the case may require) he were the plaintiff or the prosecutor or the defendant therein, and, where such action or other proceeding relates to the exercise or performance by such elective body of a reserved function of such elective body, such manager shall, in the doing of any such act, matter, or thing as aforesaid, act with the express authority of such elective body, and such authority shall be deemed to have been given unless or until the contrary is shown. [*Remainder of Act omitted.*]

FIRST SCHEDULE
Grouping of Certain Counties

Group A. This group shall consist of the counties of Carlow and Kildare.

Group B. This group shall consist of the counties of Kilkenny and Waterford.

Group C. This group shall consist of the counties of Laoighis and Offaly.

Group D. This group shall consist of the counties of Leitrim and Sligo.

Group E. This group shall consist of the counties of Longford and West-
meath.

Group F. This group shall consist of the counties of Tipperary North
Riding and Tipperary South Riding.

(c) *The position of the Elected Council made stronger*
Document 9.14 — Extracts from City and County Management
(Amendment) Act, 1955 (no. 12).

MANAGER TO GIVE PRIOR INFORMATION

2.—(1) Subject to the provisions of this section, a local authority may by
resolution direct that, before the manager performs any specified executive
function of the local authority, he shall inform the members of the local
authority of the manner in which he proposes to perform that function, and
the manager shall comply with the resolution.

(2) A resolution under subsection (1) of this section may relate to any
particular case or occasion or to every case or occasion of the performance of
the specified executive function.

(3) A resolution under subsection (1) of this section shall not apply or
extend to the performance of any function of the manager in relation to the
officers or servants of a local authority or the control, supervision, service,
remuneration, privileges or superannuation of such officers or servants or any
of them, and any resolution purporting to be passed under subsection (1) of
this section which contravenes this subsection shall be void.

(4) Every dispute arising between a local authority and the manager as to
whether a resolution passed by the local authority does or does not contravene
subsection (3) of this section shall be referred for decision—

(a) in case the local authority are a joint mental hospital board or a joint
board established by order under section 45 of the Health Act,
1953 (No. 26 of 1953)—to the Minister for Health, and

(b) in any other case—to the Minister [for Local Government].

(5) A resolution under subsection (1) of this section shall not apply or
extend to the performance of any of the individual health functions of a local
authority, and any resolution purporting to be passed under subsection (1) of
this section which contravenes this subsection shall be void.

(6) Every dispute arising between a local authority and the manager as to
whether a resolution passed by the local authority does or does not contravene
subsection (5) of this section shall be referred for decision to the Minister for
Health.

(7) The manager shall inform the members of a local authority—

    (*a*) before any works (other than works of maintenance or repair) of the local authority are undertaken, or

    (*b*) before committing the local authority to any expenditure in connection with proposed works (other than works of maintenance or repair).

(8) A local authority may by resolution define what information is to be given pursuant to this section, and how and when it is to be so given, and the manager shall comply with the resolution.

(9) Nothing in the foregoing provisions of this section shall prevent the manager from dealing forthwith with any situation which he considers is an emergency situation calling for immediate action without regard to those provisions.

COUNCIL'S POWER OF DIRECTION

3.—Where the members of a local authority are informed pursuant to section 2 of this Act of any works (not being works which the local authority are required by or under statute or by order of a Court to undertake), the local authority may by resolution direct that the works shall not be proceeded with, and the manager shall comply with the resolution.

4.—(1) Subject to the provisions of this section, a local authority may by resolution require any particular act, matter or thing specifically mentioned in the resolution and which the local authority or the manager can lawfully do or effect to be done or effected in performance of the executive functions of the local authority. [*SSs. 2-7 omitted.*]

(8) Where a resolution is passed under and in accordance with this section, the manager shall, if and when and so far as money for the purpose is or has been provided, do or effect in accordance with the resolution the act, matter or thing specified in the resolution.

(9) A resolution under this section shall not—

    (*a*) apply or extend—

        (i) to the performance of any function of a local authority generally,

        (ii) to every case or occasion of the performance of any such function or to a number or class of such cases or occasions so extended as to be substantially or in effect every case or occasion on which any such function is performed, or

        (iii) to every case or occasion of the performance of any such function in a particular area or to a number or class of such cases or occasions so extended as to be substantially or in effect every case or occasion on which any such function is performed in that area, or (*b*) apply or extend to the performance of any executive function in relation to the officers or servants of a local authority or the control, supervision, service, remuneration, privileges or superannuation of such officers or servants or any of them,

and any resolution purporting to be passed under this section which contravenes this subsection shall be void.

(10) Every dispute arising between a local authority and the manager as to whether a resolution passed by the local authority under this section does or does not contravene subsection (9) of this section shall be referred for decision—

(*a*) in case the local authority is a joint mental hospital board or a joint board established by order under section 45 of the Health Act, 1953 (No. 26 of 1953), and the dispute is as to whether the resolution does or does not contravene paragraph (*b*) of that subsection—to the Minister for Health, and

(*b*) in any other case—to the Minister.

(11) A resolution under this section shall not apply or extend to the performance of any of the individual health functions of a local authority, and any resolution purporting to be passed under this section which contravenes this subsection shall be void. [*SS.* 12 *and S.* 5 *omitted.*]

LIMITATIONS ON MANAGER'S POWERS

6.—(1) The manager shall not submit any proposal to vary the number of permanent offices under a local authority for the sanction of such Minister as may be empowered to sanction the proposal save with the consent by resolution of the local authority.

(2) The manager shall not submit any proposal to fix an increased or reduced rate of remuneration applicable to any class, description or grade of office or employment for the sanction of such Minister as may be empowered to sanction the proposal save with the consent by resolution of the local authority.

(3) The manager shall not fix an increased or reduced rate of remuneration applicable to any class, description or grade of office or employment under a local authority save with the consent by resolution of the local authority, but this restriction shall not apply if a proposal by the manager to fix that increased or reduced rate of remuneration applicable to that class, description or grade of office or employment has previously, with the consent by resolution of the local authority given pursuant to subsection (2) of this section, been submitted for the sanction of such Minister as may be empowered to sanction the proposal [*Ss.* 7-10 *omitted.*]

POWERS IN RELATION TO EXPENDITURE

11.—(1) At any time after they have adopted an estimate of expenses, a local authority may, as respects the local financial year to which the estimate relates, authorise by resolution the expenditure of money or the incurring of a liability in excess of the expenditure for any particular purpose specified in the estimate.

(2) Save with an authorisation given by resolution under subsection (1) of this section, the total amount of money expended and liability incurred by a local authority as respects any local financial year for any particular purpose specified in the estimate of expenses for that year shall not exceed the total amount specified in that estimate in respect of that purpose.

(3) Where, as respects any local financial year the manager is of opinion that the proper performance of the functions of a local authority requires the expenditure of money or the incurring of a liability in respect of any particular purpose in excess of the expenditure for that purpose specified in the estimate of expenses for that year, he may prepare an application for the authorisation by the local authority of the excess expenditure and may submit the application—

(*a*) in the case of a local authority having an estimates committee, to the committee, and

(*b*) in any other case, to the members of the local authority.

(4) Where an application is submitted to an estimates committee under subsection (3) of this section, the committee shall consider the application and shall then submit it, with their recommendation thereon, to the members of the local authority. [*Remainder of Act omitted.*]

6. OFFICERS

(a) *Powers to appoint and assign remuneration*

Document 9.15 — Extracts from Local Government Act, 1941
(no. 23) in Street, *op. cit.*, pp. 254-7.

10.—(1) Subject to the provisions of this Part of this Act—

(*a*) every local authority may appoint such officers and employ such servants as are necessary for the performance of the functions for the time being of such local authority;

(*b*) every officer appointed or servant employed by a local authority shall perform such duties and be paid such remuneration as such local authority may from time to time assign to him.

(2) Any officer of a local authority who is aggrieved by a decision of such local authority in relation to his remuneration, duties, or conditions of service may appeal against such decision to the appropriate Minister in the prescribed manner and on notice to such local authority and the appropriate Minister, after consideration of such appeal and of the representations (if any) of such local authority in relation thereto, shall either (as he thinks proper) refuse such appeal or give to such local authority such direction as the appropriate Minister considers will remedy the grievance of such officer.

(3) Any local authority to whom a direction is given under the immediately preceding sub-section of this section shall comply with such direction.

[1]*(4) For the purposes of this section, a local authority may, with the general or particular approval of the appropriate Minister, create offices either on a permanent or a temporary basis.*

(5) A local authority may, with the general or particular approval of the appropriate Minister, abolish offices, but in the case of an office held by a person in a permanent capacity, it shall not be abolished save with the consent of that person.

(6) An appeal under subsection (2) of this section shall not be brought after the expiration of six months after the decision is communicated to the officer.

11.—The appropriate Minister may by order direct the kind and number of the officers to be appointed by a local authority for any purpose, and thereupon it shall be the duty of such local authority from time to time to appoint for that purpose such and so many (and no other) officers as may be necessary to conform with the requirements of such order. [*Remainder omitted.*]

---

1. The subsections in italics were added by Local Government Act, 1955 (No. 9), section 12. Section 20 of that Act restricts a Local Authority's power to assign remuneration as follows:—

20.—(1) The power of a local authority under section 10 of the Act of 1941 to assign remuneration to an officer shall not be exercised except in accordance with such one or more of the following as may be appropriate from time to time:—

    (*a*) any order made by the appropriate Minister under section 29 of the Act of 1941,

    (*b*) any regulation made by the appropriate Minister under paragraph (*a*) of subsection (1) of section 19 of the Act of 1941,

    (*c*) any direction given by the appropriate Minister regarding the considerations that should govern levels of remuneration of officers generally,

    (*d*) any direction given by the appropriate Minister regarding the considerations that should govern levels of remuneration of officers of a specified class, description or grade, the officer being in that class, description or grade,

    (*e*) the sanction of the appropriate Minister.

(2) The power of a local authority under section 10 of the Act of 1941 to assign remuneration to a servant shall not be exercised except in accordance with such one or more of the following as may be appropriate from time to time:—

    (*a*) any direction given by the appropriate Minister regarding the considerations that should govern levels of remuneration of servants generally,

    (*b*) any direction given by the appropriate Minister regarding the considerations that should govern levels of remuneration of servants of a specified class, description or grade, the servant being in that class, description or grade,

    (*c*) the sanction of the appropriate Minister.

(3) The appropriate Minister may give directions for the purposes of this section.

(b) *The Local Appointments Commission*

Document 9.16 — Extracts from Local Authorities (Officers and Employees) Act, 1926 (no. 39) in Street, *op. cit.,* pp. 683-6.

2.—(1) In this Act the expression "office to which this Act applies" means and includes—

(a) the chief executive office under every local authority, and

[1](b) *every office (not being a temporary office, a part-time office as engineer or surveyor under the council of an urban district or the commissioners of a town or an office as a teacher) under a local authority the qualifications for which are wholly or in part professional.*

(c) all such other offices and employments under a local authority as the Minister shall from time to time with the concurrence of the Commissioners declare to be offices to which this Act applies. [*Remainder of S. 2 omitted.*]

3.—(1) It shall be lawful for the Government from time to time to appoint fit and proper persons to be Local Appointments Commissioners (in this Act referred to as "the Commissioners") to fulfil the functions assigned to such Commissioners by this Act.

(2) A person shall not be ineligible for appointment as a Commissioner under this Act by reason only of his being a Civil Service Commissioner under the Civil Service Regulation Act, 1924 (No. 5 of 1924).

(3) The Commissioners shall not at any time exceed three in number.

(4) Every person appointed under this section to be a Local Appointments Commissioner shall hold office during the pleasure of the Government.

(5) Every appointment and every removal of a Commissioner under this section shall be published immediately in the *Iris Oifigiúil*. [*S. 4 omitted.*]

---

1. The words in italics are an amendment made by Local Government Act, 1955 (No. 9), section 26. The section is further amended by the Local Authorities (Officers and Employers) (Amendment) Act, 1940 (No. 15) sections 3 and 4 which state as follows:—

    3.—Notwithstanding anything contained in sub-section (1) of section 2 of the Principal Act, that Act shall not apply to the office or employment of nurse under a local authority or to the office or employment of midwife under a local authority, and the expression "office to which this Act applies" shall, in the Principal Act, be construed and have effect accordingly.

    4.—(1) The Minister may at any time, with the concurrence of the Commissioners, revoke, either wholly or in respect of a particular office or employment or particular offices or employments, a declaration made (whether before or after the passing of this Act) by him under paragraph (c) of sub-section (1) of section 2 of the Principal Act.

5.—(1) An appointment of a person to fill an office to which this Act applies may, subject to the sanction of the Minister, be made by a local authority without requesting or obtaining a recommendation from the Commissioners under the subsequent provisions of this Act if but only if the appointment is made within three months after such office became vacant or (in the case of an appointment to a new office) was created and the person so appointed is a person who at the time when such office became vacant or was created (as the case may be) either—

(a) held a pensionable office under the said or any other local authority or any two or more local authorities the duties of which related to matters the same as or similar to the matters to which the duties of the vacant office relate, or

(b) was in receipt of an allowance from the said or any other local authority or any two or more local authorities in respect of his having ceased to hold an office under the said or any other local authority or any two or more local authorities the duties of which related to matters the same as or similar to the matters to which the duties of the vacant office relate. [*SS. 2 omitted.*]

6.—(1) Save as is otherwise authorised by this Act, every local authority shall, before making an appointment to an office to which this Act applies, request the Commissioners to recommend to them a person for appointment to such office.

(2) Whenever a local authority does not, within three months after an office to which this Act applies becomes vacant or (in the case of a new office) is created, either request the Commissioners to recommend to them a person for appointment to such office or make an appointment (other than a temporary appointment) to such office under and in accordance with a provision of this Act dispensing with such request, the Minister may on behalf of such local authority request the Commissioners to recommend to such local authority a person for appointment to such office.

(3) On receiving such request as aforesaid from the local authority or the Minister (as the case may be) the Commissioners shall select in accordance with this Act and recommend to the local authority one person for appointment to the said office or shall, if they so think proper, select in accordance with this Act and recommend to the local authority two or more persons for such appointment.

(4) On receiving from the Commissioners their recommendation under this section, the local authority shall appoint to the said office the person recommended by the Commissioners or, where more than one person is so recommended, such one of the persons so recommended as they shall think proper.

(c) *Powers of Ministers in Relation to Offices and their Holders*
Document 9.17 — Extracts from Local Government Act, 1941 (no. 23)
in Street, *op. cit.*, pp. 261-72.

EXTENT OF MINISTERIAL POWER

19.—(1) The appropriate Minister may, for all or any of the following purposes, make regulations applying to all the offices in relation to which he is the appropriate Minister and their holders or to such of those offices as belong to a specified class, description, or grade and their holders, that is to say : —

   (*a*) determining remuneration,

   (*b*) regulating the payment and amount of travelling expenses,

   (*c*) determining hours of duty,

   (*d*) providing for records of attendance,

   (*e*) regulating the granting of sick and other leave and the payment of remuneration during leave,

   (*f*) requiring holders to give security for the due and proper performance of their duties and regulating the nature and amount of such security,

   (*g*) prescribing the procedure to be followed by local authorities in making appointments otherwise than on the recommendation of the Local Appointments Commissioners and in obtaining candidates when proposing to make appointments as aforesaid,

   (*h*) regulating continuance in and cessor of office,

   (*i*) fixing periods, upon the expiration of which in relation to holders respectively, they shall cease to hold office unless they have theretofore satisfied or complied with specified requirements or conditions.

   [1](*j*) *providing, in case of holders being ill, absent or incapacitated, for the performance of their duties by deputy or substitute,*

   (*k*) *providing for restrictions on holders engaging in any other gainful occupation,*

   (*l*) *providing for the removal from office by local authorities of holders who hold in a permanent capacity and prescribing the procedure to be adopted and the conditions to be fulfilled in relation to such removals,*

   (*m*) *providing for the imposition by local authorities on holders of suspensions from performance of duties (including short-term disciplinary suspensions, not exceeding seven days), the non-payment of remuneration during the continuance of the suspensions and, upon the termination thereof, the forfeiture (in whole or in part), payment or disposal otherwise of remuneration which would, but for the suspensions, have been paid during the periods thereof,*

[1.] The words in italics are amendments made by Local Government Act, 1955 (No. 9), section 14.

(*n*) *providing for the supplementing of the regulations by directions*
(being directions for the purpose of giving effect to the regulations,
but neither extending the regulations nor widening their scope) given
from time to time by the appropriate Minister.

20.—(1) The appropriate Minister may by declaration do all or any of
the following things in respect of a specified office in relation to which he is
the appropriate Minister or in respect of such of the offices in relation to
which he is the appropriate Minister as belong to a specified class, description
or grade, that is to say : —

(*a*) define the duties of holders thereof,

(*b*) assign a particular duty to holders thereof,

(*c*) define the places or limits within which all or any of the duties of
holders thereof are to be performed.

[*SS. 2 omitted.*]

MINISTER'S POWER TO DECIDE QUALIFICATIONS

21.—(1) The appropriate Minister may declare a qualification of any of
the following classes or descriptions to be a qualification for a specified office
in relation to which he is the appropriate Minister or for such of the offices
in relation to which he is the appropriate Minister as belong to a specified
class, description or grade[1], that is to say : —

(*a*) qualifications relating to character,

(*b*) qualifications relating to age, health, or physical characteristics,

(*c*) qualifications relating to education, training, or experience,

(*d*) qualifications relating to residence[2],

(*e*) qualifications relating to sex,

(*f*) the qualification that any woman holding the office in question be
either unmarried or a widow.

(2) The appropriate Minister shall not declare under this section that any
qualification relating to sex is a qualification for any office unless he is of
opinion that the duties of such office so require.

[1.] The practice as regards qualifications has been that, on a vacancy arising,
the Department concerned consults the Local Appointment Commissioners as to
qualifications The local authority, though not always consulted, may make suggestions. On receipt of the assent of the said commissioners the qualifications are
declared. . . . During the year 1947 general qualifications were prescribed for
nearly all offices, after consultation with the said commissioners, and have been
isued with covering circular letters by the Departments by which the offices concerned are controlled. Qualifications for county surveyors (or engineers) were prescribed on 21st January, 1945. When the qualifications have been declared by the
Minister no further qualifications may be declared by the local authority (Act 24
of 1946 s. 40). . . .—Street.

[2.] Local authorities have in some cases asked for restriction of candidates to
those born or resident within a particular area — Street.

(3) Before declaring under this section that any qualification is a qualification for any office to which the Act of 1926 applies, the appropriate Minister shall consult with the Local Appointments Commissioners.

(4) Sub-sections (1) and (2) of section 7 of the Act of 1926 shall cease to have effect in relation to every office under a local authority, and every reference in that Act to the qualifications prescribed under that Act shall be construed in relation to every office under a local authority as a reference to the qualifications (if any) for the time being declared under this section to be the qualifications for such office.

(5) For the purposes of the Act of 1926, none of the following qualifications shall be deemed to be professional or technical, that is to say: —
   (a) certification as a midwife,
   (b) registration as a nurse,
   (c) any qualification relating to training or experience as a nurse or midwife,
   (d) any qualification relating to the knowledge required by a nurse or midwife.

(6) Subject to the provisions of the next following sub-section of this section, no person shall be appointed to any office for which any qualifications are for the time being declared under this section to be the qualifications unless he possesses those qualifications.

(7) Whenever it is necessary to fill immediately any office for which any qualifications are for the time being declared under this section to be the qualifications and no suitable person possessing such qualifications is available for appointment, the appropriate Minister may, on the application of the local authority concerned, authorise an appointment, limited as to its duration to a specified period, to be made to such office without reference to such qualifications and thereupon such appointment may be so made.

(8) A person appointed to any office in pursuance of an authorisation under the immediately preceding sub-section of this section shall (unless for any reason he has previously ceased to hold office) cease to hold office on the occurrence of whichever of the following events first occurs, that is to say: —
   (a) the expiration of the period specified in that behalf in such authorisation,
   (b) the appointment to such office of a person possessing the qualifications for the time being declared under this section to be the qualifications for such office.

(9) For the purposes of this section, the fact that a person has been recommended by the Local Appointments Commissioners for appointment to any office shall be conclusive evidence that he possessed at the time of such recommendation the qualifications (if any) for the time being declared under this section to be the qualifications for such office.

(10) The Local Appointments Commissioners shall, before recommending a person to a local authority for appointment to any office, satisfy themselves that such person possesses the requisite knowledge and ability for the proper discharge of the duties of such office.

[*S. 22 omitted.*]

23.—(1) The appropriate Minister may declare any specified age to be the age limit for all offices in relation to which he is the appropriate Minister or for such of those offices as belong to a specified class, description, or grade or for one or more specified such offices.

(2) Every declaration under this section shall come into force six months after the day on which it is made. [*SSs. 3 and 4 omitted.*]

RESIGNATION FROM OFFICE

24.—(1) Where the appropriate Minister is satisfied—

(*a*) that the holder of an office does not possess a qualification which before the appointment of such holder to such office, has been declared under this Part of this Act to be a qualification for such office, or

(*b*) that, on account of any alteration (whether it has already occurred or is in contemplation) in the conditions of service or the nature or extent of the duties attached to such office, it is in the public interest that the holder of such office should resign therefrom,

[1]*or*

(*c*) *that, on account of any alteration (whether it has already occurred or is in contemplation) in the nature or extent of the duties attached to such office, it is in the public interest that such office should be abolished,*

the appropriate Minister may require the holder of such office to resign within a specified period and, if such holder refuses to resign from such office or fails to resign from such office within the said period, may by order remove such holder from such office.

REMOVAL FROM OFFICE

25.—(1) For the purposes of this section, the following shall be the statutory grounds for the removal of the holder of an office from such office, that is to say:—

(*a*) unfitness of such holder for such office,

(*b*) the fact that such holder has refused to obey or carry into effect any order lawfully given to him as the holder of such office, or has otherwise misconducted himself in such office,

and, in this section, the expression "statutory grounds for removal from office" shall be construed accordingly.

---

[1] Words in italics are an amendment made by Local Government Act, 1955 (No. 9, s. 17.

(2) Where the appropriate Minister is satisfied as a result of any local inquiry that any of the statutory grounds for removal from office exists as regards the holder of an office, the appropriate Minister may by order remove such holder from such office. [SSs. 3 and 4 omitted]

SUSPENSION FROM OFFICE

[1]27.—(1) Whenever in respect of the holder of an office under a local authority there is, in the opinion of the appropriate Minister, reason to believe that such holder has failed to perform satisfactorily the duties of such office or has misconducted himself in relation to such office or is unfit to hold such office, the appropriate Minister may suspend such holder from the performance of the duties of such office while such alleged failure, misconduct, or unfitness is being inquired into and the disciplinary action (if any) to be taken in regard thereto is being determined.

(2) The appropriate Minister may terminate a suspension under this section and every such suspension shall continue until so terminated.

REMUNERATION

29.—The appropriate Minister may by order fix the amount and nature of the remuneration of holders of a specified major office [2]*or holders of such major offices as belong to a specified class, description or grade* and such order shall have the force of law in accordance with its terms in relation to such office *or offices* and holders thereof and, if and in so far as it conflicts with any regulation made under this Part of the Act, shall override such regulation. *The powers conferred by this section in relation to the holders of a specified major office may be exercised notwithstanding that such office belongs to a class, description or grade in relation to which the powers conferred by this section have already been exercised.*

7. FINANCE

Document 9.18 — Extract from *Returns of Local Taxation for the Year ended 31 March 1961.*

FINANCES—REVENUE ACCOUNTS

The income of local authorities on revenue account is derived from miscellaneous receipts, State grants and rates.

MISCELLANEOUS RECEIPTS

The principal miscellaneous receipts in the year ended 31st March, 1961, were rents received by local authorities for houses let to tenants, which

1. This section is printed as amended by Local Government Act, 1955 (No. 9) which removed certain words from the section as originally enacted.
2. The words in italics were added by Local Government Act, 1955 (No. 9) s.19.

amounted to £2,776,641, purchase annuities paid by local authority tenants buying their houses, which amounted to £475,186, rents received from corporate estate, town halls and other property which amounted to £132,565, contributions by patients towards the cost of institutional services which amounted to £976,525, water rents and water and sewerage connections which amounted to £589,743, and repayments of loan instalments by borrowers under the Small Dwellings Acquisition Acts which came to £2,016,164.

STATE GRANTS

The total amount of State grants received by local authorities in a number of years is shown in Table A at the end of this introduction[1]. It should be noted that the amount shown in these Returns for individual State grants is the amount lodged to the credit of local authorities in the financial year and is not necessarily equal to the actual amount of the grant paid or allocated for that year.

The amount of the most important grants received by local authorities on revenue account in the year ended 31st March, 1961, is as follows:—

   (a) Agricultural Grant £5,668,677
   (b) Grants from the Road Fund £6,137,111
   (c) Grants under the Health Services (Financial Provisions)
      Act, 1947 ... ... £8,804,999
   (d) Contributions towards Housing Loan Charges £2,249,997
   (e) Contributions towards Sanitary Services Loan Charges £380,417

The following is a short description of each of these grants:—

(a) *Agricultural Grant*

The agricultural grant is paid to county councils to enable them, without loss to themselves, to make allowances by way of rate abatement to the rated occupiers of agricultural land in their rating areas. The grant was first given under the Local Government (Ireland) Act, 1898. It was a fixed annual subvention of £727,655 for the whole of Ireland, this being the amount required to give relief to the extent of half the rates paid on agricultural land in the standard year 1896/97. On the setting up of the State in 1922 the twenty-six county share was fixed at £599,011. In the year 1925/26 the amount of the grant was doubled. Between that year and the year 1946/47 the basis of its distribution and the amount of the grant were altered on a number of occasions. Prior to 1946/47 the amount of the grant was always a sum fixed by each successive Act. Under the Rates on Agricultural Land (Relief) Act, 1946, it was provided that the grant would be the sum needed to give relief of rates by way of a *primary allowance* amounting to three-fifths of the general rate in the pound on the land valuation up to £20, *a supplementary allowance* of one-fifth of the general rate in the pound on the land valuation over £20 and an *employment allowance* calculated at the rate of 10/- in the pound on the land valuation over £20, subject to the limitation

---

[1.] See page 306 below.

that this allowance should not exceed £6 10s. 0d., for each adult workman at work on the holding during the whole of the preceding calendar year. The agricultural grant was continued on this basis until the passing, in 1953, of an amending Act which applied to the years 1953/54, 1954/55 and 1955/56. That Act left the *primary allowance* unchanged, abolished the *supplementary allowance* and provided for an *employment allowance* of £17 in respect of each qualified workman subject to the limitation that the total of the employment allowances would not exceed the rates on the land valuation over £20. Amending Acts in 1956 and 1959 continued the distribution of the grant on this basis for a further six years up to 31st March, 1962.

The Rates on Agricultural Land (Relief) Act, 1962, which applies to the three years ending on 31st March, 1965, increased the *primary allowance* to seven-tenths of the general rate, provided for a *supplementary allowance* of one-quarter of the general rate on land valuations over £20 and left the *employment allowance* unchanged.

The total amounts of agricultural grant received by county councils increased from £2,907,930 in 1946/47 to £4,649,720 in 1952/53 and to £5,662 millions in 1960/61. These amounts include certain fixed sums which were received by county councils but were later paid over to those urban districts and boroughs which were created or extended since 1898. In the year 1959/60, £9,273 was paid over by county councils to 26 such urban authorities.

In addition to the amount of agricultural grant payable to county councils, certain fixed sums are payable annually to four county borough corporations (Cork, Dublin, Limerick and Waterford) whose boundaries were extended since the coming into operation of the Local Government (Ireland) Act, 1898. The amounts received by these corporations in 1959/60 was £6,219.

(b) *Grants from the Road Fund*

Licence duties on mechanically propelled vehicles were first introduced by the Budget of 1909. A Road Board was set up which devoted the funds derived from the licence duties to road improvements which took the form of new roads, the straightening or widening of existing roads, and the provision of better road surfaces. The functions of the Road Board were merged in those of the Ministry of Transport in 1919 and, on the setting up of the State in 1922, were transferred to the Department of Local Government. Under the Roads Act, 1920, county councils and county borough corporations (referred to as licensing authorities), are responsible for the registration of mechanically propelled vehicles and the collection of taxation on them by way of licence duties, including the duty on driving licences. The licensing authorities act under the general direction of the Minister for Local Government and in accordance with the Roads Act, and the Orders and Regulations made thereunder and under the Finance Acts (which set out the rates of motor taxation). In addition to motor taxation, licensing authorities collect fees on petrol pumps and certain other miscellaneous fees; these receipts are also paid by them into the Road Fund. The moneys collected by licensing authorities are paid into a central Motor Tax Account, from which they are transferred through the Exchequer to the Road Fund. Fines and penalties recovered under the Roads Act and the Road Traffic Act, 1933, are also paid through the same channels into the Road Fund. Grants from the Fund were allocated to local authorities as follows for the year 1960/61 : —

   (i) one hundred per cent grants for the improvement of main and county roads divided between county councils primarily on the basis of their main and county road mileages (a main road improvement grant is also allocated to Dundalk Urban District Council and Drogheda Borough Corporation);

   (ii) main road upkeep grants representing forty per cent (increased in year 1962/63 to 50 per cent) of approved expenditure by county councils, county borough corporations, Dun Laoghaire and Drogheda Borough Corporations and Dundalk Urban District Council on the maintenance of trunk and link roads;

   (iii) special grants allocated for the construction or reconstruction of bridges and for the improvement of short sections of roads which could not be dealt with by other methods;

   (iv) grants to the county borough corporations, borough corporations and urban district councils for road improvement work.

In addition grants for the Tourist Road Scheme were made.

(c) *Grants under the Health Services (Financial Provisions) Act, 1947*

The payment of grants from central government funds towards the cost of health services has since 1st April, 1948, been governed by the provisions of the Health Services (Financial Provisions) Act, 1947. Prior to the commencement of operation of that Act State grants for specified health services were paid from various sources to different classes of local authorities. These grants included issues from the Local Taxation Account and from voted moneys towards the cost of mental treatment services, infectious diseases services, general medical and institutional services provided by public assistance authorities, maternity and child welfare services, school medical services, free milk, etc. From 1st April, 1948, a single grant became payable to health authorities (county councils and county borough councils) which became the authorities responsible for the provision of the funds to meet the direct expenditure on the various health services.

Under the Health Services (Financial Provisions) Act, 1947, each health authority receives a grant equal to the excess of the amount of the running costs of its services over the amount of the corresponding expenses met out of local funds in the year 1947/48. The expenditure on which the grant is based is the expenditure certified by the Minister for Health to have been properly incurred on recognised health services, and it does not include capital expenditure or loan charges. The expenditure in excess of that incurred in 1947/48 (the "Standard Year") is recoupable in full to each authority up to the point at which its current expenditure is equal to twice its net expenditure in respect of that year. Beyond that point expenditure is recoupable to the extent of 50 per cent. In the five years 1947/48 to 1951/52 the percenages of net expenditure recouped were 16 per cent, 28 per cent, 35 per cent, 44 per cent and 50 per cent. In the year 1952/53 the expenditure of each health authority exceeded the equivalent of twice the appropriate figure for the Standard Year, and accordingly, the grants from the Health Vote have been at the rate of 50 per cent of current expenditure in all cases since that year. The amount of State assistance for health services paid in respect of the year prior to the introduction of the new system was approximately £0.9 million. The amount of Health Grant received by Health authorities in the first year of operation of the new system was £1,681,387 and the amount in respect of 1960/61 is £8,804,999.

The Health Act, 1953, amended the Health Services (Financial Provisions) Act, 1947, by providing, inter alia, that the Minister may, in respect of a particular year and for a particular body, fix a sum which shall be the maximum expenditure which may be included in respect of a health service or part of a health service in the calculation of the net health expenditure of that body in respect of that year.

(d) *Contributions towards Housing Loan Charges*

Rural Housing—In 1891 State assistance was first made available towards the cost of the erection of houses by rural housing authorities. The nature and extent of the assistance was varied on a number of occasions. Under the Housing (Financial and Miscellaneous Provisions) Act, 1932, the assistance takes the form of annual contributions to loan charges. The subsidy is paid during the period of the loan which, up to 1948, was 35 years and since then has been 50 years. The statutory maximum subsidy is 66⅔ per cent. of annual loan charges where overcrowding has been relieved or unfit dwellings have been replaced or repaired or any other Statutory operation is carried out by the housing authority and 33⅓ per cent. for other rural housing, subject to maximum subsidisable limits of capital cost. The present subsidisable limits are £1,100 for unserviced cottages and £1,650 for serviced cottages.

Urban Housing—Prior to 1908 no subsidy was provided for urban housing schemes. As in the case of rural housing, the Housing (Financial and Miscellaneous Provisions) Act, 1932, forms the basis of financing and subsidising all urban housing at present. The statutory maximum contribution is 66⅔ per cent. of annual loan charges in the case of houses or flats provided for slum clearance, relief of overcrowding and rehousing of homeless persons, etc., and the maximum for other purposes is 33⅓ per cent. The present limits of subsidisable cost are £1,650 for houses and £2,200 for flats.

(e) *Contributions towards Sanitary Services Loan Charges*

Contributions towards loan charges are also paid in respect of Sanitary Services works. In the period from 1925 to 1950 State assistance towards such works (mainly water supply and sewerage schemes) took the form of lump sum grants, which came principally from the Employment and Emergency Schemes Vote, and to a limited extent (in the period 1946 to 1950) from the

Transition Development Fund. As from 1951 it was decided that assistance should be given by way of percentage contribution towards loan charges incurred on schemes.

Since 18th September, 1959, the ordinary rates of subsidy were 40 per cent. to 60 per cent. of annual loan charges, depending on type and location of scheme. The rates of subsidy payable in respect of schemes where loans were sanctioned or work commenced before that date ranged from 38⅓ per cent to 50 per cent.

RATES

Rates are levied annually by county councils, county borough and borough corporations, and urban district councils to supply deficiencies in their funds. Each of these authorities has exclusive rating jurisdiction within its own area. The rate levied by county councils is known as the county rate. The rate levied by the other authorities is known as the municipal rate. Town commissioners are not rating authorities, their requirements, apart from State grants and miscellaneous receipts, being obtained on demand from the county council, which collects the amount of the demand and certain incidental expenses in the town as part of the county rate. The demand and expenses are known as town charges. The total amount of rates received in a number of years is shown in Table A at the end of this introduction.

As a general rule rates are made on the occupiers of property. Exceptions to this are rates made on the landlord as immediate lessor of a house let in separate apartments or lodgings; rates made on persons receiving rent from certain charitable or public properties and rates made on the owners of "small dwellings". Broadly small dwellings are houses provided by housing authorities and owned by them, or houses with a valuation of up to £6, or higher in certain county boroughs and urban districts. Rates are also made on the owners of hereditaments which are unoccupied at the making of the rate.

VALUATION

The property which is assessed for rates is immovable property such as land, buildings, factories, shops, railways, canals, mines, woods, rights of fishery and rights and easements over land. The valuing of such property for the purpose of local taxation is done for the whole State by the Valuation Office under the direction of the Commissioner of Valuation and subject to a right of appeal to the courts. Rating authorities have no valuing powers. The basis of the valuation of houses and other building is net annual value, that is, the rent which a tenant liable for rates, repairs, insurance and maintenance might reasonably be expected to pay. The value of agricultural land varies with the prices ruling for agricultural products and in an effort to secure uniformity of valuation a fixed scale of prices for such products was specified in the Valuation (Ireland) Act, 1852. This scale was adopted for the purposes of land valuation, local circumstances being taken into consideration. The valuations of land except land in parts of the county boroughs of Dublin and Waterford have remained practically unaltered since they were determined under the 1852 Act. The valuation of railway hereditaments (which do not include hotels, refreshment rooms, dwellinghouses, town offices or receiving depots, etc., occupied by the railway company) is revised every five years. The valuation is based on an estimate, by reference to the average net receipts, of the rent at which the hereditaments might reasonably be expected to let from year to year, the probable average annual costs of repair, insurance and maintenance, and all rates and tithe rent charges being paid by the tenant. A minimum valuation is also made. This is based on the valuation which would have been made if the hereditaments had not been adopted for use as a railway. If the sum of the minimum valuation exceeds the valuation based on the net rent then those valuations are fixed. Where the valuation based on net rent is fixed the Commissioner of Valuation apportions it between all the railway hereditaments according to certain rules. The valuing of other property is done on the same basis as the valuing of buildings.

EXEMPTION FROM, AND REMISSION OF RATES

Turf banks used for the exclusive purpose of cutting and saving turf or for taking turf mould for fuel or manure are not rateable unless a rent or other valuable consideration is payable. Mines are not rateable for seven years after they have been opened. New farm buildings are exempt from rates for 20 years. Certain burial grounds and infirmaries, hospitals and other buildings used exclusively for public or charitable purposes, or for the purpose of science, literature and the fine arts, for example, Government offices, churches, libraries and national schools are deemed exempt from rating. The Exchequer, however, pays a voluntary contribution in lieu of rates to local authorities to make up the loss which they would otherwise sustain from the exemption of Government occupied property from rating. Fishery rights are deemed exempt from local authority rates, but are liable to rates struck by boards of fishery conservators. Other exemptions are lighthouses, beacons, buoys, etc., hereditaments intended to be used or occupied solely for the purpose of affording air raid protection, and certain works, for example, the Shannon Works, used exclusively for the generation, transmission and distribution of electricity.

In addition to these exemptions there are a number of partial exemptions and remissions. A local authority may remit two-thirds of the rates for ten years on premises certified by An Foras Tionscal to have been provided for an industrial undertaking in an undeveloped area, either by that body or by means of a grant from it. In the county boroughs (except Cork), boroughs and urban districts, the rate is levied on a fraction—usually three-quarters or three-fifths—of the valuation of land used as arable, meadow or pasture ground or as woodlands or market gardens or nursery grounds. In Cork County Borough only lands which became added to the Borough under the Cork City Management (Amendment) Act, 1941, are entitled to remission. Most new houses are entitled to a two-thirds remission of rates for seven years, and most improved or reconstructed houses qualify for either a complete or a two-third remission of rates for seven years on the increase in valuation following the improvement. Buildings (including hotels, shops, factories, offices and dwellinghouses) not otherwise entitled to rate remission may be entitled to a similar remission if they were erected, improved or reconstructed within the period prescribed in the Local Government (Temporary Reduction of Valuation) Act, 1960. The Housing (Amendment) Act, 1958, provides for a graduated scale of rates remission over a period of nine years in the case of new houses in respect of which grants have been paid under the Housing Acts and which appear in the valuation lists on or after 1st March, 1959.

APPORTIONMENT AND CHARGEABILITY OF EXPENSES

Save where it is otherwise provided by law the expenses of a county council are charged over the whole county including the boroughs and urban districts. The cost of services administered by the county council for the whole county is charged in this way. The principal services involved are *Main Roads, Public Assistance, Mental Health* and *Health.* The county council demands the amount chargeable on the urban area from the urban authority. This demand was calculated up to and including the year ended 31st March, 1956, in such a way that the amount of the expenses borne by a particular area bears the same relationship to the total expenses as the valuation of the area bears to the valuation of the whole county. For the year ended 31st March, 1957, and subsequent years the demand is calculated according to the produce of a rate of one penny in the pound in the different areas. (This is now the basis of apportionment of all expenses levied over different areas, unless otherwise provided by law.) The manner in which the produce of a rate of one penny in the pound is calculated is set out in the Public Bodies (Temporary Provisions) Order, 1955. The urban authority when determining its rate must provide for the county demand and also for the services which it administers itself. Generally the cost of the other services administered by county councils is charged on the county health district which consists in all counties except Cork (where there are three county health districts) of the whole county exclusive of urban districts and boroughs. In the counties of Galway, Kerry, Louth, Sligo, Wexford and Wicklow, however, the cost of vocational education is charged on an area consisting of the county health district and certain urban districts; the cost of meeting malicious injury claims is usually levied on a fairly small area in a county; and there are other separate charges levied on different areas, but these are not now of much significance.

LOAN AND STOCK ACCOUNT

The revenue accounts of local authorities include figures for a limited number of capital works such as road improvements, the cost of which is met mainly by State grants. The Loan and stock accounts cover work of a capital nature, such as the construction of houses, the provision of water supplies and sewerage systems, and the erection of hospitals, dispensaries, etc., the cost of which is met by borrowing and from State grants supplemented by miscellaneous capital receipts.

BORROWING

Local Authorities have wide borrowing powers under the Local Government (No. 2) Act, 1960, but ministerial sanction to such borrowing is normally required. Borrowing may be effected in any manner which the local authority considers suitable including mortgages, bills of exchange, stock or bonds or by means of temporary overdraft. Local authorities resort to temporary borrowing in order to meet short term deficiencies pending the receipt of rates or other revenue or pending the receipt of capital by way of long term borrowing to finance works of a capital nature, which could not be financed out of current revenue. Long term loans are obtained mainly from the Local Loans Fund which is under the control of the Minister for Finance. Local authorities also borrow to some extent from their bankers and from insurance companies. A summary of loans sanctioned in the year 1960/61 will be found in the Annual Report of the Department of Local Government for that year.

The net indebtedness of local authorities at 31st March, 1961, was £148.1 million, an increase of £4.8 million on the indebtedness at 31st March in the previous year.

GENERAL

Further details of the services provided by local authorities may be obtained in the Reports of the Departments of Local Government, Health and Social Welfare. Reports of the Departments of Agriculture and Education deal with committees of agriculture and vocational education committees.

LOCAL RECEIPTS, EXPENDITURE AND INDEBTEDNESS

SUMMARY TABLES

REVENUE ACCOUNT

TABLE A.—RECEIPTS IN YEAR ENDING 31ST MARCH

Receipts	1939	1949	1955	1956	1957	1958	1959	1960	1961	1962
	£000s	£000s	£000s	£000s	£000s	£000s	£000s	£000s	£000s	£000s
1. *Rates	6,271	10,358	17,041	17,746	19,700	20,077	20,561	21,412	22,058	23,163
2. State grants	4,697	11,139	20,054	20,647	21,121	23,384	22,230	22,948	24,807	25,903
3. Other receipts	1,672	3,590	6,417	7,030	7,821	8,495	8,753	9,460	9,904	10,813
Totals	12,640	25,087	43,512	45,423	48,642	51,956	51,544	53,820	56,769	59,879

*Includes increases in rents of small dwellings owned by rating authorities. These increases are in effect the rates for those dwellings.

Figures for the year 1961/62 are provisional.

TABLE B.—EXPENDITURE IN YEAR ENDING 31ST MARCH

Purpose	1939	1949	1955	1956	1957	1958	1959	1960	1961	1962
	£000s	£000s	£000s	£000s	£000s	£000s	£000s	£000s	£000s	£000s
1. Roads		7,760	11,174	11,609	11,568	10,724	11,002	11,558	12,090	13,896
2. Public Assistance		4,663	7,267	1,125	1,150	1,200	1,164	1,142	1,103	1,156
3. Mental Hospitals		2,259	3,420	3,674	3,947	4,110	4,475	4,534	4,865	22,097
4. Health	11,982	2,317	4,960	12,477	14,073	14,395	14,782	15,028	15,743	
5. Sanitary Services		2,019	3,121	3,408	3,722	3,856	4,146	4,389	4,669	5,073
6. Housing		3,013	6,615	7,101	8,020	8,723	9,121	9,634	10,087	10,517
7. General Purposes		3,944	6,416	7,039	7,138	6,553	6,717	7,017	7,333	8,021
Totals ..	11,982	25,975	42,973	46,433	49,618	49,561	51,407	53,302	55,890	60,760

8. AUDIT

(i) Document 9.19 — Extracts from Local Government (Ireland) Act, 1871 (34 and 35 Vict. c. 109) in Street, *op. cit.*, pp. 1254 and 1268.

12.—Every auditor acting in pursuance of this Act shall examine into the matter of every account which is to be audited by him, and shall disallow and strike out of every such account all payments, charges, and allowances made by any person and charged upon the funds of any towns contrary to law, or which he deems to be unfounded, and shall surcharge the same upon the person making or authorising the making of the illegal payment and shall certify the same to be due from such person, and upon application by any party aggrieved shall state in writing at the foot of such account the reasons for his decision in respect of such disallowance or surcharge, and also of any allowance which he may have made; and it shall be lawful for every person aggrieved by any such allowance and for every person aggrieved by such disallowance or surcharge, if such last-mentioned person have first paid or delivered over to any person authorised to receive the same all such money, goods, and chattels as are admitted by his account to be due from him or remaining in his hands, to apply to the High Court for a writ of *certiorari* to remove into the said court the said allowance, disallowance or surcharge, in the like manner and subject to the like conditions as are provided in respect of persons suing forth writs of *certiorari* for the removal of orders of justices of the peace, except that the condition of the recognizance shall be, to prosecute such *certiorari,* at the costs and charges of such person, without any wilful or affected delay, and if such allowance, disallowance or surcharge be confirmed, to pay to such auditor or his successor, within one month after the same may be confirmed, his full costs and charges, to be taxed according to the course of the said court, and except that the notice of the intended application, which shall contain a statement of the matter complained of, shall be given to such auditor or his successor, who shall in return to such writ return a copy under his hand of the entry or entries in such book of account to which such notice shall refer, and shall appear before the said court and defend the allowance, disallowance or surcharge so impeached in the said court, and shall be reimbursed all such costs and charges as he may incur in such defence out of the rates which the governing body of the town interested in the decision of the question have power to make, unless the said court make any order to the contrary; and that on the removal of such allowance, disallowance or surcharge the said court shall decide the particular matter of complaint set forth in such statement, and no other; and if it appear to such court that the decision of the said auditor was erroneous, they shall, by rule of the court, order such sum of money as may have been improperly allowed, disallowed, or surcharged to be paid to the party entitled thereto by the party who ought to repay or discharge the same; and they may also, if they see fit, by order of the court, direct the costs of the person prosecuting such *certiorari* to be paid out of rates which the governing body have power to make, as to such court may seem fit; which orders of court respectively shall be enforced in like manner as other orders of the said court are enforceable.

Provided always, that it shall be lawful for any person aggrieved as aforesaid by any allowance, disallowance or surcharge, in lieu of making application to the High Court for a writ of *certiorari,* to apply to the appropriate Minister to inquire into and to decide upon the lawfulness of the reasons stated by the auditor for such allowance, disallowance or surcharge, and it shall thereupon be lawful for the appropriate Minister to issue such order therein, under his hand, as he may deem requisite for determining the question.

[*Ss.* 13-17 *still in force omitted.*]

18.—Within fourteen days after the completion of the audit of the accounts of any town the auditor shall report upon the accounts audited and examined, and shall deliver or transmit such report, with an abstract of the accounts, to the Minister for Local Government, and a copy of the same to the governing body of such town, and the said governing body shall cause the same to be deposited in the office of the town clerk, or other proper officer, of such town, and shall publish an abstract of such accounts in some one or more of the newspapers circulated in the district in which such town is situate.

(ii) Document 9.20 — Extracts from Local Government (Ireland) Act, 1902 (2 Edw. 7 c. 38) in Street, *op. cit.,* pp. 1270-72.

20.—(1) At the audit of the accounts of any public body, the auditor shall charge, against *any member or officer of such public body*[1] the amount of any deficiency or loss incurred by his negligence or misconduct, or of any sum which ought to have been, but was not, brought into account by him, and shall, in any such case, certify the amount due from him. [*SS. 2 omitted.*]

21.—(1) Where the Local Government Board require an extraordinary audit to be held of the accounts of any public body, or of any officer, whether still continuing or upon his resignation or removal from office, the audit shall be deemed to be an audit within the meaning of the enactments relating to the audit of the accounts of public bodies, and may be held after three days' notice thereof given in the usual manner.

(2) An auditor of the Local Government Board may, at any time when authorised or required so to do by that Board, inspect the accounts and books of account of any public body or any officer liable to account to him.

(3) Any member or officer of a public body who refuses to allow such inspection, or obstructs the auditor therein, or conceals any account or book for the purpose of preventing the inspection, shall be liable, on summary conviction, to a fine not exceeding five pounds.

22.—(1) The Local Government Board may make general regulations for the audit of the accounts of public bodies and their officers, and the regulations may prescribe the form in which the accounts are to be kept, the mode of publishing the time and place for holding the audit, the person by whom, and the time within which, the accounts are to be produced for audit, and the mode of conducting the audit. [*SS. 2 omitted.*]

9. CENTRAL GOVERNMENT CONTROL OVER LOCAL AUTHORITIES

(a) *Removal of Members from Office*

Document 9.21 — Extracts from Local Government Act, 1941 (no. 23) in Street, *op. cit.,* pp. 282-87.

---

1. The words in italics were substituted for "any person accounting" by Act 5 of 1925 s.61(3).—Street.

44.—(1) If and whenever—

(a) the Minister, after holding a local inquiry into the performance by a local authority of their duties, is satisfied that such duties are not being duly and effectually performed, or

(b) a local authority refuses or neglects to comply with a judgment, order, or decree of any court, or

(c) a local authority refuses after due notice to allow their accounts to be audited by an auditor of the Minister, or

(d) the members of a local authority capable of acting are less in number than the quorum for meetings of such local authority,

[1]*or*

(e) *a local authority refuses or wilfully neglects to comply with an express requirement which is imposed on them by or under any enactment or order,*

the Minister may by order remove from office the members of such local authority. [*Ss. 45-47 omitted.*]

48.—(1) For the purposes of enabling a local authority whose members have been removed from office to function during the period between such removal from office and the coming into office of the members elected at a new election, the Minister shall from time to time appoint one or more persons[2] to be the commissioner or commissioners for such local authority. [*SSs. 2 and 3 omitted.*]

49.—(1) During the period between the removal from office of the members of a local authority and the coming into office of the members elected at a new election, every power, function, or duty which is exercisable or to be performed by the members of such local authority acting together in a meeting of such local authority or exercisable or to be performed by any one or more members of such local authority by virtue of such membership or by virtue of the office of chairman, lord mayor, or mayor shall be exercised or performed by the commissioner or commissioners for such local authority.

(b) *Minister's Powers in case of insufficiency of Rates*

Document 9.22 — Extract from section 30 of Local Government Act, 1946 (no. 24) in Street, *op. cit.,* pp. 339-40.

30.—(1) If, at any time after the rate in the pound of the rate for a local financial year has been determined by a rating authority, it appears to the Minister that such rate at such rate in the pound is likely to be insufficient

---

1. The words in italics were added by the Local Government Act, 1946 (No. 24), section 64.

2. The only instance of appointment under this section of more than one commissioner prior to date of writing is that of the Dublin Board of Assistance (April, 1942) — Street.

to meet the part defrayable out of rates of the expenses to be incurred by the rating authority in that financial year in—

(a) maintaining at a reasonable standard the public services for the maintenance of which the rating authority is responsible, and

(b) paying to any other body any sums which the rating authority are bound to supply to that body,

the Minister, after causing a local inquiry to be held by one of his inspectors into the sufficiency of such rate, may require the rating authority either to revoke such determination and determine a new rate in the pound for such rate or (if by reason of any steps already taken for the making, levying or collecting of such rate, such a course is more convenient) determine a rate in the pound of a supplementary rate for that local financial year.

(2) Within fourteen days after the date of the receipt by the secretary or clerk of a rating authority of notification that a requirement has been made under sub-section (1) of this section, the rating authority shall comply with such requirement.

(3) Where a rating authority determine pursuant to a requirement under sub-section (1) of this section a rate in the pound of a supplementary rate, it shall be the duty of the rating authority to make, levy, collect and recover such supplementary rate.

(4) Where a rating authority in relation to whom a requirement is made under sub-section (1) of this section determine and make pursuant to the direction either—

(a) a new rate in the pound of a rate, or

(b) a rate in the pound of a supplementary rate.

which in the opinion of the Minister is insufficient, the Minister may by order remove from office the members of the rating authority.

(c) *Minister's powers to obtain information*
Document 9.23 — Extracts from Local Government Act, 1941 (no. 23) in Street, *op. cit.*, pp. 309-10.

83.—(1) The Minister may cause such local inquiries to be held as he may consider necessary or desirable for the purposes of any of the powers and duties for the time being conferred or imposed on him. [*SSs. 2-6 omitted.*]

84.—(1) The Minister may require a local authority to make to him any return or report or to furnish him with any information in relation to their functions which he may consider necessary or desirable for the purposes of any of the powers and duties for the time being conferred or imposed on him in relation to such local authority, and it shall be the duty of such local authority to comply with such requirement.

(2) An inspector of the Minister[1] may require any officer of a local authority to give to such inspector any information in relation to the functions of such officer which such inspector reasonably requires for the purpose of performing the duties imposed on such inspector by the Minister, and it shall be the duty of such officer to comply with such requirement.

85.—(1) An inspector of the Minister may for the purpose of the functions imposed on him by the Minister visit and inspect any premises used by a local authority for the purposes of their powers and duties.

(2) Any person who obstructs an inspector of the Minister in the exercise of the power conferred on him by this section shall be guilty of an offence under this section and shall be liable on summary conviction thereof to a fine not exceeding five pounds.

86.—(1) An inspector holding a local inquiry pursuant to a direction of the Minister under this or any other Act or a local government auditor auditing the accounts of a local authority make take evidence on oath and for that purpose may administer oaths.

(2) Subject to the provisions of the next following sub-section of this section, an inspector holding a local inquiry pursuant to a direction of the Minister under this or any other Act or a local government auditor auditing the accounts of a local authority may, by giving notice in that behalf in writing to any person, require such person to attend at such time and place as is specified in such notice to give evidence in relation to any matter in question at such inquiry or audit (as the case may be) or to produce any books, deeds, contracts, accounts, vouchers, maps, plans, or other documents in his possession, custody or control which relate to any such matter.

READING

A. W. Bromage: 'The Council-Manager Plan in Ireland' in *Administration*, vol. 9.

J. Collins: *Local Government*, 2nd Edition by D. Roche, Dublin, 1963. (This work contains a very full bibliography).

J. Collins: 'The Genesis of City and County Management' in *Administration*, vol. 2.

J. Garvin: 'Local Government and its Problems' in *Administration*, vol. 11 (Autumn, 1963).

B. Hensey: *The Health Services of Ireland*, Institute of Public Administration, Dublin, 1959.

J. A. Robins: 'The County in the Twentieth Century' in *Administration*, vol. 9.

D. Turpin: 'The Local Government Service', two articles in *Administration*, vols. 2 and 3.

D. Walker: *Local Government Finance in Ireland*, Economic Research Institute, Dublin, 1962.

D. Walker: *Local Government Finance and County Incomes*, Economic Research Institute, Dublin, 1962.

In addition, the volumes of *Administration* contain a large number of articles on local government services, finances and administration.

---

1. Including the Ministers for Health, Social Welfare and Agriculture (S.R. & O. 58, 329 and 417 of 1947)—Street.

Chapter 10

STATE-SPONSORED BODIES

INTRODUCTION

In his book, *Cabinet Government*, Sir Ivor Jennings writes:

the administrative system has become far more complicated than is generally realised. The simple dichotomy of central departments responsible to Parliament through ministers and local authorities responsible to a local electorate no longer exists. The . . . ministers are not leaders of columns which march behind them in regular ranks, for the columns now have outriders on their flanks and a relatively unorganized mass of camp followers trailing behind.

In Ireland a term has been coined to describe the bodies in this considerable penumbra which surrounds the central administration. They are generally known as 'state-sponsored bodies'.

Difficult to define and classify, these bodies, which number between 50 and 60, include large production and service industries (what in many countries would be called 'nationalized industries'); finance and credit organizations; trading, marketing and promotional organizations; bodies charged with regulating some industry or activity; the governing bodies of certain professions; research organizations; and bodies which provide social services, particularly health services, or services which, though public, are not thought to be appropriate for departmental administration. Documents 10.1 to 10.7 give examples of some of these. Also, in the Appendix to this chapter there is a list of all Irish state-sponsored bodies compiled from the appendix to G. Fitzgerald, *State-Sponsored Bodies*, 2nd edition, Institute of Public Administration, Dublin, 1963.

As in most countries, the Irish public sector of economic enterprise includes the 'infra-structure' industries such as transport and power. There are also a number of enterprises the inclusion of which reflects a recognition of the need to stimulate and assist private enterprise in some fields in order to achieve satisfactory economic growth. There are, finally, an heterogeneous collection of bodies whose appearance in the public sector reflects a pragmatic approach to the use of public authorities for the conduct of economic activities, a pragmatism which is also evident in the statements of the Taoiseach, Mr Lemass, who has had much to do with the creation of many of them. (Document 10.8). In these respects also, Ireland does not differ very markedly from some of the developed countries of Western Europe and elsewhere.

It is, indeed to be noticed that the range and importance of public enterprise in a country is by no means governed by the strength or otherwise of socialist parties or the wide acceptance of socialist theory in that country. Ireland has not and, from the inception of the State, never has had, a socialist party of any significance. The principle enshrined in Article 45.3.1° of the Constitution, namely that 'the State shall favour and, where necessary, supplement private initiative in industry and commerce', probably states the generally accepted attitude of the community. But what is 'necessary' for Ireland is inevitably to a large extent governed, as it is in all states, by the general tendency for governments of whatever complexion to take an active and ever-increasing role in promoting steady economic growth and welfare. In addition, the growing propensity to make use of the state-sponsored body for non-commercial purposes, such as the provision of social services, and the regulation of professions and other activities, perhaps reflects a growing awareness of the limitations and the proper limits of the ministerial department.

In view of the considerable numbers and importance of these bodies, it might appear surprising that few general principles governing them seem to have been evolved. Such matters as the most appropriate legal form for a body performing a given type of activity, the composition of governing bodies and appropriate methods of providing finance seem to have been decided in the same pragmatic manner as the question of their inception. It is significant that 1927, the year which saw the setting up of the first of the giant public corporations, the Electricity Supply Board, saw also statutory provision for the first state public company, i.e. a company incorporated under the Companies Acts. Since then, this device has been much used. It is claimed to be a very flexible instrument. Certainly it has proved possible to set up such companies merely on the order of a Minister and without any statutory authority at all, and also to use this form (until 1961) to provide certain health services.

While it may probably be claimed that the pragmatism which has been so much in evidence in this area of public life has been beneficial to the community, there can be no doubt that it has had the result of leaving not only the public but also the politicians themselves very unclear about the nature, extent and methods of public control appropriate to each of these bodies. The control exercised by sponsor ministers and their relationships with the boards of the bodies for which they have some responsibility vary considerably and according to no discernible pattern or principles. In the case of some trading enterprises, this reflects a failure to define precisely their objectives. Are they to be operated as straightforward commercial concerns or as public services in the national interest ? If the latter, where is the responsibility vested for deciding when and to what extent the public interest should have priority over commercial arguments and how are the inevitable consequences of this for their management to be taken care of ? (Documents 10.9 to 10.12). More serious from the point of view of the working of democracy, this failure to define the exact relationships of some bodies to Ministers and Departments has exacerbated the unsatisfactory state of Oireachtas control. In no section of government is the Oireachtas less well informed and less able to scrutinize, comment on, or publicize the successes and failures of these bodies and their conduct of what is, after all, public business. In this area the theoretical responsibility of ministers is by no means enforced and no progress at all towards effective Oireachtas control has been made. (Document 10.13.)

DOCUMENTS

1. SOME EXAMPLES

   (a) *The Agricultural Credit Corporation—The First State Company*
   Document 10.1 — Extracts from Agricultural Credit Act, 1927 (no. 24).

   (*Note*—Much of this Act has been repealed or amended, but the document that follows is the Act *as it was first enacted*. It is included here for historical interest.)

AN ACT TO MAKE PROVISION FOR THE FORMATION AND REGISTRATION OF A COMPANY HAVING FOR ITS PRINCIPAL OBJECT THE GIVING OF CREDIT TO PERSONS ENGAGED IN AGRICULTURE AND BUSINESSES ANCILLARY TO AGRICULTURE, TO AUTHORISE THE GIVING OF GUARANTEES BY THE STATE IN RELATION TO THE CAPITAL OF SUCH COMPANY AND SECURITIES ISSUED BY IT, AND TO PROVIDE FOR CERTAIN

OTHER MATTERS RELATING TO SUCH COMPANY, AND TO FACILITATE THE BORROWING OF MONEY BY FARMERS ON MORTGAGES OF THEIR FARMING STOCK AND TO REGULATE THE OPERATION AND EFFECT OF SUCH MORTGAGES.

[*28th May,* 1927.]

FORMATION OF THE CORPORATION

3.—Immediately upon the passing of this Act the Minister [for Finance] take all such steps as appear to him to be necessary or desirable to procure that a limited company (in this Act referred to as the Corporation) conforming to the conditions laid down in this Act shall be formed and registered under the Companies Acts, 1908 to 1924 not later than the 30th day of September, 1927 to perform the functions specified in this Act.

4.—(1) The name of the Corporation shall be " The Agricultural Credit Corporation, Limited."

(2) The capital of the Corporation shall be £500,000 (five hundred thousand pounds) divided into five hundred thousand shares of one pound each of which five shillings shall be payable on application for the share and a further five shillings shall be payable not less than twenty nor more than forty days after allotment, and the residue shall be payable as and when called by the Directors on not less than thirty days notice. [*SS. 3 and S. 5(1) omitted.*]

5.—(2) All shares of the Corporation offered for subscription by the general public and not so subscribed for shall at the expiration of the time limited with the approval of the Minister for such subscription be subscribed for by the Minister.

STATE LIABILITY FOR CAPITAL AND DIVIDENDS

6.—(1) In the event of the Corporation going into liquidation (whether voluntary or compulsory) and being wound up and its assets proving on such winding-up to be insufficient to pay to the members of the Corporation the full amount of its paid-up capital, the Minister shall provide and pay to the liquidator in such winding-up such sum as will be sufficient with the assets of the Corporation available for the purpose to pay the full amount of the paid-up capital of the Corporation. [*SS. 2 omitted.*]

7.—(1) The Corporation shall pay to its members dividends at the fixed rate of five per cent per annum on the amount of its capital for the time being paid up and such dividends shall be paid by the Corporation half-yearly on such dates as shall be appointed for that purpose by the Directors with the approval of the Minister.

(2) If on any of the days appointed under this section for the payment of half-yearly dividends the Corporation have not any or sufficient moneys available for the payment of the dividend so payable on such day the Corporation shall forthwith certify to the Minister the sum which with the moneys (if any) so available is required to pay such dividend and upon receipt of such certificate the Minister shall advance to the Corporation the amount so certified by the Corporation and the moneys so advanced shall be forthwith applied by the Directors in or towards payment of such dividend.

(3) All moneys advanced to the Corporation by the Minister under this section shall be repayable by the Corporation to the Minister on demand with interest from the date of the advance at such rate as shall be fixed by the Minister and (except in the winding-up of the Corporation) shall be so repayable only out of moneys which are profits as ascertained in accordance with directions of the Minister and in the winding-up of the Corporation shall be so repayable after the creditors of the Corporation have been paid in full.

MEMORANDUM AND ARTICLES OF ASSOCIATION

8.—(1) The Memorandum of Association of the Corporation shall be in such form consistent with the provisions of this Act as shall be approved by the Minister and the Minister for Lands and Agriculture.

(2) Notwithstanding anything contained in the Companies Acts, 1908 to 1924 no alteration in the Memorandum of Association of the Corporation which is made without the previous approval of the Minister and the Minister for Lands and Agriculture or is inconsistent with any of the provisions of this Act shall be valid or effective. [*S. 9 omitted.*]

10.—(1) The Articles of Association of the Corporation shall be in such form consistent with the provisions of this Act as shall be approved by the Minister and the Minister for Lands and Agriculture.

(2) Notwithstanding anything contained in the Companies Acts, 1908 to 1924, no alteration in or addition to the Articles of Association of the Corporation which is made without the previous approval of the Minister and the Minister for Lands and Agriculture or is inconsistent with any provision of this Act shall be valid or effective.

DIRECTORS

11.—The Articles of Association of the Corporation shall provide—

(i) that the number of directors (including the Chairman) shall be seven, of whom four shall be elected by the shareholders with the usual provisions for co-option to casual vacancies and three shall be nominated by the Minister from time to time as occasion requires;

(ii) that so long as the Minister holds more than two hundred thousand shares of the Corporation the Chairman of the directors shall be nominated from time to time by the Minister from amongst the three directors nominated by him. [*Ss. 12-16 omitted.*]

ACCOUNTS

17.—The Corporation shall keep all such accounts and other records and in such form as may be prescribed by regulations made by the Minister under this section. [*Remainder omitted.*]

(b) *The Electricity Supply Board—The First Public Corporation*
Document 10.2 — Extracts from Electricity Supply Act, 1927 (no. 27).

CONSTITUTION AND MEMBERS OF THE BOARD

2.—(1) As soon as may be after the passing of this Act a board to be styled and known as the Electricity Supply Board (in this Act referred to as the Board) shall be established in accordance with this Act to fulfil the functions assigned to it by this Act.

(2) The Board shall be a body corporate having perpetual succession and may sue and be sued under its said style and name.

(3) The Board shall consist of a chairman and such number (not being less than two nor more than six) of other members as the Executive Council shall from time to time determine.

(4) The members of the Board shall be appointed by the Executive Council and every person so appointed to be a member of the Board shall hold office for such period not exceeding five years as shall be fixed by the Executive Council when appointing him and every such person shall on the expiration of his term of office be eligible for re-appointment.

(5) The chairman of the Board shall be that member of the Board who at the time of his appointment to be a member of the Board or subsequently is appointed by the Executive Council to be such chairman.

(6) The chairman of the Board shall devote the whole of his time to his duties as such chairman and each of the other members of the Board shall devote the whole or so much of his time to his duties as such member as shall be prescribed by the Executive Council at the time of his appointment.

(7) Every member of the Board shall be paid out of the funds at the disposal of the Board such remuneration and such allowances for expenses as the Executive Council shall when appointing him prescribe. [*S. 3 omitted.*]

4.—(1) The Board shall provide and have a common seal, and such seal shall be authenticated by the signature of the chairman of the Board or some other member thereof authorised by the Board to act in that behalf and the signature of an officer of the Board duly authorised by the Board to act in that behalf.

(2) All courts of justice shall take judicial notice of the seal of the Board, and every document purporting to be an order or other instrument made by the Board and to be sealed with the seal of the Board authenticated in accordance with this section shall be received in evidence and be deemed to be such order or instrument without further proof unless the contrary is shown.

5.—(1) If at any time it appears to the Executive Council that the removal from office of all or any of the members of the Board is necessary in the interests of the effective and economical performance of the functions of the Board under this Act the Executive Council may remove from office all or so many of the members of the Board as the Executive Council considers necessary in the interests aforesaid.

(2) The Executive Council may at any time remove from office any member of the Board who has become incapable through ill-health of performing efficiently his duties as such member or who has (otherwise than for a reason considered by the Executive Council to be sufficient) been absent from all meetings of the Board during a period of six months.

(3) If and whenever the Executive Council removes from office under this section any member of the Board, the Executive Council shall lay before each House of the Oireachtas a statement in writing of the fact of the removal from office of such member and of the reasons for such removal. [*S. 6 omitted.*]

ACCOUNTS AND AUDIT

7.—(1) The Board shall keep in such form as shall be approved by the Minister [for Transport and Power] after consultation with the Minister for Finance all proper and usual accounts of all moneys received or expended by them, including a capital account, revenue account, profit and loss account, and a balance sheet, and in particular shall keep in such form as aforesaid all such special accounts as the Minister on his motion or at the request of the Minister for Finance shall from time to time direct.

(2) The accounts of the Board shall in each year be audited and be the subject of a report by duly qualified auditors appointed annually for the purpose by the Minister, with the consent of the Minister for Finance, and the fees of such auditors and the expenses generally of such audits shall be paid by the Board.

(3) The Minister may with the consent of the Minister for Finance make regulations prescribing the time, place, and method of conducting the audit of the accounts of the Board under this section and may also prescribe by such regulations the accounts of which copies are to be furnished to the Minister under this section and the accounts which are to be published and put on sale under this section and the time and method of such publication and sale.

(4) Immediately after every audit under this section of the accounts of the Board, the Board shall send to the Minister a copy of the balance sheet and profit and loss account as passed by the auditors, a copy of the auditors' report, and copies of such of the accounts submitted to the auditors as are prescribed in that behalf by regulations made under this section or may be specially called for by the Minister, and shall publish and put on sale in accordance with such regulations such of the accounts submitted to the auditors as are prescribed in that behalf by such regulations.

EMPLOYEES

8.—(1) The Board shall appoint such and so many officers and servants as it shall from time to time think proper.

(2) There shall be paid by the Board to its officers and servants out of the funds at its disposal under this Act such remuneration and allowances as the Board shall determine. [*Ss. 3 and 4 and S. 9 omitted.*]

DISCLOSURE OF INTEREST

10.—A member of the Board who has any interest in any company or concern with which the Board proposes to make any contract or any interest in such contract shall disclose to the Board the fact of such interest and the nature thereof, and such member shall take no part in any deliberation or decision of the Board relating to such contract, and such disclosure shall be recorded in the minutes of the Board.

11.—(1) Every person appointed to be a member of the Board shall within three months after his appointment absolutely sell and dispose of all shares in any electrical undertaking which he shall at the time of his appointment own or be interested in for his own benefit, and if any shares in any electrical undertaking shall come to or vest in a member of the Board by will or succession for his own benefit, he shall within three months after the same shall have so come to or vested in him, absolutely sell and dispose of the same or his interest therein.   [*Remaining Subsections and Ss.* 12-16 *omitted.*]

DUTIES OF THE BOARD

19.—It shall be the duty of the Board—

(*a*) to produce and generate electricity in the Shannon works so soon as such works or a sufficient portion thereof for the purpose are handed over to the Board by the Minister, and to transmit through the transmission system of the Shannon works and any extension of that system the electricity so generated, and

(*b*) to control, manage, and maintain in good repair and condition and proper and efficient working order each and every part or section of the Shannon works as from the respective dates on which such parts or sections are respectively handed over to the Board by the Minister, and

(*c*) to distribute, utilise and sell the electricity generated by the Board in the Shannon works and to promote and encourage the purchase and use of such electricity, and

(*d*) to control, co-ordinate, and improve the supply distribution, and sale of electricity generally in Saorstát Éireann and for the purposes of such control, co-ordination, and improvement to exercise and employ the powers conferred on the Board by this Act, and

(*e*) generally to perform and exercise all duties and powers which are imposed or conferred on the Board by this Act and all such other duties and powers as may hereafter be imposed or conferred on the Board by the Oireachtas.

[*Ss.* 20 *and* 21(1) *omitted.*]

OBLIGATION TO ' BREAK EVEN '

21.—(2) All charges made by the Board after the appointed day for electricity (whether derived from the Shannon works or otherwise) sold by it in bulk or direct to consumers and for goods sold and services rendered by it shall be fixed at such rates and on such scales that the revenue derived in any year by the Board from such sales and services together with its revenue (if any) in such year from other sources will be sufficient and only sufficient (as nearly as may be) to pay all salaries, working expenses, and other outgoings of the Board properly chargeable to income in that year (including the payments falling to be made in such year by the Board to the Minister for Finance in respect of interest and sinking fund payments on advances out of the Central Fund) and such sums as the Board may think proper to set aside in that year for the reserve fund, extensions, renewals, depreciation, loans, and other like purposes. [*SS. 3 and S. 22-31 omitted.*]

ANNUAL REPORT AND INFORMATION

32.—(1) The Board shall in each year, at such date and in such form as the Minister may prescribe, make to the Minister a report of its proceedings under this Act during the preceding year.

(2) The Board shall furnish to the Minister at such times and in such form and manner as the Minister may direct such statistics and returns as the Minister may require.

(3) The Minister shall lay as soon as may be before each House of the Oireachtas a copy of every report made to him by the Board under this section together with a copy of the last capital account, revenue account, profit and loss account, and balance sheet of the Board and a copy of the auditors' report on such accounts and balance sheet and shall with every such report by the Board lay before each House of the Oireachtas copies of such statistics, returns, and accounts furnished to him by the Board under this Act as may be necessary for the proper understanding of such report.

[*Remainder omitted.*]

(c) *The Nursing Council*
Document 10.3 — Extracts from Nurses Act, 1950 (no. 27).

ESTABLISHMENT

7.—(1) On the establishment date there shall be established by virtue of this section a board to be styled and known as An Bord Altranais.

(2) The Board shall be a body corporate with perpetual succession and power to sue and be sued in their corporate name and to hold and dispose of land.

8.—(1) The Board shall provide themselves with a seal, and such seal shall be authenticated by the signature of the president of the Board or some other member thereof authorised by the Board to act in that behalf and the signature of an officer of the Board authorised by the Board to act in that behalf.

(2) Judicial notice shall be taken of the seal of the Board, and every document purporting to be an instrument made by the Board and to be sealed with the seal (purporting to be authenticated in accordance with this section) of the Board shall be received in evidence and be deemed to be such instrument without further proof unless the contrary is shown.

MEMBERS

9.—The number of the members of the Board shall be twenty-three. [*Ss.* 10 *and* 11 *omitted.*]

12.—(1) Before the establishment date and before the 1st day of December in each election year, the Minister [for Health] shall appoint thirteen persons to be members of the Board.

(2) Where an appointment is made under this section of persons to be members of the Board—

   (*a*) (i) one shall be a person who is or has been a master of a maternity hospital, or an assistant master of a maternity hospital,

     (ii) two shall be medical practitioners who are engaged in the training of nurses in training hospitals,

    (iii) one shall be a medical practitioner with experience in connection with mental nursing,

    (iv) one shall be representative of general medical practitioners,

     (v) one shall be a medical officer of health,

    (vi) one shall be a person specially experienced in educational matters,

   (vii) one shall be representative of councils of counties, and

  (viii) one shall be representative of councils of county boroughs; and

   (*b*) two shall be persons who are nurses, persons whose names are included in the register kept in pursuance of the Nurses Registration (Ireland) Act, 1919, or persons registered under the Act of 1944.

(3) Before appointing the persons referred to in paragraph (*a*) of subsection (2) of this section, the Minister shall consult such organisations or bodies as he considers suitable to advise him on the appointments, but if the Minister considers that there is no suitable organisation or body qualified to advise him on any particular appointment, he shall make that appointment without consultation.

13.—(1) Before the 1st day of December in each election year, ten persons (being nurses) shall be elected by nurses to be members of the Board.

(2) of the persons elected under subsection (1) of this section—

   (*a*) one shall be a person with such qualification or experience in public health nursing as may be prescribed;

   (*b*) two shall be persons with such qualification or experience in midwifery as may be prescribed;

(*c*) two shall be persons with such qualification or experience in mental nursing as may be prescribed;

(*d*) three shall be general trained nurses with such experience in training nurses as may be prescribed;

(*e*) one shall have such experience in private nursing as may be prescribed;

(*f*) one shall be engaged in nursing in a hospital, which is not a training hospital.

(3) Every election under this section shall be carried out in accordance with rules. [*Ss.* 14-19 *omitted.*]

20.—The Minister may at any time by order remove any member of the Board from office. [*S.* 21 *omitted.*]

ANNUAL REPORT

22.—(1) Before the 1st day of April in each year, the Board shall prepare and publish a report of their proceedings in the preceding year (in this section referred to as the report) and the report shall contain such particulars as the Minister may direct.

(2) The Board shall—

(*a*) keep copies of the report available for purchase or inspection at their principal office,

(*b*) furnish to the Minister such number of copies of the report as the Minister may require, and

(*c*) furnish to each health authority a copy of the report.

REMOVAL OF MEMBERS FROM OFFICE

23.—(1) The Minister, if he is satisfied that the Board have not performed any function which they are required by this Act to perform, may by order require the Board to perform such function and to comply with such directions as are given in the order.

(2) If the Board do not, within a period specified by the Minister, comply with an order made under subsection (1) of this section, the Minister may by order remove from office the members of the Board. [*SSs.* 3 *and* 4 *and Ss.* 24 *and* 25 *omitted*]

MIDWIVES COMMITTEE

26.—On the establishment date there shall be established by virtue of this section a committee under the Board to be styled and known as the Midwives Committee.

27.—The number of members of the Committee shall be eight. [*Ss.* 28-38 *omitted.*]

EMPLOYEES

39.—(1) The Board shall appoint such and so many persons to be officers and servants of the Board as the Board, subject to the consent of the Minister, from time to time think proper and every person so appointed shall be selected by the Board in such manner (if any) as the Minister may direct or approve. [*Remaining Subsections and S. 40 omitted.*]

REGISTRATION OF NURSES

41.—(1) The Board shall, in accordance with rules, maintain a register of nurses which shall be divided into the divisions specified in such rules and such divisions shall include a division applicable to midwives. [*SSs. 2-5 omitted.*]

42.—(1) The Board shall, in accordance with rules, register in the register of nurses every person who satisfies the Board that such person complies with the prescribed conditions for such registration.

(2) The Board may, subject to the prescribed conditions, register a person in more than one division of the register of nurses.

43.—The Board may, in accordance with rules, register in the register of nurses a person who shows to the satisfaction of the Board that such person has, outside the State, undergone such courses of training and passed such examinations as are specified for the purposes of this section in the rules. [*S. 44 omitted.*]

45.—(1) The Board may, in accordance with rules and subject to section 46 of this Act, remove the name of a person from the register of nurses, or from a division or divisions of the register of nurses, and in the case of the removal of the name of a midwife shall inform every local supervising authority concerned and the Minister.

(2) The rules made for the purposes of this section shall, in particular, provide that, where it is proposed to remove the name of any person from a division of the register of nurses other than the midwives division proceedings in that behalf shall be instituted before the Board and that in those proceedings the defendant shall have the opportunity of answering the allegations made against the defendant.

(3) The rules made for the purposes of this section shall prescribe the causes for which and the conditions under which the name of a nurse may be removed from a division of the register of nurses other than the midwives division, and different rules may be made under this section governing the removal of names from different divisions of the register of nurses.

46.—(1) The Committee may, in accordance with rules, recommend to the Board that the name of a midwife should be removed from the midwives division and the Board shall give effect to such recommendation.

(2) The Board shall not, save on the recommendation of the Committee, remove the name of a midwife from the midwives division. [*Remaining subsections and Ss. 47 and 48 omitted.*]

49.—(1) Where, under this Act, the name of a person has been removed from the register of nurses or where the Committee has refused to recommend the restoration of the name of a person to the midwives division or the Board has refused to register the name of a person in the register of nurses or refused to restore the name of a person to the register of nurses, the person may appeal from the decision of the Board or the Committee as the case may be either to the High Court or the Minister (but not to both) within three months after the notification to the person of such removal or such refusal as the case may be. [*SSs. 2 and 3 omitted.*]

TRAINING AND EXAMINATIONS

50.—The Board may, in accordance with rules, provide or make provision for the courses of training and examinations to be taken by candidates for registration in the register of nurses and may prescribe the manner in which and the conditions under which training shall be provided and such rules may, in particular, provide—
  (*a*) for the approval by the Board for the purposes of such rules of lecturers and teachers,
  (*b*) for the conditions of admission to the examinations, and
  (*c*) for the granting of certificates to persons taking the courses and passing the examinations.

51.—The Board may, in accordance with rules, provide or make provision for courses of training and examinations for nurses, and for the granting to nurses taking such courses and passing such examinations of certificates or diplomas, and may prescribe the manner in which and the conditions under which training shall be provided, and such rules may, in particular, provide—
  (*a*) for the approval by the Board for the purposes of such rules of lecturers and teachers, and
  (*b*) for the conditions of admission to the examinations.

52.—(1) The Board may hold the examinations provided for by rules and may, by such rules, regulate the conduct of such examinations.
  (2) The examiners (none of whom shall be a member of the Board) at every examination held under this section shall be appointed by the Board, shall hold such qualifications and have such experience in relation to nursing as the Board think proper, and shall be remunerated in accordance with a scale fixed by the Board with the approval of the Minister.
53.—(1) Where the Board, on application made to them in that behalf, are satisfied that a hospital or institution is suitable for the training of nurses or of candidates for registration in the register of nurses, the Board shall approve of the hospital or institution for such training. [*Remaining subsections and Ss. 54-57 omitted.*]

ACCOUNTS AND AUDIT

58.—(1) The Board shall cause the accounts of the Board to be kept in such form as the Minister directs or approves.

(2) The accounts of the Board shall be made up in respect of such periods as may be determined by the Minister.

(3) The accounts of the Board shall be audited by a local government auditor appointed from time to time by the Minister for that purpose after consultation with the Minister for Local Government.

[*Ss. 59-64 omitted.*]

ADVICE AND REPORTS

65.—(1) The Board shall furnish advice to the Minister on any matter, relating to nursing, on which he has requested the advice of the Board.

(2) The Board may furnish to the Minister such advice and reports relating to nursing as they think fit.

(3) The Board may, with the consent of the Minister, advise a health authority on the organisation of nursing services within the functional area of the health authority.

RESEARCH

66.—The Board may, and if so required by the Minister shall, conduct, or cause to be conducted, research into matters relating to the organisation or practice of nursing or the training of nurses.   [*Remainder of Act omitted.*]

(d) *The Agricultural Research Institute*
Document 10.4 — Extracts from Agriculture (An Foras Talúntais)
Act, 1958 (no. 1).

ESTABLISHMENT

3.—(1) There is hereby established an Institute to be styled and known as An Foras Talúntais to fulfil the functions assigned to it by this Act.

(2) The Institute shall be a body corporate with perpetual succession and power to sue and be sued in its corporate name and to acquire, hold and dispose of land.

FUNCTIONS

4.—(1) The functions of the Institute are to review, facilitate, encourage, assist, co-ordinate, promote and undertake agricultural research. [*SS. 2 omitted.*]

(3) The Institute shall advise the Minister [for Agriculture] on any matter relating to agricultural research or agricultural science on which its advice is requested by him.

COUNCIL

5.—(1) There shall be a council, to be known as the Council of An Foras Talúntais, to carry out the general government of the Institute and the administration of its affairs.

(2) The Council shall consist of a chairman and twelve ordinary members.

(3) The chairman shall be appointed by the President and shall hold office for such term (not exceeding three years) and on such terms and conditions (including terms of remuneration) as may be determined by the Government at the time of his appointment. [*SSs*. 4-6 *omitted*.]

(7) The ordinary members of the Council, of whom nine shall be persons nominated under subsections (8) and (9) of this section, shall be appointed by the Government and the first appointments shall be made by the Government as soon as conveniently may be after the commencement of this Act.

(8) Five persons shall be nominated by such agricultural and rural organisations and in such manner as may be determined by the Government by order to be ordinary members of the Council.

(9) One person shall be nominated to be an ordinary member of the Council by each of the following:

> the Governing Body of University College, Dublin,
> the Governing Body of University College, Cork,
> the Governing Body of University College, Galway, and
> the Board of Trinity College, Dublin.

[*SSs*. 10 *and* 11 *omitted*.]

6.—There may be paid, out of the income of the Institute, to members of the Council such expenses of travel and subsistence as the Council may determine.

DIRECTOR

7.—(1) There shall be a director of the Institute (in this Act referred to as the Director).

(2) The Director shall be the chief officer of the Institute and shall control and direct the activities and staff of the Institute subject to the direction of the Council.

(3) The first Director shall be appointed by the Government as soon as may be after the commencement of this Act and shall hold office for such term and on such terms and conditions (including terms of remuneration) as may be determined by the Government. [*Remaining subsections of S. 7 and Ss. 8 and 9 omitted*.]

FUNDS

10.—(1) The Minister for Finance shall, when requested by the Council to do so, pay to the Institute, out of the monies held in the Counterpart Special Account, a sum of eight hundred and forty thousand pounds and that sum, when paid to the Institute, shall be known as the Capital Fund of An Foras Talúntais and is in this Act referred to as the Capital Fund. [*Remaining subsections omitted*.]

11.—(1) The Minister for Finance shall, when requested by the Council to do so, pay to the Institute, out of the monies held in the Counterpart Special Account, a sum of one million pounds and that sum, when paid to the Institute, shall be known as the Endowment Fund of An Foras Talúntais and is in this Act referred to as the Endowment Fund.

(2) The Endowment Fund shall be kept invested by the Institute in such securities as may be approved from time to time by the Minister for Finance.

(3) The interest on the Endowment Fund shall accrue to the Institute as income.

12.—(1) For the purpose of assisting the Institute to carry out effectively its functions under this Act, there shall be paid to the Institute in every financial year, out of monies provided by the Oireachtas, a grant towards the expenses of the Institute the amount of which shall be determined by the Minister for Finance in consultation with the Minister and the Council after due consideration of any information furnished under subsection (2) of this section.

(2) The Council shall furnish to the Minister such information regarding its income and expenditure as he may from time to time require.

(3) In this and the next following section "expenses" does not include expenses incurred by the Institute in relation to the grants or capital costs specified in subsection (2) of section 10 of this Act. [*Ss.* 13-18 *omitted.*]

ACCOUNTS AND AUDIT

19.—(1) The Institute shall keep, in such form as may be approved by the Minister, with the concurrence of the Minister for Finance, all proper and usual accounts of all monies received or expended by it.

(2) Accounts kept in pursuance of this section shall be submitted annually by the Council to the Comptroller and Auditor General for audit at such times as the Minister, with the concurrence of the Minister for Finance, directs and the accounts when so audited shall, together with the report of the Comptroller and Auditor General thereon, be presented to the Minister who shall cause copies thereof to be laid before each House of the Oireachtas.

ANNUAL REPORT

20.—(1) The Council shall, as soon as conveniently may be after the end of every financial year, prepare and submit to the Minister a report of the work of the Institute in that financial year.

(2) A copy of every report submitted by the Council to the Minister under this section shall, within two months after its receipt from the Council, be submitted to the Government and laid before each House of the Oireachtas. [*Remaining sections omitted.*]

(e) *Radio Éireann*
    Document 10.5 — Extracts from Broadcasting Authority Act, 1960 (no. 10).

ESTABLISHMENT

3.—(1) There shall, by virtue of this section, be established on the establishment day an authority to be known as Radio Éireann (in this Act referred to as the Authority.)

(2) The Authority shall be a body corporate with perpetual succession and power to sue and be sued in its corporate name and to acquire, hold and dispose of land.

MEMBERS

4.—(1) The members of the Authority shall be appointed by the Government and shall be not less than seven and not more than nine in number.

(2) The period of office of a member of the Authority shall be such period not exceeding five years, as the Government may determine when appointing him.

(3) A member of the Authority whose term of office expires by effluxion of time shall be eligible for re-appointment.

(4) A member of the Authority may at any time resign his office as member by letter sent to the Government, and the resignation shall take effect on receipt of the letter.

(5) Where a member of the Authority is nominated either as a candidate for election to either House of the Oireachtas or as a member of Seanad Éireann, he shall thereupon cease to be a member of the Authority.

(6) A person who is for the time being entitled under the Standing Orders of either House of the Oireachtas to sit therein shall, while so entitled, be disqualified from becoming a member of the Authority.

5.—(1) A member of the Authority shall be paid, out of funds at the disposal of the Authority—

    (*a*) such remuneration as may be fixed from time to time by the Government, and

    (*b*) such amounts in respect of expenses as the Authority considers reasonable.

        [*SSs. 2 and 3 omitted.*]

6.—The Government may at any time remove a member of the Authority from office.

7.—(1) The Government shall from time to time as occasion requires appoint a member of the Authority to be chairman thereof. [*Remaining subsections and Ss. 8-10 omitted.*]

DIRECTOR-GENERAL

11.—The Authority shall from time to time appoint a person to be the chief executive officer of the Authority, and such person shall be known, and is in this Act referred to, as the Director-General.

EMPLOYEES

12.—(1) The Authority shall, as well as appointing the Director-General, appoint such and so many other persons to be officers and servants of the Authority as the Authority from time to time thinks proper, but, subject to subsection (2) of this section, a person shall not be appointed under this section to be an officer of the Authority unless he has been selected by means of a public competition. [*Remaining subsections and Ss. 13-15 omitted.*]

FUNCTIONS AND DUTIES

16.—(1) The Authority shall establish and maintain a national television and sound broadcasting service and shall have all such powers as are necessary for or incidental to that purpose. [*SS. 2 omitted.*]

17.—In performing its functions, the Authority shall bear constantly in mind the national aims of restoring the Irish language and preserving and developing the national culture and shall endeavour to promote the attainment of those aims.

18.—(1) It shall be the duty of the Authority to secure that, when it broadcasts any information, news or feature which relates to matters of public controversy or is the subject of current public debate, the information, news or feature is presented objectively and impartially and without any expression of the Authority's own views.

(2) Nothing in this section shall prevent the Authority from transmitting political party broadcasts.

19.—The periods fixed by the Authority for broadcasting shall be subject to the approval of the Minister [for Posts and Telegraphs].

ADVERTISEMENTS

20.—(1) The authorities may broadcast advertisements, may fix charges and conditions for such broadcasts and, in fixing the charges, may provide for different circumstances and for additional special charges to be made in special cases. [*SSs. 2-8 omitted.*]

ADVICE TO AUTHORITY

21.—(1) For the purpose of enabling the Authority to have advice in performing its functions, the Minister, after consultation with the Authority, may from time to time appoint advisory committees or advisers. [*SSs. 2-4 omitted.*]

FINANCES

22.—(1) Subject to subsection (2) of this section, the Minister, with the approval of the Minister for Finance, may, in respect of each of the five consecutive financial years beginning with that in which the establishment day occurs, pay to the Authority out of moneys provided by the Oireachtas—

(a) an amount equal to the total of the receipts in that year in respect of broadcasting licence fees less—

(i) any expenses certified by the Minister as having been incurred by him in that year in relation to the collection of those fees and

(ii) any expenses certified by the Minister as having been incurred by him in that year in respect of the performance of his functions under sections 12 and 12A of the Act of 1926 in relation to interfering with or injuriously affecting wireless telegraphy apparatus for receiving only, and

(*b*) such further amount as the Minister considers reasonable.

(2) The total of the amounts paid pursuant to paragraph (*b*) of subsection (1) of this section shall not exceed five hundred thousand pounds. [*S*. 23 *omitted.*]

24.—It shall be the duty of the Authority so to conduct its affairs as to secure that its revenue becomes at the earliest possible date, and thereafter continues, at least sufficient—

(*a*) to meet all sums properly chargeable to current account, and

(*b*) to make suitable provision with respect to capital expenditure.

ACCOUNTS AND AUDIT

25.—(1) The Authority shall keep in such form as shall be approved by the Minister, after consultation with the Minister for Finance, all proper and usual accounts of all moneys received or expended by it, including an income and expenditure account and a balance sheet, and, in particular, shall keep in such form as aforesaid all such special accounts as the Minister on his own motion, or at the request of the Minister for Finance, shall from time to time direct.

(2) The accounts of the Authority for each year shall be audited within ninety days or such longer time as the Minister may in any particular case allow after the end of that year and shall be the subject of a report by duly qualified auditors appointed annually for the purpose by the Minister, with the consent of the Minister for Finance, and the fees of the auditors and the expenses generally of the audits shall be paid by the Authority.

(3) The Minister may, with the consent of the Minister for Finance, appoint the time, place and method of conducting the audit of the accounts of the Authority under this section, and may also appoint the accounts of which copies are to be furnished to the Minister under this section.

(4) Immediately after every audit under this section of the accounts of the Authority, the Authority shall send to the Minister a copy of the income and expenditure account and balance sheet as certified by the auditors, a copy of the auditors' report, and copies of such of the accounts submitted to the auditors as are appointed under the foregoing subsection to be furnished to the Minister.

(5) The Minister shall cause the documents furnished to him under this section to be laid before each House of the Oireachtas.

ANNUAL REPORT AND INFORMATION

26.—(1) The Authority shall, in each year, at such date as the Minister may direct, make a report to the Minister of its proceedings under this Act during the preceding year, and the Minister shall cause copies of the report to be laid before each House of the Oireachtas.

(2) Whenever the Minister so directs, the annual report shall also include information on such particular aspects of the Authority's proceedings under this Act as the Minister may specify.

(3) The Authority shall submit to the Minister such information regarding the performance of its functions as he may from time to time require. [*Ss.* 27-30 *omitted.*]

DIRECTIONS BY THE MINISTER

31.—(1) The Minister may direct the Authority in writing to refrain from broadcasting any particular matter or matter of any particular class, and the Authority shall comply with the direction.

(2) The Minister may direct the Authority in writing to allocate broadcasting time for any announcements by or on behalf of any Minister of State in connection with the functions of that Minister of State, and the Authority shall comply with the direction. [*Remainder omitted.*]

(f) *Corporate Bodies in the Health Services*

    (i) Document 10.6 — Extract from *Health Corporate Bodies Bill, 1961*
                  —Explanatory Memorandum (issued to Members
                  of Dáil Éireann with the text of the Bill).

1.—From time to time projects have arisen in relation to the health services which, while not appropriate to be dealt with by the Department of Health, were not of a local nature and were therefore unsuitable for administration by local health authorities. The provision of blood transfusion facilities and a mass X-ray service are examples of such projects. In cases such as these the practice has been for the Minister for Health to take steps to have a company established under the Companies Acts to do the work. A number of such companies have been established in this way, their activities being, in the main, financed in whole or in part from funds in the control of the Minister or from funds provided by local authorities. The procedure under the Companies Acts is not entirely appropriate for the establishment of bodies such as these, and the Minister has for some time thought that it would be desirable for him to have a simple power to set up statutory corporations to provide appropriate health services. The Health (Corporate Bodies) Bill is designed to give the Minister such a power. [*Remainder omitted.*]

(ii) Document 10.7 — Extracts from Health Corporate Bodies Act, 1961 (no. 27).

3.—(1) The Minister may from time to time by order (in this Act referred to as an establishment order) establish a body to perform functions in, or in relation to, the provision of a health service or two or more health services.

(2) A body established under subsection (1) of this section shall be called and known by such title as may be specified in the establishment order.

(3) A body so established shall be a body corporate with perpetual succession and a seal and with power to sue and be sued in its corporate name and to hold land.

(4) All courts shall take judicial notice of the seal of a body so established and every document purporting to be an order or other instrument made by that body and to be sealed with its seal (purporting to be authenticated in the manner provided in the establishment order) shall be received in evidence and be deemed to be such order or instrument without further proof unless the contrary is shown.

(5) The Minister may from time to time by order amend an establishment order or an order made under this subsection.

4.—(1) Every establishment order shall contain such provisions as the Minister considers appropriate in relation to—

(a) the number of members of the body established by the order, the method, terms and conditions of their appointment and their tenure of office;

(b) the number, grades, method of appointment, conditions of service, tenure of office and the remuneration of the officers and servants of the body so established.

5.—An establishment order shall contain such provisions as the Minister considers appropriate defining the functions of the body established by the order in, or in relation to, the provision of the health service or health services to which the order relates, and the manner in which and the conditions under which the body so established may perform the functions so defined.

6.—An establishment order shall contain such provisions relating to the administration generally of the body established by the order as the Minister considers appropriate including provisions relating to—

(a) the meetings of the body so established and the procedure at such meetings,

(b) the use and authentication of its seal,

(c) the regulation of its finances and the keeping and auditing of its accounts, and (*d*) the furnishing to the Minister by such body from time to time of information regarding the performance of its functions, and the furnishing of such information to the Minister at any time at his request.

7.—(1) The Minister may at any time by order revoke an establishment order.

2. THE TAOISEACH REVIEWS THEIR DEVELOPMENT

Document 10.8 — Extracts from Seán F. Lemass, *The Role of the State-sponsored Bodies in the Economy,* Institute of Public Administration, Dublin, 1959. (Also published in *Administration,* vol. 6.)

The establishment of statutory boards and quasi-State corporations was a consequence of the extension of Government activity into fields which were previously regarded as the preserve of private commercial enterprise. As the area of Government responsibility became enlarged, it was realised that the normal arrangements and procedures of Government administration were not always suitable and that new agencies through which to function were required. The independent statutory board — such as the Electricity Supply Board and Coras Iompair Éireann — was the device which was deemed to be appropriate where the task was to provide essential services on a nation-wide, non-competitive basis. For the more directly commercial type of operation, the device used was the State-financed corporation, with the characteristics of a joint-stock company, registered under the Companies Acts with a Minister subscribing for capital under the authority of legislation.

In all cases the initiation and shaping of policy in the broadest sense is the prerogative of Government. The method and degree of Government control over these boards and companies is, however, to some extent still a matter of debate and controversy. Generally speaking, the extent of the control exercised in particular instances is settled on a pragmatic rather than theoretical basis, but I will have something more to say in this regard later. The aim is to provide the possibility of progressive modern business management with a proper degree of public accountability. President Roosevelt described the Tennessee Valley Authority as " A corporation clothed with the power of Government but possessed of the flexibility and initiative of private enterprise." . . .

There are, however, dangers and disadvantages associated with the growth in the number and importance of State-sponsored commercial organisations. It is desirable that realisation of these dangers should prevail not merely in Government circles but also amongst the staffs of the organisations.

There is the danger that after the initial drive, to set up a new organisation and to get it functioning properly, has expended itself the organisation may settle down to routine operation characterised by excessive caution and loss of initiative and flexibility. There is the danger that in the course of time these organisations may be directed and administered with decreasing regard for the national needs and increasing and undue concern for the benefit and convenience of their staffs. There is danger that bureaucratic procedures may stifle efficiency and delay necessary or desirable innovations and changes.

In raising this issue, I am suggesting not that these dangers have emerged in any acute form, but that they exist and that they can only be prevented from emerging by constant vigilance.

In most instances, in the case of these organisations, there is, apart from the spirit of public service, no automatic spur to efficiency. They lack the stimulus of private enterprise and competition. When it is possible that every rise in costs can be offset by higher charges, the danger is more acute and the need for some means to ensure continuing efficiency becomes clearer. The State-sponsored boards, if they are to fulfil their proper role in the national economy, require to be kept under continuous pressure, from inside and outside, to revise their procedures and costs in a continuous effort to maintain their efficiency.

In competitive private enterprise the making of profits is the acid test of economic merit, but in the case of State enterprise different considerations and tests apply. For statutory corporations like the E.S.B. there is a legislative ban on profits in the accepted sense. The revenue from sales must not be more than sufficient to balance outgoings, including depreciation and loan capital repayments. In private industry, however, there is usually the aim of accumulating in addition to profits sufficient to maintain dividend payments, a surplus which can be utilised for capital expansion. To a reasonable extent this course is justifiable by State-sponsored commercial concerns and particularly so when their products are sold at prices which equate to those which would operate if they did not exist. As shareholder in commercial concerns, the State is not avaricious for higher dividends, as the shareholders of some private concerns may be. There are obvious dangers in seeking to do too much by way of financing expansion out of retained profits where non-competitive prices are possible and where it means maintaining a price level which imposes handicaps on other private firms. In some semi-State companies the emphasis on the accumulation of reserves has, at times, been excessive.

In determining their price and profit policies, State-sponsored organisations must have regard to the effect of what they may do on the over-all economic situation as well as on the appearance of their own published accounts. As I have stated, our main reliance is on private competitive enterprise and where the expansion of private concerns or the growth of export trade is likely to be handicapped by excessive prices charged for services or supplies from State concerns, by reason of an unduly conservative financial approach or desire to tuck away reserves to finance without fresh borrowing some future development in contemplation, the over-all national interest may be prejudiced. Meeting the capital needs of State organisations is not ordinarily a problem for the Government and the possibility of having to delay some desirable development at some future time because of capital shortage is so unlikely that it is not a justification for the undue exploitation of a monopoly position by any State concern for the purpose of accumulating reserve resources.

The relationship between State boards and the Ministers who are responsible to the Dáil for their operations is not always very precisely defined and a great deal depends on the confidence which a Minister may have in the board or executives of a particular concern and on the readiness of a board to accept that the particular operations for which they are responsible should be kept in line, through the Minister as the co-ordinating authority, with the over-all development plans of the Government.

When new capital is required for expansion, involving either a direct Exchequer contribution or a Government guarantee of borrowing, the obligation to satisfy the Minister on the soundness of the proposals involved is obvious enough, although fitting the capital needs of individual boards into the State Capital Budget may occasionally involve some adjustment of plans. The Minister who has to defend the proposals to the Dáil must be fully satisfied about them, not so much in their technical aspects as in their general suitability for achieving the purposes for which the board was set up.

There is, in my experience, rarely any difficulty in securing agreement between Minister and a board when the board is progressing vigorously and intelligently to accomplish developments which both desire. The difficulty is where a board is dragging its heels, or is so excessively cautious or dilatory that it fails to keep its place in the general advance. The Minister has the task of stimulating greater activity in such cases and it is not always easy to do so without some friction. There develops a tendency in some boards to think of themselves rather as sovereign independent authorities than as integral parts of a larger organisation and they are sometimes disposed to resent pressures to keep them in line.

In the last resort, the responsibility for the failures and deficiencies of any State board rests on the Minister. Because he has the final power of changing their directors, if he fails to use that power he proclaims himself to be satisfied with their progress or administration. A Minister will not as a rule seek to get the results he desires by changing boards or managers except at a last resort. There are undesirable consequences of frequent changes. In the circumstances of this country it is not so very easy to secure the right people to undertake the direction of State concerns and it would be made still more difficult if membership carried the risk of a loss of reputation following an arbitrary removal by a Minister. A Minister who acted in that way would merely add to his own difficulties. The Minister's main instrument is criticism. His responsibility is to the public and he would fail in his responsibility if he withheld criticism where he considered it to be due. As a general guiding rule, the relations between the Minister and the board should never be too cordial. At least the board must feel that criticism will be prompt and vigorous whenever circumstances may call for it. . . .

In this regard, mention should be made of various ideas which have emerged from time to time for keeping State organisations under more effective parliamentary scrutiny. The question of the form of control to be exercised over State-sponsored bodies and of the extent of such control is raised regularly. Various public utterances imply a desire to bring the affairs of these bodies under some form of periodic Parliamentary review, particularly where their activities may have a considerable influence on the national economy.

Efforts are made from time to time by means of parliamentary questions to enquire into affairs of these bodies. In general, the ministerial practice in answering these questions is to be as informative as possible on matters of general policy, while avoiding undue interference with or taking responsibility for the day-to-day functioning of these bodies. The problem of securing parliamentary control is not peculiar to this country: it is common to democratic countries which have had to resort to State-sponsored bodies for the performance of public services. In spite of much searching, no generally accepted scheme of control has yet been evolved anywhere.

It could be argued that additional parliamentary control is unnecessary having regard to the wide ministerial powers in relation to State-sponsored bodies and to the fact that the annual report and accounts are presented to the Oireachtas. It could be said that as these bodies were set up with the deliberate intention of avoiding close State control, the case for scrutiny by a parliamentary committee cuts at the root of this idea and involves an attempt to have things two ways at once. Duplicating the systems of control or supervision could have undesirable consequences. It could force State companies into civil service procedures by which freedom of enterprise might be hampered and the initiative of management and staff might be impaired.

It would add to the difficulty of securing persons of the requisite calibre to act as directors, if their decisions, taken in good faith, were to be subject to public questioning of the kind that a parliamentary committee might indulge in. The confidence of other firms in the State-sponsored body's ability to fulfil its engagements and to keep trade secrets might be seriously lessened.

There would also be a danger that any parliamentary review would become too detailed: it would be very difficult to restrict the terms of reference of a parliamentary committee so as to avoid that possibility. There would be a danger of unenlightened criticism, publication of which could damage the standing and credit of a State-sponsored body. It would be very doubtful whether a State board could function satisfactorily if it were to be responsible to both a Minister and a parliamentary committee. These are all important considerations and, in the light of them, it will be appreciated that this is a most complex problem and that it is no wonder that no entirely satisfactory solution has so far been evolved. . . .

3. MINISTERIAL AND PARLIAMENTARY CONTROL OF PUBLIC ENTERPRISE

(a) *Minister-Board Relationships*

Document 10.9 — Extracts from Speech by Minister for Transport and
Power in *Dáil Debates,* vol. 182, cols. 999-1003
(10 June 1960).

Mr. Childers (Minister for Transport and Power): A number of Deputies
referred to the fact that the Minister for Transport and Power and his officers
do not interfere with the day to day activities of the companies over which
we exercise some general supervision. This must be examined from a common-
sense point of view. Quite obviously the State companies must be allowed to
operate as much as possible as private companies with full liberties in initiative,
with full liberties in regard to control of staff, and with full liberties in regard
to the day-to-day operations of their concerns.

The purpose of the Department is, first of all, to prepare legislation when
it is required, to examine the demands for capital for future productive purposes and the promotion of the various companies, to examine how capital
already provided is being spent and whether or not it should be remunerated
at any given stage in a company's operations, to examine the general policy of
each of these companies in relation to the national economy as a whole, to
see if they are contributing to the national economy, and to see if there are
any elements in their operations which are hindering other companies or
other interests. In that we should also have regard to the necessity of there
being reasonably good relations between employers and workers in these companies and we like to assure ourselves in every way possible that industrial
relations are operating on what might be described as an optimum basis.

It is the duty of the Department also to exhort all companies at every
possible opportunity to adopt dynamic cost reducing, output raising techniques, to lower their costs as much as possible, to provide the very best possible
service at the lowest cost, and to keep in line with modern practice but that
does not mean that we see these companies every day, that we write to them
every day, or that we are in contact with them every day. It means that we
have meetings with the Boards of the Companies and their chief officers from
time to time. We compare the progress they make with the progress made by
companies of renown in other countries. We make general comparisons—
always general comparisons—always exhorting them on a general basis, but
not interfering with the day-to-day operations of any particular company.

We also study the quality of service they give the public in a general way,
comparing it with the quality of service given by other companies abroad, to
ensure that their customers, who are the public, are being reasonably treated,
that for the money they pay they get good value. I count it entirely wrong
and against the interests of these companies, and the public in the long run,
if we were to make pin-pricking interferences with their day to day operations.
What we do is to examine these questions in a big way and, as I said, have
discussions with the Boards on the basis of general efficiency, general mode of

production, general relations with workers, and general costings. I thought that would be fairly obvious to most Deputies but I think it is just as well that I stress what is our purpose.

It would be very inadvisable for me to encourage Deputies to ask individual questions as to why railway carriages on a certain line were dirty, but what I would wish to encourage Deputies to do is to complain to the companies themselves, and to encourage the public to make complaints to these companies if the service they receive is poor. I think this procedure is fair and reasonable. I would intervene if I became aware that a large number of Deputies were getting a large number of complaints in regard to a particular company, if I became aware that quite evidently a large number of the public were complaining about the services provided by the company for them.

Then it would cease to be a day-to-day question. It would become a matter of public interest and I would certainly intervene with the Board of that company and ask why the volume of complaints had reached such a level that I had to have regard to it. That is a very different matter from my having to answer questions in detail as to whether the remuneration of certain employees of a company being transferred to another company was to be the same as the other employees of that company, when I know that the industrial tribunal—a trade union committee—had good relations with the company's management and that the men's interests were being looked after. There would be absolute chaos if I interfered unilaterally in a particular case because a Deputy asked questions.

I could repeat examples of that *ad infinitum,* showing the very great undesirability of my answering questions of a day-to-day character when it would be better for the people concerned if the Deputy addressed his questions to the companies themselves. So far as I know Deputies receive courteous replies reasonably promptly in regard to the questions they ask. There again, if there are many complaints that the replies they receive are long delayed, are discourteous, or show lack of regard for the matters complained of, it would be part of my general responsibility to see that the public relations of these companies were improved so that complaints would be properly and efficiently investigated, whether they come from Deputies, Senators or the general public at large.

I hope I have made this matter sufficiently clear. Of course, quite a considerable amount of freedom has been allowed in the course of this debate by the Ceann Comhairle and Leas-Cheann Comhairle. They have taken a liberal attitude in regard to the extent and detail of the questions asked. This would be a matter for the Ceann Comhairle and the Leas-Cheann Comhairle to control in future. Now that we have a separate Department, the position is different. I think it very proper that the Ceann Comhairle has allowed a very liberal amount of detailed comment. I think it could be useful in future years. It gives me a fair idea of what people are thinking of the general progress of these companies, and the rather detailed matters raised in these questions I can consider myself, discuss with the officers of my Department or refer to them for consideration.

Deputy Booth raised the question of the general control of State companies and he suggested that we ought to have further thoughts on this subject which has been so much discussed in other countries as to how far State companies should be free of examination by the Parliament of the country concerned, free of investigation by Committees of the Parliament and by the Minister himself. I think the best thing I can do is to remind Deputy Booth of a question asked by Deputy McQuillan in regard to this matter on the control of State and semi-State bodies.

The Taoiseach, in replying, said:

In the case of those of the principal State-sponsored bodies referred to by the Deputy which do not receive annual grants but the capital of which has been wholly or mainly subscribed or guaranteed by the State, I would, if there is a substantial demand in the House for such a procedure, be prepared to consider whether there is need for an arrangement whereby the House would be asked to allow time periodically for discussion of a motion dealing with the report and accounts of each such body which have been laid before the House pursuant to statute.

So the Taoiseach has suggested a method whereby, in addition to the debate on the Estimate, if a number of Deputies asked for a particular debate by resolution, on the presentation of the annual accounts of one of these numerous State companies, that might be arranged. The Taoiseach has said that he is prepared to consider an arrangement whereby there could be such a discussion outside the scope of the debate on the Estimate itself. I do not know if that is likely to arise in future. I hope these State companies will continue to be run and administered so as not to warrant such a particular examination but it is impossible to foretell the future.

(b) *The Minister 'strongly requests' the Board of CIE*

(i) Document 10.10 — Correspondence between the Minister for Industry and Commerce and Coras Iompair Éireann published in *Irish Times,* 2 April 1963.

Last night C.I.E. issued copies of the correspondence which led up to the postponement of strike action by the unions. The company's announcement said that yesterday afternoon the Board received the following letter from the Minister for Industry and Commerce: —

> "Office of the Minister for Industry and Commerce,
> Dublin 2,
> 1 Aibrean, 1963.

"A Chara,

"At a meeting I had with representatives of the Unions whose members are involved in the present bus dispute, the Union representatives proposed to me that that part of the proposals I put forward on Friday, 22nd March, for the settlement of the dispute dealing with the pensions, sickness benefit and travel facilities scheme be modified so as to enable the men to ballot on the recommendations of the Commission. I have informed the Unions that if they can procure the endorsement of my proposals with this modification I will direct the Board of C.I.E. to accept them. The Unions have intimated to me that they could have a ballot carried out on the amended proposals, and the results conveyed to me before Monday, 8th April, I therefore, strongly request that your Board defer the operation of one-man scheduled bus services until that date.

Mise, le meas,

J. Lynch.

M. J. Hayes, Esq.,
Secretary,
Coras Iompair Éireann,
Kingsbridge, Dublin 8."

The Board has replied to the Minister as follows:
"J. Lynch, Esq., T.D.,
Minister for Industry and Commerce,
Kildare Street, Dublin 2.

1st April, 1963.

"Dear Sir,

"I am directed by my Board to acknowledge receipt of your letter of to-day's date and to say that your intention to direct the Board in the matter of the recommendation of the proposed Commission is noted.

"In the circumstances, my Board accedes to your strong request to defer the extension of one-man buses to scheduled services until the 8th of April.

Yours Faithfully,

M. J. Hayes,
Secretary."

(ii) Document 10.11 — Extract from *Dáil Debates*, vol. 202, cols. 33-4 (23 April 1963).

49. Dr. Browne and **Mr. McQuillan** asked the Minister for Industry and Commerce under what powers vested in him by the Oireachtas he can direct the Board of CIE to accept his proposals, as referred to in a letter by him to CIE on 1st April 1963.

50. Dr. Browne and **Mr. McQuillan** asked the Minister for Industry and Commerce the conditions and powers, if any, under which he can make a strong request for action by the Board of CIE in a dispute between the company and its employees on conditions of employment and related matters.

51. Dr. Browne and **Mr. McQuillan** asked the Minister for Industry and Commerce whether he has power to direct CIE to accede to a demand by him in matters relating to a dispute between the company and its employees.

Mr. J. Lynch: I propose, with the permission of the Ceann Chomhairle, to take Questions Nos. 49 and 50 and 51 together.

I have no statutory power to issue directions to CIE in relation to trade disputes between the company and its employees. In view of the functions assigned to me under the Ministers and Secretaries Act, I do not need to have special powers to enable me to make a strong request to the company.

Dr. Browne: What is the position of the company in relation to a strong request? Do they have to accept it or can they reject it? What is the position?

Mr. J. Lynch: When I issued a direction to the company in the first place, the company knew well that I had not the power to direct them to do anything but knew I was making an attempt to solve the strike and they agreed to accept my direction in the matter. Other people also intervened to try to solve the dispute but, unfortunately, the two Deputies sabotaged their efforts.

(c) *The Government Requests the Electricity Supply Board*
Document 10.12 — Extract from *Irish Times,* 8 June 1963.

At the specific request of the Government the Board of the E.S.B. has deferred an award of 7 per cent by the E.S.B. General Employees' Tribunal to about 850 clerical workers because it is feared that the implementation would start a ninth round of wage increases by other Board staffs and in employment generally. The award had been retrospective to June 3rd, 1962.

The deferment is the first to be made since the Government White Paper on Incomes and Output last January. It will be challenged.

In a letter to the E.S.B. Board the Government stated that it aims, in consultation with the employers and the trade unions, to make arrangements for an objective study of the progress of the national economy, to enable consideration to be given, in the light of the growth in national production since salary and wage rates were last adjusted, of the wage and salary increases which could be granted without danger to the continued expansion of employment or of an inflationary increase of prices.

The letter declared that it was the considered view of the Government that the E.S.B. should "await the completion of this study before arriving at a decision regarding the implementation of the present award of the Tribunal."

The staff associations have been told by the Board of the decision but all associations have declared that the deferment "is unacceptable." It seems likely that the matter will be raised in the Dáil and will be considered also by the other clerical and professional bodies and by teachers and other State employees.

The claim for increased salaries was made by the E.S.B. salaried workers' associations in June, 1962, and part of the claim was that the previous agreement had contained a clause that there would be no claim unless there was a 5 per cent increase on the cost of living.

At the time, June, 1962, the cost-of-living had risen by over 7 per cent. The Tribunal award, therefore, is a cost-of-living award and it could be argued that it was consistent with the eighth round of wage increases.

(d) *Control by the Oireachtas*
Document 10.13 — Extract from *Dáil Debates,* vol. 119, cols. 367-70 (21 February 1950).

Note: Mr Lemass was at this time (1950) in opposition. It will be noticed that both sides seemed to be in favour of the establishment of some machinery for the systematic review of the progress of the state-sponsored enterprises and the Minister promised it. Nevertheless, no such machinery has, in fact, been set up, or indeed, proposed by any Government since then.—Editor.

Mr. Lemass: I move amendment No. 49 : —

Before sub-section (5) to insert a new sub-section as follows : —

(5) Within 21 days after a copy of the accounts and any report furnished to the Minister have been laid before each House of the Oireachtas, the Minister shall move in the Dáil for the establishment of a select committee of the House to examine the accounts and report (if any) and to report thereon to the Dáil.

This raises a matter of fairly general policy in which I know some Deputies are interested. During the course of time the number of State companies and State-sponsored boards has increased considerably. The legislation which set up these companies or boards uniformly provided for the tabling of accounts and annual reports and, in theory, it is open to the Dáil through any individual member, to have a debate upon the accounts or to query anything contained in the reports. In practice, of course, that is not so. It was all right when the first board, the Electricity Supply Board, was the sole organisation of its kind but, as the years passed and other organisations were added to it, it became obviously impossible for the Dáil to take cognisance of the trend of policy and administration revealed in these reports or even to debate adequately the financial results of the operations of these undertakings. That position was recognised by the previous Government and we had been giving consideration to the methods by which the Dáil might have these accounts and reports brought especially to its notice with a view to their detailed examination. It was not that the previous Government were dissatisfied with the way the various Acts worked out, but we felt that the efficiency of these undertakings was impaired to some extent by the absence of any such detailed examination of their accounts and reports in a manner which would ensure that they would realise that periodically they would be obliged to give to a critical audience an account of their administration.

Let it be clear that there was no desire, and there is no desire, to impose upon any of these undertakings the obligation to keep the detailed records which are necessary in a Government Department. In a Government Department any Deputy has the right to ask about the treatment of any individual citizen, even in a matter of very minor importance. There must be records so detailed that the information required to answer a question can be turned up at a day's or two days' notice, giving to the Minister the material necessary for his reply. It would clearly be a considerable handicap to the efficiency of these semi-State and State organisations if they had to keep records as elaborate as that, but it is desirable, nevertheless, that they should be subject to some periodical review here.

We had contemplated the establishment of a committee akin to the Committee of Public Accounts to which these company accounts and reports would be submitted. There is an obvious practical difficulty in that the reports appear at different times of the year and, if the committee was to function only when a volume of work had been accumulated for it, it would, in relation to some of the organisations, be dealing with material already fairly old. Nevertheless, it seems to me that if the work is to be done in a way which appears to be in line with the views of most Deputies here, it has got to be through the device of establishing something akin to the Committee of Public Accounts, to which these accounts will go with or without the prior comments of an officer like the Comptroller and Auditor-General, and where they can be examined and where the officers of the company can be brought to give any further detailed information desirable.

There are objections and difficulties, but I think most Deputies will recognise that, with the pressure of legislation and other business in the Dáil, if work of that kind has to be done it will have to be done by a Committee of the House meeting simultaneously with the House, just as the Committee of Public Accounts does.

Here we are setting up another undertaking. This time it is a board to manage our transport system. We have in the Bill the usual provisions requiring the board to keep all the proper and usual accounts, to send copies of the accounts as passed by its auditors to the Minister, and placing on him the obligation to furnish copies of the accounts to each House of the Oireachtas. It seems to me if we are ever to make progress in this matter we may as well start now and establish what I hope will become a precedent for all these State companies.

We are aware that the Taoiseach informed us last year that this matter was under consideration by the Government. I took the precaution, before this amendment came up for debate, to inquire what progress had been made. I was informed in reply to a Parliamentary Question last week that the matter was still under consideration and that no progress had been made. I do not think progress will be made if the Dáil neglects the opportunity of insisting on some arrangement which will ensure that the accounts of the board and any report furnished by the board to the Minister will be submitted to a committee for examination. If they are tabled, then any Deputy can put down a motion in relation to them or get from them information which he can use during the debate on the Minister's Estimate. Experience has shown that that power is completely insufficient and that the work of the Dáil is in a sense being neglected, because of the pressure of other business, in relation to this matter. I therefore move the amendment which provides that in relation to this board, and without raising any question of the suitability of this device to other boards, we should insist on a select committee examining its accounts and reports and giving a general report on both in a formal manner when it has done so.

Mr. Morrissey: I am in full agreement with the idea behind this amendment and I have full sympathy with the point of view that the activities, finances, and expenditure of various State companies should be brought under effective review by the Dáil. That is the view of the Government. I can say that the examination to which the Taoiseach referred has been going on as rapidly as, having regard to other work, it could be pushed. The desire of the Government in relation to these State-sponsored companies is to get the most effective machinery which will enable the Dáil systematically to consider their activities and I as a member of the Government can give an assurance to the House that it is the intention and the desire of the Government to bring in proposals which will enable the Dáil to have a systematic consideration of the activities of these various boards at the earliest possible date.

I would not be prepared to accept the amendment in the light of that knowledge, because I think there ought to be a uniform method or, if we are going to have a committee, we ought to have the same type of examination in relation to all State sponsored companies. While I am in full and complete sympathy with the idea behind this amendment, I would have to resist it going into this Bill. I am doing that in the full knowledge that the Government will have proposals to put before the Dáil in connection with what the Dáil has so frequently asked for over a number of years.

READING

B. Chubb: 'Public Control of Public Enterprise' in *Administration*, vol. 2.

G. Fitzgerald: *State-sponsored Bodies*, 2nd Edition (revised), Dublin, 1963.

S. F. Lemass: *The Role of the State-sponsored Bodies*, Dublin, 1959.

P. Lynch: 'Public Enterprise in a Free Economy' in *Administration*, vol. 2.

In addition, the volumes of *Administration* contain a large number of articles describing the work and organization of individual state-sponsored bodies. In the case of some of them, complete issues are devoted to them.

Appendix

STATE-SPONSORED BOARDS AND COMPANIES

Source: Garret Fitzgerald, *State-Sponsored Bodies*, 2nd edition (revised), 1963

PRODUCTION

1. Arramara Teo.
2. Board for the Employment of the Blind
3. Bord Iascaigh Mhara
4. Bord na Móna
5. Ceimici Teo.
6. Colucht Groighe Náisiunta na hEireann Teo.
7. Comhlucht Siúicre Eireann Teo.
8. Dairy Disposal Co.
   Subsidiaries:
   (i) Cleeves Confectionary (Limerick) Ltd.
   (ii) Condensed Milk Co. of Ireland (1928) Ltd.
   (iii) Newmarket Dairy Co.
9. Electricity Supply Board
10. Gaeltarra Eireann
11. Irish Steel Holdings Ltd.
12. Min-Fhéir (1959) Teo.
13. National Building Agency
14. Nitrigin Eireann Teo.

COMMUNICATIONS

1. Aer Rianta Teo.
2. Aer Lingus Teo.
3. Aerlinte Eireann Teo.
4. Coras Iompair Eireann
5. Ostlanna Iompair Teo.
6. Irish Shipping Ltd.
7. Radio Eireann

MARKETING

1. Bord Bainne
2. Bord Gráin
3. Cork District Milk Board
4. Dublin District Milk Board
5. Pigs and Bacon Commission

FINANCE

1. Agricultural Credit Corporation Ltd.
2. Central Bank of Ireland
3. Industrial Credit Co. Ltd.
4. Irish Film Finance Co. Ltd.
5. Shipping Finance Corporation Ltd.
6. Irish Life Assurance Co. Ltd.
7. Ilasco Subsidiary Ltd.
8. Irish Estates Ltd.

PROMOTION AND DEVELOPMENT

1. Inland Fisheries Trust Inc.
2. An Comhairle Ealaion
3. Bórd Fáilte Eireann
4. Coras Tráchtála Teo.
5. Shannon Free Airport Development Co. Ltd.

HEALTH

1. Dublin Rheumatism Clinic Association
2. St. Luke's Hospital
3. Voluntary Health Insurance Board
4. Bord Altranais
5. Bord na Radharc-mhastóiri
6. Comhlachas Náisiúnta um Thairmreith Fola
7. Dental Board
8. Hospitals Trust Board
9. Hospitals Commission
10. The Hospitals Library Council
11. Irish Red Cross Society
12. Medical Registration Council
13. Medical Research Council
14. National Mass Radiography Association
15. National Organization for Rehabilitation
16. Veterinary Council

RESEARCH

1. Foras Talúntais
2. Dublin Institute for Advanced Studies
3. Institute for Industrial Research and Standards
4. Salmon Research Trust of Ireland Inc.

OTHERS

1. Bord na gCon
2. Foyle Fisheries Commission
3. Racing Board

Chapter 11

THE COURTS AND THE LEGAL SYSTEM

INTRODUCTION

The common law and British legal institutions have been present in Ireland since the twelfth century, though, until the seventeenth century, their extent varied with the area of English influence. From that time, Irish legal institutions paralleled those in England, the close similarities being enhanced at first by the appointment of English judges to Ireland then by the close similarity in the training of the legal profession in the two countries. This parallelism was continued when the judiciary was reformed in the later nineteenth century, for the Supreme Court of Judicature Act, 1875, was closely followed by a very similar measure for Ireland (The Supreme Court of Judicature Act (Ireland), 1877), while reforms of court procedure were also similar in both countries. Moreover, appeals from the Irish courts lay ultimately to the House of Lords which was thus the apex of both systems. After a brief period in 1921 and 1922, when there was added a 'High Court of Appeal for Ireland', a sort of supreme court on the British Commonwealth model set up under the Government of Ireland Act, 1920, the whole system was carried over into the Irish Free State in 1922 with the substitution of the Judicial Committee of the Privy Council for the House of Lords. It bridged the gap until the courts envisaged in the Constitution of the Irish Free State were established in 1924.

Meanwhile, however, in 1919 a new and entirely different system of courts had come into existence. The first Dáil set up the machinery of a State and a Government with the full array of ministers and departments. Mostly these had but a shadowy existence, being intended as much for propaganda purposes as for administration. But in two fields particularly, local government and justice, the jurisdiction of Dáil Éireann was far from shadowy. Since the ordinary courts could only function where they were backed by military power and since a community must have law, the Dáil courts (which included parish, district and circuit courts and land settlement courts) were much used by all classes. (Document 11.1.) However, as we have seen, the new Irish Government took over the ordinary court system and it chose to retain this system. Accordingly, it wound up the Dáil courts, honouring their judgments and protecting the rights of those who had had recourse to them.

The Irish Free State Constitution provided for the setting up by law of a system of courts including a supreme court, and for appeal to the Privy Council in London in the manner then normal for the countries of the British Empire and Commonwealth. The independence of the Judiciary was enunciated and safeguarded so far as it is possible to do so by constitutional declarations. Further, the laws in force at the coming into operation of the Constitution were continued in force. (Document 11.2.) Following the recommendations of the Judiciary Committee, 1923, the Courts of Justice Act, 1924, provided for a new courts system, and though this system was not exactly the same as that inherited in 1922, no changes of basic principle were made. The Irish legal system still resembled the British quite closely. (Document 11.3.)

Amongst the constitutional changes carried out by the first Fianna Fáil Government in pursuance of its aim to remove objectionable links with Great Britain was the abolition of appeal from Irish courts to the Privy Council. This Act, the Constitution (Amendment no. 22) Act, 1933 (no. 45), was judged to be valid in English law under the provisions of the Statute of Westminster, 1931, by the Privy Council itself in *Moore* v. *Attorney General for the Irish Free State* [1935] A.C.484. The Irish court system was now, therefore, self-sufficient.

With this objective accomplished and since there was no dissatisfaction with the system set up under the 1924 Act, Mr de Valera saw no need to make changes when he came to prepare the new Constitution, Bunreacht na hÉireann. Accordingly, apart from the omission of any reference to the Privy Council and the inclusion of an oath, the provisions in Bunreacht na hÉireann for the setting up of courts and the appointment and tenure of judges resemble those of the Irish Free State Constitution quite closely. (Document 11.4.) One significant addition, however, is Article 37 which permits the exercise of limited functions and powers of a judicial nature by persons and bodies other than the regular courts, a provision which clearly envisages administrative tribunals (see chapter 12 below).

Until the new courts to be set up under Bunreacht na hÉireann were constituted by law, it was provided (under Article 58, one of the Transitory Provisions) that the courts in existence immediately before the coming into operation of the Constitution should continue to operate. Under this provision, the existing courts continued until as recently as 1961. It should be noticed, however, that though it continued to have legal effect, Article 58 disappeared from the official texts of the Constitution under the terms of another Transitory Provision, Article 52, which itself also disappeared. Consequently, the courts depended upon a provision not to be found in copies of the Constitution printed after 1941. Mention in the course of litigation in the 1950s was made of the fact that the courts then operating were not the courts envisaged in the Constitution, and arguments about the legality of this state of affairs were heard by the courts on a number of occasions. (Document 11.5.) In 1961, the Courts (Establishment and Constitution) Act established a new system of courts as envisaged in Article 34 of Bunreacht na hÉireann, but these are precisely the same as those which have been replaced. (Document 11.6.) At the same time, the Courts (Supplemental Provisions) Act, 1961 (no. 39), provided for the matters mentioned in Article 36, viz. the number of judges, their conditions of tenure, the distribution of jurisdiction and business, and matters of procedure.

It is beyond the scope of this work to discuss decided cases and the development of the body of Irish law. It should be noticed, however, that the new state not only took over a developed system of courts parallel to those of Great Britain, but inherited the body of United Kingdom law to which of course the Irish courts had made their contribution in the past. As Mr A. G. Donaldson has pointed out, ' the application of the doctrine of precedent and the citation of United Kingdom cases has so far prevented any radical alteration.' (*Some Comparative Aspects of Irish Law*, Durham N.C. and London, 1957, p. 35.)

DOCUMENTS

1. THE DAIL COURTS

    Document 11.1 — Extract from V. T. H. Delany, *The Administration of Justice in Ireland,* Institute of Public Administration, Dublin, 1962, pp. 38-40.

Part of the programme of the revolutionary Dáil during the period 1919-1921 involved the establishment of a system of ' courts,' designed to give colour to the theory of *de jure* sovereignty and, more important, to administer justice in those areas that the insurrectionary movement had deprived of the service of the ordinary courts. A decree of the republican government, dated June 29, 1920, established 'courts of justice and equity,' and also empowered the (republican) Ministry of Home Affairs to set up courts with criminal jurisdiction.

By September, 1920, the following judicial structure had been created: (a) 'Parish Courts,' consisting of three members, meeting once a week and dealing with small civil and criminal cases. (b) 'District Courts,' comprising five members, meeting once a month, and dealing with more important civil and criminal cases, or cases which came before them on appeal from the Parish Courts. In addition, there were three sessions during the years in which a 'circuit judge' presided over the District Court, which then became a 'Circuit Court,' with unlimited civil and criminal jurisdiction. There were four circuit judges and four circuit districts. (c) A 'Supreme Court' in Dublin, composed of not less than three members appointed for three years, functioning both as a court of first instance and as an appellate tribunal.

The legal system applicable in these courts was the law as it stood at January 2, 1919, save as amended by the Dáil. It was also provided that though British legal works were not to be used in argument, 'the early Irish law codes,' decisions of continental courts, and Roman law could be cited as persuasive authorities. The attitude of the legal profession to these arrangements was cautious. The Incorporated Law Society of Ireland considered a resolution aimed at preventing solicitors from appearing before Parish and District Courts, but the resolution was dropped. The General Council of the Bar of Ireland passed a resolution declaring it to be unprofessional for counsel to appear before the republican courts; but a general meeting of the Bar decided to take no action against counsel who ignored the resolution.

The civil authorities in Ireland, faced with the existence of this extensive system of what were regarded by them as illegal courts, were also embarrassed by the fact that the courts professed to be nothing more than arbitration tribunals. Their suppression was decided on, however, on the ground that they were functioning under the authority of a treasonable organisation, the First Dáil, and that this rendered them seditious assemblies. In the south and west of the country, however, the Dáil courts managed to function fairly regularly, and there were said to be over nine hundred Parish Courts and over seventy District Courts in operation by July, 1921.

When the Provisional Government took over the administration of what was to become the Irish Free State, under the terms of the Treaty, it found itself in possession of two separate systems of courts — these Dáil Courts, operating under the decrees of the revolutionary cabinet, and the Supreme Court of Judicature in Southern Ireland, the County Courts, and the Courts of Petty Sessions, all of which had been transferred to the new administration. The Government was thus faced with alternatives: it could either consolidate these Dáil Courts, or it could utilise the ordinary courts which had been handed over. The latter course was adopted. A decree of the 'cabinet of Dáil Éireann' — which was coextensive with the Provisional Government — abolished all the Dáil Courts, other than the District and Parish Courts, with effect from July 25, 1922. District and Parish Courts were abolished on October 26, 1922, by another decree, on the basis that 'the former British Courts were now in Irish hands.'

The ultimate fate of these tribunals is of interest. By the Dáil Éireann Courts (Winding Up) Act, 1923, the Parliament of the Irish Free State provided for the appointment of a Commissioner with wide powers to settle questions arising out of the judgments of the former Dáil Courts. The policy of this Act seems to have been to save their judgments, but it made clear that any validity those judgments might have was conferred, not recognised, by the Act. So far as the courts of the Irish Free State were concerned, the decrees of the Dáil Courts were regarded as being not only void, but also illegal; for there was no continuity, in law, between the courts of the revolution and those of the Irish Free State: *R. (Kelly) v. Maguire and O'Sheil* [1923] 2 I.R. 58.

The revolutionary Dáil had also established a 'Land Settlement Court' in 1920, aimed at carrying out re-settlement policies with respect to agricultural land. In 1924 an amending statute to the Dáil Éireann Courts (Winding-Up) Act, 1923, was passed, declaring that the decrees of this court were to be treated as arbitration awards which might be confirmed by the Irish Land Commission.

2. THE COURTS OF THE IRISH FREE STATE

(a) *Constitutional Provisions*
Document 11.2 — Extracts from *Constitution of the Irish Free State.*

Article 64
The judicial power of the Irish Free State (Saorstát Éireann) shall be exercised and justice administered in the public Courts established by the Oireachtas by judges appointed in manner hereinafter provided. These Courts shall comprise Courts of First Instance and a Court of Final Appeal to be called the Supreme Court. The Courts of First Instance shall include a High Court invested with full original jurisdiction in and power to determine all matters and questions whether of law or fact, civil or criminal, and also Courts of local and limited jurisdiction, with a right of appeal as determined by law.

Article 65
The judicial power of the High Court shall extend to the question of the validity of any law having regard to the provisions of the Constitution. In

all cases in which such matters shall come into question, the High Court alone shall exercise original jurisdiction.

Article 66

The Supreme Court of the Irish Free State (Saorstát Éireann) shall, with such exceptions (not including cases which involve questions as to the validity of any law) and subject to such regulations as may be prescribed by law, have appellate jurisdiction from all decisions of the High Court. The decision of the Supreme Court shall in all cases be final and conclusive, and shall not be reviewed or capable of being reviewed by any other Court, Tribunal or Authority whatsoever: Provided that nothing in this Constitution shall impair the right of any person to petition His Majesty for special leave to appeal from the Supreme Court to His Majesty in Council or the right of His Majesty to grant such leave.

Article 67

The number of judges, the constitution and organisation of, and distribution of business and jurisdiction among, the said Courts and judges, and all matters of procedure shall be as prescribed by the laws for the time being in force and the regulations made thereunder.

Article 68

The judges of the Supreme Court and of the High Court and of all other Courts established in pursuance of this Constitution shall be appointed by the Representative of the Crown on the advice of the Executive Council. The judges of the Supreme Court and of the High Court shall not be removed except for stated misbehaviour or incapacity, and then only by resolutions passed by both Dáil Éireann and Seanad Éireann. The age of retirement, the remuneration and the pension of such judges on retirement and the declarations to be taken by them on appointment shall be prescribed by law. Such remuneration may not be diminished during their continuance in office. The terms of appointment of the judges of such other courts as may be created shall be prescribed by law.

Article 69

All judges shall be independent in the exercise of their functions, and subject only to the Constitution and the law. A judge shall not be eligible to sit in the Oireachtas, and shall not hold any other office or position of emolument. [*Articles 70-72 omitted.*]

Article 73

Subject to this Constitution and to the extent to which they are not inconsistent therewith, the laws in force in the Irish Free State (Saorstát Éireann) at the date of the coming into operation of this Constitution shall continue to be of full force and effect until the same or any of them shall have been repealed or amended by enactment of the Oireachtas.

(b) *The System*

Document 11.3 — Extracts from V. T. H. Delany, *The Administration of Justice in Ireland*, pp. 42-4.

In order to implement these constitutional provisions, a Judiciary Committee was appointed on January 27, 1923, to advise the Executive Council as to the establishment of the new courts, and as to their jurisdiction. The committee was requested to approach these problems 'untrammelled by any regard to any of the existing systems of judicature' in the country, and the existing framework of law and justice was described as 'a standing monument of alien government.' These weighty matters were considered by the committee with commendable speed, for it was able to report on May 25, 1923, setting out the scheme which was to be enacted into law by the Courts of Justice Act, 1924.

The policy underlying this scheme appears to have been a recasting of the system of courts with a view to decentralising the administration of justice, but there was very little change in the principles involved. The following was the basis of the new judicial system:

(1) Petty Sessions were abolished and replaced by a unified District Court, presided over by a paid District Justice. The Justice of the Peace disappeared, but a new functionary, called a 'Peace Commissioner,' was created, to discharge the non-judicial functions, such as signing summonses, formerly carried out by the Justices. The jurisdiction of the criminal side of the District Court was still, in substance, that of summary jurisdiction for minor offences, together with the duty of the preliminary investigation of indictable offences. The civil jurisdiction was increased to £25 in contract and £10 in tort.

(2) County Courts were abolished, and, in their place, was set up a Circuit Court of Justice.' The State was divided into eight circuits, each under a circuit judge, and each representing about 400,000 people. The civil jurisdiction was to extend to £300 for debt or damages, with an equity jurisdiction up to £1,000. On the criminal side the Court could try all felonies and misdemeanours save murder, treason and piracy. It heard appeals from the Circuit Court. Appeals from the Circuit Court on the civil side went to the High Court, where they were heard by two judges on the written transcript of the proceedings in the lower Court. Criminal appeals went to the Court of Criminal Appeal mentioned below.

(3) The High Court of Justice consisted of six judges, one of whom, called the 'President of the High Court,' presided. This Court corresponded to the old High Court of Justice in Southern Ireland and had all the jurisdiction of that Court transferred to it. It also provided one of its number to preside at the 'Central Criminal Court' in Dublin, an extension of the old Dublin City Commission, where all serious crime from the country was to be tried.

(4) The Supreme Court of Justice was composed of three judges, one of whom was the Chief Justice of the Irish Free State. It had all the appellate jurisdiction of the old Court of Appeal, together with that prescribed by the

Constitution. The functions of the Lord Chancellor in connection with wards of court, lunatics, and the discipline of solicitors were transferred to the Chief Justice.

(5) A Court of Criminal Appeal was established, consisting of three judges, one of whom was to be the Chief Justice or a judge of the Supreme Court, the others being members of the High Court, and in special cases the Chief Justice could request additional judges of the Supreme Court or the High Court to sit. This Court corresponded to the Court of Criminal Appeal set up in England, under the Criminal Appeal Act, 1907. Its decision was final, unless the Attorney-General certified that the case involved a point of exceptional public importance, when a further appeal could be taken to the Supreme Court.

(6) Provision was also made in the Act of 1924 for the setting up of a 'Court of the High Court Circuit,' and it seems to have been contemplated that a tribunal similar to the old Court of Assize would travel through the country for the purpose of hearing criminal cases within the jurisdiction of the High Court. This was to supplement the Central Criminal Court in Dublin. This plan was never put into operation and the provisions were repealed in 1926.

These courts set up under the Courts of Justice Act, 1924, continued to operate in the Irish Free State until that political entity ceased to exist in 1937. Minor changes were carried in, but the main framework remained unchanged. A joint committee of both Houses of the Oireachtas set up to consider the working of the new courts reported in 1930 and, as a result, certain alterations were made. The strength of the Supreme Court was increased to five judges; the system of appeals from the Circuit Court was abolished and replaced by an appeal to a judge of the High Court, travelling on circuit, by way of re-hearing; the jurisdiction of the Chief Justice over wards of court and lunatics was transferred to the President of the High Court; and certain other minor amendments were carried in (Courts of Justice Act, 1936). Earlier, the Court of Criminal Appeal had been empowered to direct a re-trial in certain cases, a power not possessed by the corresponding court in England: Courts of Justice Act, 1928.

3. THE COURTS SINCE 1937

(a) *Constitutional Provisions*

Document 11.4 — Extracts from *Bunreacht na hÉireann* (*Constitution of Ireland*), as enacted by the People, 1938 (i.e. including the transitory provisions (Articles 50 ff.) subsequently omitted from official text).

Article 34

1. Justice shall be administered in public courts established by law by judges appointed in the manner provided by this Constitution.

2. The Courts shall comprise Courts of First Instance and a Court of Final Appeal.

3. 1° The Courts of First Instance shall include a High Court invested with full original jurisdiction in and power to determine all matters and questions whether of law or fact, civil or criminal.

2° The jurisdiction of the High Court shall extend to the question of the validity of any law having regard to the provisions of this Constitution, and in all cases in which any such matter shall come into question the High Court alone shall exercise original jurisdiction.

3° The Courts of First Instance shall also include Courts of local and limited jurisdiction with a right of appeal as determined by law.

4. 1° The Court of Final Appeal shall be called the Supreme Court.

2° The president of the Supreme Court shall be called the Chief Justice.

3° The Supreme Court shall, with such exceptions and subject to such regulations as may be prescribed by law, have appellate jurisdiction from all decisions of the High Court and shall also have appellate jurisdiction from such decisions of other courts as may be prescribed by law.

4° No law shall be enacted excepting from the appellate jurisdiction of the Supreme Court cases which involve questions as to the validity of any law having regard to the provisions of this Constitution.

5° The decision of the Supreme Court shall in all cases be final and conclusive.

5. 1° Every person appointed a judge under this Constitution shall make and subscribe the following declaration:

"In the presence of Almighty God I

do solemnly and sincerely promise and declare that I will duly and faithfully and to the best of my knowledge and power execute the office of Chief Justice (*or as the case may be*) without fear or favour, affection or ill-will towards any man, and that I will uphold the Constitution and the laws. May God direct and sustain me."

[*SSs. 2°-4° omitted.*]

Article 35

1. The judges of the Supreme Court, the High Court and all other Courts established in pursuance of Article 34 hereof shall be appointed by the President.

2. All judges shall be independent in the exercise of their judicial functions and subject only to this Constitution and the law.

3. No judge shall be eligible to be a member of either House of the Oireachtas or to hold any other office or position of emolument.

4.   1° A judge of the Supreme Court or the High Court shall not be removed from office except for stated misbehaviour or incapacity, and then only upon resolutions passed by Dáil Éireann and by Seanad Éireann calling for his removal. [*SSs. 2° and 3° omitted.*]

Article 36

Subject to the foregoing provisions of this Constitution relating to the Courts, the following matters shall be regulated in accordance with law, that is to say: —

i. the number of judges of the Supreme Court, and of the High Court, the remuneration, age of retirement and pensions of such judges,

ii. the number of the judges of all other Courts, and their terms of appointment, and

iii. the constitution and organization of the said Courts, the distribution of jurisdiction and business among the said Courts and judges, and all matters of procedure.

Article 37

Nothing in this Constitution shall operate to invalidate the exercise of limited functions and powers of a judicial nature, in matters other than criminal matters, by any person or body of persons duly authorised by law to exercise such functions and powers, notwithstanding that such person or such body of persons is not a judge or a court appointed or established as such under this Constitution. [*Articles 38-57 omitted.*]

Article 58

1.   On and after the coming into operation of this Constitution and until otherwise determined by law, the Supreme Court of Justice, the High Court of Justice, the Circuit Court of Justice and the District Court of Justice in existence immediately before the coming into operation of this Constitution shall, subject to the provisions of this Constitution relating to the determination of questions as to the validity of any law, continue to exercise the same jurisdictions respectively as theretofore, and any judge or justice being a member of any such Court shall, subject to compliance with the subsequent provisions of the Article, continue to be a member thereof and shall hold office by the like tenure and on the like terms as theretofore unless he signifies to the Taoiseach his desire to resign.

2.   Every such judge and justice who shall not have so signified his desire to resign shall make and subscribe the declaration set forth in section 5 of Article 34 of this Constitution.

3.   This declaration shall be made and subscribed by the Chief Justice in the presence of the Taoiseach, and by each of the other judges of the said Supreme Court, the judges of the said High Court and the judges of the said Circuit Court in the presence of the Chief Justice in open court.

4.   In the case of the justices of the said District Court the declaration shall be made and subscribed in open court.

5.   Every such declaration shall be made immediately upon the coming into operation of this Constitution, or as soon as may be thereafter.

6.   Any such judge or justice who declines or neglects to make such declaration in the manner aforesaid shall be deemed to have vacated his office.

(b) *Failure to Establish New Courts Occasions Doubts and Comment*
    Document 11.5 — Extracts from The State (Killian) v. The Minister for Justice and The Governor of Portlaoighaise Prison [1954] I.R. 207 (Murnaghan J.).

The ground upon which the present application is made is stated in para. 6 of the application and is as follows:— "I say that the said Judge J. A. McCarthy was appointed a Judge of the Circuit Court of Justice subsequent to the enactment and coming into operation of the Constitution of Ireland on the 29th December, 1937, but I say that the said Judge J. A. McCarthy was not appointed in the manner provided by Articles 34 and 35 of the Constitution or otherwise under the Constitution, or at all, and that his appointment was, has been at all material times, and is, irregular, unconstitutional, *ultra vires* and void." . . .

The principal argument relied upon in support of the application was that there was at the date of this appointment no power to fill any such vacancy. It is contended by Mr. Sheehan [Senior Counsel] that Article 34 contemplated the establishment by the Oireachtas of Courts and this contention seems to be quite correct. Article 35 reads:— "The Judges of the Supreme Court, the High Court and all other Courts established in pursuance of Article 34 hereof shall be appointed by the President." On this Article it is contended that the appointments to be made by the President under this Article are appointments of judges in the Constitutional Courts envisaged by Article 34. This submission appears likewise to be correct. The argument rightly proceeds on the view that the Courts at present existing are given force and authority by one of the transitory provisions of Article 58 which reads as follows: — "1. On and after the coming into operation of this Constitution and until otherwise determined by law, the Supreme Court of Justice, the High Court of Justice, the Circuit Court of Justice and the District Court of Justice in existence immediately before the coming into operation of this Constitution shall, subject to the provisions of this Constitution relating to the determination of questions as to the validity of any law, continue to exercise the same jurisdiction respectively as theretofore, and any judge or justice being a member of any such Court shall, subject to compliance with the subsequent provisions of this Article, continue to be a member thereof and shall hold office by the like tenure and on the like terms as theretofore unless he signifies to the Taoiseach his desire to resign." . . .

But Mr. Sheehan, without apparent foundation, asserts that it was the intention of the makers of the Constitution that vacancies in the Courts so continued either arising from failure to make the prescribed declaration, or from retirement owing to age limit, or by resignation or death were not to be filled; and he contends that there was no power to fill any such vacancy. First he contends that it was intended that Courts should be set up under Article 34 after a very short interval of time. Whatever may have been the hope at the time the Courts are by the express terms of Article 58 continued "until otherwise determined by law." No law has as yet otherwise so determined and it is manifest that the Courts can and do at the present moment exercise the same jurisdiction subject as in Article 58 as they did before the 29th December, 1937, the date of coming into operation of the Constitution.

(c) *New Courts Established*
> Document 11.6 — Extracts from Courts (Establishment and Constitution) Act, 1961 (no. 38).

SUPREME COURT

1.—(1) On the commencement of this Act, the Court of Final Appeal, which in pursuance of Article 34 of the Constitution is to be called An Chúirt Uachtarach (The Supreme Court), shall stand established.

(2) The Supreme Court shall be constituted of the following judges—

   (*a*) the president thereof, namely, An Príomh-Bhreitheamh (The Chief Justice), and

   (*b*) such number (not being less than four) of ordinary judges (each of whom shall be styled "Breitheamh den Chúirt Uachtarach" ("Judge of the Supreme Court") as may from time to time be fixed by Act of the Oireachtas.

(3) The President of the High Court shall be *ex officio* an additional judge of the Supreme Court. [*SS. 4 omitted.*]

HIGH COURT

2.—(1) On the commencement of this Act, the Court of First Instance referred to in Article 34 of the Constitution as An Ard Chúirt (The High Court) shall stand established.

(2) The High Court shall be constituted of the following judges—

   (*a*) the president thereof, who shall be styled "Uachtarán na hArd-Chúirte" ("The President of the High Court"), and

(b) such number of ordinary judges (each of whom shall be styled "Breitheamh den Ard-Chúirt" ("Judge of the High Court") as may from time to time be fixed by Act of the Oireachtas.

(3) The Chief Justice shall be *ex officio* an additional judge of the High Court.

(4) The President of the Circuit Court shall be *ex officio* an additional judge of the High Court. [*SS. 5 omitted.*]

COURT OF CRIMINAL APPEAL

3.—(1) On the commencement of this Act, a Court of Appeal, which shall be called An Chúirt Achomhairc Choiriúil (The Court of Criminal Appeal), shall stand established.

(2) For the purpose of hearing and determing any particular appeal cognisable by the Court of Criminal Appeal, the Court of Criminal Appeal shall be summoned in accordance with directions to be given by the Chief Justice, and the Court shall be duly constituted if it consists of not less than three judges—

> (a) of whom one shall be either—
>> (i) the Chief Justice, or
>>
>> (ii) an ordinary judge of the Supreme Court nominated by the Chief Justice, and
>
> (b) of whom the other two shall be either—
>> (i) two ordinary judges of the High Court nominated by the Chief Justice, or
>>
>> (ii) the President of the High Court, if nominated by the Chief Justice and willing to act, and one ordinary judge of the High Court nominated by the Chief Justice.

but any other available judge or judges of the Supreme Court or the High Court may, at the request of the Chief Justice, attend as a member or members of the Court.

CIRCUIT COURT

4.—(1) On the commencement of this Act, a Court of First Instance, which shall be called An Chúirt Chuarda (The Circuit Court) shall stand established.

(2) The Circuit Court shall be constituted of the following judges—

> (a) a judge, who shall be styled "Uachtarán na Cúirte Cuarda" ("The President of the Circuit Court"), and
>
> (b) such number of ordinary judges (each of whom shall be styled "Breitheamh den Chúirt Chuarda" ("Judge of the Circuit Court") as may from time to time be fixed by Act of the Oireachtas.

DISTRICT COURT

5.—(1) On the commencement of this Act, a Court of First Instance, which shall be called An Chúirt Dúiche (The District Court), shall stand established.

(2) The District Court shall be constituted of the following judges—

 (*a*) a judge who shall be styled "Uachtarán na Cúirte Dúiche" ("The President of the District Court"), and

 (*b*) such number of other judges (each of whom shall be styled "Breitheamh den Chúirt Dúiche" ("Justice of the District Court") as may from time to time be fixed by Act of the Oireachtas.

VACATION AND FILLING OF JUDICIAL OFFICE

6.—(1) In this section, the expression "judicial office" means an office being—

 (*a*) the office of Chief Justice, President of the High Court, ordinary judge of the Supreme Court, ordinary judge of the High Court, President of the Circuit Court or ordinary judge of the Circuit Court, or

 (*b*) the office of President of the District Court or justice of the District Court.

(2) A judicial office held by any person may be vacated by resignation in writing under his hand addressed to the President and transmitted to the Taoiseach.

(3) A judicial office held by any person shall be vacated by his being appointed, with his consent, to another judicial office.

(4) The office held by each person who, immediately before the commencement of this Act, was a judge or justice of any of the courts of justice mentioned in Article 58 of the Constitution shall be vacated by his being appointed, with his consent, to a judicial office. [*SSs. 5-7 omitted.*]

EXISTING COURTS ABOLISHED

7.—(1) In this section, the expression "the existing courts" means the several courts of justice mentioned in Article 58 of the Constitution.

(2) The existing courts shall, on the commencement of this Act, cease to exercise any jurisdiction.

(3) When every person who immediately before the commencement of this Act held the office of judge or justice of any of the existing courts has vacated that office—

 (*a*) the existing courts shall cease to be established,

 (*b*) every such office shall stand abolished.

[*Remainder omitted.*]

READING

V. T. H. Delany: *The Administration of Justice in Ireland*, Dublin, 1962.
A. G. Donaldson: *Some Comparative Aspects of Irish Law*, Durham N.C. and London, 1957.

Chapter 12

ADMINISTRATIVE POWERS

INTRODUCTION

Bunreacht na hÉireann is couched in traditional terms and in a number of places it conventionally enunciates a division of powers. Nevertheless, a division of functions and powers strictly on conventional lines does not, and could not, obtain in Ireland. As everywhere else, the development of the welfare state 'has given rise, on the one hand, to an increasing delegation of law-making powers to the Executive, and, on the other, to the conferring of functions of adjudication upon the Executive itself or upon agencies responsible to it or directly or indirectly under its control.' (Vincent Grogan, *Administrative Tribunals in the Public Service*, p. 45.) Although Article 15.2.1° of the Constitution states that no authority other than the Oireachtas has power 'to make laws for the State', legal rules which in normal speech we refer to in bulk as 'delegated legislation' and individually as 'statutory instruments', are every day made by the Government, by ministers, either singly or jointly, and by many other public authorities endowed with statutory powers so to do. (Documents 12.1 and 12.2).

Such a body of law presents a considerable constitutional problem. Normally we think of the courts as the great safeguard of the citizen, but if the Oireachtas specifically gives ministers and others powers to make law, the courts tend to be restricted to ensuring that the rule-maker is within his powers and that he has made no errors of procedure. 'The true constitutional problem presented by delegated legislation', as Professor H. W. R. Wade has said, is 'that its enormous growth has made it difficult for Parliament to watch over it'. In order to ensure that a necessary minimum of formality will attend the making of this type of law, we have the Statutory Instruments Act, 1947, which makes provision for the presentation of instruments to the Oireachtas; for a period of twenty-one sitting days during which members can move to annul; and for publication and deposit in certain libraries. (Document 12.1)

361

However, these requirements do not go very far and, as was the case in Great Britain also, the real problem was to devise more direct and efficient methods by which Parliament could in fact scrutinize this flow of legislation and sieve out *prima facie* objectionable items for further enquiry. In 1944, the British House of Commons set up a Select Committee on Statutory Rules and Orders (later called the Select Committee on Statutory Instruments) and, in 1948, Seanad Éireann followed suit with a committee with similar terms of reference and powers. It is this committee, since 1954 known as the Select Committee on Statutory Instruments (as is the British one), which has had, in the words of Senator Luke Duffy, who proposed it, 'the function of preventing abuses creeping in'. (Document 12.3).

As Griffith and Street say of the British Committee in their *Principles of Administrative Law*, 'the value and importance of the work are undeniable. The very existence of the Committee must prevent more short-comings than the Committee detect.' What they do detect in Ireland is illustrated below. (Documents 12.4 to 12.10) The evidence provided by the series of reports which have appeared suggests that some administrative faults are not easily prevented. Although a report of the Committee in 1961 mentioned 'a praiseworthy effort by instrument-making authorities to conform with the standards formulated by Statutory Instruments Committees over the years', it nevertheless recorded that of the 501 instruments it had examined, 42 (8 per cent) had to be reported to the Seanad for one reason or another. Of these, 22 (4 per cent of the total examined) were obscure and needed elucidation, and in the case of 10 (2 per cent), there was unjustifiable delay in laying or publishing. That continuous vigilance by the Committee is necessary seems clear enough from this evidence alone. It becomes clear beyond doubt when one reads the following answer which the Secretary of a Department gave to the Committee some years ago to explain why an order had been drafted to give wholesale powers, though he could not conceive (he said) of the Department using them:

> the difficulty is that if we try to enumerate specifically the various categories, that enumeration might not be exhaustive . . . we have found in our experience that when one commences to refine in order to specify aims in greater detail, one is very often placed in difficulty.

The road to bureaucracy is paved with just well-intentioned orders couched in just such convenient terms to avoid a Department being 'placed in difficulty'.

The device of delegated legislation is necessary to produce the complicated services of the welfare state. These give rise to innumerable rights and duties, and they in turn produce disputes. The resolution of these disputes has necessitated the creation of adjudication authorities, both persons and bodies, which are not part of the system of the ordinary courts of the land, but which are, on the contrary, connected with, or which seem to be connected with, the Government or Administration. Bodies exercising such functions are, indeed, usually known as 'administrative tribunals', and this term has also often been stretched to cover persons exercising similar functions. (Document 12.11)

In his book *Administrative Tribunals in the Public Service*, Mr Vincent Grogan surveyed about eighty such 'tribunals' endowed with judicial powers. These included, first, powers given to Ministers to decide issues (i) between the state and private interests, (ii) between local authorities and private interests, (iii) between two local authorities in dispute, and (iv) between private parties in dispute, together with appellate powers of various kinds. They included, secondly, powers vested in 'departmental tribunals' i.e. designated officers of departments; and, thirdly, powers given to tribunals the members of which are not officers of the departments responsible for the administration of the legislation concerned, but who are appointed by the Government or a Minister. Some examples of these administrative powers of adjudication are given below (Document 12.12 to 12.14).

The Committee on Tribunals and Enquiries (the Franks Committee), in Great Britain, concluded that 'despite the haphazard way in which they have developed, this method of decision by tribunals works on the whole reasonably well', and such a conclusion seems justified in Ireland too. But that Committee enunciated important principles which also have as much relevance here as they have in Britain:

> Administration must not only be efficient in the sense that the objectives of policy are securely attained without delay. It must also satisfy the general body of citizens that it is proceeding with reasonable regard to the balance between the public interest which it promotes and the private interest which it disturbs. Parliament has, we infer, intended in relation to the subject-matter of our terms of reference that the further decisions or, as they might rightly be termed in this context, adjudications must be acceptable as having been properly made . . .
> When we regard our subject in this light, it is clear that there are certain general and closely linked characteristics which should mark

these special procedures. We call these characteristics openness, fairness and impartiality.

Further, the specific matters to which the Franks Committee drew attention also merit attention here. These include such matters as methods of appointment and personnel. They include, too, attention to rules of operation and procedure in order to ensure that everyone has full knowledge of the case he has to meet; that both parties to a dispute should be heard; that proceedings should be in public except for some good reason; that proper records should be kept; that reasons should be given for decisions; and that there should be adequate right of appeal.

Above all, perhaps, there is the danger that the Government and public servants might come to regard such tribunals as 'appendages of Government Departments'. 'Much of the official evidence', said the Franks Committee, 'appeared to reflect the view that tribunals should properly be regarded as part of the machinery of administration, for which the Government must retain a close and continuing responsibility . . . We do not accept this view. We consider that tribunals should properly be regarded as machinery provided by Parliament for adjudication rather than as part of the machinery of administration.' As Document 12.15 shows, the Irish courts at least are concerned to make this point quite clear too.

DOCUMENTS

1. DELEGATED LEGISLATION
   (a) *The Constitution and the Statutory Instruments Act,* 1947
   Document 12.1—Extract from Paul Jackson, 'Delegated Legislation in Ireland' in *Public Law,* 1962, pp. 418-22.

Note—The footnotes in this extract are all Mr Jackson's—Editor.

THE CONSTITUTION AND DELEGATED LEGISLATION

To speak of delegated legislation, except as a convenient name for ministerial and other administrative regulations, orders, schemes, rules, etc., is, in the light of the 1937 Constitution, a complete misnomer. Article 15.2.1° provides:

"The sole and exclusive power of making law for the state is hereby vested in the Oireachtas: no other legislative authority has power to make laws for the state."

Article 15.2.2° provides:

"Provision may, however, be made by law for the creation or recognition of subordinate legislatures and for the powers and functions of these legislatures."

No such legislatures have, as yet, been established. Therefore in this connection the only relevant provision is Article 15.2.1°. Hence when a Minister, the Government or any administrative body makes rules or issues regulations the question is whether this is "making law for the state." In Ireland, as in America, and unlike, to a large degree, in England, the definition of legislation is of practical importance and not merely academic interest. The Irish courts, like the American, have had to decide what is legislation. Various criteria have been proposed by writers[1]:

    (1) the authority making the rule;

    (2) the generality of the rule;

    (3) whether the rule affects private rights.

The first test is circular at best, and in the Irish context positively valueless, for since only the Oireachtas makes law, any regulation made by a Minister cannot be law and thus by definition cannot offend Article 15.2.1°.

The third test[2] has certain attractions: by using it de Smith, for example, explains why concessions by the revenue authorities are not legislation, while a Finance Act which affects legal rights is. But this test surely would include a ministerial order relating to, say, one particular house. Although such an order clearly affects legal rights, such a regulation is not usually regarded as legislation. It is precisely this type of order which is said to be the obstacle to the second test. An Act of Parliament, however specific,[3] is legislation. Is not the answer that in determining what is, or is not, legislation it is necessary to look not at the scope of the actual ordinance, but at the power of the rule-making authority? Thus, a rule made by Parliament or the Oireachtas is legislation, however specific, because of the extremely wide powers of these bodies. But a ministerial regulation is not legislation if the Minister's discretion is hedged about. This approach seems to accord with the established use of the word "legislation," and with the case law.[4] The leading Irish case is *Pig Marketing Board* v. *Donnelly (Dublin), Ltd.*[5] The Pigs and Bacon Acts, 1935 and 1937, established a board which had the power to fix a "hypothetical price" for bacon. It also fixed an "appointed price." When the latter was

---

1. Griffith and Street, *Principles of Administrative Law*, 2nd ed., pp. 50-51.
2. De Smith, *Judicial Review of Administrative Action*, p. 33; Gordon, 49 L.Q.R. 94, 112.
3. The Committee on Ministers' Powers (Cmd. 4060) cites as an example of such legislation the Act of 1530 providing for the boiling alive of the Bishop of Rochester's cook. For a more modern (and more humane) example see Charles Beattie Indemnity Act, 1956 (4 & 5 Eliz. 2, c. 27).
4. The American courts have dealt with this problem in the two leading cases of *Schechter Poultry Corporation* v. *U.S.* (1935) 295 U.S. 495 (cited in *Donnelly's Case*, 1939 I.R. 413) and *Yakus* v. *U.S.* (1943) 321 U.S. 414, 88 L.Ed. 834.
5. *Supra*, note.

lower than the former the difference was payable to the board by the purchaser. On being sued for payment of such a sum the defendants claimed that the Pigs and Bacon Acts infringed the provision of the Constitution, prohibiting the delegation of legislative powers. Hanna J. held that the Acts were valid.[6] "The legislature has directed them to fix, not any price, but the price which, in their opinion, would be the proper price under normal conditions. That is a statutory direction. It is a matter of such detail and upon which such expert knowledge is necessarily required, that the legislature, being unable to fix such a price itself, is entitled to say, 'We shall leave this to a body of experts in the trade who shall in the first place determine what the normal conditions in the trade would be apart from the abnormal conditions prescribed by the statute, and then form an opinion as to what the proper price in pounds, shillings and pence would be under such normal conditions.' The Pig Marketing Board, in doing so, is not making a new law: it is giving effect to the statutory provisions as to how they should determine that price."[7] Earlier in his judgment the learned judge pointed out with reference to this type of body "such bodies are not law makers; they put into execution the law as made by the governing authority and strictly in pursuance therewith, so as to bring about, not their own views, but the result directed by the Government."[8]

In so far as Hanna J. did not accept the source of the rule as determining whether it was legislation or not, the Irish courts have rejected the first of the three criteria mentioned above. Rather does the second criterion seem acceptable— as it was ultimately to the U.S. Supreme Court in *Yakus* v. *U.S.*[9] The court said: "The essentials of the legislative functions are the determination of the legislative policy and its formulation and promulgation as a defined and binding rule of conduct . . . These essentials are satisfied when Congress has specified the basic conditions of fact upon whose existence or occurrence . . . it directs that its statutory command shall be effective . . . what matters is not the breadth of the definition of the facts upon which the officer is to take action but upon the determination whether the definition sufficiently marks the field within which he is to act so that the court can tell whether he has kept within it in compliance with the legislative will."

STATUTORY INSTRUMENTS ACT, 1947

By the Statutory Instruments Act, 1947,[10] "Statutory Instrument" is defined as meaning "an order, regulation, rule, scheme or by-law made in exercise of a power conferred by statute."[11]

---

6. A judgment interesting for the almost complete abdication of any powers of judicial review of legislation for infringement of rights guaranteed by the Constitution.
7. [1939] I.R. 413, 422.
8. [1939] I.R. 413, 421.
9. (1943) 321 U.S. 414, 88 L.Ed. 834 at p. 838.
10. No. 44 of 1947.
11. s.1(1).

This comprehensive definition has the merit of not making the question whether a ministerial regulation is a Statutory Instrument or not depend on the wording of the statute under which the Minister acts—a danger not avoided by the English statute, which provides that a document is only a Statutory Instrument if made under a power "expressed

    (*a*) in the case of a power conferred on Her Majesty to be exercisable by Order in Council;

    (*b*) in the case of a power conferred on a Minister of the Crown to be exercisable by Statutory Instrument."[12]

Thus whether the safeguards of the Act are applicable in any given case is made to depend on the draftsman's choice of phraseology in the enabling statute.

The generality of the Irish definition has the second merit that it avoids the need for tortuous and lengthy reasoning before determining whether documents made under pre-1948 Acts are Statutory Instruments.[13]

The Irish Act does, however, distinguish between Statutory Instruments made before January 1, 1948, and those made after that date.[14] Statutory Instruments are divided into two types: those to which the Act primarily applies, in which case the provisions of the Act must be complied with unless exempted under section 2, and secondly, other instruments, in which case the provisions *may* apply.[15]

For a Statutory Instrument to fall in the former class it must satisfy four requirements:

(1) Have been made on or after 1.1.48;

(2) by (a) President;

     (b) Government[16];

     (c) any member of the Government;

     (d) any Parliamentary Secretary;

     (e) any person or body whether corporate or unincorporate exercising throughout the state any functions of government or discharging throughout the state any public duties in relation to public administration[17];

     (f) any authority having for the time being power to make rules of court;

(3) and is either

     (a) required by statute to be laid before both or either of the Houses of the Oireachtas, or

---

12. Statutory Instruments Act, 1946, s.1(1).
13. See *Griffith and Street*, p. 45, for difficulties of English law.
14. The English distinction is based on date of enabling Act, not date of making of instrument.
15. s.2(1). Dáil Debates, Vol. 109, col. 278.
16. *i.e.*, the Irish Cabinet Act 28 of Irish Constitution.
17. Any question as to whether a body falls within this section is to be settled by Att.-Gen.'s Certificate—s. 2 (1).

(b) is of such a character as affects the public generally or any particular class or classes of the public;

(4) is not a Statutory Instrument which is required by statute to be published in the Iris Oifigiúil.

The Attorney-General is given power to exempt from the provisions of the Act a particular instrument of a type or class on the grounds that it is only of local or personal or temporary application or for any reason.[18] This last ground of exemption is so vague as to give a virtually unfettered discretion to the Attorney-General—a deplorable provision in an Act aimed at providing certain and clear publicity of delegated legislation.

Publicity is ensured by providing that within seven days of its being made, a copy of each Statutory Instrument must be sent to ten listed libraries.[19] Curiously, the list does not include any library of either House of the Oireachtas. Each Statutory Instrument must be printed as soon as possible after being made and notice given of making and the place where copies may be obtained.[20] The Irish statute, no more than the English, deals with the effect of failure to publish. Indeed, it expressly preserves uncertainty by providing: "Nothing in this section shall affect any enactment or rule of law relating to the time at which any Statutory Instrument comes into effect.[21]

In criminal cases, as in England, non-publication is made a defence, unless the prosecutor can prove reasonable steps had been taken to bring the Statutory Instrument to the notice of the public or persons likely to be affected.[22] But whereas under the English statute the prisoner must prove non-publication before the Crown need assume the burden of proving that it took other steps to bring the instrument to the notice of persons affected, the Irish statute places the burden of proving publication on the prosecution. For this the Senate must take the credit. The original Bill required the prisoner to prove non-publication; the Minister admitted that he "resisted" the proposed change "for a long time."[23]

The Irish Act differs from its English counterpart in not establishing a uniform period for laying instruments before both Houses. In practice in the case of instruments laid subject to annulment most statutes follow the provisions of the Local Government (Sanitary Services) Act, 1948,[24] which provides for a period of twenty-one sitting days.

---

18. s.2(3), (4). By s.2(5) a notice of such exemption must be published in Iris Oifigiuil; for a discussion of the constitutional validity of these provisions see Dail Debates, Vol. 109, col. 275; Senate Debates, Vol. 34, col. 1481.
19. s.3(1). As to antecedent publicity see Dáil Debates, Vol. 109, col. 269.
20. S.I. (Amendment) Act, 1955.
21. s.3(3). For the allied question of the effect of failure to lay see under Parliamentary Control.
22. s.3(3).
23. Senate Debates, Vol. 34, cols. 1492 and 1517; Dáil Debates, Vol. 109, col. 861.
24. No. 3 of 1948, s.7. Instruments requiring positive resolutions are rare, Donaldson, *op. cit.*, p. 188.

(b) *Example of a Statutory Instrument*

Document 12.2—The Office Premises (Overcrowding) Regulations, S.I. No. 30 of 1959, in *Statutory Instruments,* 1959, vol. 1.

S.I. No. 30 of 1959

OFFICE PREMISES (OVERCROWDING) REGULATIONS

1959

I, SEAN F. LEMASS, Minister for Industry and Commerce, in exercise of the powers conferred on me by subsection (2) of section 9 of the Office Premises Act, 1958 (No. 3 of 1958), after consultation with the Minister for Health and having referred the proposals to which effect is given by the following regulations to the Advisory Council, hereby make the following regulations:

1. (1) These Regulations may be cited as the Office Premises (Overcrowding) Regulations, 1959.

(2) These Regulations shall come into operation on the 1st day of September, 1959.

2. For the purposes of subsection (2) of section 9 of the Office Premises Act, 1958 (No. 3 of 1958), fifty square feet shall be the minimum amount of floor space allowed for every person employed in any room.

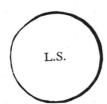

GIVEN under my Official Seal, this 28th day of February, 1959.

L.S.

(Signed) SEAN F. LEMASS, Minister for Industry and Commerce.

EXPLANATORY NOTE

(This note is not part of the Instrument and does not purport to be a legal interpretation.)

The purpose of this Order is to prescribe a minimum floor space for workers in offices.

Notice of the making of this Statutory Instrument was published in " Iris Oifigiúil " of 6th March, 1959.

(c) *Seanad Select Committee on Statutory Instruments*

(i) Terms of reference

Document 12.3—Extract from *First Report of the Select Committee on Statutory Instruments appointed 4 July 1957* (T.162), 16 July 1958.

ORDER OF REFERENCE

4th July, 1957:—*Resolved*: (1) That a Select Committee, to be nominated by the Committee of Selection, be appointed to consider every Statutory Instrument laid, or laid in draft, before Seanad Éireann, in pursuance of statutory requirement with a view to determining whether the special attention of Seanad Éireann, should be drawn to it on any of the following grounds : —

(i) that it imposes a charge on the public revenues or contains provisions requiring payments to be made to the Exchequer or any Government Department or to any local or public authority in consideration of any licence or consent, or of any services to be rendered, or prescribes the amount of any such charge or payments;

(ii) that it is made in pursuance of any enactment containing specific provisions excluding it from challenge in the Courts either at all times or after the expiration of a specified period;

(iii) that it appears to make some unusual or unexpected use of the powers conferred by the Statute under which it is made;

(iv) that it purports to have retrospective effect where the parent Statute confers no express authority so to provide;

(v) that there appears to have been unjustifiable delay either in the laying of it before Seanad Éireann or in its publication;

(vi) that for any special reason its form or purport calls for elucidation.

(2) That the Select Committee consist of nine members of whom three shall form a quorum.

(3) That the Select Committee have power to report from time to time and to require any Government Department concerned to submit a memorandum explaining any Statutory Instrument which may be under their consideration or to depute a representative to appear before them as a witness for the purpose of explaining any such Statutory Instrument.

(4) That it be the duty of the Committee before reporting that the special attention of Seanad Éireann should be drawn to any Statutory Instrument to afford to any Government Department concerned therewith an opportunity of furnishing orally or in writing such explanations as the Department may think fit and the Select Committee have power to report to Seanad Éireann, from time to time, any memoranda submitted or other evidence given to them by any Government Department in explanation of any Statutory Instrument [*Senator O'Brien*].

(ii) Examples of Matters Referred to in Reports

(1) *Instrument imposes a charge*

Document 12.4—Paragraph 6 of *First Report of the Select Committee on Statutory Instruments appointed* 4 *July* 1957, (T.162) 16 July 1958.

6. On ground (i), viz. " that it imposes a charge on the public revenues or contains provisions requiring payments to be made to the Exchequer or any

Government Department or to any local or public authority in consideration of any licence or consent, or of any services to be rendered, or prescribes the amount of any such charge or payments ", the special attention of Seanad Éireann is drawn to the following instrument : —

> Newspapers (Special Service for Conveyance by Post Office Mail Vans) Warrant, 1957 [S.I. No. 37 of 1957].

This warrant, which authorises the conveyance of bundles of newly published daily newspapers by Post Office mail vans on rural services and fixes the scale of charges therefor, was made under the authority of the Post Office Act, 1908. It will be noted from the minute submitted by the Department of Finance (*see* Appendix II) that the Attorney General is satisfied as to the legality of the instrument. As it might not be generally expected, however, that the fixing of a scale of charges for a service of the type indicated would come within the ambit of the Post Office Act, 1908, the Committee has decided that the special attention of Seanad Éireann should be drawn to the instrument.

(2) *Instrument appears to make unexpected use of power*

Document 12.5—Paragraph 5 of *First Report of the Select Committee on Statutory Instruments appointed* 16 *December* 1954, (T.152) 11 May 1955.

5. On ground (iii), viz., " that it appears to make some unusual or unexpected use of the powers conferred by the Statute under which it is made," the special attention of Seanad Éireann is drawn to the following two instruments : —

> Housing (Grants to Housing Authorities) Regulations, 1954 (S.I. No. 174 of 1954).

Article 4 (2) of these regulations purports to enable the Minister for Local Government to dispense with certain prescribed conditions in relation to the making of housing grants. The evidence given by the Departmental representatives (*see* Minutes of Evidence, Questions 1 to 6) suggests that this provision is *ultra vires* the parent Statute.

The Select Committee appreciate that a dispensing clause may be administratively indispensable for the effective operation of the grant provisions (*see* minute from Department, Appendix I). They are of opinion, however, that an unrestricted dispensing power is undesirable in the context. Members of the Seanad may, therefore, consider that the proper course to follow where there is need for such a dispensing power, is for the Minister to put suitable legislative proposals before the Oireachtas.

> Housing (Repair and Improvement Works) Regulations, 1954 (S.I. No. 200 of 1954).

(*a*) Section 12 (4) of the enabling Act specifies the ground on which an appeal lies to the Minister for the purpose of grants under the section, viz., refusal by a housing authority to issue a certificate. The regulations purport to specify an additional ground, viz., neglect by a housing authority to certify. The Select Committee appreciate that the additional ground may be necessary in order not to render the section inoperative in a particular case. Their view, however, is that the Minister's power to make regulations for the purposes of the section does not extend to the prescription of the additional ground.

(*b*) The Schedules to these regulations appear below the signature of the Minister and might be thought not to have been themselves attested by the Minister (*see*, in this connection, paragraph 10, *Attesting of Schedules*).

(3) *Instrument Purports to give Retrospective Effect*
Document 12.6—Paragraph 7 of *First Report of the Select Committee on Statutory Instruments appointed* 4 *July*, 1957, (T.162) 16 July 1958.

7. On ground (iv), viz. " that it purports to have retrospective effect where the parent Statute confers no express authority so to provide ", the special attention of Seanad Éireann is drawn to the following instrument: —

Garda Síochána Pensions Order, 1957 [S.I. No. 231 of 1957].

This Order, which was made under section 13 of the Police Forces Amalgamation Act, 1925, amends the Garda Síochána Pensions Order, 1925, as amended, so as to provide that a Garda pensioner who is in receipt of Army retired pay may be given the benefit of the provisions of the Pensions (Increase) Act, 1956. The Order was made on 8th November, 1957, but it purports to have effect from 1st August, 1956, the date from which the increases authorised by the Pensions (Increase) Act, 1956, were payable. As will be observed from the correspondence with the Department of Justice (*see* Appendix III), the necessity for making the Order arose from the fact that the case of the particular pensioner was not adverted to before the Act of 1956 was passed.

As the Police Forces Amalgamation Act, 1925, confers no express authority for the making of such an Order, with retrospective effect, the special attention of Seanad Éireann is drawn to the instrument.

(4) *Unjustifiable Delay in Laying Instruments before House*
Document 12.7—Paragraph 12 of *Second Report of the Select Committee on Statutory Instruments appointed* 16 *December* 1954, (T.154) 28 November 1956.

Notwithstanding the recommendation contained in Paragraph 13 of its First Report in regard to the period within which Instruments should be laid before the House, the Select Committee is concerned to find that it has again to draw the special attention of Seanad Éireann to the fact that in its opinion unjustifiable delay occurred in the laying of seventeen Instruments. It notes, however, that in the majority of replies furnished by the various Departments assurances have been given that steps will be taken to meet the wishes of the Select Committee in future. It feels confident that save in rare cases it will not be called upon to draw the special attention of Seanad Éireann in future to unjustifiable delay in the laying of instruments.

(5) Instrument Calls for Elucidation

Document 12.8—Paragraph 9 of *First Report of the Select Committee on Statutory Instruments appointed* 4 *July* 1957, (T.162) 16 July 1958.

9. On ground (vi), viz. " that for any reason its form or purport calls for elucidation ", the special attention of Seanad Éireann is drawn to the following . . . instruments : —

Emergency Powers (Córas Iompair Éireann) (Reduction of Railway Services) Order, 1944 (Revocation) Order, 1957 [S.I. No. 60 of 1957].
Game Preservation Act, 1930 (Period under Section 27) (Extension) Order, 1957 [S.I. No. 76 of 1957].
Solicitors' Accounts Regulations, 1957 [S.I. No. 252 of 1957].

A previous Select Committee made certain recommendations in regard to the precise citation of the statutory authority under which an instrument is made and, in particular, recommended the discontinuance of the use of the phrase " every and any power in this behalf enabling." The Committee agrees with the view that the use of this phrase tends to make a citation valueless as a means of ascertaining the precise authority under which an instrument is made. It has, therefore, decided to draw the special attention of Seanad Éireann to the foregoing three instruments because, in each, the citation of authority includes a phrase of the type referred to, the necessity for which is not readily apparent. It will be seen from the correspondence with the authorities concerned (*see* Appendix VIII) that, in the present instances, the phrases were included through failure to advert to the earlier recommendations.

(6) Legislation by Reference

Document 12.9—Paragraph 12 of *First Report of the Select Committee on Statutory Instruments appointed* 4 *July* 1957, (T.162) 16 July 1958.

When extensive amendment of a statutory instrument becomes necessary the Select Committee would like, where possible, to see the instrument repealed and replaced by one embodying the required amendments. The Committee has in mind a case such as that of the Poultry Hatcheries Regulations, 1957, which consists entirely of detailed amendments of the Poultry Hatcheries Regulations, 1953 and of which no one article can be understood without reference to the earlier regulations. In this particular case the Committee feels that the interests of clarity would have been better served if the 1953 regulations were replaced by comprehensive regulations incorporating the amendments and it is to be noted (*see* Appendix XV) that the Department concerned agrees with this view but is unable to proceed with the preparation of such regulations until the question of enacting amending legislation has been settled.

In the case of instruments which have been subject to amendments over a period of years such as the Defence Forces (Pensions) Scheme, 1937, the Select Committee is of the opinion that there is a need for consolidation and it would be glad to see this work undertaken at a convenient opportunity.

(7) *Explanatory Notes*
Document 12.10—Paragraph 10 of *Second Report of the Select Com-mittee on Statutory Instruments appointed* 4 *July* 1957, (T.170) 18 November 1959.

The explanatory note, which is now appended to nearly every statutory instrument, is of great assistance to all who have to construe delegated legislation. The value of the note depends entirely on the clarity with which the purport of the instrument is explained. The Committee readily appreciates the difficulty of drafting a statutory instrument, dealing with a technically complex subject, in terms that will be immediately intelligible to all, but it feels that it ought to be possible to word the explanatory note, which has no legal significance, so that the intention of the instrument can be easily understood by everybody concerned. The more persons affected by the provisions of an instrument the greater the necessity for clarity in the note. In this regard, the Committee is not satisfied that the notes appended to some of the health regulations mentioned in the preceding paragraph are as helpful as they might be. The explanatory note dealing with the General Institutional and Specialist Services (Amendment) Regulations, 1958 [S.I. No. 266 of 1958], for example, is in the following terms:

"These regulations make amendments in the regulations governing Institutional and Specialist Services arising from the alterations in the classes eligible for these services made by the Health and Mental Treatment (Amendment) Act, 1958 and the Social Welfare (Amendment) Act, 1958."

As the instrument itself consists entirely of amendments of details in earlier regulations and cannot be understood without reference to the latter it will be appreciated that the note is of little assistance to a reader towards a quick understanding of its provisions. The Committee, in drawing specific attention to this example, does so with the object of impressing on all instrument-making authorities the need for providing, with every instrument, a clear and adequate explanatory note.

2. ADMINISTRATIVE POWERS OF ADJUDICATION

  (a) *The Constitution and Administrative Tribunals*

  Document 12.11—Extracts from V. Grogan, *Administrative Tribunals in the Public Service,* Institute of Public Administration, Dublin n.d.

The term "administrative tribunal" calls for explanation. In the strict sense it may be defined as a person or body of persons, other than a court of justice, established under statute to adjudicate upon issues arising in the course of administration of that body of legislation, original and delegated, which is termed administrative law, where the result of the adjudication is to confer or deny a benefit or to impose or absolve from an obligation created by statute. This function of adjudication is an exercise of the judicial power, and constitutes an exception to the rule that justice is to be administered in courts established by law by judges appointed in the manner provided by the Constitution.

The term is also commonly used to include any person or body of persons given the statutory function of holding a fact-finding inquiry as a necessary preliminary to the exercise of an act of public administration. In this class of case no issue of legal right or obligation is involved in the exercise of the act itself, but the investigation or inquiry bears at least some of the essential characteristics of a judicial process. A person adversely affected by the exercise of the act will not be heard by a court to complain of illegality in the decision taken, but he may be heard to complain of irregularity, such as want of due form, or infringement of natural justice, in the preliminary procedure. . . .

It might appear to follow from the provisions of the Constitution . . . that the judicial power must be exercised by a Court, and could not be delegated to any other person or body. Article 37 of the Constitution, however, introduces an important modification: " Nothing in this Constitution shall operate to invalidate the exercise of limited functions and powers of a judicial nature, in matters other than criminal matters, by any person or body of persons duly authorised by law to exercise such functions and powers, notwithstanding that such person or such body of persons is not a judge or a court appointed or established as such under the Constitution." That provision expressly justifies the assignment of certain judicial functions to administrative tribunals.

The Article contains two important qualifications: the matter must not be a criminal matter, and the functions and powers must be of a limited nature. As to the first: it would appear that a matter may be criminal, although the tribunal is not concerned with determining the guilt or innocence of a person charged with an offence against the law of the State, provided that the effect of the decision given is disciplinary and punitive, as, for example, the striking of a solicitor off the Roll. As to the second: " the test as to whether a power is or is not 'limited' . . . lies in the effect of the assigned power when exercised. If the exercise of the assigned powers and functions is calculated ordinarily to affect in the most profound and far reaching way the lives, liberties, fortunes or reputations of those against whom they are exercised they cannot properly be described as 'limited'".[1] Each "power and function" given must be limited in its character and effect. The limitation is qualitative.

(b) *Examples of Administrative Powers*

(i) Document 12.12—Extracts from Social Welfare Act, 1952 (No. 11).

MINISTER MAY APPOINT DECIDING OFFICERS

41.—The Minister may appoint from his officers such and so many persons as he thinks proper to be deciding officers for the purposes of this Act, and every person so appointed shall hold office as a deciding officer during the pleasure of the Minister.

POWERS OF DECIDING OFFICERS

42.—(1) Subject to the provisions of this Act and in accordance with any relevant regulations, every question arising—

    (*a*) in relation to a claim for benefit,

    (*b*) as to whether a person is *or was*[2] disqualified for benefit;

    (*c*) as to the period of any disqualification for benefit,

    (*d*) as to whether an employment is *or was* insurable employment,

---

1. *In re the Solicitors Act*, 1954, *O'Farrell and Gorman, Solicitors* (not yet reported), in which the Supreme Court reviews the nature of judicial power. There is no question here, the decision points out, of a domestic tribunal with a jurisdiction based solely on contract, such as the power given to the committee of a club or trade union, *under its own rules*, to expel a member. There the jurisdiction is not given by legislation. The member, by joining, agrees to abide by a code of rules which constitutes a contract between himself and the other members. Other useful cases on the nature of judicial power are: *Fisher v. Irish Land Commission* [1948], I.R. 3; 82 I.L.T.R. 50; *State (Crowley) v. Irish Land Commission* [1951], I.R. 250; *Foley v. Irish Land Commission* [1952], I.R. 118.—Grogan.

2. Words in italics are amendments made by Social Welfare (Miscellaneous Provisions) Act, 1961 (no. 22), section 16.

(*dd*) *as to whether a person is or was employed in an insurable employment,*

(*e*) as to what rate of employment contribution is *or was* payable by an employer in respect of an employed contributor,

(*f*) as to who is *or was* the employer of an employed contributor,

(*g*) as to whether a person is *or was* entitled to become a voluntary contributor, or

(*h*) on any such other matter relating to this Act as may be prescribed, shall be decided by a deciding officer.

(2) A reference in this section to a question arising in relation to a claim for benefit includes a reference to a question whether benefit is or is not *or was or was not* payable.

43.—(1) The Minister may appoint from his officers such and so many persons as he thinks proper to be appeals officers for the purposes of this Act, and every person so appointed shall hold office as an appeals officer during the pleasure of the Minister.

(2) One of the appeals officers shall be designated by the Minister to be the Chief Appeals Officer and another of them shall be designated by the Minister to act as the deputy for the Chief Appeals Officer when that Officer is not available.

(3) The Chief Appeals Officer shall be responsible for the distribution, amongst the appeals officers, of the references to them and for the prompt consideration of such references.

APPEALS OFFICERS

44.—(1) If any person is dissatisfied with the decision given by a deciding officer under section 42 of this Act, the question shall, on notice of appeal being given to the Minister within the prescribed time, be referred to an appeals officer.

(2) A deciding officer may, if he so thinks proper, instead of deciding it himself, refer in the prescribed manner any question which falls to be decided by him under section 42 to an appeals officer.

(3) Regulations may provide for the procedure to be followed on appeals and references under this section.

(4) An appeals officer, when deciding a question referred under subsection (1) of this section, shall not be confined to the grounds on which the decision of the deciding officer was based, but may decide the question as if it were being decided for the first time.

(5) The decision of an appeals officer on any question specified in paragraph (*a*), (*b*) or (*c*) of subsection (1) of section 42 of this Act which is referred to him under this section shall, subject to subsections (3) and (4) of section 46 of this Act, be final and conclusive.

(6) An appeals officer shall, on the hearing of any matter referred to him under this section, have power to take evidence on oath and for that purpose may administer oaths to persons attending as witnesses at such hearing.

(7) An appeals officer may, by giving notice in that behalf in writing to any person, require such person to attend at such time and place as is specified in the notice to give evidence in relation to any matter referred to such appeals officer under this section or to produce any documents in his possession, custody or control which relate to any such matter. [*SSs. 8 and 9 omitted.*]

(10) An appeals officer may, in relation to any matter referred to him under this section, award to any person any costs or expenses (including expenses representing loss of remunerative time) which he considers reasonable, and the award shall be payable by the Minister.

(11) (*a*) The Minister may appoint any person whom he considers suitable to sit as an assessor with an appeals officer when any question which appears to the Minister to require the assistance of assessors is heard.

   (*b*) The Minister may constitute, on the basis of districts or otherwise as he considers appropriate, panels of persons to sit as assessors with appeals officers and members may be selected in the prescribed manner from such panels to sit as aforesaid when any question which is of a class prescribed as being appropriate for the assistance of assessors is heard.

   (*c*) Any matter referred to an appeals officer under this section and to be heard by the appeals officer sitting with any such assessor may, with the consent of the parties appearing at the hearing, but not otherwise, be proceeded with in the absence of the assessor.

[*SS. 12 omitted.*]

APPEALS TO HIGH COURT

45.—Where any question other than a question specified in paragraph (*a*), (*b*) or (*c*) of subsection (1) of section 42 of this Act is referred to an appeals officer—

   (*a*) the Minister may, on the request of the Chief Appeals Officer, refer the question for the decision of the High Court, and

   (*b*) if the question is decided by an appeals officer, any person who is dissatisfied with the decision may appeal therefrom to the High Court on any question of law.

REVISION OF DECISIONS

46.—(1) A deciding officer may, at any time and from time to time, revise any decision of a deciding officer, if it appears to him that the decision was erroneous in the light of new evidence or of new facts which have been brought to his notice since the date on which it was given or by reason of some mistake having been made with respect to the law or the facts, or if it appears to him in a case where benefit has been payable that there has been any relevant change of circumstances since the decision was given, and the provisions of this Act as to appeals shall apply to such revised decision in the same manner as they apply to an original decision.

(2) The provisions of subsection (1) of this section shall not apply to a decision relating to a matter which is on appeal or reference under section 44 of this Act unless the revised decision would be in favour of a claimant for benefit.

(3) An appeals officer may, at any time and from time to time, revise any decision of an appeals officer, if it appears to him that the decision was erroneous in the light of new evidence or of new facts brought to his notice since the date on which it was given, or if it appears to him in a case where a claim for benefit has been allowed that there has been any relevant change of circumstances since the decision was given.

(4) The Chief Appeals Officer may, at any time and from time to time, revise any decision of an appeals officer, if it appears to him that the decision was erroneous by reason of some mistake having been made with respect to the law or the facts, and, save where the question is a question specified in paragraph (*a*), (*b*) or (*c*) of subsection (1) of section 42 of this Act, any person who is dissatisfied with the revised decision may appeal therefrom to the High Court on any question of law. [*Remainder omitted.*]

(ii) Document 12.13—Extract from Town and Regional Planning Act, 1934 (No. 22).

59.—(1) Any person aggrieved by the grant or the refusal by a planning authority of a special permission or a general permission or by the making of a special prohibition by such planning authority may appeal within the prescribed time to the Minister and thereupon the Minister may do such one or more of the following things as are applicable to the case and he thinks proper, that is to say : —

(*a*) confirm the grant, refusal or prohibition the subject of such appeal;

(*b*) revoke the grant of the permission or the making of the prohibition which is the subject of such appeal;

(c) in the case of an appeal from a refusal to grant a permission, give the said permission with such (if any) omissions, and variations and subject to such (if any) conditions as he shall think proper;

(d) in the case of an appeal from the grant of a general or special permission, amend (by deletion, addition, or variation) such permission or the conditions attached to such permission and confirm such permission with and subject to such amendments;

(e) in the case of an appeal from the grant of a general permission or the making of a special prohibition, amend (by deletion, addition, or variation) the permission or prohibition (as the case may be) in relation to the statement therein of the area, lands, structures, work, and uses to which such permission or prohibition applies and confirm such permission or prohibition with and subject to such amendment);

(f) in the case of an appeal from the making of a special prohibition amend such special prohibition by inserting conditions therein or deleting conditions therefrom or varying conditions contained therein and confirm such special prohibition with and subject to such amendments.

(2) Where on an appeal under this section from the making of a special prohibition, such prohibition is revoked by the Minister, or is confirmed by the Minister with new conditions inserted therein or with amendments of the conditions contained therein, the Minister may, if he thinks proper, as part of his determination of the matters the subject of such appeal, direct the planning authority by whom such prohibition was made to pay to the person by whom such appeal was brought such sum as the Minister shall think proper to specify by way of compensation for loss suffered by such person by reason of such prohibition during the period between the making of such prohibition and the determination of such appeal.

(3) The determination by the Minister of an appeal under this section shall be final and, in so far as it directs a planning authority to do any act or thing, shall be complied with by such planning authority.

(iii) Document 12.14—Extract from Section 3 of Military Service Pensions Act, 1924 (No. 48).

3.—(1) A board of assessors (in this Act referred to as "the board of assessors") shall be constituted under this Act and shall consist of three members who shall be appointed by the Minister with the approval of the Executive Council and one of whom shall be a person who at the date of his apointment is a Judge of the Supreme Court, High Court, Circuit Court, or

District Court of Saorstát Éireann or is a practising barrister of not less than ten years standing.

(2) The board of assessors shall examine every application for a certificate of military service referred to them by the Minister, and they shall for that purpose make all such enquiries, summon all such witnesses, and take all such evidence, whether on oath or otherwise, as may appear to them necessary or proper for the purpose of making a report to the Minister as to the military service of the applicant.

(3) Every report as to military service of any applicant for a certificate of military service shall contain findings upon the following matters, that is to say : —

    (*a*) the military service of such applicant in Oglaigh na hÉireann or in the Irish Volunteers or in the Irish Citizen Army or in Fianna Éireann or in the Hibernian Rifles; and

    (*b*) the military service of such applicant in the National Forces or the Defence Forces of Saorstát Éireann; and

    (*c*) the period of the service of such applicant in each such force or body as aforesaid.

(4) Every report made by the board of assessors as to the military service of any applicant for a certificate of military service shall be in the prescribed form.

(5) The onus of proof shall rest on the applicant for a certificate of military service, and he shall be at liberty to offer such evidence as may be necessary to enable him to discharge such onus.

(6) The findings of the board of assessors set out in their report shall in all cases be final and conclusive and binding upon the applicant, provided however that the board may at any time re-open any or all of their findings at the request of the Minister on the ground that evidence not available prior to the making of their report had since become available, and upon hearing such additional evidence the board of assessors may amend their report and alter or discharge any findings therein as may seem to them just having regard to such further evidence.

(c) *The Courts and Administrative Justice*
Document 12.15—Extract from McLoughlin v Minister for Social Welfare [1958] I.R. 27 (O'Daly J).

(This case is an appeal from the decision of an Appeals Officer provided for under the Special Welfare Act, 1952—see Document 12.12 above.)

Counsel for the appellant has submitted that there was a flagrant disregard of the appellant's right by the appeals officer. The direction of the Minister for Finance he characterised in the words of Juvenal, "Hoc volo, sic jubeo." He has submitted that there was a complete failure to hear the appellant's case and that the decision of the appeals officer should be quashed and the matter remitted for a proper hearing.

Counsel for the respondent Minister has argued that there was no more than a mistake on the part of the appeals officer as to the evidential value of a document, viz., the direction of the Minister for Finance, amounting only to error of law and that by reason of the rehearing which the appellant sought in the High Court any objection based on failure of natural justice is no longer open to the appellant.

I cannot accept it that the appeals officer was merely mistaken as to the evidential value of the direction of the Minister for Finance. He has not said so himself. What he did say was that he was bound to adhere to a direction, purported to have been given to him by the Minister for Finance, an observation which disclosed not a concern for the niceties of the probative value, but the belief that a public servant in his position had no option but to act on the direction of a Minister of State. Such a belief on his part was an abdication by him from his duty as an appeals officer. That duty is laid upon him by the Oireachtas and he is required to perform it as between the parties that appear before him freely and fairly as becomes anyone who is called upon to decide on matters of right or obligation.

The appellant is in my opinion right in his submission that there was a failure on the part of the appeals officer to hear his appeal, and if he had chosen he might have moved the High Court simply for an order quashing the pretended decision of the appeals officer. He chose instead to appeal to the High Court and there to re-argue the point of law upon which there was no proper hearing before the appeals officer. In this circumstance there is no purpose in sending the matter back to the appeals officer; but the appeal will serve to make it known, although it is indeed regrettable that it should be necessary to come thus far for the purpose, that appeals officers under the Social Welfare Act, 1952, and equally deciding officers, are, and are required to be, free and unrestricted in discharging their functions under the Act.

READING

M. W. Abrahamson: 'The Grievance Man—in Ireland?' in *Administration*, vol. 8.
V. Grogan: *Administrative Tribunals in the Public Service*, Dublin, n.d.
Paul Jackson: 'Delegated Legislation in Ireland' in *Public Law*, 1962.

A